COMPUTERS AND PROFITS:

Quantifying Financial
Benefits of Information

ADDISON-WESLEY SERIES ON DECISION SUPPORT

Consulting Editors
Peter G. W. Keen
Charles B. Stabell

Decision Support Systems: An Organizational Perspective
Peter G. W. Keen and Michael S. Scott Morton

*Decision Support Systems: Current Practice
and Continuing Challenges*
Steven L. Alter

Electronic Meetings: Technical Alternatives and Social Choices
Robert Johansen, Jacques Valee, and Kathleen Spangler

*Computers and Profits: Quantifying Financial
Benefits of Information*
Jack P. C. Kleijnen

COMPUTERS AND PROFITS:

*Quantifying Financial
Benefits of Information*

Jack P. C. Kleijnen

Katholieke Hogeschool, Tilburg
The Netherlands

ADDISON-WESLEY PUBLISHING COMPANY
**Reading, Massachusetts • Menlo Park, California
London • Amsterdam • Don Mills, Ontario • Sydney**

Library of Congress Cataloging in Publication Data

Kleijnen, Jacobus Petrus Catharinus.
    Computers & profits.

    (Addison-Wesley series on decision support)
    Bibliography: p.
    Includes indexes.
    1. Management information systems. 2. Decision-
making. 3. Managerial economics. I. Title.
II. Series.
T58.6.K58   658.4´03   79-14097
ISBN 0-201-03813-7

ISBN 0-201-03813-7
ABCDEFGHIJ-HA-89876543210

To those who made it possible
. . . and worthwhile:
Mai,
Wilma,
Mara, and Jakko.

SERIES FOREWORD

Determining the value of information is an elusive topic and central to the evaluation of any computer-based decision aid. *Computers and Profits* provides an in-depth review of this issue as it relates to the value of information systems and to the use of formal, analytic methods for evaluation. It assembles in a single book a number of different approaches that are generally treated separately. This book provides a broader, a new, and, we hope, a more useful perspective, both in terms of the potential for application of each approach and of its conceptual assumptions.

The scope of the book covers more than the issues of Decision Support and the evaluation of the benefits of decision support systems. *Computers and Profits* emphasizes the benefits and value-added effects of information systems, rather than cost reduction and displacement effects. The topics the book discusses are fundamental to the aims of decision support: They are the application of interactive technologies to management decision making through the development of tools that

- address nonstructured rather than structured tasks;
- support rather than replace managerial judgment; and
- focus on effectiveness rather than efficiency in decision processes.

As the book demonstrates, the issue of identifying and estimating benefits cannot be resolved through any straightforward application of simple techniques. This is true even in the relatively constrained case in which we solely consider the effects of changes in the quality of the information available to the decision maker. For decision support systems the evaluation process can be extraordinarily complex. Therefore, the primary use of formal analytic techniques for evaluation is to provide a conceptual and methodological base to help us organize our efforts in this area.

Evaluation is a key activity throughout any successful effort to improve the quality of information systems and the effectiveness of decision making. Evaluation is more than an input to a decision to proceed or not to proceed with the development of an information system. Evaluation is required both to guide and control the design and implementation effort. We, therefore, need to continuously evaluate and reevaluate both what the benefits to be achieved are and to what extent the desired benefits are being obtained. This obviously requires both concepts and techniques. *Computers and Profits* brings together, for the first time, the best available research that can be utilized in evaluation processes.

Peter G. W. Keen
Charles B. Stabell

PREFACE

As a guide to the reader, a brief summary of the contents and organization of this book precedes a discussion of the book's uses and aims. Chapter One delimits the *scope* of this book: the quantification of the financial benefits of computerized information used in managerial decision making.

Chapter Two discusses various types of managerial decision making, including operational and strategic decisions. It distinguishes between the data processing system (a production process transforming data) and the *information system*. The worth of the information yielded depends on its effects on decisions influencing the company's economic performance. At the operational level, formal models are readily available to relate information, decisions, and performance. At the strategic level, such models are more problematic. Several approaches to the benefit problem are surveyed in subsequent chapters.

Chapter Three concentrates on the *technical* performance of *computer* systems. This performance is measured by response times, CPU (Central Processing Unit) utilization, etc. Relevant techniques and models are benchmarks, queuing theory, simulation, and so on. Discussion of this topic is brief because computer systems are only a subsystem of the information system, the focus of this book.

Chapter Four emphasizes computer users' growing awareness of factors beyond technical performance, factors such as costs and flexibility. *Scoring methods* for the *selection* of a computer system are a special case of more general utility models popular in economic theory and are comparable to *multicriteria* decision making in management sciences. None of these models, however, provides causal, predictive models, which relate computerization effects, such as increased accuracy and timeliness, to the economic performance of the company.

Chapter Five provides an *economic framework* for the discussion of economic benefits. Economic benefits are determined by prices, which in turn depend on supply and demand. Therefore the chapter discusses the *price and market* mechanism and its limitations: external effects, monopolies, etc. Replacement of labor by capital (computers) is also examined. A microeconomic issue is the price the computer department charges its users within the same company. Among various principles surveyed are cost versus loss, and marginal versus integral pricing. *Costing and pricing* can be used for efficiency control and for resource allocation. Another relevant topic is the *investment* character of computer and information projects. Related matters include net present value, the purchase versus lease issue, risk analysis for coping with uncertainty in investments, and sensitivity analysis for testing model validity and for optimizing model output. This sensitivity analysis uses regression analysis and experimental designs, such as fractional factorial designs.

Chapter Six contains a list of *information attributes* that determine the quality of information: timeliness, accuracy, aggregation, report mode, retention time, security and privacy, reliability and recovery, scope, user-machine modes, flexibility, and multiple users. These information characteristics are defined quantitatively; their costs and benefits are discussed qualitatively. Quantitative analysis techniques are postponed until subsequent chapters.

Chapter Seven summarizes *information economics*, a theory based on *Bayesian* decision analysis. The simple "newsboy" inventory exemplifies the calculus of the theory and its presentation through decision trees. Team theory for multiple-person organizations, and dynamic variants for multiple-period decision making are extensions of the basic theory. Applications of information economics demonstrate that despite its limitations, examined critically in the text, this theory provides an interesting conceptual framework.

Chapter Eight surveys some miscellaneous research and simulation experiments. Ad hoc studies of the benefits of information have used linear programming, inventory modeling, the Shannon–Weaver entropy concept, control engineering, empirics, and so on. The simulation experiments have comprised discrete-event *simulation*, difference-equation models like those used in corporate models, *industrial dynamics* or system dynamics, and management *games*. Simulation is only a tool for examining concepts derived from theories such as information economics. System dynamics is more than a technique; it is a world view, a conceptual framework. The chapter summarizes several experiments using simulation, gaming, or system dynamics. It also presents a general framework called CYSDEM, developed by R. Welke.

Chapter Nine details a simulation based on a business game, the "IBM Management Decision-Making Laboratory." The simulation experiment focuses on the role of accurate information in tactical and strategic decision making. A special computer program is developed to play the IBM game; i.e., human players (managers) are modeled by this program. The chapter examines varying degrees of information accuracy with regard to information on sales volume and production cost. Accuracy shows a significant linear effect on the economic benefits, as measured by the company's return on investment, market share, and balance sheet total.

Chapter Ten mentions some related research efforts, not covered in previous chapters. It recapitulates the main ideas and points to future research.

An extensive list of references facilitates further study of aspects of reader interest. Notes at the end of each chapter collect most references to the literature. Each chapter includes a number of simple exercises with solutions at the end of the book. Each chapter is self-contained and can be read individually. Author and subject indexes further facilitate use of the book.

Not an instruction manual for calculating the financial benefits of a planned information system, this book provides a conceptual framework and presents a number of tools. A few selected theories, such as information economics and system dynamics, shape this framework. These theories are themselves embedded in a larger framework of economic theory and management science. Ideas from computer science amplify the theoretical concepts. The tools suggested in this book are mathematical techniques, such as simulation, gaming, and other operations research techniques and models.

The benefits of information systems interest a variety of experts, users, and managers. This book is relevant to students and practitioners of

- informatics[1] and computer science;

- management science, operations research, and business administration;

- economics; and

- engineering, especially industrial engineering.

Reading this book requires an elementary knowledge of management and computers. The author's background includes a formal education in management science and economics. Although this book is on quantification and modeling, it reduces to a minimum the use of mathematics.

As yet there exists no comprehensive theory with well-accepted models and techniques on which to base the financial evaluation of a management information system. Nevertheless, this book endeavors to move toward such a theory.

Tilburg, The Netherlands   J.P.C.K.
March 1980

NOTE

1. Informatics may be defined as follows:

"Informatics encompasses the design, the construction, the evaluation, the use and maintenance of information processing systems including hardware, software, organizational and human aspects as well as the complex of their industrial commercial administrative social and political impact."

See the Main Working Document of the 1978 IBI-Unesco Conference on "Strategies and Policies for Informatics." (Address: IBI, 23 Viale Civilta del Lavoro, 00144 Roma—E.U.R., Italy.)

ACKNOWLEDGMENTS

My interest in the economic evaluation of information systems was aroused when I visited the IBM Research Laboratory in San Jose, California, in 1974. This twelve-month visit with IBM was made possible by an IBM postdoctoral fellowship, a fellowship from the Netherlands Organization for the Advancement of Pure Research (Z.W.O.), and the cooperation of my home university, Katholieke Hogeschool Tilburg. On the simulation experiment with the IBM management game, presented in Chapter Nine, I worked together with my temporary IBM colleague Dr. L. Barbosa and our manager, Dr. J. Jacob. I had many stimulating discussions with them and with Dr. T. Naylor, professor in the department of economics, Duke University, Durham, North Carolina. After my return to Tilburg, a preliminary experiment with a computerized player in an ICL business game was performed by P. van Drunen and P. Zijlmans, students in the department of business and economics, Katholieke Hogeschool Tilburg.

In 1977 I had the opportunity of working with Dr. R. Welke, associate professor in the faculty of business, McMaster University, Hamilton, Ontario, Canada. His visit to the Katholieke Hogeschool Tilburg during the first half of 1977 was made possible by a fellowship from Z.W.O. Dr. Welke commented both generally and specifically on a preliminary draft of my manuscript.

In the final stages of manuscript preparation, I had several long-distance telephone discussions with the co-editor of this series, Dr. C. Stabell, the Norwegian School of Economics and Business Administration, Bergen, Norway. His comments led to a drastic reorganization of Chapter Eight on miscellaneous models and to the expansion of Chapter Ten. His comments on the other chapters were also helpful.

Chapter Four on scoring methods benefited from the criticisms of Dr. J. Dujmovic, faculty of electrical engineering, University of Belgrade, Belgrade, Yugoslavia, and from the comments by P. van Loon, my colleague at the Katholieke Hogeschool. Chapter Six on information attributes profited from the comments made by Dr. G. Nielen, professor and chairman of the Informatics Group, of which I am a member. Of course, any deficiencies in this book remain my sole responsibility.

The various versions of the manuscript have been typed under the guidance of Mrs. J. Peeters at the Katholieke Hogeschool Tilburg. The artwork was prepared by A. van Helfteren, Katholieke Hogeschool. In the retrieval of the many references and their bibliographic data, I was assisted first by L. van den Brule and then by M. Meulendijks, students at the Katholieke Hogeschool. The writing style of this book benefited greatly from the copy editing by Dr. Claire Edwards Yskamp.

The Institute of Management Sciences (TIMS) granted permission to reproduce Table 1 on the Minnesota gaming experiments in Chapter Eight. A Dutch version of Chapter Nine on the simulation with an IBM management game was previously published in *Maandblad voor Accountancy en Bedrijfshuishoudkunde*, 50(8):453–470.

CONTENTS

Chapter 1   SCOPE OF STUDY   1

Exercises   2

Notes   2

Chapter 2   INFORMATION AND MANAGERIAL DECISION
MAKING   5

Introduction   5

Decision Types and Information Needs   6

Computers and Decision Making   7

Data Processing, Information, and Decision Systems   9

Additional Research and Data   11

Appendix 2.1: Point-of-sale (POS) Systems   12

Appendix 2.2: Inventory Management and Computers   13

Exercises   15

Notes   16

Chapter 3   TECHNICAL COMPUTER PERFORMANCE   19

Introduction   19

Miscellaneous Techniques   19

Analytical OR Models   22

Simulation   24

Related Issues   28

Exercises   29

Notes   30

Chapter 4   SCORING METHODS, MULTIPLE CRITERIA, AND UTILITY
ANALYSIS   33

Introduction   33

Scoring Methods in Computer Selection   33

Utility Analysis in Economics   36

Multiple Criteria in Management Science   43

Summary   44

Exercises   45

Notes   47

Chapter 5   MICROECONOMIC FRAMEWORK   51

Introduction   51

The Market Factors of Supply and Demand   51

Supply and Demand of Computers   53

Limitations of the Market Mechanism   62

Charging and Pricing Computer Jobs   65

Investment Analysis   69

Risk Analysis and Sensitivity Analysis   73

Summary   79

Appendix 5.1: Regression Analysis   79

Appendix 5.2: Some Useful Formulas for Means and
Variances   81

Exercises   81

Notes   84

Chapter 6   INFORMATION ATTRIBUTES   89

Introduction   89

Timeliness   92

Accuracy   98

Aggregation   101

Report Mode   102

Retention Time   104

Security and Privacy   105

Reliability and Recovery   105

Scope   106

User-machine Modes   106

Flexibility   107

Multiple Users   108

Miscellaneous Attributes   109

Conclusion   109

Exercises   110

Notes   111

Chapter 7   INFORMATION ECONOMICS: BAYESIAN DECISION
THEORETIC APPROACH   115

Introduction   115

The "Newsboy" Example   116

More about Information Economics   121

Applications   125

Limitations of the IE Approach   127

Benefits of the IE Framework   130

Exercises   132

Notes   133

Chapter 8   MISCELLANEOUS MODELS   135

Introduction   135

Control Theory   135

System Dynamics   137

Simulation   139

Gaming   143

Linear Programming   146

Inventory Models   147

Entropy   147

Empirical Studies   148

Epilogue   148

Appendix 8.1: System Dynamics Studies   149

Appendix 8.2: Simulation Studies   149

Appendix 8.3: Gaming Studies   150

Appendix 8.4: More Studies   151

Exercises   152

Notes   153

Chapter 9   SIMULATION WITH AN IBM MANAGEMENT GAME   157

Introduction   157

The IBM Management Game   158

The DUMMY Player   159

Inaccurate Production Information   166

Inaccurate Sales Information   172

Conclusion   174

Appendix 9.1: Details on the DUMMY Player   174

Appendix 9.2: The R^2 Statistic   178

Appendix 9.3: F-tests and t-tests   179

Appendix 9.4: A Model for Inaccurate Sales Data   181

Exercises   182

Notes   184

Chapter 10   CONCLUSION   187

Introduction   187

Related Research   187

Overview of Preceding Chapters   189

Final Evaluation   190

Notes   193

SOLUTIONS TO EXERCISES   195

Chapter One   195

Chapter Two   195

Chapter Three   196

Chapter Four   196

Chapter Five   197

Chapter Six   199

Chapter Seven   200

Chapter Eight   200

Chapter Nine   201

BIBLIOGRAPHY   203

AUTHOR INDEX   245

SUBJECT INDEX   255

CHAPTER ONE

The scope of this book is limited to a discussion of several approaches to the quantification of the financial benefits of a computerized information system (IS). Let us examine the key words in this description.

Quantification is based on formal models of the system studied. Quantification and modeling are not meant to make purely automatic the selection of a particular IS. In the much wider context of systems analysis for military decisions, Fisher (1971, p. 7) said,

> Rather the objective [of quantification] is to provide a better basis for exercising that judgement [of the decision makers] through the more precise statement of problems, the discovery and outlining of alternatives, the making of comparisons among alternatives, and the like.

Keeney and Raiffa (1976, p. 9) mention the following advantages of a formal analysis:

> Psychological comfort—The decision maker may find reassurance on the correctness of intuition.

> Communication—In the discussions with others, assumptions, goals, and restrictions are clarified.

> Advocacy—The formal analysis may serve to gain the support of others.

Financial benefits are those of a purely economic nature; for example, profit, return on investment, market share, balance sheet total, and earnings per share. Because these benefits interest profit-oriented companies primarily, nonprofit organizations, like government agencies, universities, and hospitals, are not included. Kraemer et al. (1973) found that cost–benefit aspects are much neglected in nonprofit organizations, such as local governments. Limiting discussion to financial benefits means not investigating benefits such as job satisfaction and service even though they are of interest to managers, employees, and customers.[1]

Limiting investigation to ISs that are *computerized* or can be computerized means restricting attention to the *formal* part of the total information system. The informal part comprises coffee-break communication, company gossip, and the like.[2] The total IS, the nervous system connecting all parts of the organization, consists of people, procedures, and technical devices, such as computers.[3] The IS is part of a larger system, the inquiry system, which provides knowledge, adaptability, and new goals.[4] Chapter Two will explore the IS and its relations with the data processing and the decision systems within the organization.

The examples of financial benefits given above are all closely related to the company's profit. For instance, the balance sheet total increases as profit increases. Net benefits (profit) can accrue from an increase in gross benefits or from a decrease in costs. The emphasis in this study is on the effects on *gross benefits* although costs will not be totally excluded. The reason for this emphasis is that the quantification of cost reductions has already been discussed in most textbooks on data processing. Scientifically its quantification is straightforward although in practice it may be awkward. (See Chapter Five.) These textbooks, however, mention only briefly the effects of computers on gross benefits, mostly as "intangibles." This book in breaking ground for research on gross benefits of an IS offers no recipes for their quantification.

Besides the scientific challenge posed by benefit quantification, practical developments have stimulated interest in this topic. As the computer matured, its applications moved from mere cost saving to benefit generation. Unfortunately—but not surprisingly because of the lack of knowledge—quantification of benefits is usually missing in practice. Constable (1972) studies a specific British industry and provides empirical data on the number of companies that actually performed a formal financial justification for their investments in process control computers. He does not specify *how* this justification was done when it was done. In the Davis (1975) survey on database systems, evaluations are usually *technical* and based on benchmarks (see Chapter Three) and on other companies' experience.[5]

What is also lacking in most cases is an ex post evaluation, i.e., an evaluation after the system has been installed. INFOTECH (1973, p. 98) states that 40 percent of United Kingdom users does not perform such an evaluation. The same situation was reported for other countries. Ex ante and ex post quantifications in United Kingdom government practice are discussed by J.G. Head (1975). For the selection of computer systems by the United States government, see Joslin (1977).[6]

Recently economic benefit evaluation has received more emphasis in the literature.[7] Boehm and Bell (1975) give the legendary example of a computerized income-tax system with very poor technical performance but extremely good economic performance because the taxpayers were led to believe that tax evaders would be caught by the computer. So the emphasis in both practice and theory is shifting from "doing the thing right" (efficiency) to "doing the right thing" (effectiveness). Many practical examples of doing the right thing can be found in an interesting book by two consultants, Grindley and Humble (1973). The growing interest in benefit evaluation is further demonstrated by recent curriculum recommendations.[8]

EXERCISES

1. What are the effects of sales revenues and sales expenses on the various financial benefits?
2. Give examples of cost savings and gross benefit generation by computers.
3. Do you think that a single model will predict all criteria?

NOTES

1. Baumgarten et al. (1975), Easton (1973, pp. 8–12), Hawgood (1975), Land (1976, pp. 3–5), and Mumford (1979). See also E.D. Carlson (1974), Crozier (1976), McLean (1976). An extensive list of references is given by Welke (1977) in his section 8.

2. For a discussion of what can or cannot be computerized, see Van de Wouw (1977, pp. 56–59).

3. Nielen (1972); see also Bosman (1976).

4. Churchman (1971) and Jewett (1973).

5. Davis (1975, pp. 18–23, 47).

6. For German practice see Bottler et al. (1972, p. 14). The importance of ex post evaluation is emphasized by Sollenberger and Arens (1973); see also Burpo (1973).

7. Specific references will be given in later chapters. Some general references are Baumgarten et al. (1975, pp. 56–57), Butterworth and Ziemba (1978), Diebold (1977), Jacquin and Mevellec (1978), Radford (1973, pp. 138–142), Stabell (1978), Verrijn Stuart (1976). One of the first books emphasizing the benefit aspects of information was McDonough (1963). A recent bibliography is Welke (1978a). Refer also to the *Quarterly Bibliography on Computers and Data Processing* published by Applied Computer Research (P.O. Box 9280, Phoenix, AZ, 85068).

8. Ashenhurst (1972) and Brittan (1974); also Vazsonyi (1975).

INFORMATION AND MANAGERIAL DECISION MAKING

CHAPTER **TWO**

INTRODUCTION

This chapter briefly surveys the role of computers in organizations of primary interest, namely in profit-oriented companies. Computers were invented in the 1940s for *technical* reasons to do things people could not do within a comparable time span. Examples include ballistic computations and other scientific number crunching. An economic analysis was hardly needed because no realistic technical alternative existed; yet the applications were thought worthwhile for noneconomic reasons such as defense and science. In the 1950s computers were purchased by some companies to handle payroll preparation and accounts receivable and payable. This second application area does require an economic analysis to determine whether clerks, using simple instruments like pencils and calculators, should be replaced by computers, a more capital intensive method of production. Such investment analysis is relatively simple because only the costs of alternative production techniques need be compared. (Chapter Five details investment analysis or capital budgeting.) Occasionally cost changes are accompanied by revenue (gross benefit) increases; for example, payments may be received earlier because of faster computerized invoicing.[1] These "negative" costs, however, are not due to better decision making.

As the computer matured, people realized that another reason for computerization was that "better quality of information" improved decision making and increased net benefits.[2] Grindley and Humble's (1973) many real-life examples of computer projects illustrate that the major benefits of computers are not in clerical cost displacement. An explicit definition of net benefits is

$$\text{Net benefits} = \text{gross benefits} - \text{total costs}$$
$$= \text{gross benefits} - (\text{information costs} + \text{operating costs}). \quad (2.1)$$

For a private company gross benefits equal sales revenues. Operating costs are all costs, such as transportation costs, except the costs of the IS, e.g., record keeping costs. More precisely, in this terminology the operating costs are the costs of the physical subsystem, and exclude the costs of the information, the data processing, and the decision making subsystems (see Fig. 2.1). This definition of operating cost is not standard but serves for lack of better terminology. For clerical cost replacement, subdivide information costs into worker costs and machine costs; computerization is economical if the machine cost increase is smaller than (the absolute value of) the worker cost decrease. It is important to recognize that computers can improve net

5

benefits by decreasing the operating cost and increasing the gross benefits. Understanding these relationships requires examining the various types of decisions and the information needed.

DECISION TYPES AND INFORMATION NEEDS

Decisions can be categorized at the *operational*, the *tactical*, and the *strategic* level of management although the distinction among these three levels is not always clear.[3] The daily scheduling of a manufacturing company is an operational decision; a price change is a tactical decision; a new plant investment is a strategic decision. Based on Anthony (1965), the characterization of the three decision levels is as follows:

Operational = low management = short term.

Tactical = middle management = medium term.

Strategic = top management = long term.

A related typification is that introduced by Simon (1960): structured or programmed versus *unstructured* or unprogrammed decision making. Unstructured problems are those that are hard to define. The crux of these problems is not the right answer but the right question. [See Pounds (1969, p. 16).]

These classifications have been elaborated in subsequent publications. Gorry and Morton (1971) combined the Anthony and Simon categorizations into an interesting framework for management information systems (MISs). Schonberger (1977) extends this framework recommending the bottom-up approach for an operational MIS, and the top-down approach for strategic decisions. (The bottom-up versus top-down controversy will be discussed later.) Several more classifications are reviewed by Lucas et al. (1974).[4] Strategic decisions are investigated and characterized in an interesting empirical study by Mintzberg et al. (1976). Unstructured decision making is modeled using Petri nets by Hackathorn (1977). Zijlker (1974) distinguishes "change" as it occurs in project management as a separate decision type.

What kinds of information are needed for each decision type? *Information* for *strategic* decisions has the following characteristics[5]:

It concerns the long term as noted above.

It is needed irregularly.

It concerns future, external events. (Internal data reflect events within the company.)

It requires human judgment because of the unstructured problem formulation. [Simon (1960).]

Operational decisions are the opposite: they concern the short time (seconds in air traffic control); are regular (as in daily scheduling); concern internal, past events; and can be computerized. In this rather fluid area, counterexamples can, of course, be found: top management might need internal data if a major strike breaks out within the company; operational management needs aperiodic data on machine breakdowns.

Tactical decisions, the middle level, are even more difficult to define rigorously. Verhelst (1974) groups tactical decisions with operational decisions, the former being based on aggregated operational data in his definition. Minsky (1975) emphasizes the informal character of top-management information. Note that Mason and Mitroff (1973) point out that different psychological types of users need different information: e.g., numerical data or verbal descriptions. (See Chapter Six for behavioral aspects of information.)

Clearly not all information needs, especially those at the strategic level, can be satisfied by the aggregation of detailed operational data, the *bottom-up* approach to a MIS. For instance, a corporate model[6], constructed to assist in strategic decision making, may use especially collected, highly aggregated data, the top-down approach. The literature further elaborates both approaches.[7] Both methods are compared empirically in a small field study by Munro and Davis (1974). Because different kinds of decisions require fundamentally different kinds of information, the idea of a "total system" based on the bottom-up approach is unrealistic.

Note that a special case of highly aggregated data is formed by economic data available in external, public data banks. A survey is provided by Treille (1978). In 1978 there were 362 public databases. The major systems containing national and international economic data are managed by Data Resources Inc. (DRI) and Chase Econometrics. Besides raw data such tools as econometric models can be provided. Public data banks are accessible through telecommunication networks like TYMSHARE and EURONET.[8]

COMPUTERS AND DECISION MAKING

Traditionally the application areas of computers are divided into two groups:

Electronic data processing (EDP), also known as automatic data processing (ADP); and

Scientific applications or *number crunching*.

The term EDP emphasizes the capability of computers to store data, which, of course, must first be collected and can later be retrieved. Examples include a file with employee data, and a file with inventory records. Nowadays this function is associated with database management systems (DBMSs), in which physical files are replaced by individual records that are linked together. (See the first section of Chapter Six.) In this book data bank or database are neutral words for a company's pool of data, organized either by files or by DBMS. EDP is the field of the administrative or accounting applications of computers.

The term number crunching emphasizes computer performance of very many, possibly complicated, mathematical operations on the data in order to solve mathematical models, such as those for engineering and chemical problems. Such models can also represent the company, either the whole system or a subsystem within the company. This is the area of operations research (OR) and management science. This book concentrates on the EDP function of computers, i.e., on the improvement of decisions through better quality of the data per se, not through the application of management models! The role of computers in operations research is discussed elsewhere. Here note that interactive decision support systems (DSSs) combine both capabilities of modern computer systems, and that OR techniques such as linear programming (LP) and simulation involve not only number crunching but also extensive data manipulation.[9]

The brief descriptions that follow exemplify how computerized information improves decision making at each of the three decision levels.

Operational Decisions

For the ordering of inventory items in a retail store, special terminals for data capture at the source, the check-out counter of the store, have been developed and are known as point-of-sale (POS) equipment. (The reader unfamiliar with these systems should refer to Appendix 2.1.) POS improves the quality of the data: more accurate, timely, and detailed data are obtained. Besides this EDP capability, computers provide number-crunching facilities. Hence inventory models can include scientifically computed safety stocks, forecasting subroutines, and so on. Altogether, these computerizations result in improved decision making, which reduces the operating costs in Eq. (2.1). Specified service percentages can be realized with less inventory and hence lower inventory carrying cost. A less expensive purchasing pattern results if orders are combined so that higher quantity discounts are realized. Sales revenues, gross benefits in Eq. (2.1), can increase if fewer stockouts occur; moreover, fewer stockouts stimulate the company's goodwill. Appendix 2.2 gives more details on the role of computers in inventory management.

Other examples in the operational decision-making area are numerous. Inventory control may be combined with production management into an integrated logistics system including material requirement planning (MRP).[10] Unfavorable cost trends may be detected earlier through a fast MIS.[11] Interest loss and risk are diminished in the management of cash and accounts receivable.[12] Capital cost is decreased when production fluctuations are dampened so that less (maximum) capacity is needed. Sales revenues are increased by better utilization of existing capacity as real-time reservation systems operated by airlines, hotel chains, and railroads have demonstrated: BOAC's reservation system yielded a 22 percent return on the investment of 50 million pounds [INFOTECH (1973, p. 100)]. Sales revenues may increase when customers are supplied (and tempted) with more information on services available from, say, a bank or a travel agent.[13] Wimbrow (1971) describes a system installed at IBM and used in order entry, delivery scheduling, payroll, accounts receivable, inventory control, billing, etc.

Tactical and Strategic Decisions

Here the benefits of computerizing data are not so clear. Computers have not been applied so much in this area; in light of the characteristics for strategic decisions given above, this situation is not surprising: irregular, external data are not so well suited for computerization. Long-term decisions do not require data of perfect recency. The role of human judgment in unstructured high-level decisions and the informal character of much of this strategic information exclude completely computerized decision making. Insofar as computers have been applied, number-crunching applications exceed EDP applications. For instance, corporate simulation models are used to answer "What if?" questions for new products and new plant investments. Recent studies show that top managers use computers more and more.[14] In the course of time, decisions move from the area of unstructured decisions into the area of routine, computerized decisions (consider inventory management); and higher management is freed for solving new, unstructured problems.[15] A case study by Trill (1977) illustrates how EDP can free lower-level managers and operators from many data processing (clerical) activities so that more time remains for the actual job (in this case, negotiation and vendor selection).

Quantifying the financial benefits of an IS in strategic and tactical decision making is extremely difficult. The types of decision making are so poorly understood that it is hard to model the relationships among the inputs and outputs of the process. These decisions concern not the internal processes of the company (closed system), but the external relations with the environment of customers, competitors, labor unions, capital suppliers, and government (open system).[16] The danger exists that emphasizing the quantification of benefits might give priority to the simplest clerical applications of computers.[17] In more sophisticated applications there is the danger of concentrating on the easily quantifiable factors (say, inventory cost) at the expense of possibly more important, but more difficult to quantify factors (say, goodwill).[18] Wallace (1975, p. 409) claims that quantifying uncertainty—through risk analysis, discussed in Chapter Ten—reveals possible MIS benefits that otherwise would be designated as intangibles and consequently ignored. The consensus is that modern applications of computers cannot be left to the technical computer staff because selection and guidance of applications require top-management involvement.[19]

DATA PROCESSING, INFORMATION, AND DECISION SYSTEMS

Some authors distinguish between data and information. Raw data can be selected for input into the computer's memory. These data may be transmitted to a central database. The computer may perform basic operations on the data, e.g., insert the new data item into a file, or update an average. Later the computer retrieves data, performs on them simple or sophisticated operations (such as the computation of totals or the construction of tables and graphs), and presents output data, which are then called information. There is a fluid continuum between raw data and information. In EDP the emphasis is on the collection of data, and their storage, simple manipulation, and presentation. In operations research the accent is on sophisticated data manipulations, providing information for deciding on alternatives. In this book the terms data and information are used interchangeably.[20]

The IS selects data, and stores and retrieves information that is the basis for decisions that control the "physical" subsystem, which is one more part of the organization. This physical subsystem actually furnishes the products of the company; e.g., metal goods or transportation services. Such a picture of an IS, superimposed upon the physical production subsystem, is well accepted in the literature.[21]

The "product" of some companies may be a document, i.e., a carrier of data. Such companies include banks, insurance companies, travel agents, and government agencies, which provide checks, account statements, insurance policies, and travel documents. In these organizations the physical production process is mainly administrative in nature; i.e., it is data processing.[22]

Data processing (DP) and information systems are related but should be distinguished. DP may yield such documents as invoices and paychecks, which are not meant as information for managerial decision making. On the other side the IS needs physical actions for its selection, storage, and retrieval of data. Consider a sales agent who has to look up some data in a ledger, or who has to type an instruction at a terminal; these physical actions within the IS are part of the DP. The computer is then like any other machine that generates physical output, but the DP output is documents, such as payroll checks, invoices, and production reports. Part of this output is not needed for managerial decision making but is required by employees (paychecks), customers (invoices), stockholders (profit-and-loss account), and government (tax reports). Computers are useful here for their reduction of human, physical labor. An example of the computer as a production machine is provided by the United States Bureau of Labor Statistics; Mendelssohn (1976) describes how the computer produces a great variety of statistical reports from a mass of raw data. Computers have affected national employment mainly through this clerical cost displacement, but other effects also exist [Kleijnen (1975)].

In decision making, computers have an indirect utility, the improvement of decision making. Churchman (1972, pp. 210–212) contrasts "routine data systems" for meeting "legal and bureaucratic" requirements with MISs for decision making. (His further remarks on MISs are quite controversial.)[23] Van Zutphen (1976), on the other hand, lumps the functions together; he contends that an IS is needed not only for decision making but also for the realization of basic "transactions" in the organization.

Besides the DP system, the IS, and the physical system, a fourth logical component is the *decision system* (DS). Everybody in an organization is engaged in some decision making. Top executives spend most of their time in decision making and only a little time in "secretarial" transactions, such as telephoning and writing. At a lower level the typist spends most of the time on physical activities, but also some time on decision making. The typist has to select the kind of paper on which to type a report. The typist's decision to start a new paragraph may change the author's meaning. Physical activities require some decision making, and so does data processing. Conversely, decisions require some DP; e.g., find and read a procedure. Baumgarten et al. (1975, p. 32) and Trill (1977, p. 65) discuss the various degrees of DP performed by different personnel.

Observe that an IS requires an IS to control itself. It may be argued that this book treats those aspects that should be inspected and controlled by such a meta-IS: how accurate should the information be, how recent, and so on. Chapter Six discusses these information attributes in more detail. The meta-IS may be compared to "Control in the Large," a metasystem for "Control in the Small," discussed in Van Aken (1978, p. 196). A further analog is provided by a DBMS, in which the data dictionary provides metadata on the data stored in the database: which data are available and what is their source.[24]

A tentative picture of the relationships among the various subsystems within the organization is shown in Fig. 2.1. In "administrative plants," such as banks and insurance companies, the physical system almost completely overlaps the DP system. To avoid information overload, Fig. 2.1 ignores physical flows (machines, products, workers, and money) in and out of the organization, and certain immaterial flows (knowledge and informal communication). Some minor relationships are shown by dotted arrows. Basically, data are transformed by DP into information. This information is input into formal OR models and informal models, which yield decisions. These decisions are communicated to the physical system (and to the DP and IS systems) and result in commands for these systems. The figure does not show how these commands lead to actions that provide results. On all these systems, data must be captured for control purposes (and for other purposes, such as legal ones). And so on. In a different, yet related approach, De Blasis (1976) applies general systems theory to IS design.[25]

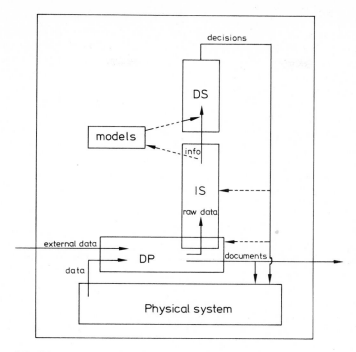

FIGURE 2–1.   *Subsystems within the Organization.*

ADDITIONAL RESEARCH AND DATA

Decisions and their information needs could be classified in several other ways. For instance, decisions might be distinguished by their function in the company, i.e., purchasing, production, sales, money receipts, or payments.[26] LeMoigne (1975) distinguishes four major flows:

- logistics; e.g., inventories, supplies

- monetary; e.g., bank accounts, accounts receivable

- assets; e.g., machines, buildings

- personnel; e.g., payroll

Van Aken (1978, p. 155) notes that "specialization" may be created by principles such as type of product, geographical area, customer type (consumer versus professional), etc.

The various reasons for using computers have been discussed in a number of publications.[27] Some empirical data on actual computer expenditures in relation to profits include a specification of how much of the EDP budget is spent on marketing, planning, and finance. These are the well-known surveys by Booz-Allen and Hamilton, and by the Diebold corporation.[28] Computer usage per industry group in the United States is discussed by Gilchrist and Weber (1973, p. 25).[29] General data sources for the computer industry are supplied in the references.[30] A plethora of data can be found in the voluminous book (six hundred pages) by Phister (1976), who emphasizes the inaccuracy of these data. (Economists accustomed to the GNP data used in econometric models will feel at ease with such inaccuracy.)

APPENDIX 2.1: POINT-OF-SALE (POS) SYSTEMS

In the most sophisticated POS systems each type of item (say, soft drink, brand X, bottle size Y) has a unique code that can be read optically by a scanner at the check-out stand. This identification is fed into a computer, on-line. The computer retrieves the item's price and feeds it back to the check-out stand so that the customer receives an invoice, pays, and leaves. At the same time the computer subtracts one unit of this particular item from the bookkeeping inventory. Technical variants are possible. For instance, the checkout may be on-line with a minicomputer; periodically (say, daily) the central computer is fed all transactions that have occurred.[31] In a Belgian self-service wholesale organization, customers (i.e., retailers) hand in a punched card per article so that no sophisticated, optical reading equipment is needed.[32] The reader can see the references for a detailed description of the basics of POS.[33]

The unique code mentioned above has been realized in the United States by the universal product code (UPC): each item has a small sticker, the size of a large postage stamp, with a graphical code. Heijn (1978) mentions that depending on the assortment, 75 to 80 percent of all items already has this UPC. In Europe, the European Article Numbering Association (EAN) has been active since 1977. Each European country has its own system.[34]

The on-line connection of the optical scanner to the CPU permits continuous stockkeeping. Besides being completely up to date, the information on the sales becomes more accurate. Without POS equipment, only total sales revenues are known at the end of the day. The sales volume per item can be determined only indirectly by periodically counting the physical inventory (sales volume = old inventory + orders received − new inventory). The effects of more timely, accurate, and detailed information on inventory management are discussed in Appendix 2.2. Note that if the organization comprises multiple stores, the stock information may be used to ship stock from one store with excess inventories to another store with a pending stockout situation.

Walsh (1976) lists no less than thirty-one potential benefits of POS systems. Besides the inventory management benefits, the following aspects of POS systems may justify such systems economically.

Avoiding Price Errors

Without POS equipment the price of an item is keyed in manually at the cash register. Errors can and do arise. These errors do not have zero expectation because only those errors to the customer's disadvantage are protested. Ricker and Krueckeberg (1971, pp. 5–6, 18) specify various errors in this category: misinterpretation of price mark, overlooked items, and "typing" errors. Losses due to these errors range from 0.2 to 1.4 percent of sales revenues. (For the Netherlands this number is estimated to be 0.5 percent.) POS systems can reduce these errors by 57 percent. SMI (Super Market Institute) estimates that in European supermarkets errors occur in 2.0 to 2.5 percent of all items.[35] In an experimental system in Switzerland, this number decreased to 0.0014 percent.

Labor Saving at Checkout

With a POS system installed, personnel may handle more customers. Ricker and Krueckeberg (1971, pp. 12, 17–18) report that customer throughput at the checkout increased 19 percent. SMI (1972, p. 13), despite reports of insignificant savings in a Swiss experiment, expects significant savings in supermarkets in the United States, where sales tax must be computed, personal checks verified, etc. Credit verification is discussed in the other references also. Reportedly training of checkout personnel is easier with POS systems.

Labor Saving in Price Marking

Labor cost for price marking of articles amounts to 0.15 percent of sales revenues, and later price changes affect 2 to 5 percent of all items.[36] With the UPC individual items need not be price marked; the price is posted on the shelf for the customers and is also stored in computer memory. UPC reduces price-marking costs from $5.00 to $0.33 per thousand items.[37]

Management Information System (MIS)

POS systems show exactly when an item was sold whereas traditional systems record only total sales revenues per day. Hence with POS systems the effects of sales promotions can be detected.[38] Ricker and Krueckeberg (1971, pp. 2–3, 24) report many additional uses of this detailed information: shelf space allocation, labor scheduling, product mix selection, and delivery scheduling. Actually management's use of the detailed information provided by POS systems is the crucial part of such systems.[39]

POS systems may result in a variety of economic benefits in addition to those just listed. POS system costs, like those for many electronic "tools," are expected to decrease further in the near future. Any decrease in operating costs is crucial for supermarkets because of their very low profit margins: net profits amounted to only 0.92 percent of sales in the United States in 1969.[40] Jones's (1977) monograph on POS in the retail business covers these topics in much more detail. For the relationships between POS and future EFT (electronic funds transfer, a cashless society), the reader can consult the references.[41]

APPENDIX 2.2: INVENTORY MANAGEMENT AND COMPUTERS

Any textbook on operations research contains both simple and more sophisticated mathematical inventory models. The simplest and oldest model concerns the well-known Wilson or Camp square-root formula for the economic order quantity, EOQ. Nowadays computer manufacturers and software houses furnish inventory management packages, based on more practical, less restrictive assumptions. These packages use heuristics to derive a satisficing, not necessarily optimal solution. IMPACT, one package made available by IBM (1967), is meant for managing a multitude of items as is necessary in supermarkets and the wholesale trade. Procedures as sophisticated as dynamic programming seem inappropriate for real-life applications, at least for now.

There are several advantages to using computers in inventory management. First, computers can serve as *decision aids* because computers facilitate scientific modeling. For instance, even the simple square-root formula, when applied to thousands of different articles, requires a small computer. Elaborated packages like IMPACT have provisions for interactions among articles (joint orders or quantity discounts) and forecast routines for trend and seasonal articles. Such packages definitely require a computer. The value of a computer can be determined by comparing the inventory cost of a simple inventory management system to the inventory cost plus computer cost of a more sophisticated inventory system.

A second advantage is that computers provide better *data* and data processing. It can be proved that the "order point" (the minimum inventory level that requires reordering) is equal to the *expected* demand during a lead time plus review time plus record-keeping time-lag, increased with the *safety* stock over that total period. Lead time is the time required by the supplier to deliver the order. Review time is the time during which stock is not monitored; e.g., if stock is measured (and possibly reordered) only on Mondays, review time is one week. The record-keeping time-lag is the time needed to update inventory records. Safety stock is meant for demand in excess of the average. Hence computers can affect inventories in the following ways.

The review period and record-keeping time-lag can be reduced by computers that facilitate monitoring inventories more frequently, the limit being continuous monitoring through on-line, point-of-sale equipment. In this way both working stock and safety stock are reduced. Without a POS system *physical* stock counting is necessary and lengthens the review period to, say, at least one week.

Computers decrease bookkeeping errors. Decreased inaccuracy means that less uncertainty remains and therefore less safety stock is required. (See Exercise 12.)

Decisions on whether a new order should be placed require knowledge of future demand as well as of current inventory status. Computers can revise estimated demand more frequently. Moreover, the input data may be more accurate, the prediction period may decrease, and the forecast procedure can be more sophisticated. Usually the forecast frequency is lower than the review frequency; e.g., monthly forecasts may be combined with weekly review.

The *variability* of the lead time may decrease if delivery times are specified when an order is placed. [See IBM (1967).] The *mean* lead time may decrease if there is an on-line computer connection with the supplier, whether an outside supplier or a company-owned central warehouse. Such on-line connections eliminate some components of the lead time. An example of on-line connections in the aircraft industry is given in IBM (1974). Computers may also be used to speed up warehouse operations.[42] Gross and Soriano (1972) studied the effects of reduced lead times. Specified delivery times also reduce the so-called early-order stock [IBM (1967)].

The literature on inventory models is overwhelming. Nahmias's (1978) survey includes 131 references. Also recommended is the survey by Hax (1976). A recent, highly practical book is Brown (1977). Taylor (1979) presents a sample survey on the practical use of computerized models. Kleijnen and Rens (1978) critically evaluate a standard, inventory-control computer package, IBM's IMPACT system.

The American Production and Inventory Control Society (APICS) recently concluded that the need for basic information is paramount in inventory management.[43] Data accuracy is improved not only by POS equipment but also by computer procedures such as input verification.[44] For a theoretical study on the role of accuracy in inventory management, see Iglehart and Morey (1972) and Chapter Seven.

EXERCISES

1. Give some more examples of decisions at the operational, tactical, and strategic levels.

2. Why have some decisions moved from the tactical–strategic level to the operational level?

3. The solution of the optimal route for a traveling salesperson might be classified as operational but nonstructured. Explain.

4. Tactical and strategic decisions may not be fully programmable. Nevertheless modern computers can be useful in their number-crunching capability. Explain.

5. A computer with a data bank and on-line terminals (like a cathode ray tube, CRT) can be used in urban planning. Is this operational, structured decision making?

6. What is risk analysis?

7. What are the effects on data quality of on-line terminals in retail stores, banks, etc.?

8. Which is more important, good data or good models?

9. What is the purpose of chain addresses in the records of a DBMS?

10. How would you define a MIS?

11. What would be the ideal solution to determine which data to incorporate in a MIS, and how to use the data?

12. Assume that safety stock (SS) is set equal to $k\sigma_d$ where σ_d denotes the standard error of (measured) demand during the next relevant period. Derive that book errors increase the required safety stock.

13. What are the effects of more frequent inventory reviews?

14. In POS systems with universal product code (UPC), prices are displayed not on the articles themselves but on the shelf. What might be the customers' reaction?

15. Why does POS equipment not give exact data on the inventory status even if such equipment were to give 100 percent correct data on sales volume?

16. If inventory is reviewed once a week, what is the average age of the information?

17. What might be a relationship between forecast frequency and order size? (Hint: When can a forecast be utilized?)

18. Management wants to examine the productivity of, say, tellers in the bank or cashiers in the grocery store. Which computer hardware would enable such studies?

NOTES

1. Bonney (1969, p. 119), McLean (1973, p. 21), Verhelst (1974, p. 194).

2. Etz (1965) offers this explanation for the shift in emphasis from clerical cost replacement to information aid in decision making: before the 1960s lack of information caused economic theory to concentrate on the supply side; now that information is more plentiful, the demand side (i.e., the utility of information) is studied. More adequate explanations include the fact that computers' clerical applications require less sophistication because they are restricted to a limited part of the organization, e.g., payroll administration.

3. See Brevoord (1971, p. 12), Eldin and Croft (1974, pp. 88–90), and Verhelst (1974, pp. 95–111).

4. See also Ansoff (1971), Le Moigne (1974), and Taggart and Tharp (1977).

5. See Verhelst (1974, pp. 99–103), Blumenthal (1969), Brevoord (1971, pp. 13, 33), Frielink (1978), Grindley and Humble (1973), Grochla (1970, p. 335), Hayes and Radosevich (1974), Hax (1976, pp. 63–67), Jones (1977, pp. 14–19), W. R. King (1977, pp. 2–3), Korteweg (1978), Lucas et al. (1974, p. 248), van Aken (1978, pp. 164–165), and Wissema (1978).

6. For corporate models see Highland et al. (1976), Naylor and Jeffress (1975), Naylor and Schauland (1976), and Schrieber (1970). For an application of corporate models in a MIS see W. R. King (1977, pp. 4–10).

7. Blumenthal (1969, p. 19), Bosman (1976, p. 13), Brevoord (1971, p. 25), Ein-Dor and Segev (1978b, pp. 1633–1635), Gorry and Morton (1971), Mertens and Griese (1972, pp. 235–236), Stern (1970), van de Wouw (1977, pp. 67–72), Verhelst (1974, pp. 238–240), and Zijlker (1974). See also Dearden (1972).

8. See also Penniman et al. (1978).

9. Kleijnen (1976c) and (1978a) discuss DBMS, MIS, and types of models, and give many references. See also Carlson (1979) and the articles in House (1977), Keen and Morton (1978), Mantey et al. (1977), Stabell (1978) and Thesen (1978). Dutton and Kraemer (1978, p. 207) distinguish two MIS conceptions: "decision-based" (OR modeling) versus "data-based" (DP view).

10. See Goddard (1977), Holden (1976), and also the references in Appendix 2.1.

11. Verhelst (1974, p. 194).

12. Lieber and Orgler (1975), and van Zanten (1975, p. 13).

13. van Zanten (1975, pp. 17–18).

14. Adams (1975, p. 338), and Dutton and Kraemer (1978).

15. Gorry and Morton (1971, p. 62), Hofer (1970, p. 169), and G. M. Hoffmann (1975). See also the survey among middle management by Shaul (1964).

16. Emery (1971, pp. 39–42), Knutsen and Nolan (1974, pp. 33–34), and Verhelst (1974, pp. 195–197).

17. Grochla (1970), and Knutsen and Nolan (1974, p. 30).

18. Lincoln (1977).

19. Brevoord (1971, pp. 17–19), Grindley and Humble (1973), and Hertz (1969, pp. 179–197).

20. See also Debons (1974) for a recent survey on the theory of information syntax, semantics, pragmatics, and this theory's relation to "knowledge." See also Gould (1971) and Nielen (1972) for a discussion of the information concept.

21. For instance, Nielen (1972).

22. Baumgarten et al. (1975, pp. 23, 33) and van Dinten (1978, p. 12).

23. See also Peterson (1977).

24. Plagman and Altshuler (1972).

25. See also Welke (1977a, pp. 5–6).

26. Verhelst (1974, pp. 86–88, 127). He also distinguishes "operational" and "management" ISs besides the "accounting" system. See also Blumenthal (1969), Bosman (1976, p. 12), Emery (1977, p. 8), Hax (1976, pp. 67–71), and van Belkum (1978).

27. A selection of references includes Bénay (1965, pp. 10–14), Bonney (1969), Boutell (1968, pp. 113–114), Chervany and Dickson (1970, p. 303), J. Diebold (1969), Eldin and Croft (1974, p. 37), Emery (1969, pp. 35–36) and (1971, pp. 6–8), Gregory and Van Horn (1963, pp. 552–554), Knutsen and Nolan (1974), and McLean (1973).

28. Dean (1968) and Diebold (1973), respectively. See also Phister (1976, pp. 135–138).

29. Avolio (1975) discusses the Italian situation.

30. Carter (1974), Sharpe (1969, pp. 199–210, 494–540), and Van Horn (1973, p. 173).

31. Power (1971).

32. Heijn (1978).

33. ACM (1974), Ricker and Krueckeberg (1971), and Walsh (1976). Computer aspects are discussed by Power (1971). The most detailed exposition is by Jones (1977).

34. See Dreesmann (1978).

35. SMI (1972, p. 14).

36. Ricker and Krueckeberg (1971, pp. 18–22).

37. Myers (1972, p. 142).

38. Little and Shapiro (1977), SMI (1972, p. 15).

39. SMI (1972, pp. 15–16); see also Power (1971).

40. Ricker and Krueckeberg (1971, p. 3).

41. Kling (1978); see also Heijn (1978).

42. Mertens (1972, pp. 155, 159–162), and Parks (1972, pp. 237, 241).

43. APICS (1974, p. 11).

44. See Grupp (1974, p. 179), and Chapter Six.

TECHNICAL COMPUTER PERFORMANCE

CHAPTER THREE

INTRODUCTION

Technical performance measures merit only brief discussion because financial performance is the focus of this book. Nevertheless technical performance cannot be omitted altogether because economic performance is affected by technical variables. For instance, bad response times lead to outdated information, which—as coming chapters demonstrate—affects the economic performance of the company. Moreover, this chapter informs the management-oriented reader about a related, yet different school of research. This school has its own organizations; e.g., the Special Interest Group on Measurement and Evaluation (SIGMETRICS) of the Association of Computing Machinery (ACM), with its own publication *Performance Evaluation Review*, and its regular conferences.[1] The abundance of publications in this area is demonstrated by the long bibliographies by Agajanian (1976) and Miller (1973).

The *technical* performance of a computer system or a subsystem, such as the central processing unit (CPU), can be measured in different ways:

- number of instructions executed per time unit;

- throughput; i.e., number of jobs per time unit;

- response time; i.e., completion time minus submittal time; and

- reliability; i.e., probability of the computer's being operative.

Phister (1976, p. 89) lists several more technical performance measures and provides real-life data. These criteria (performance variables) represent the traditional approach to the performance of computers. Even management-oriented books list such technical characteristics as criteria of effectiveness.[2] This chapter briefly surveys a number of techniques for the prediction of technical performance.

MISCELLANEOUS TECHNIQUES

Originally a computer's performance was measured by the execution time per computer instruction, e.g., the time per add-instruction. The user needed no techniques because these execution times were taken from the manufacturers' manuals.

This approach can be improved by weighing various types of instructions (add, shift, etc.) by their relative use, the *instruction mix*. If this mix represents a complete program, such as a payroll system or a matrix inversion, the mix is called a *kernel.* An alternative is to program and execute an actual job (or at least the core of the job) and to measure the total execution time, the *benchmark* evaluation. Note that these definitions are not standard; the terms benchmark and kernel are sometimes interchanged.

The techniques above concentrate on the performance of a specific subsystem, especially the CPU; but database management system (DBMS) oriented studies also have been performed.[3] Other techniques try to measure the whole system, hardware and software. Such a technique may develop formulas for the time required to execute a program: *formula timing.* A simple example follows: let T denote the time to compile a job, C the number of cards in the source deck, S the number of subprograms; and let the β's be constants. Then this equation might be postulated:

$$T = \beta_0 + \beta_1 C + \beta_2 S. \tag{3.1}$$

An alternative technique is to obtain *improvement factors* per subsystem and to determine how much total execution time decreases. Improving a subsystem has an effect only if that subsystem is a bottleneck during part of the total process. To depict such bottlenecks, a graph, called the *system profile,* is prepared. A simple example is displayed in Fig. 3.1. This system profile is only a summary of the system's activities, and does not show the order in which events occur. Hence, Fig. 3.1 means that during 32 percent of the total elapsed time the CPU works nonoverlapped with channel activities. Figure 3.1 does not indicate a sequence in which first the CPU works for 32 time units, and then the channels become active during 40 + 28 time units.

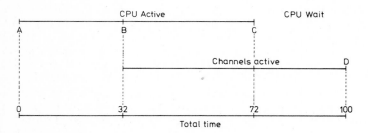

FIGURE 3–1.   *A System Profile Example.*

Suppose CPU speed is improved by a factor 4. Wrong reasoning is shown in Fig. 3.2, in which $A'C'$ equals $72/4 = 18$, and $B'D'$ equals BD ($= 100 - 32 = 68$), so that between CPU and Channels no overlap remains ($B'C' = 0$). Figure 3.1 had to distinguish parts during which the CPU is dominant (AB), the channels are dominant (CD), and both subsystems are active (BC). The improvement in CPU yields Fig. 3.3, in which $A'B'$ equals $32/4 = 8$, and $B'D'$ equals the original BD. (See also Exercise 9.)

An alternative to "profile conversion" is the *synthetic model.* It, like a simulation model (see the section on simulation), combines subsystems to evaluate the total system. However, the synthetic model is based on a gross model. Summary statistics (say, cards per minute) are used together with *overlap factors,* which express roughly how subsystems can operate simultaneously during at least part of the total system time.

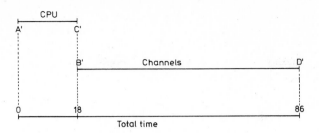

FIGURE 3-2.   Wrong New System Profile.

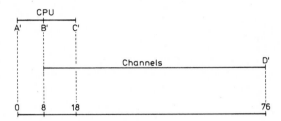

FIGURE 3-3.   Correct New System Profile.

Consider the following simplistic example. The configuration is composed of a CPU, a card reader/puncher, and a line printer. Cards are read at 500 cards per minute; reading 400 cards takes 0.8 minutes or 48 seconds. Lines are printed at a speed of 1000 lines per minute; the output of 100 lines takes 0.1 minutes or 6 seconds. Assume that a kernel evaluation shows that the CPU needs 27 seconds to execute the application. As a next step consider the overlap between the card reader and line printer, the two components of the input/output (I/O) subsystem. Knowledge of the data channels and control units leads one to assume a particular overlap factor, called k, between the card reader and the line printer; i.e., both devices can be active simultaneously. Without any overlap ($k = 0$), the total time needed by the two devices would be 48 + 6 = 54 seconds. With complete overlap ($k = 1$), the total time would be reduced to 48 seconds. If k were 0.8, total time becomes 48 + 0.2 × 6 = 49.2 seconds. In general, two devices with execution times t_i and overlap k yield

$$\text{Total time} = \max (t_1, t_2) + (1 - k) \cdot \min (t_1, t_2). \tag{3.2}$$

Next again using overlap factors, combine the I/O and the CPU subsystems. If the CPU needs 27 seconds, the I/O subsystem needs 49.2 seconds, and the overlap factor is 0.9, applying Eq. (3.2) yields a total time of 49.2 + (0.1)(27) = 51.9 seconds. Usually the exact interaction between components cannot be expressed by the overlap factors. To remedy these shortcomings, simulation is required.

The simple techniques discussed so far are explained in detail by Drummond (1973) and in more advanced textbooks such as Hellerman and Conroy (1975). Summaries are given by several authors.[4] These references indicate in which situations the simple techniques above are adequate to predict technical performance. Many more references appear in these publications and in a number of bibliographies.[5]

ANALYTICAL OR MODELS

Operations research (OR) techniques offer a different approach to the technical evaluation of computers. In many situations these techniques are more accurate because they can represent interactions among programs in a multiprogramming system. OR techniques do not require the system's physical availability as benchmark programs do. A discussion of the adequacy of OR techniques versus the other methods can be found in the literature cited above. Consider some of these techniques in more detail.

Queuing theory has been applied to *time-sharing* computer systems. Scherr (1967) derives the following simplified time-sharing model. A user may be either "thinking" or "waiting for output" at the terminal. The average think time is λ so that requests for service arrive at the computer with an average speed of $1/\lambda$. Suppose it takes the computer μ time units at the average to serve requests. Let n denote the number of users signed on. The system is in state j if j users are in the waiting status (waiting includes being served); hence $n - j$ users are in the thinking state. Only these latter $n - j$ customers can generate requests for service. Hence, the probability that during a short time interval h, a request for service is generated is

$$\frac{1}{\lambda} (n - j)h$$

if the system is in state j. The probability that a user completes service during h equals

$$\frac{1}{\mu} h.$$

(This simple model does not account for time slicing, a fundamental characteristic of time-sharing computer systems.) For the subsequent, tedious computations of basic queuing theory, consult any textbook on OR in general or queuing in particular. This computation yields the results summarized in Fig. 3.4, in which ϱ denotes traffic intensity μ/λ. See also Hellermann and Conroy (1975, pp. 137–140).

A more realistic model of time sharing accounts for the "round-robin" queuing discipline; i.e., after a time slice the customer is put at the end of the queue, the queue discipline being first-in, first-out (FIFO). An alternative is that the customer, after having been served the jth time ($j = 1, 2, \ldots$) during one time slice, is put at the end of queue $j + 1$; queue j has priority over $j + 1$ while each queue has the FIFO discipline. A different factor of interest is the length of the time slice. A larger time slice decreases the probability of having to remove the current customer and having to fetch a new customer whose program may reside on disc and so require "swapping" between primary and secondary storage. An interesting formal model of various priority schemes is presented in Ruschitzka and Fabry (1977). Note that queuing theory has been advanced by the needs of computer science. Computer scientists have analyzed and developed the theory on *networks* of queues.

The approach above concentrates on CPU scheduling algorithms. Other models represent *data management* problems; e.g., how should data be distributed over primary and secondary memory. The concept of the working set is important in data management. In paging, a program including its data is divided into "pages,"

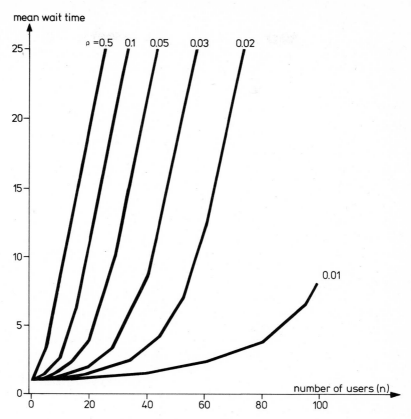

FIGURE 3–4. Mean Wait Time in a Simplified Time-sharing Queuing Model.

which may be stored either in main memory or on disc. Let X_i be the identification number of page i ($i = 1,. . .,n$) of a program. Consider the page-address stream 1, 1, 1, 2, 2, 2 versus 1, 2, 1, 2, 1, 2. The frequency of each X_i-value is the same, namely 3/6. The working sets W, however, are different where

> $W(i, ,h)$: set of *different* page numbers between the
> current page reference i and the old reference $i - h$
> (h is called the window size).

Hence the example results in Table 3.1. (For another example refer to Exercise 10.)
    The few analytical models, including queuing models, for the computer system as a *whole* must necessarily be rather coarse. The *maintenance* of computers presents a different problem area: reliability engineering. The literature on analytic models includes discussions of on-line computer systems, computer networks, and storage devices.[6]

TABLE 3.1.   Working Set Example

i	X_i	h = 2 W(i, 2)	h = 3 W(i, 3)	X_i	h = 2 W(i, 2)	h = 3 W(i, 3)
1	1	1	1	1	1	1
2	1	1	1	2	1, 2	1, 2
3	1	1	1	1	1, 2	1, 2
4	2	1, 2	1, 2	2	1, 2	1, 2
5	2	2	1, 2	1	1, 2	1, 2
6	2	2	2	2	1, 2	1, 2
Average size:		$\frac{7}{6} = 1\frac{1}{6}$	$\frac{8}{6} = 1\frac{1}{3}$		$\frac{11}{6} = 1\frac{5}{6}$	$\frac{11}{6} = 1\frac{5}{6}$

SIMULATION

The OR technique of simulation should not be confused with the computer technique of "simulation": a program written for computer 1 can be executed on computer 2 (possibly a newer computer) using special software. "Emulation" means that this software is assisted by special hardware.[7]

The OR simulation technique is usually applied if the model has to be more realistic than an analytical model permits. The simulation model may represent the effects of specific subsystems. Simulation is an extremely versatile technique that can mimic the behavior of any dynamic, possibly stochastic system.[8] Chapter Eight discusses the simulation of information and decision systems; here the emphasis is on the simulation of computer systems per se.

Queuing systems are a most important class of simulated systems. Figure 3.5 shows a simple queuing simulation of a one-server queuing system with FIFO queuing discipline. In this example the time axis is sliced into intervals of fixed length; at each interval, whether an event will happen is checked. An alternative programming technique is "event sequencing": the simulation jumps to the next, most imminent event and skips periods of time during which nothing happens. Readers unfamiliar with simulation may skip the next paragraph and the example of Fig. 3.6.

Figure 3.6 sketches the simulation of a simplified time-sharing computer model, which uses the matrices QUEUE and SERVER shown in Table 3.2. Note that AT denotes not the interarrival time but the absolute arrival time. PRI may be identical to the last time the job was served during a time slice. (In a FIFO queuing rule, PRI would equal AT.) The SERVER table allows for m servers ($m \geq 1$), but Fig. 3.6 assumes a single server ($m = 1$). In Fig. 3.6 a job is served during a time slice of length TS unless the remaining service time is smaller than TS. (Refer also to Exercise 15.)

In a computer there are many queuing problems; e.g., in a time-sharing system customers are waiting for service from a single CPU. Additional problems in a time-sharing system include job shop and allocation problems like when to execute which program, and where to store programs and data.[9]

Besides stochastic simulation, *trace-driven simulation* is a special approach for computer evaluation. A trace is a diagnostic program used for performing a check on another program or for demonstrating its operation.[10] Trace-driven simulation

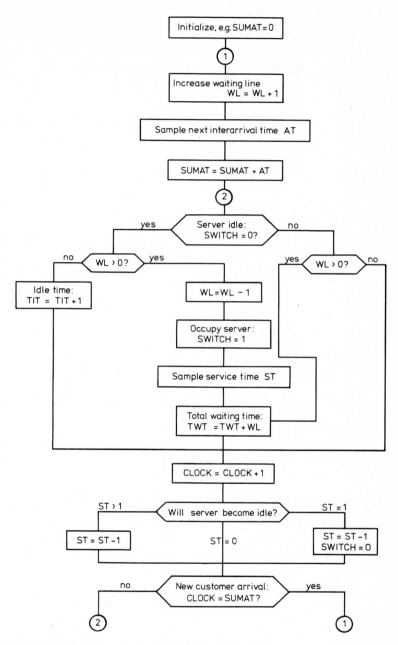

FIGURE 3-5. *One-server FIFO Simulation.*

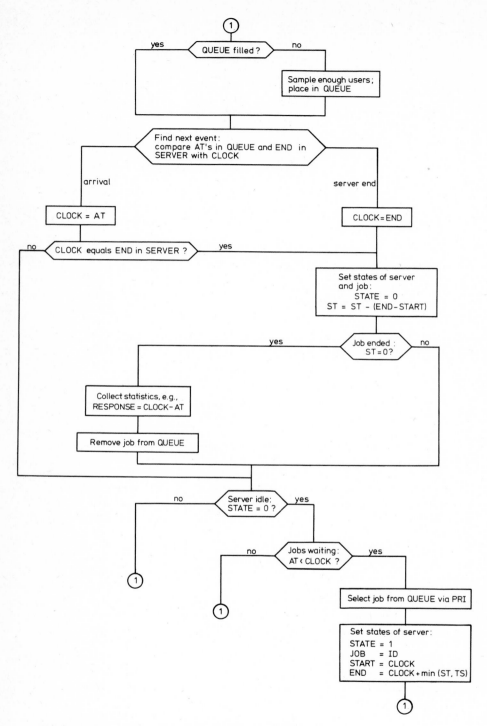

FIGURE 3–6.   Simulation of Time-sharing Computer System.

TABLE 3.2.   Tables Used in Simulation of Fig. 3.6

Queue

	ID (1)	AT (2)	ST (3)	PRI (4)
1				
2				
•				
•				
•				
n				

Legend:

ID = job number
AT = arrival time
ST = remaining service time
PRI = priority

Server

	STATE (1)	JOB (2)	START (3)	END (4)
l				
•				
•				
•				
m				

STATE = idle (0) or busy (1)
JOB   = ID of job being
            served
START = time service started
END   = time service will end

utilizes as input the deterministic, empirical data obtained through the execution of actual programs on a particular computer, these data being generated by tracing the computer programs. This input is then processed by a model simulating alternative computer systems. Usually this model is less detailed than a stochastic simulation model. Figure 3.7 shows part of a larger trace-driven simulation presented in Drummond (1973, pp. 172–197). In this example the CPU may be engaged in computing (left branch) or in I/O handling. In the former case the observed, traced time is re-computed by using a general improvement factor. In the latter case a special time is looked up. A comprehensive survey of trace-driven simulation can be found in Sherman (1976). A related simulation approach is discussed by Kumar & Davidson (1978).

To facilitate simulation modeling and programming, much software is available. Besides general programming languages like FORTRAN and ALGOL, many special languages, like GPSS and SIMSCRIPT[11], enable discrete-event simulation of any system, not just a computer system. There are also languages such as DYNAMO and CSMP for difference-equation simulation models, which are less relevant to computer evaluation; Chapter Eight returns to this type of models. Simulation languages developed especially for computer evaluation include ECSS (Extendable Computer System Simulation), CTSS, LOMUSS, OSSL, and QAL.[12] A "precanned" simulation model, one in which the user has to specify input parameters only, has been developed by the System Development Corporation. This interactive, discrete-event simulation is called IMSIM. [See SDC (1975).] A simulation package that does not follow the discrete-event approach is SCERT (System Computer Evaluation and Review Technique). Moreover SCERT contains a file with data on technical and economic characteristics of hardware and software components

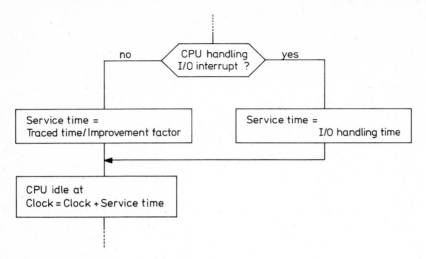

FIGURE 3–7.   Trace-driven Simulation Example.

available on the EDP market.[13] Numerous simulation studies on the technical performance of DBMSs appear in Highland et al. (1976). Clearly the simulation of computer systems is a well established practice.[14] Of course, simulation and analytical
modeling can be performed together: simulation results can be checked against
theoretical results, and can also guide analytical research; analytical results may reduce simulation effort.[15]

RELATED ISSUES

For an existing system the computer can measure its own activities through hardware
and software *monitors*.[16] The resulting data may be compared to the model's output: model validation. The input data for alternative models may also be provided
by monitors. Nevertheless uncertainty on how to formulate the input creates a
workload characterization problem: level of detail may vary; different distribution
functions can be formulated for queuing models; and empirical data can be used for
simulation.[17] In the experimentation with existing computer configurations, statistical problems arise on which techniques (regression or analysis of variance) and
which measures to use.[18]

Lyons (1978) describes the use of gaming to teach configuring computer systems. Players confronted with a hypothetical job mix have to make decisions on the
computer's configuration. A simulation model computes the technical and economic
consequences of the players' decisions. Chapter Eight discusses extensively the use of
gaming in the economic evaluation of information systems.

Schneidewind's (1967) survey found that in practice scientific methods were
rarely used, at least at that time.[19] Very few of the seven hundred papers E. F.
Miller (1973) lists on "computer performance" concern the *economic* performance
(effectiveness as opposed to efficiency). Unlike the technical performance of computer systems, the economic performance of information systems forms a very un-

structured problem area. In the technical area the questions are clear; the challenge is to develop the right answers. Economic analysis has not yet reached the stage of developing appropriate techniques; the correct frameworks (what to look for) must be developed. The following chapters gradually sharpen the focus on the economic aspects of computer systems.

EXERCISES

1. Mean response time equals mean service time plus what? Define the 90 percent quantile of the response time.

2. Denote the arrival (submittal) time of a job by a_i and the completion time by c_i $(i = 1, . . .,n)$. Give formulas for the average response time $\bar{r}$ and throughput T.

3. Will the mean response time be smaller for the first-in-first-out rule or for the small-jobs-first rule? How about throughput? The results that Vasicek (1977) derived for the mean and variance of waiting times hold for any queuing discipline, provided the discipline is "independent of the service time of the customers in the queue at the instant of selection." Give an example of a queue discipline that violates this assumption.

4. Which of these criteria interest the user and which criteria interest the computer center's management: mean response time, throughput, and utilization percentage of CPU?

5. In a computer composed of two parallel CPUs, what is the probability that the system is available, i.e., that at least one CPU works? What is the reliability of a computer system composed of n components (CPU, channel, etc.) in series?

6. System 1 is composed of n parallel processors, each with a speed of $1/n$ of the speed of system 2, which has a single fast processor. Which system has the higher reliability? Which has the better mean response time? [For a general discussion see Sauer and Chandy (1979).]

7. From a statistical point of view, discuss benchmark programs.

8. Does the example of formula timing in Eq. (3.1) account for multiprogramming?

9. If the channels in the system profile of Fig. 3.1 improve by a factor 2, and the CPU shows no improvement, what is the resulting system profile? Derive the system profile if both improvement factors apply. How might the improvement factors be determined?

10. Some analytical computer models use the processor sharing (PS) queuing discipline: each job $i(i = 1, . . ., n)$ is assumed to receive service at $(1/n)$th the rate of a single job. Which actual priority scheme is approximated by the artificial PS rule?

11. Using $h = 2, 5$, and 10, respectively, compute the average working set size for the following page-address stream, taken from Hellerman and Conroy (1976, p. 288): 4, 22, 4, 22, 4, 23, 5, 23, 5, 24.

12. If an address is denoted by n bits, and the page size is 2^s, how many pages result?

13. Monitors can disturb the process that is being measured because they themselves require computer time. Do software monitors take more time or less than hardware monitors?

14. It is well known that a computer's input/output is much slower than its computing. If you want to improve throughput in a multiprogramming system, should you give priority to I/O-bound jobs or to CPU-bound jobs?

15. In considering the organization of data on a disc, which two criteria have to be balanced?

16. Let the priority of a job in a time-sharing system be determined by setting PRI in Table 3.2 equal to the job's arrival time AT. After a job has received a time slice, PRI equals END. Will new arrivals always have priority over older jobs?

17. Devise a simulation for a simple model of your own computer system.

Note: For more exercises see Ferrari (1978) and Hellerman and Conroy (1975).

NOTES

1. For instance Chandy and Reiser (1978), and PROCEEDINGS (1976). For European activities see Beilner and Gelenbe (1978), and Gelenbe (1976).

2. For instance, Eldin and Croft (1974, p. 140), and Seiler (1969, pp. 45–68).

3. See Highland et al. (1976), INFOTECH (1977), Joyce et al. (1974), and the discussion in the next sections.

4. Joslin (1968, pp. 67–115), Lucas (1971), Sharpe (1969, pp. 295–314), and Timmreck (1973, pp. 207–209).

5. To the above references, add Buchholz (1969), Scull (1973), and Walkowicz (1974). See also the contributions in Part Four of McFarlan and Nolan (1975).

6. General surveys of queuing theory are given by Bhat (1969) and Crabill et al. (1977). An excellent (but rather old) introduction to and survey of analytical time-sharing models is McKinney (1969). Fine textbooks on analytical (including queuing) models for computers are Hellerman and Conroy (1975) and Kobayashi (1978); see also Ferrari (1978), INFOTECH (1977d) and (1978b), and Svobodova (1976). Queuing theory is summarized and applied to on-line computer systems by Pritchard (1976). Networks of computers are analyzed by Kleinrock (1976); a comprehensive survey of networks of queues is provided by Graham (1978) and Le Moine (1977). Denning (1970) discusses the storage allocation problem in two-level memory systems; see also the references in Kimbleton (1972). Stochastic models for the time to access data, randomly or sequentially, on various memory devices are given in Hanssmann (1971, pp. 119–158) and Sharpe (1969, pp. 363–441); a recent, extensive survey is given by Severance and Carlis (1977). The performance of the total computer system is studied by a few authors; see de Lutis (1977), Hellerman and Smith (1970), Kimbleton (1972), Kriebel (1967), and Silver et al. (1971). For reliability studies see Barlow and Proschan (1975), Drummond (1973, pp. 9–15), Hellerman and Conroy (1975, pp. 80–90), Hsu (1968), Pritchard (1976, pp. 183–209), and Chapter Six. Extensive bibliographies including analytical models are Agajanian (1976), and E. F. Miller (1973); see also *Computing Reviews*. Some German references are Baugut (1973) and Osswald (1973). A recent synopsis of analytical work in computer science is given by Greenberg et al. (1978).

7. See Drummond (1973, pp. 197–199), Gould (1971), and Leventhal (1977). Proprietary simulation packages are surveyed by Howard (1977).

8. The literature on simulation and its applications is overwhelming. We refer to Kleijnen (1975, pp. 28–29) and (1976b) for literature including bibliographies. A recent, outstanding book on simulation is Zeigler (1976). Chapter Eight gives more references.

9. For a simple outline of time sharing see Meadow (1970, pp. 99–110). For tutorials on the simulation approach as applied to computer evaluation see Drummond (1973, pp. 147–172), Hellerman and Conroy (1975, pp. 112–118), MacDougall (1970), and Maisel and Gnugnoli (1972, pp. 317–341).

10. See T. E. Bell (1971, p. 22), and Gould (1971).

11. There is much literature on simulation languages. A recent survey is Kreutzer (1976); see also Kleijnen (1976b) for references.

12. See Hart (1970), Highland (1976), Huesmann and Goldberg (1967), Leroudier and Parent (1976, pp. 12–14), Maguire (1972), Nunamaker et al. (1976, p. 682), and Wyatt (1975).

13. See Dearden et al. (1971, pp. 98–124), Evans (1972), and Huesmann and Goldberg (1967).

14. To the references in notes 7 through 13 add T. E. Bell (1972), Chanson and Bishop (1977), Coppus et al. (1976), de Lutis (1977), Hanssmann (1971), Howard (1977, pp. 28–29), Hultén and Söderlund (1977), Lucas (1971), and E. F. Miller (1973, p. 10). See also Highland et al. (1976, pp. 281–330, 364–385, 460–471, 513–536). The recent article by Unger (1978) is recommended.

15. Examples are Estrin and Kleinrock (1967), Scherr (1967), and Schwetman (1978).

16. Auerbach (1975), T. E. Bell (1971), Drummond (1973, pp. 219–280), Hart (1970), Hellerman and Conroy (1975), Howard (1977, pp. 30–32), Maguire (1972), Maynard (1974), E. F. Miller (1973), Nutt (1973), and Rose (1978).

17. See Agrawala and Mohr (1978), Boehm and Bell (1975, pp. 32–34), Dujmovic (1978, pp. 6, 8–10), Joslin (1977, pp. 158–170), and Phister (1976, pp. 88–96).

18. See Carlson (1974), Frane (1975, pp. 447–508), Freiberger (1972), and Jain (1977).

19. See also Timmreck (1973, pp. 215–217).

SCORING METHODS, MULTIPLE CRITERIA, AND UTILITY ANALYSIS

CHAPTER **FOUR**

INTRODUCTION

Technical performance measures like throughput and response times were of major interest in the early years of computerization. Moreover, scientific evaluation methods like simulation and queuing analysis tend to concentrate on such single performance measures. Gradually, however, the computer buyer came to realize that relevant aspects of a computer are many: hardware and software characteristics determining technical performance, conversion effort, availability of additional hardware and software from the vendor in the future, flexibility of capacity increase, training facilities, delivery date, costs, and so on. W. G. Miller's (1969) checklist gives 82 relevant characteristics (see Table 4.1), and many such lists can be found in the literature.[1] Certainly there is no single, relevant performance characteristic.

Scoring methods were introduced to quantify the process of selecting computer systems. The next section treats these computer scoring methods. The subsequent section shows that such scoring is a special case of the more general problem of utility analysis, addressed in economics, especially in the theory on consumer behavior. The section thereafter shows how management science approaches the issue of multiple criteria, especially in mathematical programming. Note that multiple criteria affect not only computer selection, but also information system evaluation, in which areas of interest include various financial benefits, such as profit and market share, and job satisfaction. Clearly utility trade-offs among criteria must be addressed by many disciplines, especially economics, management science, and psychometry, i.e., conjoint measurement theory.[2]

SCORING METHODS IN COMPUTER SELECTION

Scoring methods found in the computer selection literature can be described as follows. First prepare a list of computer characteristics (attributes, aspects) that appear relevant for the selection of a computer. The introduction has already mentioned some of these attributes. Let s_{ij} denote how well computer j scores on characteristic i. The relative importance or weight assigned to characteristic i is denoted by w_i. No index j is needed for the weight. Then the performance of computer j is

$$P_j = w_1 \cdot s_{1j} + w_2 \cdot s_{2j} + \cdots + w_n \cdot s_{nj} \tag{4.1}$$

where the weights satisfy the obvious conditions

$$\sum_{i=1}^{n} w_i = 1 \text{ and } w_i \geq 0. \tag{4.2}$$

TABLE 4.1.   *Computer Characteristics*

Cost Data
Total cost
Maintenance cost

Performance Data
Compilation time, by compiler, on benchmark tasks
Sort timings (from sequential and random access files)
Readability of printed output

Hardware Characteristics
Average machine instruction time
Channel speed (total and per channel)
Total storage—random access
Average access speed—random access storage for data
Floating point and decimal arithmetic hardware
Character coding (6 or 8 bit bytes)
Expandability of memory
Virtual memory capability
Total number of channels available to high speed devices
Total number of remote terminals capable of support with a response delay of less than
    three seconds
Compatibility to smaller or larger machine models
Total floor space (square feet) required
Memory-protect features

Software Support
Application programs available
Conversion assistance
Utility programs available and their features
Memory utilized by operating system
Debugging facilities of each language
Automatic restart (recovery) procedures available

Miscellaneous Data
Delay before system may be delivered
Proximity to other similar systems available for backup support
Reputation of the vendor for technical and maintenance support
Training programs offered by the vendor
Availability of software developed by independent software houses for the bid system
Expandability of the total system and potential for use in systems with faster processors
Main time between failure for each system component
Purchase options, long-term lease arrangements, guaranteed pricing for anticipated life,
    and other benefits

Which characteristics are relevant? From the 82 attributes listed by W. G. Miller (1969), Table 4.1 shows a selection, grouped into five classes. The terminology in this table is taken verbatim from Miller (1969).

The scores in Eq. (4.1) may be based on either objective measurements or subjective estimates. For instance, in Table 4.1 benchmark programs may measure compilation time objectively, vendor's documentation yields total storage, and queuing and simulation models provide estimates of response delays (see Chapter Three). Subjective estimates of readability of printed output and of the vendor's reputation may be collected.

Reliance on such subjective judgments can be criticized because of the subjectiveness of the *scores,* not of the *weights* attributed to these scores. The variability of subjective estimates can be quantified by (subjective) probability distributions: for instance, the expert may state an 80 percent probability of the vendor's still being in business in five years.[3] The problem of assigning weights to uncertain outcomes will be treated again in the next section. Note that subjective measures are also used extensively in cost–benefit analyses like those performed for library services for research and development.[4]

Besides problems in quantification of the scores, a *basic fault* exists in the scoring approach presented in the computer literature. Not all of the many characteristics in Table 4.1 can possibly be considered as criteria! Some of those characteristics should merely serve to determine the value or score of the final criteria. For instance, maintenance costs contribute to total cost; average machine instruction time and total storage determine the response delay at the terminals. Whether a particular characteristic is an *input* or an *output* variable in the computer selection process is not always clear. For example, are training facilities a criterion or should such facilities be converted into costs, another criterion? "Overlapping criteria" are further discussed in the references.[5] Many publications, not necessarily on computer selection, recommend restricting the number of criteria in practical studies to, say, five.[6]

Brocato (1971, p. 14) encounters the problem of whether to compare only equal-cost systems, and if not, how to weight costs. One approach is to impose a restriction (side condition) on the input variable "cost," and to determine the costs and benefits of the various systems. More generally one must determine which output (response) variables to consider as criteria (see Fig. 4.1), and how these output variables depend on input variables. These input variables may be either controllable—decision variables such as memory size—or uncontrollable—environmental variables such as future vendor support. How sensitive the resulting choice is to changes in the uncontrollable environmental variables should be investigated. The control variables should be selected so that the criterion variables are favorably

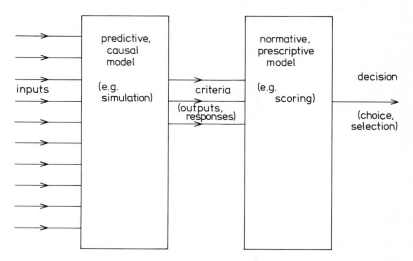

FIGURE 4–1. Predictive versus Normative Models.

affected. The input and output variables may be subjected to certain restrictions, generated by user requirements (say, maximum response delays), corporate policy (diversified suppliers, no leasing), government regulations (privacy protection), labor unions, and so on.

A related issue is the organization of attributes into a *hierarchy:* in Table 4.1 the 82 attributes were grouped into a two-level hierarchy with a five-branch upper level. (The upper level is printed in bold type; the lower level, in light face.) More generally, the large number of attributes may be organized into a multilevel hierarchy in which several subcriteria contribute to a single higher criterion, which with other criteria contributes to a higher-level criterion.[7] At the bottom of the hierarchy of objectives are attributes that are not ends, but simply means to an end.[8] Again the issue is to determine causal relationships between input and output variables.

A computer system—or more generally an information system (IS)—should be evaluated on more than a single criterion. Relevant criteria and subcriteria for an IS include financial benefits (subdivided into profits and market shares), job satisfaction (with subcriteria of intellectual challenge and fatigue), privacy and security, and service to customers. First, however, causal methods (discussed in other chapters) must determine how each criterion is affected by decision variables, such as interactive versus batch computer system, and maximum expenditure. Next, scoring methods must reconcile conflicting criteria. Equation (4.1) is a highly simplified model for reconciliation. Actually, multiple-criteria decision making is a traditional topic in economics and management science. The computer selection model of Eq. (4.1) must be evaluated in the much wider context of multiple criteria decisions in general.

One *benefit* of the scoring method is the elicitation and communication of experts' opinions. A list of possibly important factors, not only technical factors, is generated. Another advantage of the scoring method is its inherent simplicity. The literature demonstrates the popularity of the scoring method in computer selection practice. The main criticism is that the method customarily neglects the need for determining the *causal* relationships between decision variables and criterion variables.

After the selection of a particular computer system, the system must be continually *tuned;* i.e., parameters of the operating system have to be adapted as the environment changes, additional disc drives can be connected, and so on. One tuning approach related to scoring models is based on *Kiviat graphs.* On a prepared list good and bad attributes [e.g., memory used by user programs versus memory used by the operating system (overhead)] alternate. Good attributes should show high scores; bad attributes should yield low scores; and an attractive overall system results in a starlike graph. (See Fig. 4.2 in which the good attributes are on axes 1, 3, 5, and 7.)[9] This section on scoring models and the next on utility theory will enable the reader to evaluate a simple approach like the Kiviat graph.

UTILITY ANALYSIS IN ECONOMICS

The economist's view of the utility (value, worth) of goods and services has three main subdivisions:

> the utility of different amounts of a single good,
>
> the trade-offs among two or more goods, and
>
> utility under uncertainty (risk).

Remember that scoring methods and utility theory do not explain causality. Their models are descriptive and prescriptive, not predictive.

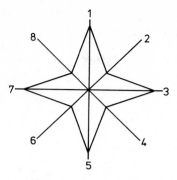

FIGURE 4-2.   A Kiviat Graph.

Utility of a Single Good

First consider a single good. In economics the term "goods" may include services. Possible relationships between the quantity of a particular item and its utility are pictured in Fig. 4.3. Note that the figure does not show the units in which utility is measured. Figure 4.3(a) demonstrates Gossen's first "law of decreasing marginal utility": as one acquires more of a particular good, the increase in utility diminishes. Figure 4.3(b) illustrates that in real-time applications, response delays above a critical level lead to a sharp drop in value. Figure 4.3(c) shows that there may be an optimal quantity of a good. Figure 4.3(d) demonstrates disutility: utility may become negative; i.e., losses lead to bankruptcy.

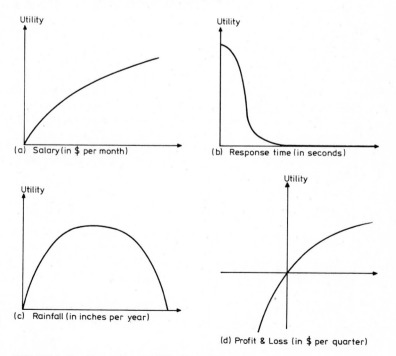

FIGURE 4-3.   Examples of Utility Functions.

Trade-offs among Several Goods

Recall the previous discussion on the choice among several information systems, each of which scored differently on criteria ("goods") such as financial benefits, job satisfaction, and privacy. These scores were denoted by s_{ij}. A system can be immediately eliminated from consideration if it is "dominated" by some other system; i.e., if $s_{i1} \geq s_{i2}$ for all criteria i, and $s_{i1} > s_{i2}$ for at least one criterion. For the nondominated systems the choice problem may be modeled through indifference curves.

An *indifference curve* is a set of values of characteristics (quantities of goods) that yield the same utility. For illustrative purposes Fig. 4.4 distinguishes only two goods: throughput and flexibility in (a); or throughput and cost (negative utility) in (b). In Fig. 4.4 indifference curves are shown by broken lines, and increasing order of utility U is denoted by a higher index of U. If such indifference curves can be specified by the decision maker, the optimal choice is the point P where an indifference curve touches the solid "budget line," which in Fig. 4.4(a) shows which combinations of throughput and flexibility can be purchased for a fixed budget. In Fig. 4.4(b) this solid line becomes the cost–throughput curve; i.e., the curve shows the minimum cost for each throughput level.[10]

An extremely simple example of an indifference curve can be drawn from Eq. (4.1): keeping the performance index (utility) P fixed means that various linear combinations of the scores s_{ij} can yield the same (indifferent) utility. Figure 4.5 pictures

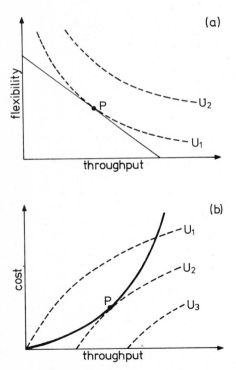

FIGURE 4–4.   Indifference Curves.

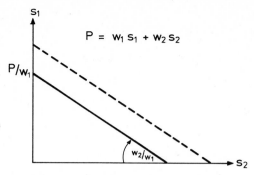

FIGURE 4–5.   *A Linear Indifference Curve.*

the case for only two attributes with scores s_1 and s_2; a higher utility is shown by the dashed line. The scoring model in Eq. (4.1) is a special case of more general utility models.[11] A *linear* utility function, however, conflicts with an assumption usually made in economics; substitution between two attributes does not remain constant. [12] For example, Eq. (4.1) implies that total absence of software (a zero score) can be perfectly compensated by other factors; but actually such a computer could not function. Functions more complicated than purely linear functions must be examined.

A simple, mathematically inspired transformation can ensure that a system with a zero score for one particular attribute becomes unattractive. Replace s_{ij} in Eq (4.1) by its logarithm:

$$P_j = w_1 \cdot \ell n s_{1j} + w_2 \cdot \ell n s_{2j} + \cdots + w_n \cdot \ell n s_{nj}, \tag{4.3}$$

which is equivalent to the multiplicative model

$$P'_j = s_{1j}^{w_1} \cdot s_{2j}^{w_2} \cdots s_{nj}^{w_n} \tag{4.4}$$

where P' is a monotonic transformation of P, $P' = \exp(P)$. Similar scoring models can be found in the literature; e.g., in White et al. (1963, p. 180).

A more sophisticated mathematical apparatus has been derived by Dujmovic (1975). His *extended continuous logic* synthesizes into an overall score P the scores realized by elementary attributes. His mathematical tools permit specification that at least one elementary criteria be fulfilled sufficiently; "the resulting global effectiveness . . . is realized by taking into account the logic relationships among the elementary effectivenesses" [Dujmovic (1975, p. 213)]. In his approach the scores satisfy the condition

$$0 \leq s_{ij} \leq 1 \tag{4.5}$$

because they "represent the degree of truth in the statement: the value of the component for evaluation x_i completely fulfils the requirements of the ith elementary criterion[13]." Dujmovic assumes that "complex criteria decompose into a sequence of independent elementary criteria." In a subsequent publication, Dujmovic (1976) discusses the application of his technique to the evaluation of a hybrid computer system, characterized by 84 attributes grouped into four classes. The reader interested in the rather complicated, mathematical details of Dujmovic's approach should first read White et al. (1963). Bemelmans (1976, pp. 112–125) surveys other approaches that try to take cause-effect relationships into account; for instance, QUEST (Quantitative Utility Estimates for Science and Technology) developed by Cetron (1969). In system selection, although scoring models serve to quantify the trade-offs among criteria, the scoring models cannot determine cause–effect relationships between criteria (output) and decision (input) variables.

The discussion thus far has demonstrated that trade-offs among goods or criteria can be modeled by indifference curves (Fig. 4.4). Specific indifference curves are the linear models of Eq. (4.1) and Fig. 4.5. To remedy the shortcomings of simple linear models, the multiplicative model in Eq. (4.4) was presented. A digression was made to approaches that try to incorporate logic relationships among a great many attributes.

In economics a large body of literature on utility theory is based on rigid mathematical principles. A recent, excellent survey, provided by Keeney and Raiffa (1976), inspired the following discussion.

For the practical evaluation of utility functions, some assumptions about their *shapes* must be made. A fundamental issue is whether multiattribute utility functions $U(x_1, x_2, \ldots, x_n)$ can be separated into independent parts. An *independence* model with an *additive* structure[14] is

$$U(x_1, \ldots, x_n) = \sum_{i=1}^{n} w_i \cdot u_i(x_i) \tag{4.6}$$

with the technical conditions

$$0 \le u_i \le 1 \qquad 0 \le w_i \le 1 \qquad \sum_{1}^{n} w_i = 1. \tag{4.7}$$

Equation (4.6) means that u_i, the utility of attribute i, does not depend on the value of the other attributes. Moreover, Eq. (4.6) specifies that elementary utilities $u_i(x_i)$ can be simply added after scaling by means of w_i. A graphic example of additive independent utilities is Fig. 4.6. Figure 4.6(a) relates back to general utility functions as presented in Fig. 4.4(a). If x_1 is fixed at a particular value, and a "low" value of x_1 is denoted by x_1^- and a "high" value by x_1^+, Fig. 4.6(b) shows the utility effects of changes in x_2. The additive independence implies that the curves in (b) are *parallel!*

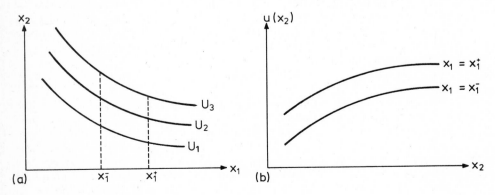

(a)   (b)

FIGURE 4–6.   Independent Utilities.

Equation (4.6) is a special case of a slightly more complicated utility function, the *multilinear* function. This function for just two attributes[15] is

$$U(x_1, x_2) = w_1 \cdot u_1(x_1) + w_2 \cdot u_2(x_2) + w_{12} \cdot u_1(x_1) \cdot u_2(x_2). \qquad (4.8)$$

Indeed, for $w_{12} = 0$, Eq. (4.8) reduces to Eq. (4.6). For $w_{12} \neq 0$, Eq. (4.8) reflects *interaction* between the two components x_1 and x_2. If $w_{12} > 0$, both attributes are "complementary"; if $w_{12} < 0$, they are "substitutes." For instance, a left shoe yields much higher utility when the left is acquired together with a right shoe; but a pair of sandals may substitute for a pair of shoes. Figure 4.7 demonstrates the role of inter-action: (a) duplicates Fig. 4.6(b); (b) shows that the increase of $u(x_2)$ is stimulated as the increase of x_2 is accompanied by an increase in x_1. In Fig. 4.7(c) the marginal util-ity of x_2 is much smaller when more of x_1 is available to substitute for x_2. Comple-mentarity in a computer system is exemplified by response time and availability; the response time of a real-time subsystem and the throughput of a batch subsystem exemplify substitutes. More applications of the multilinear utility function can be found in Huber (1974a, b). For many years models with interactions like those in the multilinear utility function have been used in the statistical theory on experimental design in agriculture, chemistry, and simulation.[16] Relationships between "frac-tional" experimental designs and utility functions can be found in Farquhar (1975).

Keeney and Raiffa (1976, pp. 238, 324) prove that the multilinear function, Eq. (4.8), can be represented also as the *product* of utility functions per attribute:

$$U'(x_1, x_2) = u_1'(x_1) \cdot u_2'(x_2) \qquad (4.9)$$

provided $w_{12} \neq 0$ in Eq. (4.8); otherwise the additive Eq. (4.6) holds. An example is provided by Eq. (4.4) where

$$u_1'(x_1) = s_1^{w_1} \quad \text{and} \quad u_2'(x_2) = s_2^{w_2}.$$

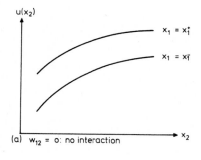

(a) $w_{12} = 0$: no interaction

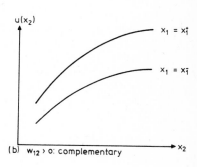

(b) $w_{12} > 0$: complementary

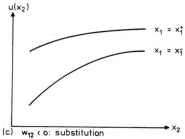

(c) $w_{12} < 0$: substitution

FIGURE 4-7.   Interactions.

Even when two criteria interact as in Eqs. (4.8) and (4.9), the overall utility can still be measured by establishing unidimensional utility curves $u_i(x_i)$ and $u_i'(x_i)$, so-called utility independence. Such a construct somewhat simplifies the practical measurement of the overall utility function (U or U'). When x_1 is utility independent of x_2, this independence does *not* imply the converse: x_2 is not necessarily utility independent of x_1. For instance Grochow (1972) studied a time-sharing system and found that the utility of response time was independent of availability. However, the utility of availability was not independent of response time, for if response time is bad, availability is not critical.[17]

Several more types of utility curves are presented in a simple survey by Easton (1973, pp. 183–283) and in an interesting article by Zeleny (1976a).

Empirical Utility Measurements

The *empirical* determination of multiattribute utility functions $U(x_1, \ldots, x_n)$ is facilitated by certain assumptions about the shape of the utility function; e.g., utility independence [see Eq. (4.9)]; or more restrictively additivity [see Eq. (4.6)]; or even more specifically forms like Eqs. (4.4) and (4.1). The more general the form of the utility function is, the more observations need to be made [see Keeney and Raiffa (1976, p. 253)].

One method for quantifying the trade-offs among criteria is to assign specific values s_{ij} to the criteria (attributes) i of system j, and ask the decision maker to rank the resulting systems j. This ranking implicitly determines the weights w_i, which can be estimated through statistical procedures analogous to multiple regression analysis. An example of such a regression model is

$$\hat{y} = \hat{\beta}_0 + \hat{\beta}_1 \cdot x_1 + \hat{\beta}_2 \cdot x_2 + \cdots + \hat{\beta}_n \cdot x_n, \tag{4.10}$$

which is obviously analogous to Eq. (4.1) if $\hat{\beta}$ is replaced by the estimated weights $\hat{w}$, and x by the specified scores s. For details see the literature.[18]

In an alternative method, no specific systems are compared, but the decision maker is asked to consider n attributes per se. The decision maker may be asked to make all $n(n-1)/2$ pairwise comparisons separately or to assign weights to all n attributes in a single shot. It is important to check for consistency in the answers. For example, if the procedural request to assign weights to each of four attributes results in the weights $w_1 = 28$, $w_2 = 17$, $w_3 = 7$, and $w_4 = 60$, the decision maker is asked later whether attribute four is more important than the aggregate of the first three attributes. If the later answer is inconsistent, the weights should be adjusted. For related approaches refer to the references.[19]

If *several* persons are asked for their utility functions, reconciliation of significant differences is necessary. Turban and Metersky (1971) provide more details.[20] Weights may be specified *a priori* or may be elicited by *interactive*, user-machine systems.[21] The weight determination problem is also addressed in the literature on computer selection.[22] Keeney and Raiffa (1976) and the review by Huber (1974a) provide excellent, elaborate discussions and case studies of the empirical evaluation of utility functions.

Although the trade-offs among criteria are a personal, subjective matter, empirical, statistical work can be done to measure personal preferences. Because of the personal character of utility, the scientific (reproducible) determination of utility functions remains difficult.

Uncertain Goods

Another problem is the choice among *uncertain* attributes; e.g., response time shows stochastic variation so that this attribute is uncertain. The axiomatic approach to the uncertainty issue is based on the utility theory of von Neumann and Morgenstern, and is virtually ignored in the computer and information systems literature. To understand this axiomatic approach, first consider the following simplistic example: a person may choose either to take $150 or to flip a coin and receive $200 for heads or $100 for tails. Are these two options indifferent to the decision maker? Would desperate need cause preference for certainty? Do preferences remain unchanged when $100 and $200 are replaced by $1 million and $2 million? The axiomatic approach to these problems can be summarized as follows.[23] If option one is preferred over option two, the utility of option one must be higher. The option may be characterized by a single (uncertain) attribute, such as money in this example, or by multiple attributes, such as money and job satisfaction. These utilities must be so scaled that the selection is based on *maximization* of the *expected* utility. (Chapter Seven briefly discusses alternative approaches such as a maximin strategy.)

A fundamental issue in utility theory is the introduction of a *lottery*.[24] Confronted with a certainty option—100 percent certainty of receiving $150—and with two extremes—a chance p of receiving $500 or a chance $1 - p$ of receiving $10—the decision maker is asked what value of the probability p would make the choice between the certainty option and the lottery *indifferent*. A "rational" decision maker, one for whom the lottery stakes are not extremely high, will select p according to this equation:

$$150 = p \cdot 500 + (1 - p) \cdot 10 \qquad \text{or} \qquad p = \frac{14}{49}. \tag{4.11}$$

A risk-averse person, however, will trade in the certainty option only if the chance of a good outcome increases above 14/49. A risk-prone person prefers the lottery even if $p < 14/49$. The decision maker's *risk attitude* is measured by the value of p in the lottery that is substituted for the certainty option. The reader may or may not like this lottery idea, but it is the basis of utility theory under uncertainty. Keeney and Raiffa (1976, pp. 198–200) suggest many checks to determine whether the decision maker's preference statements remain consistent.

Preferences between present and *future* attributes involve the role of the time dimension, and can be discussed from a strict utility-theoretical point of view.[25] The next chapter presents practical business techniques, like Net Present Value (NPV).

Keeney and Raiffa (1976) summarize a number of practical studies using utility theory: air pollution control in New York City, choice of educational programs, fire department options, selecting business objectives in a consulting company, nuclear power site selection, and airport development in Mexico City. Keefer (1978) presents an application to R&D planning. See also the survey article by Huber (1974a) and the proceedings edited by D. E. Bell et al. (1977). Easton (1973) gives many realistic exercises.

MULTIPLE CRITERIA IN MANAGEMENT SCIENCE

Some approaches to multiple-criteria decision making are associated more with management science than with economics although the distinction is not always clear. The discussion of Fig. 4.4 examined the *optimal* combination (trade-off) of several attributes or criteria. However, the behavioral school of management suggests that each criterion should satisfy specific *aspiration levels*, and that therefore a "satisficing" solution, rather than "the" optimal solution, should be sought. [See Cyert and March (1963) and also Easton (1973, pp. 72–78).] Chapter Eight discusses Bonini's (1963) simulation study based on this satisficing approach.

The "aspiration" approach has been further formalized in mathematical programming (linear programming, for example), which has led to *goal programming*. The literature provides more details.[26] One can decide to concentrate attention on a single criterion, say cost, while the other criteria meet specific minimum values (aspiration levels). These minimum values create side conditions in a classical minimization problem.[27] Interactive assessment of utility functions is usually based on mathematical programming algorithms.[28] The literature on multiple criteria is growing rapidly in the mathematical programming area.[29] Recently the problem of multiple-criteria decision making has been approached using the new mathematical apparatus of *fuzzy set theory*, pioneered by Zadeh (1975).[30]

A limiting case arises when a single criterion is investigated in a formal model while trade-offs with other criteria are performed intuitively by the manager. In *computer selection* the single criterion selected is usually the cost. One must decide on the computer configuration that can execute a given set of applications at minimal cost while satisfying certain restrictions on, say, response time. The few linear programming solutions offered for this problem remain very theoretical.[31] An alternative approach is to fix the cost (the budget) and to maximize the gross benefits. Both cost minimization and benefit maximization are found in the literature.[32] Ideally neither the applications nor the cost should be fixed *a priori*; instead the net benefit should be maximized. For a private corporation this net benefit may be profit, i.e., sales revenues minus costs, which vary with both the applications and the computer configurations; see also Eq. (2.1).

SUMMARY

Although multiattribute utility theory remains quite theoretical, time spent on this topic is worthwhile because utility theory provides a sound foundation for the more practical approaches followed in computer selection and information system evaluation. In the practice of computer selection, scoring methods have long been in use. Kiviat graphs, a related approach, have gained popularity in computer tuning. In the area of information system evaluation the multicriteria character of such systems has been emphasized in a few publications. For instance, Hawgood (1975) divides those affected by an information system into five groups (e.g., users and personnel) each with separate criteria (e.g., money and job satisfaction).[33] Note that Mintzberg et al. (1976, pp. 258–259) argue that utility functions are irrelevant in *strategic* decision making.

The major error in scoring methods as presented in the computer selection literature is the equating of excessively numerous characteristics with selection criteria. Many of these attributes are simply input variables that determine the final, limited set of true criteria. Predictive cause–effect models are often needed to determine the resulting criteria values or scores. Outside the computer selection area, scoring models are not meant to predict the performance of alternative systems; these models start from known values s_{ij} for the (relatively few) criteria i realized by alternative j; and scoring models are then used to select an alternative.

Another criticism of the computer scoring approach is the extreme simplicity of the linear model of Eq. (4.1). However, outside the computer field more complicated models, like the multilinear model of Eq. (4.8), account for interactions. Nevertheless, some authors argue in favor of simple linear models.[34]

Some authors point out that the ultimate, overall performance P is a dimensionless number without intuitive meaning. How important is it that system one scores five units higher than system two?[35]

Major benefits of scoring approaches are the elicitation and communication of the opinions of experts and users, the generation of a list of possibly important attributes (not only technical criteria), and the approach's simplicity (cost–benefit of the methods themselves).

Proponents and opponents of the scoring approach, not limited to computer selection, have produced a substantial literature.[36] The most up-to-date and detailed survey of more general utility models is Keeney and Raiffa's (1976).[37] The single, biggest computer user, the United States government, bases its computer selection on Joslin's "cost-value" approach; see Joslin (1968) for details. After the computer selection stage, both parties—buyer and vendor—have to negotiate the final contract; see Brandon and Segelstein (1976).

How does this chapter relate to the remaining chapters? In scoring models the n attributes are supposed to be given. Chapter Six discusses specific information attributes, such as timeliness and accuracy. Instead of being combined in a linear scoring model or in a more general indifference curve, these attributes serve as the user's decision variables; their effect on the ultimate criteria, say, profit and market share, is investigated in subsequent chapters. Causality models are needed more urgently than models describing and prescribing how to choose among alternatives. (For the selection of a system, scoring models are indeed of practical relevance.)

In computer selection the information requirements, i.e., the applications, are considered to be given so that no attention is paid to gross benefit evaluation. For instance, in Table 4.1 none of the characteristics is an economic benefit. A genuine interest in the *ultimate* criteria for computer system effectiveness shifts the focus of concentration from the computer system itself (the scoring model focus) to the benefits generated by the computer as part of the information system serving its users within the organization. As Dujmovic (1977b) suggests, the computer selection problem should be solved only *after* the economic benefits of computerized information systems have been determined. This latter problem is the central issue of the next chapters.

EXERCISES

1. Consider Table 4.1, based on W. G. Miller (1969). Which other category reflects the consequences of the hardware characteristics (the third category in Table 4.1)?

2. Why does $w_i = 0$ or $w_i = 1$ in Eq. (4.2) or Eq. (4.7) represent a degenerate case?

3. The weights w and the scores s in Eq. (4.1) contribute to the overall performance P in the same way. Why would you nevertheless criticize a subjective assessment of s more strongly than you would a subjective assessment of w?

4. Give a few criteria and input factors in the selection of an automobile.

5. How is technical progress shown in Fig. 4.4(b)?

6. How is a decrease in the price of flexibility shown in Fig. 4.4(a)?

7. Suppose the indifference curve is specified by Eq. (4.1) with $n = 2$. Denote the prices of s_1 and s_2 by p_1 and p_2. Show that if $p_2/p_1 > w_2/w_1$, the whole budget should be spent on s_1.

8. The linearity of the utility function is mentioned as a disadvantage of the scoring approach. Why is this linearity a less serious disadvantage when the characteristics can assume values in a small range only?

9. Give the second-degree polynomial aproximation to a function in the scores s_i.

10. How many pairs must a person judge in evaluating ten attributes, presented in pairs?

11. What are some criterion variables in computer selection that assume uncertain (probabilistic) values and that demonstrate the relevance of the discussion around Eq. (4.11)?

12. Bromley (1965, p. 40) found that the end score P in Eq. (4.1) was insensitive to drastic changes in the weights. (He gave one score a weight of one, and the other scores weights of zero.) Do you consider this insensitivity an advantage or a disadvantage?

13. The end score P is a dimensionless number without intuitive meaning. Give examples of criteria that do not have this disadvantage.

14. Taking the logarithm of s in Eq. (4.1) means $P' = (s_1^{w_1}) \cdot (s_2^{w_2}) \ldots$ with P' being a monotonic transformation of P. Prove.

15. A nonlinear relationship between a characteristic and its utility may sometimes be postulated. Do you expect this situation to hold for the throughput of a batch system or for the response time of a time-sharing system?

16. Gossen's first law states that the marginal utility of a good decreases. Does this law imply that taking one dollar from a rich man and giving it to a poor man improves social utility?

17. In research areas such as marketing, it has been suggested that "scores" should have some ideal value, say $s_i^o (i = 1, \ldots, n)$; see Zeleny (1976a, p. 17). (a) Which formula would correspond with such a scoring model? (b) Why is such a model unrealistic for computer and information systems?

18. Zeleny (1976a, pp. 17–18) proposes the following solution to the problem raised at the end of the preceding exercise: define the ideal scores s_i^o upon the set (say, J) of *feasible* alternatives; e.g., $s_i^o = \max_{j \in J} s_{ij}$. What disadvantage do you see?

19. In Coppus et al. (1976) a computer center's manager, interested in minimizing queuing (waiting) times of customers, partitions jobs into small, medium, and large jobs. (a) Devise an overall performance function that reflects queuing times of each of the three job classes. (b) Propose measures other than *average* queuing time. (c) What is the direction of the effects from changing the borderline between small and medium jobs?

20. Microeconomics examines the selection of the "economic" production technique when several techniques are available to produce a given output volume. To which concepts is this problem related: gross benefit generation, net benefit maximization, cost minimization, or linear programming?

21. A company, characterized by a linear relationship between total cost C and total production x, shows a linear relationship between price P and sales volume (x). When are gross benefits maximized? When are net benefits maximized?

22. Which characteristics do you personally feel are important in computer selection? What weights would you assign? How does the computer system you are currently using score on these characteristics?

NOTES

1. The following references provide lists of computer attributes, computer scoring examples, and discussions of the scoring method itself: Barber and Abbott (1972, p. 69), Bottler et al. (1972, pp. 109–117), Brandon and Segelstein (1976), Brocato (1971, p. 16), Canning (1966, p. 3), Dowkont et al. (1967), Dujmovic (1978, p. 7), Eldin and Croft (1974, pp. 208–213, 223–230), Fife (1968, pp. 7–8), Gregory and Van Horn (1963, pp. 634–636), Gritten (1975), Joslin (1968, pp. 3–9, 20–45, 65–67), Keller and Denham (1968), H. C. Lucas (1973, pp. 111–122), Parkin (1978), Scharf (1969), and Yearsley and Graham (1973, pp. 41–48). For slightly different performance criteria, see Schussel (1974). See also the bibliography with 138 references in Dujmovic (1977a).

2. D. E. Bell et al. (1977, pp. 4–10), and Morse (1976a).

3. Bemelmans (1976, pp. 110, 125–130) discusses the probability that a score is realized; see also Dujmovic (1977a) and White et al. (1963, pp. 180–181). See also the discussion of risk analysis in the next chapter and Bayesian decision theory in Chapter Seven. Sensitivity analysis of scoring is also discussed by Land (1976, p. 7).

4. J. N. Wolfe (1974).

5. Easton (1973, pp. 304–313), and J. R. Moore and Baker (1969, p. 93).

6. Keeney and Raiffa (1976, pp. 29, 52), G. A. Miller (1956), and Turban and Metersky (1971, p. 827).

7. Dujmovic (1975) and (1977a), Keeney and Raiffa (1976, pp. 41–49, 115–116, 123–125, 332–343), and White et al. (1963). The hierarchy concept itself is discussed in detail by Saaty (1977).

8. Keeney and Raiffa (1976, p. 52), and Easton (1973, pp. 64–69). See also the discussion on overlapping criteria in J. R. Moore and Baker (1969, p. 93).

9. See, for instance Borovits and Ein-Dor (1977, p. 186).

10. See also Keeney and Raiffa (1976, pp. 79–82), and Zeleny (1976a, pp. 13, 16).

11. The relationships between scoring methods and utility theory are discussed by Bemelmans (1976, pp. 148–151) and Sharpe (1969, pp. 287–292); see also Keeney and Raiffa (1976, p. 81).

12. Keeney and Raiffa (1976, p. 84), and Sharpe (1969, pp. 287–292).

13. See also Dujmovic (1977a) and (1977b), Jarvis et al. (1972, p. 15), and White et al. (1963, p. 178).

14. Keeney and Raiffa (1976, pp. 91, 101, 116–117, 224–281).

15. Keeney and Raiffa (1976, p. 234, 240–241).

16. Kleijnen (1975, pp. 207–450) and (1979b).

17. Grochow's studies are also discussed by Keeney and Raiffa (1976, pp. 408–412).

18. Easton (1973, pp. 303–304), Green and Carmone (1974), Hopkins et al. (1977, p. 368), Huber (1974a), Parker and Srinivasan (1976), Schwartz and Vertinsky (1977), Scott and Wright (1976), Van Raaij (1978), and Wind and Spitz (1976).

19. Easton (1973, pp. 292–296), Hopkins et al. (1977, p. 367), Saaty (1977), and Van Raaij (1978).

20. Obtaining weights from several persons is also discussed by Bemelmans (1976, p. 132), Jarvis et al. (1972, pp. 19–20), Land (1976, pp. 6–7), W. G. Miller (1969, p. 14), and Senn (1974); see also the bibliography by Dujmovic (1977a). A different area is that of group decision making and social welfare; see Keeney (1976), Keeney and Raiffa (1976, pp. 515–547), and also Hanken and Reuver (1977, pp. 97–117).

21. D. E. Bell et al. (1977), Keeney and Raiffa (1976, pp. 83, 209–210, 349–353), Nijkamp and Rietveld (1978, p. 45), Oppenheimer (1978), Van Loon (1975), Wehrung (1978), Zangemeister (1975), and Zionts and Wallenius (1976).

22. In the computer literature sometimes different goals are distinguished with different weights; to these goals the many attributes contribute in different proportions; see Bottler et al. (1972, pp. 67–74, 109–117), Bromley (1965), Jewett (1973), Land (1976, pp. 6–7), Sharpe (1969, pp. 284–286), Timmreck (1973, pp. 210–211), and Zangemeister (1975). See also the discussion on indifference curves in Sharpe (1969, pp. 5–8) and Seiler (1969, pp. 77–83). Many references to the German literature are provided by Bottler et al. (1972) and Zangemeister (1975).

23. Keeney and Raiffa (1976, p. 131).

24. Keeney and Raiffa (1976, pp. 133, 140). See also W. D. Rowe (1977, pp. 179–189, 221–223, 245).

25. The contribution by Meyer in Keeney and Raiffa (1976, pp. 473–514) is recommended. See also Bernhard (1977), and Hanken and Reuver (1977, pp. 51–58).

26. D. E. Bell et al. (1977), Ignizio and Satterfield (1977), and Keeney and Raiffa (1976, p. 72).

27. Keeney and Raiffa (1976, pp. 73–74).

28. Oppenheimer (1978); see also note 21.

29. D. E. Bell et al (1977), Charnes and Cooper (1977), Keeney and Raiffa (1976, pp. 72–77), Montgomery and Bettencourt (1977), Morse (1976b), Starr and Zeleny (1977), Thiriez and Zionts (1976), Van Lommel (1968, pp. 247–263), Van Loon (1975), and Zeleny (1976).

30. See Orlovsky (1978), and the bibliography in Dujmovic (1977a).

31. Ramer (1973), and Sharpe (1969, pp. 279–284).

32. Fisher (1971, pp. 10–11, 38–39) discusses both approaches in the context of military systems analysis. Related to Fisher (1971) is the work by Eldin and Croft (1974, pp. 140–144), and Seiler (1969, p. 74). In the computer area gross benefit evaluation, as opposed to cost minimization, is emphasized by Cooper

(1973, pp. 23–25), Grochla (1970, p. 331), and Welke (1975a, pp. 6–7); see also Chapters One and Two.

33. See also Bottler et al. (1972, pp. 13–30).

34. N. Baker and Freeland (1975, p. 169), Goodwin (1972, pp. 16–18), Green and Carmone (1974), Huber (1974a), Keeney and Raiffa (1976, pp. 295–297). Parker and Srinivasan (1976), S. L. Schwartz and Vertinsky (1977), and Van Loon (1975, pp. 396–397).

35. E. D. Carlson (1974, p. 60), Keefer (1977, p. 16), and Zangemeister (1975, p. 443).

36. A fine introduction to scoring is White et al. (1963). An excellent survey of scoring in a research and development context is given by Baker and Freeland (1975); see also Bemelmans (1976, pp. 99–154). Critical discussions are given by Fife (1968), Goodwin (1972), Gritten (1975), Joslin (1968, pp. 211–212), W. G. Miller (1969), W. D. Rowe (1977), Sharpe (1969), and Van Loon (1975).

37. Another textbook on utility theory is Fishburn (1970). A good text on multi-criteria decision making is provided by Hanken and Reuver (1977, pp. 26–58). Many references can be found in Butterworth and Ziemba (1978), and Glauque and Peebles (1976). See also Hauser (1978), Krishnan (1979), Fishburn (1977), Kirkwood (1976), and the journal *Operations Research*, September/October 1976, pp. 933–1025.

CHAPTER FIVE

INTRODUCTION

This chapter, meant primarily—but not exclusively—for computer users without a firm background in economics, discusses the following basic economic concepts. In general, the price of products and services, such as computers and information systems, is determined by the market factors of supply and demand. Within a company, computer services can also be made available at a price, but such pricing does not solve the problem of benefit evaluation. Charging for computer services is a cost accounting problem involving fixed and joint costs. Opposed to this ex post charging is the ex ante decision making on proposed computerization projects. Such projects require an investment analysis, including discounting (time value of future money streams) and risk analysis. Besides risk analysis, a sensitivity analysis should be performed. Two statistical appendixes and nearly forty exercises are included in this chapter.

THE MARKET FACTORS OF SUPPLY AND DEMAND

The economic environment is usually a given and cannot be noticeably influenced by an individual company. Nevertheless it is useful to gain some insight into the laws that govern this environment. A most important interface between a company and its environment is the *marketplace.* (See Exercise 1.) In economics the market with its price mechanism plays a crucial role. A company is confronted with two types of markets: one for its outputs and one for its inputs. On the output market the company is a seller of its final product, like steel products or banking services. Similarly a computer hardware manufacturer sells main frames, and a service bureau offers software and CPU time. On the input market the company buys its production factors; i.e., labor, capital goods, land, and management. Prices are determined simultaneously by supply and by demand.

The way supply and demand interact depends on the characteristics of the market, the extremes being perfect competition and monopoly. Figure 5.1 demonstrates some possible relationships. Under perfect or free competition the individual supplier is only an atomistic part of the total market and cannot affect the price by changing supply (Fig. 5.1, lower left). Higher prices generate higher total supply (Fig. 5.1, upper left) as new suppliers are attracted and old suppliers increase their production volumes. Such higher prices may result as a consequence of a "shift in demand"; i.e., at the same price level more units are demanded (see the broken lines in Fig. 5.1). A demand shift may result from an increase in income (see also Exercise 2). In a

Total market:

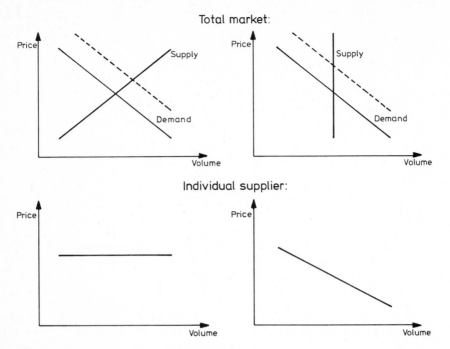

Individual supplier:

FIGURE 5–1.   Supply-and-demand Relationships.

pure monopoly (Fig. 5.1, right) there is a single supplier of the product. Examples are provided by public utilities. The supplier who increases production must accept lower prices, all else being equal.

In real life pure monopolies do not exist because partial substitutes are always available: coal can replace oil for heating purposes; margarine is a substitute for butter. The supplier may try to reduce this substitutability by creating a technically unique product, such as a supercomputer for large-scale meteorological computations. What really matters, however, is not the technical qualities of the product, but the degree to which the consumer (user) differentiates among products. A well-known method to create an economically unique product is the creation of brand names—product differentiation. As Brock (1975, p. 47) points out, substantial brand loyalty does exist in computer selection practice. In general, oligopolistic markets are characterized by the presence of a few suppliers. The number of competitors may be limited by product differentiation. For highly technological products like computers, the entrance of new suppliers is further limited by the large amounts of capital required for research and production. The modeling of oligopolistic markets is quite difficult and will not be pursued in this chapter. (Chapter Nine, however, does include an oligopolistic market.)

Within a company, certain supply-and-demand relationships exist among the various departments. If a company were organized on a pure profit-center basis, the departments would be completely independent, separate economic "households"; and the classical economic laws could be applied straightforwardly. Actually departments operate under a more or less restrictive, corporate organizational policy that usually provides the data processing (DP) department with a monopoly: the user departments operate within a "captive market" because they are not permitted to buy services outside the company. The normal (complicated) monopoly theory, however, cannot be applied directly to this captive situation because the supplier (DP department) and the customers (user departments) have a common ultimate goal, the organization's prosperity. This issue will be reexamined later in this chapter.

Unlike classical economics, which emphasizes the function of the price mechanism, Keynesian economics stresses the role played by income. For example, classical economics explains consumption by its price relative to the price for competitive usage of income (savings); Keynesian economics explains consumption as a function of available income. The role of income budgets will enter the discussion of pricing of computer jobs in a later section.

Space does not allow full presentation of the theory of economics. An excellent textbook on economic theory, Sharpe (1969) emphasizes its applications to the computer field. Shorter expositions are also available.[1] The reader may also attempt Exercises 1 through 6. The next section concentrates on how supply-and-demand factors affect the price of computers.

SUPPLY AND DEMAND OF COMPUTERS

Because the price of a product is determined by its supply and demand, the cost of a computer bought to support a company's information and data processing system is partly explained by the computer supply. Cost is defined here as the price paid for a production factor. (A later section treats other cost concepts such as opportunity costs and out-of-pocket expenses.) The supply of computers is influenced by two technical phenomena: technological progress and economies of scale.

Technological progress means that for the production of the same quantity of goods, a smaller quantity of production factors is required. Hence the product becomes cheaper if market competition stimulates the supplier to lower the price when the costs decrease. In the computer field an excellent example of technological progress is the Large-Scale Integration (LSI) technique. In the course of time, systems with the same computing power have indeed become dramatically cheaper. Communication costs have shown some decline, but much less than computer hardware costs. See Brock (1975, pp. 185–215) and Phister (1976).

Economies of scale mean that a large quantity is cheaper to produce than a small quantity because of the *indivisibility* of certain production factors. For example, a blast furnace has a certain minimum size; no minifurnace can be built to produce just an ounce of steel. If production costs are reflected in the selling price, economies of scale imply that a machine that is twice as big costs less than twice the price of the smaller machine. In the computer field this phenomenon is known as *Grosch's Law:* $C = K\sqrt{E}$ with cost C, effectiveness E, and constant K. Examples are provided by the prices charged for various CPUs within the same machine type, say, the IBM System 370.

Diseconomies of scale also exist. For instance, a company may become so big that it becomes difficult to manage. Computer systems, too, show certain diseconomies of scale. For its utilization, a large computer system usually needs data transmission facilities: terminals, modems, lines, and teleprocessing software. Moreover, one large system offers less protection against breakdown than several, parallel, smaller systems offer. Users may prefer their own little pet system. Computer software, as opposed to hardware, is most certainly suspect of diseconomies of scale. The production of big software products, such as an operating system, requires so many programmers that management of the total effort becomes a serious problem; see the famous article by Brooks (1974).

Knight's (1968) empirical studies demonstrate that both economies of scale and technological progress have indeed affected the price paid for computers. Nevertheless diseconomies of scale have also been pointed out in the literature.[2] Brock (1975, pp. 27–41) presents an interesting discussion and data on economies of scale in the computer area.

Economies of scale refer to technological factors affecting the most efficient production size. Economic factors, however, may lead to *underutilization* of the technical capacity; the producer may find that profit is maximized by limiting output. Figure 5.2 shows a simple cost function consisting of fixed costs A and constant

Demand function: $p = a + bx$ $(a > 0, b < 0)$
$\therefore$ Revenue function: $r \equiv px = ax + bx^2$
$\therefore$ Marginal revenues: $dr/dx = a + 2bx$

Total cost function: $c = A + Bx$ $(A > 0, B > 0)$
$\therefore$ Marginal cost function: $dc/dx = B$

Profit: $P = r - c$
$\therefore$ Maximum profit if $dP/dx = dr/dx - dc/dx = 0$

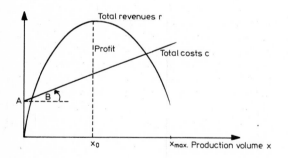

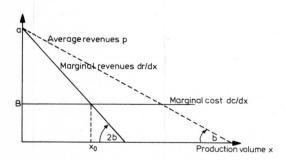

FIGURE 5–2.   Profit Maximization.

variable costs B. (See also Exercise 7.) Profit is maximized when *marginal revenues equal marginal costs.* This law follows from the definition

$$\text{Profit} = \text{Revenues} - \text{Costs}. \tag{5.1}$$

The product volume x that maximizes profit satisfies

$$\frac{d\,(\text{Profit})}{dx} = \frac{d\,(\text{Revenues})}{dx} - \frac{d\,(\text{Costs})}{dx} = 0 \tag{5.2}$$

or equivalently

$$\frac{d\,(\text{Revenues})}{dx} = \frac{d\,(\text{Costs})}{dx}\,. \tag{5.3}$$

In Fig. 5.2, Eq. (5.3) is satisfied by $x = x_0$; see also Exercises 8 and 9. Kriebel et al. (1974, p. 12) derive a similar "marginal law" for optimal pricing in a complicated computer system.

A different economic reason for temporary underutilization is a growth in demand and concomittant production volume that needs some time to materialize. Figure 5.3 shows that as the ultimate production volume approaches x_2, a larger capacity with higher fixed costs pays off. (See also Exercise 10.) In the computer area large installations do need some time to become fully utilized; see also Emery (1971, pp. 10–12).

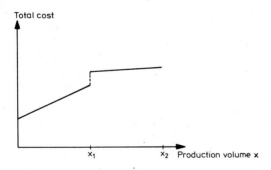

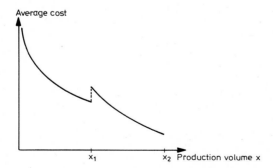

FIGURE 5–3.   *Costs for Various Capacities.*

Figure 5.4 demonstrates that for small production volumes $(x < x_1)$, it is economical to utilize a production technique with relatively low fixed costs, say machine costs, and relatively high variable costs, say labor costs. Hence small information systems may not be computerized because high fixed costs require massive production volumes. Note that software utilization has few variable costs but does have high fixed development costs; a centralized computer system may spread these software costs over many users. Minicomputers have reduced the fixed hardware costs so that decentralization may become economically feasible. Software costs, too, can be spread over many users by using standardized software packages instead of custom-made software. Such standard software is used in inventory control, mathematical programming, and corporate modeling. For the pros and cons of such packages, for a buy-or-make decision, refer to the references.[4]

Each type of product has its own production cost curve with resulting optimum production volume; compare steel production with strawberry production. *Integration,* the production of several products within a single company, may mean that the production capacity is not optimal for each product. The products involved in integration may be intermediate products used in a next production phase; e.g., iron ore is used in steel production. In the computer field, software can be produced in much smaller production units (companies) than hardware can.[5]

Costs can be reduced further by *division of labor;* i.e., employees specialize in a specific type of labor. Hence a software house may specialize in a particular product like software monitors. Modular programming permits work on particular modules by those programmers best qualified by education, natural skills, and experience. For the "chief programmer team" approach, developed at IBM, see Zelkowitz (1978, p. 204).

Marginal costs may decrease because of a *learning* effect: the variable costs decrease as more units are produced and the employees learn to improve their skills [Ebert (1976), and McIntyre (1977)].

In spreading fixed costs over many product units, a dynamic dimension is the *life expectancy* of a production unit. The costs of a computer system can be spread over more users by increasing the system's flexibility and thus permitting longer use.

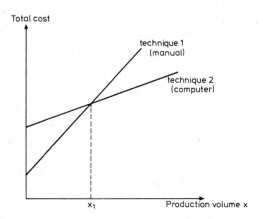

FIGURE 5–4.   Mass Production and Choice of Production Technique.

Such flexibility is improved by modular software and higher level languages. The life expectancy of software is lengthened also by using microprograms (firmware, stored logic) to emulate the old hardware on the new machine. (See note 7 in Chapter Three.)

Before one examines the demand for computers, a recapitulation of this section seems useful. The price paid for computers is determined by supply and demand. Supply is affected by technological progress, like LSI, and economies of scale (Grosch's Law). Economies of scale determine the technically optimal production capacity. Economic factors (law of marginal revenues equaling marginal costs) may make underutilization of technical capacity optimal. Underutilization may be temporary if demand for the product takes time to materialize. Fixed costs require a high production volume.

Demand for a product is affected by its value to the buyer: consumer goods serve immediate consumption; capital goods or investments are used as input into a production process. The value of consumer goods is governed by *Gossen's Laws:* his first law states that increased quantities of a specific consumption good have decreasing marginal utilities. Figure 5.5 demonstrates that the marginal utility may become negative (as in eating too many strawberries). Gossen's second law states that consumers will spend their incomes so that the marginal utilities of the various goods become equal. Since computers (apart from hobby kits) are not consumption goods, refer to Sharpe (1969, pp. 29–50) for more details on demand and utility.

When a company buys a production factor, its value is either an increase in revenues or a decrease in costs. [The reader may merely skim the discussion of Eqs. (5.4) through (5.11) if the material seems too complicated.]

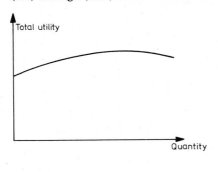

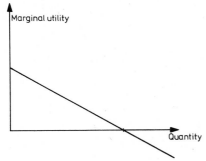

FIGURE 5–5. Gossen's First Law.

Alternative 1: Increased production.   A *revenue increase* equals the value of the increased physicial output of the company's product at the price at which the increased output can be sold. In symbols, the production function is

$$x = f(y, z) \tag{5.4}$$

where x is output volume, y and z are two production factors (say capital and labor), and f denotes the production function. Hence the marginal physical output of production factor y (or z) is denoted by $\partial x/\partial y$ (or $\partial x/\partial z$). The demand curve specifies at which price p_x the output x can be sold. Hence the marginal revenues of production factor y are

$$\text{Marginal revenues} = (\partial x/\partial y) \bullet p_x. \tag{5.5}$$

The optimal quantity of production factor y can be determined by equalizing marginal revenues and costs as in Eq. (5.3):

$$\frac{\partial x}{\partial y} \bullet p_x = p_y \tag{5.6}$$

where p_y is the price the company pays for a marginal unit of the production factor y.

Alternative 2: Constant production.   The physical output volume can be kept constant, but a *different combination of inputs* is used so that the total cost is reduced. In symbols, replace original input volumes y_1 and z_1 by y_2 and z_2 where $y_1 > y_2$ and hence $z_1 < z_2$. The total production cost is

$$c = y \bullet p_y + z \bullet p_z. \tag{5.7}$$

The isocost line follows from Eq. (5.7); in Fig. 5.6 production factor costs p_y and p_z are assumed constant. Given the relative factor costs p_z/p_y specified in Fig. 5.6, technique 1 is optimal because it results in minimum total cost c; see point A in Fig. 5.6. If p_y increases, it becomes attractive to produce according to technique 2, which uses more of factor z; see point B. The two techniques would become indifferent when the factor cost ratio p_z/p_y had a very special value, namely $(y_1 - y_2)/(z_2 - z_1)$; see the broken line between the points A and B.

The second alternative can also be formulated as a linear programming (LP) model: let x_i be the output volume produced by technique i ($i = 1,2$). Let γ_i be its unit production cost:

$$\gamma_i = \alpha_i \bullet p_y + \beta_i \bullet p_z \qquad (i = 1, 2) \tag{5.8}$$

where α_i denotes the y quantity needed to produce one unit of x_i. Hence as the upper part of Fig. 5.6 shows, $\alpha_i = y_i/x_0$. Likewise $\beta_i = z_i/x_0$. The corresponding LP model is

$$\text{Minimize } c = \gamma_1 \bullet x_1 + \gamma_2 \bullet x_2 \tag{5.9}$$

under the constraints of Eq. (5.10):

$$\alpha_1 x_1 + \alpha_2 x_2 \le y$$
$$\beta_1 x_1 + \beta_2 x_2 \le z$$
$$x_1 \ge 0 \qquad x_2 \ge 0. \tag{5.10}$$

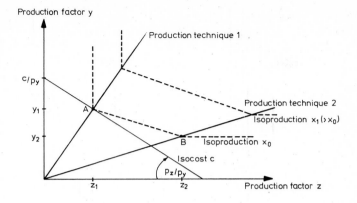

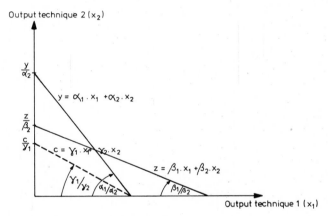

FIGURE 5–6.   *Optimal Production Technique.*

Exercise 12 suggests additional relationships between the upper and lower parts of Fig. 5.6.

Whereas Fig. 5.6 assumes only two production techniques to choose from, another extreme is to suppose *infinitely* many techniques. This situation may be modeled by the *Cobb–Douglas* production function

$$x = y^\alpha \cdot z^\beta \tag{5.11}$$

where α and β represent production elasticities (productivities). (See Exercise 13.) Then the cost function Eq. (5.7) can be minimized under the restriction that a specific production volume x be produced using the production function Eq. (5.11). Sharpe (1969, pp. 151–162) gives a more detailed exposition of the general microeconomic theory of the minimum cost combination of production factors.[6]

Consider applications of this economic theory to the computer field. The buyer of a computer system purchases a production factor. As indicated above this production factor can be used to increase revenues (gross sales) or to decrease production costs by production factor substitution. Chapter Two has already discussed some reasons for purchasing a computer.

Production cost reduction, substituting capital for labor, corresponds to the clerical cost displacement of Chapter Two. Capital-labor substitution *within* a DP system is exemplified by the increased use of high-level languages, which take less programming time (labor) and more computation and running time, besides additional memory space (capital). Such substitution is stimulated by rising labor costs. (Note that a higher p_y value in Fig. 5.6 moves the optimum from point A to B.) A different example is the computerized generation not only of some program but also of a complete information system; see the ISDOS project.[7]

In practice substitution of capital (computers) for labor has been intrinsically connected with technological progress. In symbols, substitution means that technique 1, characterized by the pair α_1, β_1 is replaced by technique 2, with α_2, β_2 where, say, $\alpha_2 < \alpha_1$ so that $\beta_2 > \beta_1$. Technological progress means that α_2, β_2 is replaced by α_3, β_3 with, say, $\alpha_2 = \alpha_3$ and $\beta_3 < \beta_2$. When substitution and technological progress occur in practice, the production volume is not necessarily kept constant. In the past postwar period of computerization, most firms experienced a growing demand for their products. Increased demand is one reason why computerization is not necessarily accompanied by growing unemployment. For a more detailed economic analysis of the effects of computers on national employment, see Kleijnen (1975a). Baumgarten et al. (1975) discuss the productivity of data processing.

The alternative reason for buying production factors is to increase (gross) revenues. Computers—or, better, computerized information systems—can improve decision making so that revenues increase. For instance, real-time airline reservation systems stimulate the sales of airline seats; see Chapter Two. The optimum degree of computerization follows from Eq. (5.6); i.e., marginal revenues must be equal to marginal costs; see also Fig. 5.2. For information systems Emery (1971, p. 19) suggests a cost/revenue relationship as shown in Fig. 5.7.[8] Refer also to Exercise 15, to Phister (1976, pp. 157–160), and to the next chapters.

Improved decision making, especially at the operational level, may decrease costs. For instance, because the same customer service (output volume) can be provided with smaller inventories, inventory carrying costs are lower. Such a cost decrease is not a simple capital–labor substitution, but implies technological progress. Whether one considers cost reductions or revenue increases or their combination, clearly the value of a computer system, or more generally an information system, *cannot be measured directly because there is no separate market where its output is sold.* Exceptions are companies, such as time-sharing bureaus, that offer computer services as their final product; see also Cotton (1975). The next section returns to this problem.

Substitution between production factors can be studied at a more detailed level *within* the computer system. In that case the production factors y and z in, say, the Cobb–Douglas production function of Eq. (5.11) do not denote gross categories like capital (computers) and labor, but may represent the production factors software, hardware, and personnel. It might be interesting to use such a model to study the share of each production factor in the total data processing budget if the firm is minimizing its total costs.[9] Empirical data on these budget shares are provided by Diebold (1973), Dorn (1979), and Phister (1976, pp. 146–154).

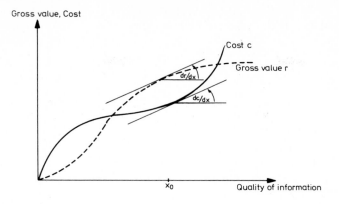

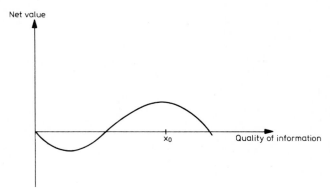

FIGURE 5–7.   Emery's Cost/Revenue Relationships.

Kriebel et al. (1974) apply production functions in an interesting nonlinear programming model of investments in computer equipment and of charging for computer usage. (See also the next two sections.) Their production function provides for economies of scale and for technological progress. Moreover, they distinguish among capital goods (computers) of various vintages (ages).[10]

Of a different nature are studies on *computer center management,* which involves job scheduling, hardware tuning, and so on. Such studies have a management science/computer science flavor. For instance, the computer system can be compared to a job shop because there are a number of jobs, each with its own requirements for CPU and printer. Jobs compete for the limited capacities of these "machines" so that when to execute which job must be decided. Usually this problem is solved intuitively, but models can replace the rule-of-thumb approach.[11] Other problems in running a computer center include how often to dump or reorganize a database, and how to balance seek time and storage space. The Special Interest Group on Computer Systems Installation Management (SIGCOSIM) of the Association for Computing Machinery (ACM) publishes a special *Installation Management Review.* Additional literature can be found in the references.[12]

LIMITATIONS OF THE MARKET MECHANISM

The classical model in economics assumes a *perfect competition* system with many supply-and-demand parties and a homogeneous product so that the "free forces" of demand and supply generate an equilibrium price. Supply-and-demand parties act purely rationally (as homo economicus) with perfect knowledge, no uncertainties. The market mechanism acts as an "invisible hand" that ensures optimum welfare for the economy as a whole. For example, in the long run the market mechanism will eliminate inefficient suppliers. In practice many of the assumptions of the classical economic model do not hold: suppliers differentiate their products (brand names), the limited number of suppliers may collude, inefficient production units may be supported by other divisions of a company, new suppliers cannot enter the market because of high research and development expenses, consumers buy only locally, payoffs are uncertain, and decision makers do not maximize but satisfice. These factors cause the market to function less than optimally. (A Pareto optimum is meant. As long as this optimum is not realized, some economic households can improve their welfare without decreasing other households' utilities.)

For some products additional causes make the market inadequate. The product may not be marketable in separate units. Examples of such *public goods* are national defense, natural scenery, highways, street lighting, and broadcasting. These products cannot be sold in units to individual consumers. Consumption by one individual does not necessarily mean that other consumers have less. Products may further have *external effects* or spillovers; i.e., they have unintended effects on other producers or consumers. Negative external effects include ecological pollution by a steel plant, health risks created by nuclear plants, and waiting caused by other customers in a queuing system. Negative external effects are usually not reflected in the producer's costs. (This situation is changing: oil refineries are being charged for their damage to the natural skyline.) The external effects can be positive: the economic infrastructure is improved, and hence investments are stimulated by the possibility of buying certain products such as railway transportation service. Production of articles with positive spillovers may be stimulated by subsidies (negative taxes). Mishan (1971) surveys economic analysis of externalities. The proceedings of a 1974 conference on externalities can be found in Lin (1976). A product may further have value both as a consumption good and as an investment; e.g., educational systems and library services. In modern economics, goods for which the market mechanism is inadequate are evaluated using *cost–benefit analysis*. Some of its techniques, such as Net Present Value, are borrowed from other areas and will be discussed in this book. As a whole, however, the cost–benefit approach does not seem to contribute much to the analysis of the benefits of computerized information systems. Refer to the literature for more detail.[13]

Obviously the product "information" suffers from many of the complications mentioned above: there is no unit of information. The unit "bit" developed in the Shannon–Weaver "information" theory—a more accurate term would be "communication" theory—is irrelevant when one focuses on meaning of information. Two messages of the same length may have quite different importance: "your match burns" versus "your house burns" or "dog bites man" versus "man bites dog." Hence the producer cannot supply the consumer with a specific amount of information because how much information is contained in a report supplied is unknown and depends on the receiver's prior knowledge (see Chapter Seven). Other consumers' reading the report does not reduce the information content for the original consumer (*public good*), but may affect the economic benefits of that information: inside information has different effects when it becomes public information. So the competitive advantage is affected by the number of people using the information. Negative external effects of information production may be risks to security and privacy. Positive external effects of information systems are clear because such systems form part of the necessary infrastructure. Information not only serves decision making but also may be appreciated ("consumed") per se. For discussion of the product "information" from an economic viewpoint refer to the references[14].

The product *computers* does not show the problems just discussed for the product "information." Computers *are* a product comparable to many other products. As with other capital goods, the market mechanism does not work exactly as the classical economic theory assumes. Actually, no other industry shows such single-supplier domination as that of IBM. The computer industry is further characterized by product differentiation; but a countervailing factor is plug-to-plug compatible equipment. Tremendous research expenses prevent new suppliers' entrance to the market and eliminate some old suppliers. Consumers cannot always shop around; they may be "locked in" with a specific computer manufacturer because of conversion problems. For these reasons the market mechanism does not function optimally.

In addition to the market for computers are the markets for the product "information." These markets might include those for library services, software houses, consulting companies, and the like. Economic models for the analysis of the manufacturer of computer hardware and software are far outside the scope of this book; see the references for details.[15]

Next consider *the market within the firm,* a market in which suppliers and users of information meet. Some authors feel that the problem of benefit evaluation for information systems can be solved by referring to the market mechanism[16] and by emphasizing that the data processing department sells a product to the other departments (users) on the "marketplace" within the company. This approach has serious limitations:

The product is ill defined.

The market mechanism works correctly only if the company is organized according to the profit center principle.

Ill-defined product   The previous discussions have already characterized the many peculiarities of the product information: lack of a unit of measurement, nondestructive usage, competitive benefits, negative external effects on security and privacy, positive external effects through the economic infrastructure, and consumptive versus productive usage. More specifically the DP department offers an ambiguous product, namely DP services and data. The services may be interactive computing facilities to which the user can subscribe. The data may be weekly reports or a database that can be queried interactively. Nevertheless, in principle the production costs for each individual type of service and product can still be determined; the cost accounting problems involved will be discussed in the next section. Another issue is that the user is often a supplier of the raw materials (data) on which the DP department works. For instance, the inventory manager supplies weekly sales data from which the DP department computes forecasts and order proposals. Such a consumer–producer relationship is rather unusual in modern industry. (The relationship often exists in handicrafts; consider house painters and tailors.) The supplier offers not a product but a (transformation) service. The supplier's market situation is affected because production can be done only on order, and staple production is impossible.

Market mechanism deviations   The market mechanism is supposed to bring together producers and consumers. In a free-competition model there are a great many suppliers who are not colluding. In the case of a single DP department, a monopoly situation exists. The monopoly model does not pretend to lead to maximum welfare for the economy as a whole, here the total company.[17] The company may decide to permit the users to go outside the company for their data processing needs: a user may buy, say, number-crunching services from a time-sharing bureau. Usually, however, the company prefers to have most DP done in-house to protect security and privacy, and to increase flexibility (control over rush jobs, informal procedures). The preference for in-house DP is not surprising because DP, computerized or not, is an essential part of the production process: one basic production factor of any production process is management based on information, which in turn requires data processing. (See Chapter Two, especially Fig. 2.1.)

As well as being affected by the DP department's monopoly, the market mechanism is drastically affected by the *common* goal of the DP supplier and the DP customers. Unlike a classic model in which the two market parties have conflicting objectives, in the present situation both parties are members of the same organization and share an ultimate goal or goals. Only if the departments were pure *profit centers* would they strive towards their own goals without regard for the overall goal. Such a construction, however, could mean the disintegration of the organization. It can be shown that if the DP department maximizes its own profit, a suboptimum for the organization as a whole results.[18]

Modern systems with their distributed computing and networks of computers complicate this picture: the DP department becomes decentralized into geographical subdivisions. (Logically local minis are part of the DP department although organizationally they may be managed by the local user department.) The user may then choose between local and remote computing services. Nevertheless, if the DP department serves a single firm, the firm's components are supposed to have a common, ultimate goal.[19]

A further complication is that the users may be too naive to evaluate properly the value of the DP services offered. If so, the DP department may be able to sell services it finds easy or interesting enough to develop.

How should the DP price be determined? Under a pure profit-center approach, the users could be charged at the external market price.[20] However, if the market is to serve as a mechanism for determining the benefits of information, the price should depend on the supply function of the supplier (the DP department and possibly external suppliers) and the demand functions of the buyers (user departments). Hence, one factor is the DP department costs, which include a rather arbitrary allocation of part of the company's overhead costs, such as top-management salaries and heating; see the next section. The other factor should be the benefits (value) to the user-departments. But *how* can these benefits be computed? The original problem has returned; the pricing of computer services *within* a company is not the answer to the problem of evaluating benefits *to* the company. Internal pricing of DP products is a relevant cost accounting problem, to be discussed in the next section. For a critical discussion of the price mechanism as a "solution" to benefit evaluation, see Welke (1977b, section 8).

Much has been published on a related issue: how decentralized subsystems can be coordinated through, e.g., transfer prices. Examples of such subsystems are the departments of a company, and the industries of a national economy. Often a linear programming framework is used for the study of the "decomposition" approach; see Sweeney et al. (1978). Chapter Eight discusses "team theory," an issue related to decentralization.

CHARGING AND PRICING COMPUTER JOBS

The emphasis in this chapter—and in this book as a whole—is on the ex ante quantification of benefits generated by computerized information systems. The preceding section demonstrated the impossibility of using the market mechanism with its resulting price as a means for ex ante benefit evaluation. In practice, computer services and products are often priced, but such computer pricing or charging is a cost accounting practice, concerned with the ex post calculation of the cost per unit of production. The reader who feels ignorant on this topic, which is tangential to this book, may first consult the short surveys in Fisher (1971, pp. 24–63) and Sharpe (1969). A review of some general concepts of cost accounting follows.

Costs versus expenses   Expenses are cash outlays made at a certain point of time. Examples are payments for a shipment of raw materials, or for machines such as computers. These expenses should be distributed over the product units: depreciation charges for machinery may employ various depreciation schedules; inventory evaluation of material costs may be based on first-in-first-out (FIFO) or last-in-first-out (LIFO). Expenses not necessary for production are not costs: personal expenses of the company's owner, and dividends (part of profit, not cost). On the other hand, costs may require no expenses at all: labor costs of the manager–owner and interest on the owner's invested funds. Expenses for machinery are made as a lump sum at specific points of time whereas the corresponding costs are spread over longer periods of time. Salary and material costs, however, are synchronized with their corresponding expenses, called out-of-pocket expenses.

Cost versus loss   Inefficient use of production factors is not cost. Loss includes not only waste of material but also unplanned underutilization of capacity such as computer capacity. Cost is restricted to standard (normative) use of production factors.

Variable versus fixed costs   Variable costs vary with the production volume. Examples are material costs, and paper and punched cards for computer output. These costs may vary linearly (Figs. 5.2, 5.4, and 5.6) or nonlinearly (Fig. 5.7). Fixed costs do not vary with the production volume (Fig. 5.2) unless a critical boundary is exceeded where the capacity must be expanded (Fig. 5.3). Examples of fixed costs are CPU cost and software development costs. (See also Exercise 17.)

Direct versus indirect (overhead) costs   Direct costs can be identified with a particular activity as can most material use. Management "labor" is an example of indirect costs. This distinction is closely related to the dichotomy between variable and fixed costs. Nevertheless the two distinctions are not identical: if two products are produced in two separate plants, plant depreciation is a fixed but direct cost item. If in a job shop more jobs are processed and require overtime, the extra light and heating are variable but indirect cost items. (The job processed during overtime could have been interchanged with the other jobs.) Overhead costs may be identified with indirect costs. A finer distinction is possible but not very relevant here.[21]

Joint costs   Joint costs arise if two or more products are produced simultaneously. The distillery process in oil refineries yields many products at the same time: kerosene, tar, and others. In the computer area a database can provide inputs to many applications.[22] When a product is delivered during both the daytime and nighttime by the same technical production unit, the two are economically different: electricity, air flights, and CPU time.

Historical versus replacement (current) costs   The cost charged for materials taken from inventory may be based on the actual, historical price paid. (If several lots are in inventory, the choice is among FIFO, LIFO, or average cost.) An alternative is to determine the present cost of new materials to replace the inventory used in current production. In Germany and the Netherlands the strong preference has always been for the substitution cost principle.[23] (See also Exercise 18.)

Marginal (differential) versus integral costing   Marginal costing means that only variable costs are calculated. Integral cost means that part of the fixed (indirect, overhead) costs is included. (See Exercise 19.)

Price differentiation and discrimination   Products may be the same technically but not economically. An example is computer services offered during either the daytime or the nighttime. When the price difference is based on differences in costs only, there is pure price differentiation. Such cost differences may arise if one product (daytime computer service) is charged the integral costs, and the other product is charged marginal costs only. When price variations are based not on cost differences but on differences in demand functions (value to the customers), there is price discrimination. To make it impossible to buy at the lower price only, price differentiation and discrimination require a "barrier" between the markets: geographic distance, day–night barrier.[24]

Opportunity costs   In economics (as opposed to, say, financial accounting) the cost of buying a product is the utility missed by not buying other products; money can be spent only once. Hence buying consumption good 1 means missing the utility provided by consumption good 2. (Remember Gossen's second law, that marginal utilities of the various goods should be equalized). There is an opportunity cost in buying production factor 1 because that money cannot be spent on production factor 2, and its marginal output is lost.

Shadow prices   Linear programming demonstrates that the revenues (to be maximized) increase when the quantity of a production factor (the right-hand side of a constraint) is increased by one unit, provided that this production factor was a bottleneck. Underutilized resources have zero shadow prices; in other words, the marginal opportunity cost for these resources is zero.[25]

Cost accounting is needed to compute the profit, i.e., to determine how well the company as a whole is doing "recently," say, over the past year or quarter. This accounting uses costs instead of expenses, and distributes fixed costs among product units over time. Nominal profits have to be avoided, using replacement cost. The resulting overall picture should be differentiated by product line and by department so that products yielding losses can be discontinued and inefficient departments can be concentrated on, an example of *management by exception.* This accounting necessitates understanding concepts like standard cost versus loss, and joint costs. Multiplying standard cost per unit by standard or expected capacity utilization results in a *budget* for the department or product line or more precisely for the "cost center." (Such a cost center may be "data entry.") Comparing budget estimates to actual costs is the work of "variance analysis." Determining standards for DP processes is discussed by Baumgarten et al. (1975, pp. 53–55). An interesting variance analysis within a LP framework is provided by Itami (1972, pp. 154–177).[26]

Costs are also needed as a basis for *pricing.* Theoretically, profit maximization requires that prices be set so that marginal costs equal marginal revenues; see Eq. (5.3). In practice a markup approach is often followed: the price is set equal to, say, 110 percent of the average cost. Such a policy is certainly reasonable for nonprofit organizations.

Concentrate now on cost accounting specifically in the *computer* area. Calculating the "exact" cost becomes difficult in the presence of fixed and joint costs.[27] Unfortunately most computer costs are fixed indeed: CPU rent, software development costs, and so on. Few costs are variable: input/output costs such as punched cards and paper, and the like. Joint costs are abundant too: the operating system and the database system support many applications. In general, modern computer systems are characterized by "shared" resources. Lists of computer cost categories can be found in the literature.[28] Recently guidelines for computer cost accounting were developed by a group of practitioners; see Statland (1977).

Notwithstanding the problems of calculating the "exact" cost, computer charging is recommended so that the *efficiency* of user departments, projects, product lines, and the DP department itself can be measured and hence controlled. Moreover, if computer capacity is limited—especially during peak periods—this capacity must be *allocated* somehow. One solution is to have users buy computer resources from their budget, and possibly to charge a higher price at peak hours. Alternatives include assigning each user a fixed number of CPU time units, or utilizing a first-come-first-served rule. Sharpe's (1969) discussion of price mechanisms for the allocation of scarce resources includes price discrimination and quantity discounts, and price versus cost.[29] Smidt (1968) discusses "hard" budgets (those that can be spent either on computer services or on other goods) and "soft" budgets ("funny" money to be spent on computer services only).[30]

If ex ante benefit evaluation is to be followed by ex post evaluation of a DP project, an accounting system is needed to determine costs besides gross benefits.

Moreover, ex post recording of costs may provide a basis for cost projections for similar, future DP activities; see the next section on investment analysis.

Algorithms for charging computer costs have a number of aspects that are typical for this field.

Reproducibility   The job should be charged the same amount when it is run at another time with a different work load or job mix.[31] Related is the stability of the charging rules: the rules should not be changed too frequently.

Demurrage   A job may be charged for resources that it did not actually use, but which it blocked so that other jobs had to wait. Refer back to the discussion on "externalities" in the previous section.[32] Note that resources may have to be blocked by a job in order to prevent deadlock.[33]

Equitability   The user should feel that the charge is fair.[34] Therefore the user must understand the algorithm. Only if the bill gives insight into the way costs were built up can the user try to utilize resources more efficiently in future runs. Efficiency improvements are indeed possible, provided the cost elements are controllable by the users. Cost elements representing overheads are not under user control!

Obviously it would be too crude to base the charge on CPU time only; think of input/output bound jobs. Consequently job-accounting routines must collect more data than just CPU time. However, these routines can definitely be less detailed than software and hardware monitors used for performance improvement; see Chapter Three. The user would just get confused by billing that was too detailed. Note that developing and running the job-accounting routine cost money. For additional discussion, see the extensive literature. A recent, recommended publication is Statland (1977).

Instead of a charge for computer resources (CPU or disc) used, the charge may be for computer services rendered: charge per paycheck or per sales order processed. (See Exercise 33.) Such a procedure satisfies the requirements of understandability and user's control.[35]

Observe that this discussion is of the costs of computer operations, not of the costs of system development. Because peculiarities such as demurrage do not occur in system development, the general cost accounting principles discussed at the beginning of this section apply. The next section discusses the *prediction* of future system development.[36]

Cost accounting and *pricing* are related but not identical. If the DP department were a pure profit center, it might maximize its own profit, guided by the law of equalizing marginal costs and revenues. If the department uses a markup policy, the goal may be cost recovery plus a modest profit. For the organization as a whole, pricing can serve as an allocation mechanism for scarce resources. Hence in peak hours higher prices may be charged. Elnicki (1977) discusses a case study in which five or six priority classes were created with a price difference up to a factor four or eight, respectively. In the early phase of a new computer system low prices may stimulate usage. The user's reactions to these prices depend on the user's demand curve (value function)—direct price elasticity—and on the prices for alternative production techniques, such as manual methods or outside DP services—indirect price elasticities. As in a national economy, top management may amend the price mechanism by imposing maximum price limits or by subsidizing certain users. Such intervention is necessary because the price mechanism does not work so perfectly as classical economic theory assumes. For instance, a user may have very valuable applications in mind but may not have the income (budget) to pay the price. (An analogy is provided by food prices and low-income consumers in starvation areas.) External effects (spillovers) may be compensated by taxes and subsidies (negative taxes). For instance, pioneering applications may be subsidized whereas peak-load usage that creates congestion can be charged extra.[37] Other imperfections of the price mechanism in general and for information in particular were discussed in the preceding section. Additional discussion on the pricing of computer services appears in the extensive literature on both pricing and charging. A recent, recommended publication is Hootman (1977, pp. 7–8).

In summary, in data processing, cost accounting is needed by the DP department, the user departments, and top management. The DP department and the user departments need such information for their individual cost-effectiveness evaluation. Top management needs this information in order to weigh DP investments against competing activities.

This section concludes with a brief discussion of the extensive literature on pricing and cost accounting for computers. Already mentioned were general surveys on costs and prices: Fisher (1971) and Sharpe (1969). Recent publications on computer charging and pricing are a monograph by Bernard et al. (1977) and the publications by Hootman (1977), Popadic (1975), and Statland (1977). Proprietary software packages for job accounting are surveyed by P. C. Howard (1977, pp. 13–16). Guidelines for cost accounting in the United States government data processing were developed by a special task group; see C. R. Palmer (1975).[38] Interesting reading is provided by the SIGCOSIM Symposium proceedings, edited by Squires (1971); some papers were individually referenced above. Many publications of interest are collected in an annotated bibliography prepared for a United States General Accounting Office Task Group.[39] A bibliography with 374 entries is provided by K. L. Hamilton (1977). Pricing computer services is further discussed by Canning (1976b), Cotton (1975, pp. 102–109), Habermann (1975), K. L. Hamilton (1978), and Sharpe (1969, pp. 53–60, 442–493). Many references can be found in Cotton (1975), J. B. Moore (1973), SIGMETRICS (1976), and Willoughby (1975). An industrial dynamics model for evaluating the effects of pricing is proposed by Weil (1971, pp. 1208–1209); Loomis (1976) uses discrete simulation to study the effects of price changes on users' demands for different computer resources, and hence on the computer center's revenues. Pricing in computer networks is discussed by Berg (1975), Kimbleton (1975), and Kriebel and Mikhail (1975). Price setting by a computer center in a competitive market may be solved by mathematical programming; see Balanchandran and Stohr (1977). There are many more references.[40]

INVESTMENT ANALYSIS

Cost accounting, discussed in the preceding section, concerns the calculation of the (standard) cost per product unit. Cost accounting should be distinguished from the issues arising when management has to choose among various possible computer projects. Many authors[41] emphasize that buying a computer or initiating a DP project is an investment; money is paid now for revenues that will materialize later.

Hence the classical problems of investment analysis or capital budgeting arise: the time value and the risk of future streams of expenses and revenues.

Several criteria have been proposed for comparing different *time patterns* of future cash flows. Let C_t denote the cash flow (gross revenues minus expenses but not necessarily costs) over period t. (See also Exercise 31.) One criterion then is the *payback* period: the number of periods required before the initial investment is recovered from the accumulated cash flows. Figure 5.8 demonstrates the inadequacy of this criterion: although all three cash flow patterns have the same payback period, alternative 2 is obviously superior to 1, which is in turn superior to alternative 3. Management might consider the payback period not as a criterion but as a side condition.

Another popular criterion is the *internal rate of return:* the interest rate that makes the Net Present Value of future cash flows and initial investment equal to zero. For the interest rate x solve Eq. (5.12):

$$\sum_{t=0}^{n} \frac{C_t}{(1+x)^t} = 0 \tag{5.12}$$

where C_t may be positive (revenues) or negative (expenses), and where n denotes the planning horizon of the company. (See also Exercise 32.) In practice the planning horizon is determined by corporate tradition. For instance, the company's general long-term planning may be 25 years ahead; in computer projects the horizon may be limited to five years to allow for new technologies developed in that time. Richard F. Meyer in Keeney and Raiffa (1976, pp. 474, 497) offers a theoretical discussion of the horizon problem. Note that Eq. (5.12) treats time as a discrete variable, but in Fig. 5.8 time is continuous. Economists are used to the discrete formulation; engineers often prefer the continuous representation.

Nowadays most authors agree that the *Net Present Value* (NPV) or Discounted Cash Flow (DCF) is the most satisfying criterion:

$$\text{NPV} = \sum_{t=0}^{n} \frac{C_t}{(1+p)^t} \tag{5.13}$$

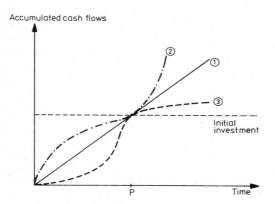

FIGURE 5–8.   *Payback Period P.*

where p denotes the cost of capital. One opinion is that this cost equals the interest rate the company made on its investments in the recent past, but other opinions can be found in the literature.[42] Projects with a positive NPV are economically justified. The project with the highest NPV is most attractive. Exercise 36 presents a simple example comparing the three criteria: payback, rate of return, and NPV. In certain circumstances and with certain goals, the NPV may *not* be a better guideline than the internal rate of return.[43]

If software expenses, for example, are made in a particular period, those expenses are not spread over the useful life of that software as they are in cost accounting to calculate the cost of a unit of computer service. For computer projects the pattern of the cash flows over time depends on the *system life cycle:* the phases of feasibility study, systems design, installation (implementation), operation (including maintenance), and phase-out. [See Palmer (1975, pp. 6, 12–15).]

In the computer literature some authors[44] favor the *relative NPV*. Let *PC* denote positive cash flows or revenues, and *NC* negative cash flows or expenses. Then the relative NPV (RNPV) is defined as

$$\text{RNPV} = \frac{\sum_{t=0}^{n} PC_t/(1 + p)^t}{\sum_{t=0}^{n} NC_t/(1 + p)^t} . \tag{5.14}$$

The idea is that if two projects have the same NPV, but project 1 requires a payment of \$10K and project 2 takes only \$1K, the less expensive project 2 is more attractive. However, a different argument can be made. If the company can make \$10K available for investments, project 1 generates a positive NPV, but project 2 leaves \$9K without a positive NPV. To incorporate the availability of financial funds explicitly, one can turn to linear programming, or mathematical programming in general. Such an approach may also be called for to take account of a variety of investment opportunities over time. However, these complications are far removed from the basics; recent textbooks can be found in the references.[45]

What is the *practical* use of the investment analysis techniques given above? The references[46] discuss the application of these techniques outside the computer area. Dean (1968, p. 90) shows how many companies actually formalize the view that computer projects are investments. Hall and Lincoln (1976) applied the rate of return criterion in an extensive DP case study. Discounted cash flows are used by the English government; see J. G. Head (1975, p. 184).

Part of the investment decision is the choice between *purchasing and leasing* the computer system. Both alternatives have their own cash flow streams, including tax payments, and both have their own risk elements; for instance, the company might purchase and be stuck with an obsolete machine. A thorough analysis of lease versus purchase from both the buyer's and the supplier's viewpoint is given by Sharpe (1969). Many more publications have discussed this topic.[47] Actual figures, provided by Diebold (1973), show a small but rising percentage of purchases.

A decision with consequences beyond cash flow is the *buy-or-make* option for application software. Cost accounting is needed to find the true costs of in-house development. GAO (1978a, p. 14) gives the example of developing a system in-house at an actual cost of \$662,000 when a similar system could have been purchased for only \$20,000.

Once a computer project has been decided upon, its *scheduling* may be done using a PERT network or some other technique to evaluate project progress.[49] Grindley and Humble (1973) suggest planning procedures and philosophy.

In the formulas for NPV, the predicted, future cash flows must be quantified. These cash flows comprise DP expenses, savings in operating costs, and revenue increases; see also Eq. (2.1). The quantification of revenues (gross benefits) is the main topic of this book and will be discussed in later chapters. Estimating the decrease in operating costs requires the same kind of approach. The estimation of the future DP expenses incurred by a particular project is greatly facilitated by the recording of *past* costs and expenses for similar DP projects, i.e., by doing cost accounting as discussed in the preceding section.[50] Regression analysis can then be applied to predict expenses for a future project if that project is similar to past projects for which data have been accumulated. For instance, in past projects direct labor (the dependent variable) may be determined mainly by such variables as the number of I/O devices and the number of jobs (independent, explanatory variables). Appendix 5.1 summarizes regression analysis. Case studies using regression analysis for the prediction of programming costs can be found in the references.[51] Fisher (1971, pp. 120–190) provides a general, not a computer oriented, exposition on cost relationship estimation, based mainly on regression analysis.[52]

If no previous, similar projects are available, expert opinions can provide *subjective or personal probabilities.* Ask an expert (manager, user, staff member) how likely it is that specific outcomes will be realized. The expert might state that the most likely lifetime of the project is five years, and that 10 percent probabilities exist for a lifetime greater than seven years and for a lifetime smaller than two years. Soliciting such subjective probabilities has become quite common, especially in Bayesian statistics and DELPHI techniques. The quantification of subjective probabilities is discussed in many publications.[53]

Objective probabilities can be computed by use of regression analysis based on past objective data. Besides an estimate of the future expenses, regression analysis provides standard errors for the regression parameters; see Appendix 5.1, especially Eq. (A5.1.6). This analysis yields standard errors and confidence bands for the predicted value of the dependent variable, say, total DP cost; see Eq. (A5.1.10).

Chrysler (1979) emphasizes that cash flow estimates should be revised as the project continues and actual cash data signal significant errors in the forecasts. Note, however, that for the decision whether to kill the project or to continue, the actual expenses are "spilled milk" and should be ignored.

In summary, DP projects are investments that generate future expenses and revenues. Future cash flows imply uncertainty, which can be quantified by means of either objective or subjective probabilities. Some authors associate the term *risk* with situations in which objective probabilities are available, and the term *uncertainty* with situations requiring subjective probabilities. Although risk can be insured against (e.g., life insurance), coping with uncertainty is management's task.[54] How to account for risk and uncertainty in investment analysis will be discussed in the next section. First, one should consider the "time resolution of uncertainty."

The NPV equation (5.13) takes into account the times at which the cash flows become available, and the next section will show how to account for the probabilities of various values realized for the cash flow C_t. However, a different aspect is *when* one will know the exact value of C_t. For instance, will one know at $t = 2$ that

C in period 5 will be minus one million dollars? Or must one wait until $t = 5$? In general, early resolution of uncertainty is preferred because hedging measures can then be taken. Moreover, psychologically people prefer shorter periods of anxiety to longer periods. For more discussion of this issue, see Meyer in Keeney and Raiffa (1976, pp. 475, 509–512).

RISK ANALYSIS AND SENSITIVITY ANALYSIS

Regarding the cash flows in the NPV computation of Eq. (5.13) as *stochastic* or probabilistic variables leads to a number of problems.

Computation of the expected NPV Mathematical statistics shows that the expected value of a function is not equal to the function of the expected value unless the function is linear. So in general

$$\mathcal{E}[f(x)] \neq f[\mathcal{E}(x)] \tag{5.15}$$

where $\mathcal{E}$ denotes the expected value. Since NPV is a linear function in the cash flows C_t, computing the NPV expectation seems to be no problem. However, the cash flows may in turn be nonlinear functions of variables that must be predicted. In that case those stochastic variables cannot simply be replaced by their expected values. Examples of such nonlinear functions are corporate simulation models, which yield the NPV as a function of a variety of input variables.

NPV quantiles and percentiles Instead of the expected or mean value, the median might characterize the location of the NPV distribution. By definition there is a 50–50 chance that the NPV is smaller or larger than its median value, denoted by q_{50} in Fig. 5.9. For nonsymmetric distributions, the median and the expected value are not identical; the mean is influenced much more by extreme values. Hence if some extreme cash flows are possible, the mean NPV is higher than the median NPV. One needs to estimate the complete distribution if one wants to estimate the median and other quantiles, such as the 10 percent quantile, denoted by q_{10}:

$$P(\text{NPV} < q_{10}) = 0.10. \tag{5.16}$$

One may also wish to estimate percentiles p, such as the probability p_0 of a negative NPV:

$$P(\text{NPV} < 0) = p_0. \tag{5.17}$$

For a normal or Gaussian distribution quantiles and percentiles can be estimated once the variance, in addition to the mean, has been estimated; see any textbook with tables for the normal distribution. Appendix 5.2 gives some useful formulas for the estimation of expectations and variances, and includes formulas that apply when the lifetime n is stochastic.

When the NPV depends on probabilistic variables, the distribution of the resulting NPV should be estimated. The complete distribution may be characterized by a few measures like the median and the 10 percent quantile. This distribution may also be used to estimate the probability of extremes, for instance, the probability of a

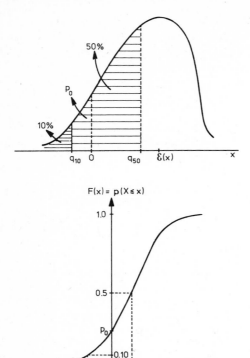

FIGURE 5–9. Characterizing the Location of a Distribution.

negative NPV. How does one obtain the distribution of NPV? A simple way is to use *simulation* or *Monte Carlo sampling.*

1. Determine the distributions of the input factors x_1, x_2 . . . in period 1. These distributions may be based on objective or subjective probabilities. For instance, lifetime may be subjectively estimated; operating DP cost may be based on regression analysis of similar projects.

2. Using random numbers, sample one value for each x in period 1. This sampling might induce correlation between, say, x_1 and x_2; i.e., if one samples a relatively high value of x_1, one tends to sample a relatively high (low) value for x_2 and thus induces a positive (negative) correlation. Techniques to sample correlated variables are discussed in the literature.[55]

3. Using the sampled values of the input variables x_1, x_2. . ., compute the resulting cash flow in period 1. This computation may be very straightforward or may use a corporate model to produce pro forma financial reports.[56]

4. Repeat steps 1 through 3 for the next period. Note that the distributions of the input factors may change over time; for instance, they may show

a growth pattern (life cycle). The variables may also affect each other. For instance, the variable inventory increases in period 1 if the sales variable turns out to be low; then this inventory is available for sales in period 2.

5.   After n periods (the planning horizon), compute the resulting NPV. If the planning horizon equals the lifetime of a computer, n may be a stochastic variable.

6.   Repeat steps 1 through 5 a number of times, say a thousand times, and form a frequency diagram of the thousand NPVs. How to determine the number of replications (here a thousand) is discussed at length in Kleijnen (1975b).

In investment analysis this Monte Carlo sampling is known as *risk analysis*; see the pioneering article by Herz (1964), and the other references.[57] In the literature[58] techniques other than risk analysis have been proposed. For instance, the more uncertain a cash flow is, the higher a discount rate p is used. These techniques seem less adequate.

Risk analysis should be distinguished from *sensitivity analysis*. The latter analysis investigates the effects of changes in specific *assumptions* of the model. For instance, a normal distribution or a growth curve may be replaced by some other specification (qualitative change); or the cost of capital p may be changed from 10 to 15 percent (quantitative change). Sensitivity analysis is also a first step in *optimization* and *satisficing*. The satisficing approach is less ambitious but more practical than optimization, and is associated with the "What if?" approach. To optimize or satisfice, first determine which decision variables (price, sales promotion, R&D) have important effects on the criterion (NPV). Factors to which the criterion is not very sensitive can be ignored in the search for an optimal or satisficing solution. In sensitivity analysis the input variables and model assumptions are changed systematically, not randomly as in Monte Carlo sampling; and the values of variables and parameters vary over a wide range. Fisher (1971) gives several approaches and examples of sensitivity analysis.[59] His examples demonstrate that if many factors (variables, parameters, assumptions) are studied, it becomes difficult to determine *which* factor combinations to investigate and how to *interpret* and *generalize* the great mass (or mess?) of output data.

Later in this section the use of a "metamodel" or auxiliary model will be proposed and discussed. Such an approach formalizes and extends the following commonsense procedure. A practitioner might change one variable x, observe the resulting output y, repeat this procedure, plot the (x, y) combinations, fit a curve by hand, and decide whether x affects y. The suggested metamodel approach formalizes this handfitting by the use of the least-squares algorithm, extends the procedure to multiple inputs, and systematizes the steps.[60]

This suggested approach is not needed if the response can be expressed as a simple, explicit function of the input variables. An example is provided by the total inventory cost in a straightforward Economic Order Quantity (EOQ) model:

$$\text{Minimum total cost} = \sqrt{2\,S\cdot C_1\cdot C_2} \qquad (5.18)$$

with yearly sales S, inventory carrying cost C_1 and setup cost C_2.[61] Another special case is parametric linear programming in which it is determined whether the optimal response changes when certain coefficients in the LP program change. Examples are provided by Emery (1969, pp. 91–98), and Rappaport (1970). However, as a rule, NPV calculations do not belong to these categories.

The criterion NPV is a function of a number of inputs, some quantitative (expected values, variances, growth rates) and some qualitative (shapes of production and demand functions). Denote the criterion or output by y, and the inputs by x_1 through x_k. [Qualitative inputs can be represented by dummy variables; see Kleijnen (1977) for details.] Scaling measures the quantitative inputs in such units that the corresponding variable x ranges between minus one and plus one. Some inputs are decision variables, under the decision maker's control, and might be optimized. Other inputs, environmental variables, are not under management's control, and are assigned hypothetical values in the model.[62] A special input is the random number seed R, used to sample from the input distributions; this stochastic factor represents all factors not explicitly modeled. The metamodel approach holds also if no sampling is used and so no R applies. Hence

$$y = f(x_1, . . .,x_k,R) \tag{5.19}$$

where f is a more or less complicated function, specified by the original model. For instance, f equals Eq. (5.13) with $y = $ NPV, $x_1 = p$, etc.

A very simple *metamodel* to express the effects of the k factors in Eq. (5.19) would be

$$y_i = \beta_0 + \beta_1 x_{i1} + . . . + \beta_k x_{ik} + e_i \qquad (i = 1, . . .N) \tag{5.20}$$

where in observation i the k factors assume the values x_{ij} $(j = 1, . . .,k)$, and are supposed to determine y_i linearly, except for a noise term e_i. This metamodel implies that a change in x_j has a constant effect on the expected response $\mathcal{E}(y)$:

$$\frac{\partial[\mathcal{E}(y)]}{\partial x_j} = \beta_j \qquad (j = 1, . . . , k). \tag{5.21}$$

A more general metamodel assumes that the effect of factor j also depends on the values of the other factors j' $(j' \neq j)$. This assumption can be expressed as in Eq. (5.22), in which illustratively $k = 3$:

$$\begin{aligned}
y_i = \beta_0 + \beta_1 x_{i1} + \beta_2 x_{i2} + \beta_3 x_{i3} + \\
+ \beta_{12} x_{i1} x_{i2} + \beta_{13} x_{i1} x_{i3} + \beta_{23} x_{i2} x_{i3} + e_i.
\end{aligned} \tag{5.22}$$

Here the coefficients β_{12}, β_{13}, and β_{23} denote *interactions* between the factors 1 and 2, 1 and 3, and 2 and 3. The interaction concept is illustrated by Fig. 5.10. (See also Chapter Four, especially Fig. 4.7). The importance of interactions in MIS is emphasized by Ein-Dor and Segev (1978a).

How can a metamodel like Eq. (5.22) be used? Proceed as follows.

1. Select N combinations of the three factors x_1, x_2, and x_3. The "optimal" choice of these combinations will be discussed later. This selection fixes x_{ij} $(i = 1, . . .,N)$ $(j = 1, . . .,3)$.

2. Use the original model of Eq. (5.19) to compute the criterion y_i for each combination i. In the NPV example use Eq. (5.13).

3. Use the N observations on the output y (step 2), together with the corresponding values of the input variables x_j (step 1), to estimate the

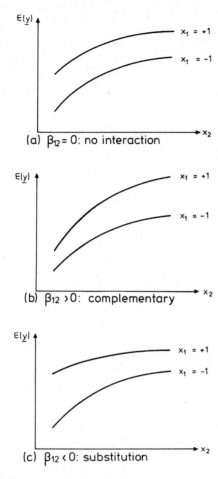

FIGURE 5-10. Interactions.

coefficients or effects β_0, β_1,. . .,β_{23} in Eq. (5.22). One can use simple regression analysis because Eq. (5.22) is linear in the parameters β. (The reader might wish to consult Appendix 5.1 on regression analysis.)

4. Test whether the assumed metamodel of Eq. (5.22) is indeed an adequate explanation of the changes in y as the x_j vary. The validity of the metamodel may be tested by using the metamodel (5.22) with estimated parameters $\hat{\beta}$ to predict y for some *new* combination of the x's, and then comparing this prediction $\hat{y}$ to the value y obtained from the original model (5.19).

5. If the metamodel does not pass the test of step 4, try other specifications for the metamodel.[63]

6. If the metamodel is accepted, proceed as follows. If the output is sensitive to specific *assumptions* (say, the value of the cost of capital p), one should spend more time on the determination of the exact value of this model parameter. If the exact value cannot be determined, one may give solutions for a variety of p values. In trying to optimize or just improve the output, one can concentrate on the important factors. The signs of their estimated coefficients $\hat{\beta}$ show in which direction these factors should be changed. Relative values like $\hat{\beta}_1/\hat{\beta}_2$ indicate the relative magnitude of the changes in the various factors, such as x_1 and x_2.

The use of metamodels to help explain the more detailed and complicated original model has also been advocated in other areas, especially in mathematical programming; see Geoffrion (1976, p. 82).[64]

The selection of the N combinations of x_1 through x_k is part of traditional statistical theory, and is known as *experimental design*. The following requirements for this selection are highlighted.

The number of combinations N should be small in order to save time and money. However, to estimate q effects, N must satisfy $N \geq q$.

Given N, the statistical inaccuracy measured by the standard errors $\hat{\sigma}$ should be minimal.

The selection should take into account the possibility of an inadequately specified metamodel. See Kleijnen (1975b) for a discussion of "lack of fit" tests and bias (confounding, alias patterns).

The design should be flexible; it should be possible to proceed in small steps (sequentialization).

To study the effects of a few factors, say three, start by letting each factor assume only two extreme values, denoted by $x = +1$ and $x = -1$; then evaluate the responses at *all* combinations, i.e., at $2^3 = 8$ combinations. However, if one assumes that the first order model of Eq. (5.20) is adequate, then one need estimate only four effects namely β_0, β_1, β_2, β_3—so that less than eight combinations may suffice. Before reading on, the reader is challenged to specify a personal selection of the x combinations; next compare this selection to Table 5.1. This table is constructed using a gimmick developed in experimental design theory: the last column x_3 is obtained by multiplying the elements in the x_1 and x_2 columns. Such tricks become necessary as the number of factors increases because the number of combinations then grows dramatically. For instance, for seven factors, $N =$

TABLE 5.1. *Experimental Design for Three Factors*

Combination	x_1	x_2	$x_3 \, (= x_1 x_2)$
1	$+1$	$+1$	$+1$
2	-1	$+1$	-1
3	$+1$	-1	-1
4	-1	-1	$+1$

TABLE 5.2.   Experimental Design for Seven Factors

Combination	x_1	x_2	x_3	x_4	x_5	x_6	x_7
1	−	−	−	+	+	+	−
2	+	−	−	−	−	+	+
3	−	+	−	−	+	−	+
4	+	+	−	+	−	−	−
5	−	−	+	+	−	−	+
6	+	−	+	−	+	−	−
7	−	+	+	−	−	+	−
8	+	+	+	+	+	+	+
9	+	+	+	−	−	−	+
10	−	+	+	+	+	−	−
11	+	−	+	+	−	+	−
12	−	−	+	−	+	+	+
13	+	+	−	−	+	+	+
14	−	+	−	+	−	+	+
15	+	−	−	+	+	−	+
16	−	−	−	−	−	−	−

$2^7 = 128$. Table 5.2 displays a design for seven factors. If a first-order model is postulated, only the first eight combinations need to be evaluated in order to estimate the eight effects $\beta_0, \beta_1, \ldots, \beta_7$. If one leaves open the possibility of an inadequate metamodel (see the third requirement above), the next eight combinations should be evaluated, too. The first eight combinations form a 2^{7-4} fractional factorial design. The sixteen combinations together form a 2^{7-3} fractional factorial; see Kleijnen (1975b) for more details.

SUMMARY

This chapter surveyed a number of topics taken mainly from microeconomic theory. The market mechanism, which yields a price determined by supply-and-demand functions, was explained and criticized. How this general economic theory applies to the products "information" and "computers" was indicated. Special attention was paid to the inadequacy of the market mechanism for solving the benefit evaluation problem for information products *within* a company. This topic led to the charging and pricing of computer jobs. Such a practice is useful for efficiency control and resource allocation. Next the discussion treated the investment character of data processing projects, using Net Present Value, risk analysis (Monte Carlo sampling), and sensitivity studies (with a metamodel).

APPENDIX 5.1: REGRESSION ANALYSIS

The linear regression model is

$$\mathbf{y} = \mathbf{X}\boldsymbol{\beta} + \mathbf{e}. \tag{A5.1.1}$$

Here boldface characters denote matrices or vectors. $\mathbf{y}$ is the vector of n observations on the dependent (endogenous) variable y_i ($i = 1, \ldots, n$). The vector $\boldsymbol{\beta}$ refers to the regression parameters $\beta_0, \beta_1, \ldots, \beta_m$ corresponding to the dummy variable $x_0 = 1$, the independent (exogenous, explanatory) variable 1, etc. X is an $n \times m$ matrix, where row i corresponds to the values of the m independent variables in observation i. The vector e denotes noise (disturbance, error). Equation (A5.1.1) yields the "normal equations"

$$X'y = X'X\hat{\beta} \qquad (A5.1.2)$$

where the prime denotes transposed matrices or vectors, and $\hat{\beta}$ denotes estimated regression parameters. Equation (A5.1.2) results in the least-squares estimators for the regression parameters:

$$\hat{\beta} = (X'X)^{-1}X'y = Wy \qquad (A5.1.3)$$

where $W = (X'X)^{-1}X'$. Next consider a linear transformation Z_2 of some stochastic variables Z_1:

$$Z_2 = AZ_1. \qquad (A5.1.4)$$

When Z_1 has covariance matrix Ω_1, the covariance matrix Ω_2 of Z_2 is given by

$$\Omega_2 = A\Omega_1 A'. \qquad (A5.1.5)$$

Applying this result to Eq. (A5.1.3) yields

$$\Omega_{\hat{\beta}} = W\Omega_y W' = \sigma_e^2(X'X)^{-1} \qquad (A5.1.6)$$

where the last equality holds if one assumes independent observations with constant variances:

$$\Omega_y = \Omega_e = \sigma_e^2 I. \qquad (A5.1.7)$$

One can estimate σ_e^2 by the Mean Squared Residuals (MSR):

$$\hat{\sigma}_e^2 = \sum_1^n (y_i - \hat{y}_i)^2/(n - m). \qquad (A5.1.8)$$

The least-squares estimators are given by Eq. (A5.1.3), and their standard errors follow from the Eqs. (A5.1.6) and (A5.1.8).

The estimated regression coefficients $\hat{\beta}$ can be used to predict the expected value of the dependent variable y for given values of the independent variables denoted by the vector x_0:

$$\hat{y}_0 = x_0\hat{\beta}. \qquad (A5.1.9)$$

Its variance follows from Eq. (A5.1.4):

$$\text{var}(\hat{y}_0) = x_0 \Omega_{\hat{\beta}} x_0'. \qquad (A5.1.10)$$

Note that Eq. (A5.1.1) assumes that the regression model is linear in its parameters β, but not necessarily in its independent variables x. Hence the following example satisfies Eq. (A5.1.1):

$$\ell n\, y = \beta_0 + \beta_1 \ell n\, x_1 + \beta_2 \ell n\, x_2 + e. \qquad (A5.1.11)$$

Another example is

$$y = \beta_0 + \beta_1 x + \beta_2 x^2 + e. \qquad (A5.1.12)$$

The numerous publications on regression analysis include Draper and Smith (1966), and Johnston (1963).

APPENDIX 5.2: SOME USEFUL FORMULAS FOR MEANS AND VARIANCES

In general

$$\mathcal{E}[f(\mathbf{x})] \neq f[\mathcal{E}(\mathbf{x})].$$ (A5.2.1)

However, for linear $f(\mathbf{x})$ one obtains

$$\mathcal{E}[\mathbf{ax}] = \mathbf{a}\,\mathcal{E}(\mathbf{x}).$$ (A5.2.2)

For instance, if $\mathbf{a}' = (1,\ldots,1)$, Eq. (A5.2.2) becomes

$$\mathcal{E}\left[\sum_i x_i\right] = \sum_i [\mathcal{E}(x_i)].$$ (A5.2.3)

A further useful formula is

$$\mathcal{E}(x) = \mathcal{E}_y\left[\mathcal{E}_x(x|y)\right].$$ (A5.2.4)

For instance, for stochastic n—and constant expectation $\mathcal{E}(x_i) = \mu$—one obtains

$$\mathcal{E}\left(\sum_1^n x_i\right) = \mathcal{E}_n\left[\mathcal{E}_x\left(\sum x_i|n\right)\right] = \mathcal{E}_n\left[\sum_1^n \mathcal{E}(x_i)\right] = \mathcal{E}_n[n\mu] = \mu\,\mathcal{E}(n).$$ (A5.2.5)

For the variance a useful formula is

$$\text{var}(\mathbf{Ax}) = \mathbf{A}\Omega_x\mathbf{A}'$$ (A5.2.6)

where Ω_x is the covariance matrix of $\mathbf{x}$; see Eq. (A5.1.5). If the x_i are independent with variances σ_i^2, and $A' = (1,\ldots,1)$, Eq. (A5.2.6) reduces to a familiar result:

$$\text{var}\sum_i x_i = \sum_i \text{var}(x_i) = \sum_i \sigma_i^2.$$ (A5.2.7)

Another handy formula is

$$\text{var}(x) = \mathcal{E}_y[\text{var}(x|y)] + \text{var}_y[\mathcal{E}(x|y)].$$ (A5.2.8)

Hence for stochastic n—and constant $\mathcal{E}(x_i) = \mu$ and var $(x_i) = \sigma_i^2$—one obtains

$$\text{var}\left(\sum_{i=1}^n x_i\right) = \mathcal{E}_n \text{var}\left[\left(\sum x|n\right)\right] + \text{var}_n\left[\mathcal{E}\left(\sum x|n\right)\right]$$

$$= \mathcal{E}_n[n\sigma^2] + \text{var}_n[n\mu]$$

$$= \sigma^2\,\mathcal{E}(n) + \mu^2\,\text{var}(n).$$ (A5.2.9)

For a constant n this equation reduces to $n\sigma^2$; see also Eq. (A5.2.7). For nonlinear functions in x, approximations to $\mathcal{E}[f(x)]$ and var$[f(x)]$ can be found in Kendall and Stuart (1963).

EXERCISES

1. Are all interfaces between a company and its environment markets?
2. Why can a shift in demand occur?
3. A "normal" demand curve is down sloping. Give counterexamples.

4. (a) Define a linear supply function. (b) How do you express a supply shift? (c) What effects does a positive supply shift (increased supply) have on price and market volume?

5. How can a time-sharing bureau differentiate its product?

6. Price elasticity is defined as $(dx/x)/(dp/p)$ where demand (or supply) x is a function of price p.
    (a) Compute the elasticity for a linear function, $x = a + bp$. (b) Compute the elasticity for $x + p^b$. (c) Why would you use a logarithmic transformation when applying regression analysis to estimate a demand function?

7. Does the demand function in Fig. 5.2 apply to a monopolistic or to a free competition market?

8. Compute the production volume x that maximizes profit in Fig. 5.2.

9. Is the revenue function r in Fig. 5.2 symmetric relative to the optimal production volume x_0?

10. Economies of scale imply that a production volume $x = 2x_1$ requires less than twice the production costs at $x = x_1$. In light of Fig. 5.3, what does this mean for the fixed costs if the variable costs remain constant over the whole production range?

11. Explain Gossen's second law.

12. Consider Fig. 5.6 and answer the following questions:
    (a) If z is fixed at z_1, and y increases above y_1, what is the marginal output? (b) If in the upper part of Fig. 5.6, $p_z/p_y = (y_1 - y_2)/(z_2 - z_1)$, what does this imply for γ_1 and γ_2 in Eq. (5.8)? (c) Both the upper and lower parts of Fig. 5.6 show that it is optimal to apply technique 1 only. Which inequalities hold among the coefficients α_i, β_i, and γ_i?

13. Derive the elasticity coefficient $(\partial x/x)/(\partial y/y)$ for the Cobb–Douglas production function specified by Eq. (5.11).

14. Consider a national clearinghouse where money checks are collected and processed. Why would management acquire a computer? For improved decision making or for cost reduction? Can you think of other reasons?

15. Consider the shape of the cost function proposed by Emery (1971) and pictured in Fig. 5.7.
    (a) Which shape has the marginal cost function? (b) Propose a simple algebraic formula to represent the total cost curve. (c) What is the area of inefficient (wasteful) information systems? (d) Does $dr/dx = dc/dx$ give a unique solution?

16. Mention a group of products that does not show much product differentiation by means of brand names.

17. Would you consider a computer operator as a variable or a fixed cost relative to punched cards? And relative to a CPU?

18. Would you expect replacement cost concepts to be more popular in countries with high inflation or in those without?

19. Consider the total cost relation, $c = A + Bx$ in Fig. 5.2. Give the formulas for the marginal and for the integral (average) costs. Does this latter formula really denote the average cost?

20. Sheep "produce" both meat and wool. Which cost problem does this create?

21. A job uses x_1 units of CPU time, and spends x_2 time units in the wait state. Why should not all x_2 units be charged to this particular job?

22. Does marginal pricing of computer services within a company reflect the long-run cost of the service? Does marginal pricing stimulate or restrict computer use?

23. Are depreciation charges joint, fixed, or variable costs?

24. Which product is, in general, more suited to monopolistic price setting: software or hardware?

25. Consider special student prices for airline tickets. (a) Are these lower prices based on average cost or marginal cost? (b) Is cost the only explanation for the price difference?

26. Why can price discrimination be realized in Exercise 25?

27. A company has information available on such items as its yearly sales volume, but only for the past ten years. Suppose you use regression analysis to forecast the reaction of sales to a contemplated price change.
(a) Why would you limit the number of explanatory variables in your regression model? (b) If you were to select three explanatory variables, which ones would you propose?

28. Suppose that computer jobs are charged not at standard cost but at actual average "cost." Why would such a practice stimulate underutilization?

29. Give a number of reasons why the standard capacity of a CPU is smaller than the product of number of days times number of hours per day.

30. Is the overhead caused by multiprogramming a cost or a loss?

31. A university operated its computer center without a budgeting and charging system. What effect would the introduction of charges for computer usage have on the users' demand for programming assistance by the computer center?

32. The computer center expects that its capacity will be underutilized during the next budget period. (a) How can the center attract customers through its charging system? (b) Which effect can the new customers exercise on the old customers? (c) How can old customers be protected against this effect? (d) What is the cost of such protective measures?

33. Consider charging computer resources used versus computer services rendered. Would you expect the latter system to be effective in a university research environment or in an administrative EDP center?

34. How can a deadlock situation arise at an intersection under a priority-to-the-right scheme?

35. Consider a company's profit and loss (P&L) account. How would you express the company's cash flow in some of its P&L items (profit, depreciation)?

36. In general how many solutions are there for Eq. (5.12) for the rate of return?

37. Consider the following buy versus lease option. Buying the computer requires a cash layout in period 1. Leasing the computer requires payments in periods 1 through 5. Do you need a depreciation scheme to decide between the two options?

38. Consider two investment projects with cash flows C_t. Suppose $C_t = A$ for project 1 $(t = 1, 2, \ldots)$ and $C_t = B$ for project 2, with $A > B$. Which project is favored by each of these criteria: NPV, payback, and rate of return? Next consider project 1 with $C_1 = -10$, $C_2 = C_3 = C_4 = 4$, $C_5 = \ldots = C_{11} = 1$; and project 2 with $C_1 = -10$, $C_2 = \ldots = C_9 = 1$, $C_{10} = C_{11} = 11$. When the cost of capital p is 5 percent, which project is selected by each criterion?

39. In a risk analysis problem the expert feels that if $C_1 > \mathcal{E}(C_1)$, then $C_2 > \mathcal{E}(C_2)$ where $\mathcal{E}$ denotes expected value, and the indices denote time. The expert has specified $\mathcal{E}(C_i)$ and var (C_i) $(i = 1, 2)$. With Gaussian distributions what more needs to be specified?

NOTES

1. Cotton (1975); see further Olsen (1971, p. 13), Selwyn (1971a), and Welke (1977b, section 8). The price elasticity of computers is also discussed by Phister (1976, pp. 160–166).

2. Bucci and Streeter (1979, p. 234), Cale et al. (1979), Campbell (1971), Cotton (1975, pp. 97–98), Kriebel and Mikhail (1975, p. 107), Selwyn (1971a, pp. 51–52), Sharpe (1969, pp. 314–348), and Willoughby (1975, pp. 431–432). A mass of data is provided by Phister (1976); see also Chapter Two.

3. See also Kriebel and Mikhail (1975).

4. Hoyt (1975), Rullo (1970), and Snyders (1973).

5. See also Selwyn (1971a, pp. 50–51).

6. Shephard (1976) gives an economics-oriented discussion, including references.

7. See, e.g., Couger and Knapp (1974).

8. A similar cost curve can be found in Kriebel and Mikhail (1975, pp. 107–108).

9. Dr. J. P. Jacob, IBM Research Laboratory, San Jose, California, 95193 (personal communication).

10. See also Kriebel and Mikhail (1975).

11. Coffman (1976), and Cook (1974); see also Bovet (1972). For a general discussion of job-shop scheduling refer to K. R. Baker (1974), and Conway et al. (1967). Proprietary software packages for scheduling computer centers are surveyed by P. C. Howard (1977, pp. 21–23).

12. References on the management of the EDP function in general are given by Emery (1972, pp. 246–247), Grindley and Humble (1973), McFarlan and Nolan (1975), and the *Computing Newsletter*, 1974, p. 13. For reorganizing databases see, for instance, Davis (1975, p. 52), and Sibley (1974, p. 99). See also the references in Chapter Three.

13. For a review of cost–benefit analysis refer to Cooper (1973, pp. 17–20), and Keeney and Raiffa (1976). See also T. E. Bell et al. (1977, pp. 8–9), Dewhurst (1972), Easton (1973, pp. 123–127), Fisher (1971, p. 21), J. L. King (1975), Nijkamp and Rietveld (1978, pp. 39–41), and Olsen (1971, pp. 12–13), Sassone and Schaffer (1978), Seiler (1969), and Wessel and Moore (1969).

14. Flowerdew and Whitehead (1975), Hirshleifer (1973), and Lamberton (1971).

15. Balachandran and Stohr (1977), Chow (1967), Cotton (1975, pp. 98–100), Harman (1971), Layton (1965), Molnar (1965), and Sharpe (1969, pp. 357–362). Data on the size of the computer service industry are given by Phister (1976, pp. 28–29). A most interesting book is Brock (1975). Treille (1978) discusses public data banks.

16. Cuninghame-Green (1973, pp. 104, 200–201); see also Willoughby (1975).

17. See, e.g., Brock (1975, p. 220).

18. Haberman (1975, pp. 15–16), and Sharpe (1969). For profit centers in MIS also refer to Bernard et al. (1977, pp. 48–49), and Diebold (1977, pp. 1–14, 40). See further Kriebel and Mikhail (1975, pp. 109–110).

19. See also Bernard et al. (1977, pp. 44–46, 96–99).

20. Bernard et al. (1977, p. 48), and K. L. Hamilton (1978, p. 23).

21. For a discussion in a computer center, refer to GAO (1978b, pp. 22–23).

22. Emery and Morgan (1973).

23. Bottler et al. (1972, pp. 191–196).

24. See Selwyn (1971b, pp. 18–19).

25. See also Bernard et al. (1977, pp. 61–62).

26. For variance analysis see also Bernard et al. (1977, p. 47).

27. Joint and fixed costs in general are discussed in Fisher (1971, pp. 24–40). For discussions in a computer context refer to Cotton (1975, p. 102), J. C. Emery (1969, p. 102) and (1971, pp. 8–12), J. C. Emery and Morgan (1974, p. 189), GAO (1978b, p. 25), Gregory and Van Horn (1963, pp. 581–583), Habermann (1975, pp. 20–21), and Sharpe (1969, pp. 162–170). See Cooper (1973, pp. 25–29) for case studies, and Van Zanten (1975) for batch versus on-line costs. For standard costs see Baumgarten et al. (1975, pp. 53–55) and Campise (1973).

28. Statland (1977). See also Bonney (1969), Bottler et al. (1972, pp. 187–189), GAO (1978b), Hollingworth (1971), J. L. King and Schrems (1978, p. 24), and Willoughby (1975).

29. More specifically Sharpe (1969, pp. 26–28, 61–81, 170–180, 252–278, 348–350).

30. See also Bernard et al. (1977, pp. 29–46), and Rogers and Van Horn (1976).

31. See, e.g., K. L. Hamilton (1978, p 17–18, 24–25).

32. See also Cicchetti and Smith (1976), and Harubi et al. (1977).

33. Hellerman and Conroy (1975) discuss deadlock in detail.

34. Refer to Savas (1978) for an interesting, but not computer-oriented discussion on equity. See also Mishan (1971, pp. 24–26).

35. See also Bernard et al. (1977, pp. 77–80).

36. See also Bernard et al. (1977).

37. See also Bernard et al. (1977, pp. 59–60, 83–87).

38. Also GAO (1978a) and (1978b).

39. See GAO (1976, pp. 17–19, 22–24, 28–38).

40. Canning (1973) and (1974a), De Coster (1975), Diebold (1977), Gotlieb (1973), Graham (1976, pp. 91–96), Grindley and Humble (1973, pp. 112–114), Nielsen (1970), Nolan (1973) and (1977), Rettus and Smith (1972), Schaller (1974), Shaftel and Zmud (1973), Singer et al. (1968), Stevens (1970c, pp. 7–8), ter Linde (1978), Wiorkowski and Wiorkowski (1973), and Yearsley and Graham (1973, pp. 107–115).

41. Boutell (1968, p. 114), Emery (1971, p. 39), GAO (1978a) and (1978b), Hollingworth (1971), Reichardt (1974), and Verhelst (1974, pp. 7, 230–232).

42. Johnson and Lewellen (1972), King and Schrems (1978, pp. 24–25), Rosenblatt and Jucker (1979, pp. 65–66), and Sharpe (1969, pp. 131–134).

43. Lesourne (1973, p. 178), and King and Schrems (1978, p. 26).

44. Menkhaus (1969, p. 50), M. H. Schwartz (1969, p. 37), and also Fisher (1971, p. 11), and Seiler (1969, pp. 74–76). For a different view see Bottler et al. (1972, pp. 49–50).

45. Bussey (1978), Levy and Sarnat (1978), and Wilkes (1977); see also Rosenblatt and Jucker (1979, pp. 66–67). Excellent introductions to investment analysis are Fisher (1971, pp. 51–59, 201–241) and Sharpe (1969, pp. 94–136). Meyer gives a theoretical but salient exposition from the utility point of view; see Keeney and Raiffa (1976, pp. 473–514). For a discussion incorporating the German (and Dutch) preoccupation with cost accounting, see Bottler et al. (1971, pp. 31–128).

46. Brigham (1976), Gitman and Forrester (1977), and Rosenblatt and Jucker (1979).

47. See Johnson and Lewellen (1972), and Sharpe (1969, pp. 81–93, 211–278, 494–501). Also refer to Bottler et al. (1972, pp. 129–142), Chaplin (1969), Corum (1975), De Bruijn (1965), GAO (1978), Joslin (1977, pp. 150–157), Moneta (1965), Sharpe (1965), and Timmreck (1973, pp. 214–215).

48. See also Graham (1976, pp. 122–131), Hoyt (1975), Rullo (1970), and Snyders (1973). More references can be found in GAO (1976, p. 10).

49. For PERT see Brooks (1974), and Thesen (1978, pp. 103–138); for a PERT application see Trill (1977, p. 80). Other techniques are reviewed in Britney (1976), Burt (1977), Elmaghraby (1977), Graham (1976), Harris (1971), McFarlan and Nolan (1975, pp. 491–646), and Wiest and Levy (1977). More references can be found in GAO (1976, pp. 11–14).

50. See also GAO (1978a).

51. Chrysler (1978), Gayle (1971), and Walston and Felix (1977).

52. For additional discussion see Aron (1969), Bernard et al. (1977, pp. 87–92), Eldin and Croft (1974, pp. 148, 213–216, 237–241), Estes (1969), Fried (1969), Grindley and Humble (1973, pp. 114–115), Hollingworth (1971), Infotech (1973, pp. 91–98), Land (1976), Pope (1975), Rosenkranz and Pelligrini (1976, p. 265), and Zelkowitz (1978, pp. 205–206). Also recommended is the bibliography prepared for the GAO Task Group; see GAO (1976).

53. Chesley (1975), Conrath (1973), Harrison (1977), Hogarth (1977), Huber (1974), Matheson and Winkler (1976), Morris (1977), Rubinstein and Schröder (1977), Spetzler and Staël von Holstein (1975). See Chapters Four and Seven.

54. Boodman (1977), Easton (1973, pp. 130–136), Fisher (1971, pp. 202–203), and also Mason and Mitroff (1973, p. 479).

55. Kleijnen (1975b, pp. 46–48); see also Bussey and Stevens (1972), and Tenenbein and Gargano (1978).

56. References were given in Chapter Two, note 6.

57. Estes (1969), Fisher (1971, pp. 201–217), Fried (1971), Hespos and Strassmann (1970), Lincoln (1977), Parkin (1977), Stone (1978), Timmreck (1973, p. 213), Wallace (1975), and Wallace and Boyd (1971).

58. Bottler et al. (1972, pp. 75–79), Fisher (1971, pp. 213–215), Gitman and Forrester (1977, p. 70), Rosenblatt and Jucker (1979, p. 67), Johnson and Lewellen (1972), and Sharpe (1969). See also Bernhard (1977). A quite complicated analytical treatment of the risk analysis problem is proposed by Perrakis and Sahin (1976).

59. Fisher (1971, pp. 12–13, 73–76, 166–190, 212–217, 242–283). See also Estes (1969), Hespos and Strassmann (1970), Stone (1978), Wallace and Boyd (1971, pp. 1217–1218), and Wilkes (1977).

60. Various types of metamodels are discussed in Kleijnen (1979a).

61. See, for instance, Churchman et al. (1957, p. 204).

62. See also Ein-Dor and Segev (1978a).

63. For details refer to Kleijnen (1979b) and Kleijnen et al. (1979).

64. See also Kleijnen (1979a).

CHAPTER **SIX**

INTRODUCTION

The present chapter presents the many attributes or characteristics that determine the quality of information. Subsequent chapters will investigate how some of these characteristics can be studied through the use of specific techniques and models. A discussion of the results of such studies will be postponed until those chapters. The present chapter will try to define independent or "orthogonal" information attributes. For instance, late information will be distinguished from inaccurate information although common practice collapses all kinds of imperfections together under the term "inaccuracy." Moreover most definitions of the information characteristics will be quantitative. In the relatively scarce literature[1] various categorizations are used. Of these attributes

- Timeliness (age, recency, delay)
- Accuracy (errors)
- Aggregation
- Report mode (exception reports, queries, formats)
- Retention time
- Privacy and security
- Reliability and recovery
- Scope
- User-machine modes
- Flexibility
- Multiple users

only timeliness of information will be analyzed in detail; the other attribute analyses will be less detailed.

As noted in previous chapters, some data are required for nondecision purposes. For instance, the employee's address is needed for forwarding a paycheck. The focus here, however, is on data needed for managerial decision making. Little attention will be paid to "peripheral" observations, the many impressions uncon-sciously filtered for future relevance. [See Nielen (1976) for a further discussion of this peripheral attitude.] The value of peripheral information would be extremely hard to quantify because its goal is not clearly defined. Therefore this discussion con-centrates on those aspects of the managerial information system that are sufficiently formalized to be computerized.

Before a discussion of the attributes of information, it is useful to consider the following *framework*. Let an event—a transaction in data processing terminology—occur at the point of time t_0. Then this event leads to the creation of a data image (one or more records), or to the change of existing records, at a time t_1 with $t_1 \geq t_0$. In on-line data-capture systems $t_1 \downarrow t_0$ where the symbol $\downarrow$ means that t_1 approaches t_0 "from above." These data, together with other data, influence a deci-sion made at time t_2 with $t_2 \geq t_1$. In real-time systems it is possible that $t_2 \downarrow t_1$. The decision, together with noncontrollable (environmental) variables, changes the real world including the organization at a time t_3 with $t_3 \geq t_2$. As van Aken (1978, p. 160) points out, it is the "inertia of technology" that creates this delay. The lag $t_3 - t_2$ depends primarily on the characteristics of the real-world system, not on the DP system, although relations with the DP system are possible. (See Exercise 1.) The state of the real-world system at a time t_4 (with $t_4 \geq t_3$) depends on the history or time path of decisions and environmental variables up to t_4. (In Markov systems the state at time t_4 depends only on the state at a single prior point of time, say, $t_4 - 1$.) In summary

t_0 : event (transaction) occurs

t_1 : data created

t_2 : decision made

t_3 : decision effective

t_4 : a future point of time.

Use of terms like on-line and real-time requires definition because no standard *terminology* exists. Real-time information systems may be described as systems in which the value of the information decreases drastically if the user has to wait "too long" for information. The critical length depends on the physical system that is to be managed. For instance, this length is much shorter in air traffic control than in air-line reservation systems. "On-line" means that the peripheral input–output device at the user's location is directly connected by wires or telecommunication channels to the central part of the computer system. Normally real-time systems require on-line processing. For economic reasons many on-line users may share one central com-puter, running under a "time-sharing" operating system. Under such an operating system the CPU works on each job during only a short period of time (time-slice); yet because of the short response time, each user has the impression of exclusive computer use. Although the terms real-time, on-line, and time sharing are often con-nected with each other, each emphasizes a different aspect. (Note that the users may share a central DP system because they wish to use a common database; but such a multiaccess system is not a time-sharing system.) In the "batch" mode several jobs accumulate over a period of time before these jobs are submitted to the computer. (Usually the jobs are rearranged before being processed by the computer.) Batch processing eliminates the real-time mode in most applications. In real-time processing a job is usually a single transaction; in other types of processing a job comprises several job steps. In "multiprogramming" the average turnaround time of jobs is improved because the CPU can start on the next job (which must reside in main memory) while waiting for input or output for the current job. In modern computers batch operations can be combined with real-time operations by giving batch operations low priority in the operating system. Batch operations may be executed mainly at night. The recent development of inexpensive minicomputers, however, has created a trend towards computer systems dedicated exclusively to a single application, either in batch mode or in real-time mode. See also Table 6.1.[2]

Database management systems (DBMSs), frequently mentioned in this chapter, merit preliminary discussion.

Traditionally an EDP system contains a number of *files*, ordered collections of records; e.g., a file on inventory, or a file on accounts receivable. Phister (1976, pp. 126–127) discusses a variety of files, their typical size, and their frequency of usage. Certain data, e.g, an article's part number and description, occur in more than one file. Because simultaneous updating of duplicated information is impossible, data discrepancies among files are created: different files may contain data of different recency.

In a DBMS, however, data occur only once. Logical relationships among the records formerly forming a physical file are now created by links or pointers: the address of the next record is contained in the current record. Physically the records are stored on random-access devices, such as discs, and can be retrieved from them using the records' addresses. Because the records are linked to form data structures such as networks, the user can question the database to answer ad hoc questions: "How many employees work in a warehouse receiving less than x articles per month?" or "In which assemblies is product A utilized?" The software needed to maintain such a database is very sophisticated, and processing and data storage overhead is incurred. For example, if a new record is created, the DBMS must update all links with other records. In addition, the user should be able to use various programming languages to operate on a single database: the data should have "program independence." On the other hand, there should be data independence: changes in the physical storage of data should not affect the user's programs. An innovative study on such systems was done by the CODASYL Data Base Task Group. Nowadays, a variety of operational systems is available on the market; e.g., ADABAS, DMS-1100, IDMS, IMS, SYSTEM-2000, and TOTAL. The number of publications on DBMSs is amazing.[3]

TABLE 6.1. *Computer Terminology*

User-oriented (Response Times)	Computer-oriented (Operating Systems)	
	Monoprogramming	Multiprogramming
Real-time	Dedicated system, e.g., minicomputer	Time sharing
Not real-time	Old generation system	Newer generation

The subject of information attributes is closely related to the problem of *what* information the user needs, the problem of *information requirements analysis*. The question, "Does this manager need information on the backlog of orders?" immediately raises other questions: "When is this information needed?" "How accurate and detailed should the information be?" The attribute "scope," discussed later, explicitly raises the issue of what data to store in the database. Information requirements analysis covers a variety of techniques: interviews with users, decision scenarios (artificial decision situations), prototypes (an actual information system of limited scope), and analyses of past data usage.[4] These techniques have practical relevance only insofar as they are able to improve existing practices. Scientifically speaking, these techniques do not provide sound analysis and prediction capabilities, nor yield normative conclusions as is illustrated by the following analogy: the doctor (information scientist) does not ask the patient which medicine (information) the patient needs.

TIMELINESS

The timeliness of information is associated with terms like currency, recency, age, delay, and response time. It is useful to distinguish between decision making triggered by some external event, like the arrival of a customer, and decision making scheduled at fixed points of time. Unscheduled decisions occur at stochastic (probabilistic) points of time. According to Blumenthal (1969) decisions made by middle management are primarily periodic, those by top management are irregular, and those by lower management are real-time.[5]

Unscheduled Decisions

Consider the various elements affecting the recency of information.

Update processing delay P   When data are submitted to the computer, it requires P time units to process them. Included in this delay is the *input time* needed by human operators, such as keypunch typists. In batch systems P is certainly not negligible, and is known as turnaround time. In on-line systems individual transactions can be processed, and P is small.

Update interval I   Data can be collected over I time units before submission for processing. In on-line data-capture systems (for instance, point-of-sale systems) this interval is virtually zero because individual transactions are processed. In batch systems, by their definition, I is not negligible. In an organization the magnitude of I is often based on tradition.

Retrieval delay R   If the decision maker asks information at time t, the information comes available at time $t + R$. R is known as response time in real-time systems. As mentioned above, the turnaround time in batch systems is associated with the processing time P. If an ad hoc question arises in a batch system, a special program might be submitted, and the time required for an answer might be denoted by R rather than by P. In the normal batch situation, however, R is the time required to retrieve manually the desired data in the output that was produced in P time units. Observe that a system may combine on-line retrieval (R small) with periodic (say, weekly) batch updating of the database ($I = 1$ week, P not small).[6]

Decision delay D   When the information is available, the decision maker needs time to reach a decision. A separate component is the time required for the decision reached to affect the physical system itself. For instance, in production scheduling this time component comprises machine setup times. In inventory control the delivery or lead time is such a time lag; see the lag $t_3 - t_2$ in the chapter introduction. Here this *reaction delay* is included within D.[7]

These four subdivisions differ from those of classical EDP categorization: data collection, recording, transmission, processing, storage, retrieval, and display.[8]

In a batch system the *minimum* total delay occurs if the decision is required immediately after the information has been updated and processed; see Fig. 6.1. (None of the following figures is drawn to scale.) Hence, at the moment the physical system changes, the decision is based on information of age $P + R + D$. (See Table 6.2.) This minimum age holds if the information reflects the *status* of a variable like inventory, not if the information reflects individual events—such as orders—over the update interval I. The status variable is important in, say, ordering new stock. The individual events may be of interest in finding out the maximum size of an individual order. In banking individual events may be relevant because of a rule like, "If the maximum account withdrawal is larger than x, then do immediately. . . ." For individual events the minimum age is the same as that for status information: $P + R + D$. The maximum age is I units higher if all previous events are available

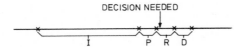

FIGURE 6–1.   *Minimum Total Delay.*

TABLE 6.2.   *Recency of Information*
(Unscheduled Decisions, Batch Processing)

	Information on	
	Status	**Events**
Decision just after processing ends	$P + R + D$	$P + R + D$ (minimum) $P + R + D + I$ (maximum)
(Minimum age)		$P + R + D + \frac{1}{2}I$ (average)
Decision just before processing ends	$P + R + D + I$	$P + R + D + I$ (minimum) $P + R + D + 2I$ (maximum)
(Maximum age)		$P + R + D + \frac{3}{2}I$ (average)
Average age	$P + R + D + \frac{1}{2}I$	$P + R + D + I$

at an update point in an appropriate summarized form, such as a frequency diagram. Hence, if events occur at a constant rate, the average or expected age is $P + R + D + \frac{1}{2} I$.[9]

The *maximum* total delay occurs if the decision is triggered immediately before new information has been processed; see Fig. 6.2. Hence, the status information has age $P + R + D + I$. The individual events have a minimum age of $P + R + D + I$; a maximum of $P + R + D + 2I$; and an average of $P + R + D + \frac{3}{2} I$. If the probability of triggered decisions is constant over time, the expected delay is the average of the corresponding minimum and maximum total delays; see the last row of Table 6.2. In general the component I will be large relative to the other components.

In *on-line* systems individual events can be immediately processed so that the update and processing times become virtually zero: $I \downarrow 0$, $P \downarrow 0$. Hence Table 6.2 reduces to a simple relation: the age of the information is approximately $R + D$. In on-line systems attention is concentrated on the retrieval delay R. In some systems such as airline reservation systems, the decision-making delay D is indeed negligible because the decision is simple. In other systems the situation may be so complicated that the decision maker can benefit very much from computer assistance in arriving at a decision: D can be reduced by computerized decision models, report mode (e.g., queries), or format (graphics), discussed in later sections of this chapter. Morton (1971) describes a system in which D was reduced from six days to half a day by means of a graphic decision-making system. See also note 9 in Chapter Two.

Some questions may need not the most recent information but information concerning a specific, historic point of time. For a question like "What did Mr. John Smith order on September 7, 1956?" only $R + D$ matters. Other queries of this type are library searches like "List all publications on computer storage techniques published before 1955."

From Table 6.2 it follows that in order to realize a desired *total* delay, one or more of *components P, R, D,* and *I* may be changed. In this simplified model, the same effect is achieved by changing either P, R, or D; but the effect of I varies: Table 6.2 shows that the weight of I may be 0, 1/2, 1, 3/2, or 2. Although the effect of the various components may be the same, their *technical* realization is different and hence implies different economic costs. The update interval I is virtually eliminated when a batch system is replaced by an on-line data-capture system. In an on-line system, the processing time P for a single event is small compared to processing a batch that reflects events over a whole period I. In an on-line retrieval system, R will be smaller than in a batch system. D may be thought of as independent of the computer system in certain situations. However, the computer may assist in reaching and realizing a decision so that D decreases. Given a specific computer system operating in batch mode, the organization can still choose among several values for the update interval I. The following discussion of the economic costs and benefits of changing the values of the age components will be rather qualitative; more exact techniques will be presented in later chapters.

FIGURE 6–2.   *Maximum Total Delay.*

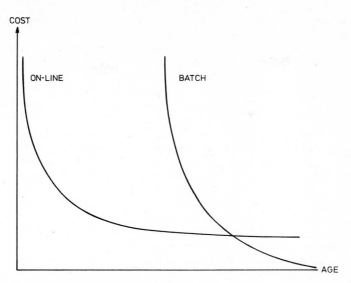

FIGURE 6–3.   Cost–age Relations.

Figure 6.3 illustrates possible relationships between the timeliness of information and its *costs*. In on-line systems delays technically can be reduced to zero (or better, to the decision delay D). However, queuing theory shows that reducing waiting times (involved in the response time R) toward zero requires exponentially increasing computer capacity. In the batch mode the information's age can be drastically reduced by decreasing the update interval I. In that case the number of batch runs per year increases and hence results in increased yearly costs fixed per run. By definition these fixed costs are costs that do not vary with the number of transactions per run; an example is the cost of mounting the appropriate disc pack.[10] In Fig. 6.3 the assumption is that these increased fixed costs are not offset by a decrease in the per-batch costs of processing the individual transactions. Note that the number of transactions also affects the update processing delay P. Apart from this effect, P can be reduced by a more powerful computer, which involves higher cost. Economies of scale (see Chapter Five) would make the cost increase less than proportional and would contradict the shape of the curve in Fig. 6.3. Therefore specifying the exact shape of the curves in Fig. 6.3 is difficult. The literature on cost curves is very scarce. In an old batch-oriented article, Gregory and Atwater (1957) propose cost curves that are U-shaped relative to the update interval I, and that show drastic increases relative to the processing delay P. Brenner (1965), too, claims that cost is a U-shaped function of age because very old, off-line information requires long searches; Gregory and Van Horn (1963, pp. 586–588) propose such a U-shape because keeping old information increases the database size. However, these arguments concern the data retention period (how long to keep data within the database), discussed in a later section. More study is needed to determine whether general relations can be postulated between the cost and the timeliness of information, or whether one must resort to case studies. Remember that the cost dimension in Fig. 6.3 involves hardware, software, operator, and user costs; the timeliness dimension is composed of the different elements displayed in Table 6.2.[11]

Several authors have suggested hill-shaped curves for the relationship between the *value* and the recency of information.[12] However, under the assumption of "adequate knowledge," more recent data cannot be less valuable than older data. The condition of adequate knowledge means that the user knows how to use the data in an optimal, or at least a satisfactory, way. Without such knowledge there is indeed the possibility of *overreaction*; i.e., too frequent decision making may destabilize a system. If the user determines that monthly decisions on production are better than weekly decisions, it is still possible to aggregate weekly data on sales and inventory into monthly data (and to ignore weekly data of the current, incomplete month). Consequently, more timely information has no negative gross value. Besides adequate decision rules, adequate forecasting routines are needed. For example, weekly data may show a more erratic pattern than monthly data show. Hence the user should be capable of determining an optimal or satisfactory update interval I, or an adequate value for the smoothing constant α in exponential smoothing.

In information economics it has been proven mathematically that information cannot have negative gross value.[13] As the next chapter shows, information economics assumes that the user has perfect knowledge about the system's structure and acts in an optimal way. A theoretical discussion on the optimal control of systems can be found in the literature on control engineering.[14] Chapter Eight treats control engineering. In practice, managers may deviate from a theoretically optimal policy. A gaming experiment found that decision-making frequency did not increase with the variability of the environment as one might have expected; however, it is possible that the players did not act optimally.[15] Although a hill-shaped curve seems unrealistic for the gross value of information, such a curve may very well hold for the *marginal* increase of value, or for the *net* value.

A different situation exists if in an on-line *retrieval* system the emphasis is not on the recency of the information, but on the response time of the computer system once a query has been started. In that case the user may want fast response time in order to give a fast answer to customers, but the data retrieved from the database does not have to be completely up to date.

An instantaneous response time is not desirable psychologically because without a (small) pause between the question and the computer's answer, the operator gets confused. Another practical point is that the value of the turnaround time may depend on the time of day the job is submitted for processing. For instance, if the job is submitted at the end of the work day, it does not matter whether the job is completed at 1 A.M. or at 2 A.M.[16]

In general the value–age relationship depends on the use of the information in the management of the organization, and not on the data processing subsystem itself. In environments in which important changes occur frequently, the value of recent information is high. For instance, in air navigation recency is of ultimate importance. In inventory systems more recent information may or may not be worth its cost. In tactical or strategic decisions the planning period is so long that the recency of information has less effect on the accuracy of the forecasts needed for these decisions; see also the section on accuracy below.[17]

Scheduled Decisions

The optimal frequency of decision making is studied in control theory. Traditional practice adheres to a rhythm of daily, weekly, monthly, or yearly decision making. Strategic and tactical decisions are often made in weekly or monthly meetings. Long-term planning may be done only once a year. Operational decisions like inventory and production planning may be restricted to weekly revisions.[18]

If one assumes, as a conceptual framework, that all information is generated only by the computer, revising decisions before new, updated information becomes available makes no sense. The *decision interval T* should satisfy the condition

$$T \geq I. \tag{6.1}$$

Unexpected information from outside the computer system might trigger the need for a new interpretation of the computer output, but such triggered decisions belong under unscheduled decisions. Greater frequency in updating than in decision making ($T > I$) makes sense because more frequent computer runs (small I) may be made for other purposes, such as decisions at lower levels, and accounting applications like payroll and invoicing. For the periodic decisions themselves it is most efficient to have $T = I$. Note that Verhelst (1974, p. 65) postulates that $T \leq I$.

As in the case of nonperiodic decisions a processing delay P and a decision delay D are distinguished. The retrieval time R vanishes when computer operations are scheduled so that the information is available at the time of the periodic decision making; see Fig. 6.4. The recency of *status* information is $P + D$ at the moment this information affects the system. Comparison with Table 6.2 shows that now decisions are scheduled to be made immediately after processing ends: the R in $P + R + D$ vanishes in the present case. The recency of *events* has a minimum of $P + D$; a maximum of $P + D + T$; and an average of $P + D + \frac{1}{2}T$. (See Table 6.3.)

In the information on *events* in Table 6.3, the assumption is that in periodic decision making, decisions are far apart so that D is small compared to T, and P is small compared to T. Therefore *the* way to decrease the average delay of information is more frequent decision making. On-line data capture is wasteful in this respect because the data are not used until the next decision-making session. On-line computer systems can be useful for reducing the decision delay time D: on-line data retrieval permits fast ad hoc questioning of the database; on-line data manipulation facilitates computerized modeling. Table 6.3 shows that the timeliness of informa-

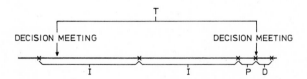

FIGURE 6–4. The Components Determining the Age of Information.

TABLE 6.3.   *Recency of Information (Periodic Decisions)*

Information on		
Status	**Events**	
$P+D$	$P+D$	(minimum)
	$P+D+T$	(maximum)
	$P+D+\frac{1}{2}T$	(average)

tion on *status* variables is not affected by the decision interval T. Because reactions to changes in the value of a status variable are possible only with intervals of length T, the most important variable in periodic decision making is T. The magnitude of T depends on the organization, not on the computer. As far as the recency of information is concerned, P and D are negligible compared to the organizational variable T.

The role of T can be investigated by simulating systems that use different values of T; see Chapter Eight. In such a simulation the state of the system to be controlled may be determined by difference equations with time lags much smaller than T. However, only every T time units can decisions for the next T time units be made. It does not seem interesting to simulate periodic decisions based on information with varying processing delays P because for any computer system, P is much smaller than T. For instance, in many business games T equals one quarter. Nevertheless, Chapter Eight shows that Boyd and Krasnow (1963, p. 13) simulated a system with P *not* much smaller than T.

Does it make sense to have a situation in which, contrary to the above assumption, $P > T$? Suppose a market survey is updated daily; fourteen days are required to process all the data, and decisions are taken daily, $I = 1$, $P = 14$, and $T = 1$. Thus daily decisions are based on old information, updated daily. The frequency of observations ($I = 1$) suggests that the environment changes frequently. Old information ($P = 14$), however, does not permit good control over such an environment. Obviously the lag P must be decreased drastically. If this decrease cannot be effected, the frequency of decision making (T) may still be maintained because the decision itself may be *not* to change previous decisions.

Industrial dynamics studies have shown that delayed information can create business cycles; see also Chapter Eight. Delays can be shortened not only by faster computers and by more frequent decision making, but also by changing the information flows within the company.[19] The effects of having more than one decision maker will be examined in the section on multiple users. Observe that periodic decision making is analogous to "sampled data control systems," i.e., systems observed only at regular points of time. These systems form the subject matter of traditional control theory.[20]

ACCURACY

As mentioned at the beginning of this chapter, when an event (transaction) occurs, it creates or changes a record. An event may have several aspects, each of which corresponds to an item (field) in the record. For instance, a customer's purchase may involve several articles; further name, address, and credit limit may be recorded. To avoid the complication of generalization to multivariable statistical distributions, the following discussion concentrates on a single record item. Of the several error sources possible, the five most relevant in a DP context[21] are

sampling errors

measurement errors

transcription errors

transformation errors, and

logical errors.

Before a discussion of each of these error sources, errors should be distinguished from the *precision* with which the computer presents its results. For instance, total sales revenues may be presented in cents or in thousands of dollars. Precision will be discussed in the section on report mode.

Sampling Errors

Sampling errors arise if only a sample from the whole population is measured. In a marketing survey such errors normally occur. In bookkeeping, accounting applications the whole population is usually measured so that these errors do not occur. In auditing, however, it is efficient to collect only a sample of possible internal events.[22] Computers do not directly affect the sample size; but for a given monetary budget or available time period, data processing may make larger samples possible.[23]

A different kind of sampling is *time sampling*: although a variable changes over time, the value is observed only at discrete points of time. See the update interval *I*, already discussed in the section on timeliness of information. In technical systems such as the process industry, in which a variable changes *continuously* over time, time sampling misses the value of the variable between two consecutive points of time, and therefore creates not only time lags but also errors. For instance, if a variable showing sinusoidal movements over time is observed only at the end of a full cycle, the observations suggest that no oscillations occur.[24]

Measurement Errors

In the collection of either a sample or a whole population, wrong measurements can be made on the aspects of the event; for instance, a wrong number may be registered for the physical inventory count. Such measurement or bookkeeping errors can be modeled by some statistical distribution, such as a normal distribution with mean μ and variance σ^2. The mean of these errors need not be zero: in supermarkets customers accept favorable errors but protest against unfavorable errors. If $\mu \neq 0$, the measurements are *biased*. Even for unbiased measurements, there still exists *variability*, or $\sigma^2 > 0$. Note that various measurement scales exist; e.g., metric, ordinal, and nominal.[25]

In data processing, checking for errors in the input data is known variously as validation, verification, editing, and screening. Computers can improve the accuracy of data by straightforward procedures that check whether the input data have values within reasonable limits, are complete, and so on. The distinction between measurement errors and transcription errors is not always clear.

Transcription Errors

Transcription errors occur when data are copied from one medium to another medium, say, from handwritten code sheets to punched cards, or from magnetic tape to disc. A special *theory of coding* studies how, say, check digits can be added to data in order to detect or even correct errors in data transmission among components of a computer system (or more generally, a communication system). Reducing human operations can drastically reduce transcription errors. For example point-of-scale systems in supermarkets can automatically read price tags with article codes and prices by means of optical character reading (OCR); see Appendix 2.1. Transcription and measurement errors are reduced by on-line data-capture, data systems with visual displays, intelligent minicomputers, and conversational facilities including "menu selection." In practice data may be so surprisingly inaccurate that DP appeals to the users for its capabilities for improving accuracy. On the other hand, DP may create ridiculous errors such as monthly paychecks of $1 million.[26]

Transformation Errors

Transformation errors occur not in the original data input, but in the intermediate or final output data *after* the computer has processed (transformed) the input. Such errors may be truncation errors, programming errors, and computer errors.

- *Truncation* is unavoidable because of the limited word-length of digital computers. These errors form a main concern in numerical mathematics: propagation of truncation errors in matrix computations, integration, etc.

- *Programming errors* or "bugs" can be fought by program tracing, interactive programming, structured programming, and correctness proofs of programs. In a DBMS one tries to ensure that concurrent processes do not adversely affect the contents and relationships of records, their integrity. See also the section on reliability.

- *Computer errors* may be caused by a malfunctioning of the "hard" software (like the operating system) or the hardware itself.

In summary, transformation errors are the area of software engineering and reliability engineering.[24]

Logical Errors

Logical errors leading to inaccurate data may be illustrated by the following example. Let sales be computed by the formula

$$\text{Sales} = \text{Initial inventory} - \text{end inventory} + \text{replenishments}. \tag{6.2}$$

Actually this formula is incorrect because pilferage, shrinkage, and the like imply that Eq. (6.2) overestimates sales. Another example is provided by the cost of a product: many formulas (definitions) exist, some of them obviously incorrect; see the preceding chapter.

Consider briefly the *cost and benefit* aspects of accuracy. Each of the error sources can be fought by spending more money. Sampling errors can be reduced by increasing the sample size, but unfortunately these errors decrease only with the square root of the sample size. Reducing measurement errors by verification procedures requires additional programming and running time, memory space, and input volume (because of redundancy in the input data). Hardware for on-line data capture is more expensive than that for batch processing. However, point-of-sale terminals also show some "negative costs" since relabeling articles for price changes is no longer necessary; fewer checkout lanes may be needed because of increased throughput; and so on; see Appendix 2.1. A DBMS requires sophisticated software and also incurs processing and data storage overhead. Truncation errors are reduced by developing good numerical procedures and by double-precision hardware. Tracing a program requires dramatically more computer time. Interactive programming takes much more computer time (interpreters are used instead of more efficient compilers), but takes less programming time. The same arguments hold for programming in higher level languages, including simulation languages and packages. For a further discussion see the recent handbook on data input accuracy by Gilb and Weinberg (1977).[28]

The *benefits* or value of more accurate information in managerial decision making must be distinguished from its value in "accounting" applications, such as tax payments and invoicing. Sterling (1979) discusses the benefits of accuracy in the company's contacts with the "public." In decision making, however, historical data are useful only to forecast the future. The *predictability of the future* is affected by the following factors:

The accuracy of the input data.

The appropriateness of the forecasting model (transformation).   In concentrating on the value of information *per se*, one may ignore the various degrees of sophistication computers make possible in forecasting models.

The planning horizon.   The accuracy of predictions decreases as the time for which a variable's value is forecast moves further into the future (see Exercise 6). Improved accuracy of the input data may or may not pay off as the planning period increases. High-level decisions require less accuracy than operational decisions do because the former concern the long run.

The recency of the input data.   The accuracy of the forecast is affected also by the recency of the input information as seen above.

Following chapters will discuss accuracy in detail. Apart from its accuracy, a DBMS with multiple users, like those systems in multinational companies, may be attractive because the users know that everybody uses the *same* data. Certain data-capture techniques not only reduce errors but also increase labor productivity as mentioned before.

AGGREGATION

To limit the data volume, one may aggregate or summarize detailed data and retain only the aggregate. For instance, one may decide to store sales not per shop but only per region if a region comprises several shops. Obviously, detailed data can always be transformed into summary data in order to answer unexpected needs for some aggregated information. However, aggregation of data means that the details are lost. A DBMS, as opposed to a traditional system of separate files, makes it easier to aggregate data in an unexpected dimension. Using aggregated data when detailed data are needed creates errors, investigated above. The degree of aggregation might be quantified by the average number of elements falling into a class. In the example just mentioned, this number is the average number of shops per region.[29]

A different kind of aggregation occurs in the recording of *time series*. A variable may be measured only at discrete intervals (update interval I); and this time series of observations (made at times t, $t + I$, $t + 2I$, $t + 3I$. . .) may be summarized through a few statistics such as its average, its average and variance, or its average and autocorrelations (spectrum). The degree of detail can then be quantified by the number of statistics used to characterize the time path of a variable.

Cost increases with the level of detail because the data volume increases. The costs of the storage medium itself (fixed cost) and the costs for retrieving and storing data (variable operating cost) are higher. The *value* of detailed data cannot be determined so simply. In programmed decision making which data are needed is known. One may experiment with different decision rules requiring more or less information. In nonprogrammed, unstructured decision making which data is needed is not known. Detailed data may provide a hunch but may also confuse the user (negative value). This behavioral aspect leads to a conclusion different from that of Marschak (1971, p. 201): "adding detail (at no cost!) cannot do damage, since the detail can be ignored." In general, in decision making at higher levels, a certain level of aggregation is definitely desirable. The bottom-up approach to a MIS tries to provide all management information by such an aggregation process; see Chapter Two. Chapters Seven and Eight present some studies on the value of detailed information. Note that recently Courtois (1977) developed a theory concerning the degree of aggregation that still permits control of "decomposable" systems. He builds on work by Simon and Ando (1961).[30] The costs and benefits of detailed information are further discussed in other references.[31]

REPORT MODE

The data within the computer can be displayed to the user in various ways. The following discussion includes these issues:

> periodic versus exception reporting
>
> query facilities versus standard reporting
>
> the displayed data format or layout, which includes human engineering aspects.

Periodic versus Exception Reporting

Examples of periodic reports include profit and loss (P&L) statements per quarter, and inventory reports per week. In exception reporting, however, data are displayed only if they exceed prespecified limits, i.e., if they are "relevant." The underlying assumption is that new decisions are required only if these limits are violated. Management-by-exception is a common management practice and is traditional in statistical quality control. De Blasis (1976, p. 29) presents a case study in which a special person was assigned to determine which computer output higher management should or should not see. An exception report means that the information has "surprise content," it may further lead to a new decision, and this decision may affect the net benefits noticeably; i.e., the information satisfies the conditions for valuable information as derived in information economics; see the next chapter.

Usually, the decision process is not so formalized and analyzed that the effect of the improved decision is calculated before an exception model decides to display an exception report. A practical approach is to determine which variables are conjectured to be so crucial that they should be continuously monitored: zero-width control limits. The remaining variables can then be handled on an exception basis. Rowe (1968, pp. 71–72) claims that in most cases 80 to 90 percent of all activities belong to the latter category, exception reporting only. For these variables one must determine when an unusual situation exists.

Exceptions can be defined either as a single data item's deviation from a limit, or as several items' deviation pattern. An example of the latter case is found in forecasting: if the forecast errors all show the same sign for a number of consecutive periods, a "tracking signal" is produced to indicate the need for a revised forecast model.[32] Periodic reports and exception reports can be combined by displaying periodically, say, the ten highest observations only. In inventory reporting the articles traditionally are arranged in the order in which they contribute to total sales revenues: A, B, and C classifications. An exception report may display only the "fast movers," those contributing to 20 percent of the total sales revenues: 20–80 rule.[33]

Queries versus Standard Reports

A standard report, intended to serve several users at several points of time, may contain data irrelevant for a particular user, and at the same time may lack data of interest to that user. The query capability of a database management system (DBMS) is meant to solve this problem. See also the introductory discussion on DBMSs. With such a capability the user can ask all kinds of questions, planned and unplanned (ad hoc). An example is "Which articles were purchased from supplier A *and* stored in warehouse Z?" Although the displayed data may be highly aggregated, an interested user can ask for the detailed data.[34]

In terms of the costs and benefits, *exception reports* have the advantage of displaying fewer irrelevant data, but the disadvantage of possibly failing to display some relevant data. An optimum balance between displayed irrelevant and nondisplayed relevant data seems hard to realize in practice. This optimization problem is analogous to the classical problem of "recall" and "precision" in literature retrieval systems[35], in which

$$\text{Recall} = \frac{\text{Number of relevant documents retrieved}}{\text{Number of relevant documents in system}} \qquad (6.3)$$

and

$$\text{Precision} = \frac{\text{Number of relevant documents retrieved}}{\text{Number of total documents retrieved}}. \qquad (6.4)$$

Exception-reporting systems require more initial analysis, which costs more. However, their saving human analysis during the operation of the system lowers operating cost; and the improved decision making increases benefits. The *query* capability tries to reduce the amount of irrelevant data displayed by standard reports, and to provide additional detailed data if desired. Unfortunately, such a capability requires a sophisticated database management system.[36]

Report Format

The same data may be displayed in several ways. The good human engineering required takes account of the following factors:

- *Standard layouts* allow immediate use without an elaborate search for the desired information in the report, and without the user's having to learn new definitions.

- *Graphs* are valuable because "one picture is worth a thousand words." Unlike computers, people are skillful at interpreting pictures.

- *Relative numbers* are used because a number gains meaning in relation to another number.

- *Adequate precision* depends on the situation. It is useless for the computer to give its output, such as average sales, to eight decimals when only the two decimals representing cents are meaningful. It might even be desirable to present sales in thousands of dollars only. Refer also to Exercise 11.

Observe that an appropriate format makes it possible to combine periodic and exception reporting: exceptional data can be indicated in the periodic report by special lettering, color, or place.

Good human engineering requires an initial investment but may pay off in reduced operating costs and increased benefits: faster and more effective decision making. Chapter Eight discusses some studies on the benefits of various report modes.[37]

One further step is the investigation of the *cognitive styles* of different users. Such studies examine not only how to present data but also which data to present to different personalities with different needs: to an analytic personality compared to an intuitive personality. Refer also to the section on multiple users.

RETENTION TIME

The retention time of data is the time span during which data are kept available. As time moves on, the oldest data may be dumped on off-line storage media such as dismounted discs or microfilm, a process called purging. Other strategies may be selected to keep the database size within specified limits. For instance, rather than dumping the oldest data, one may delete the least-used data. Another alternative is to retain only a randomly selected sample. Individual data not retained can be kept in the database in summarized form. Because normally the value of data diminishes as their age increases, not much value of old data is sacrificed by retaining only an aggregation.

Increasing the retention time of data increases the database size and hence augments costs; see the discussion on data aggregation. A benefit is that it takes less time to retrieve data stored on on-line storage media; see the discussion on the recency of information, especially the components response time R and processing time P. Retention is more a technical computer science problem than an "informatics" problem.[38]

SECURITY AND PRIVACY

Security means that data are not available to unauthorized users and cannot be changed by them. *Privacy* is a related concept with the emphasis on the moral consequences arising from personal data availability to unauthorized users, especially if various personal data can be collected and combined relatively easily by means of a modern DBMS. This study on the effects of information in managerial decision making will skip the privacy dilemma. Security can be improved by proper architecture of the computer center building itself, and by organizational procedures and legal measures. Computer-related measures are adequate hardware and software: for instance, requiring a password for user-identification at a terminal, and limiting subsequent access to only a part of the database. Because a salesperson needs a different part of the database from that a personnel manager needs, the DBMS software may present different images to different users; compare the "sub-schemas" in Codasyl (1971).[39] Note that security shows relationships with auditing.[40]

Obviously security costs money. The costs of privacy, a closely related characteristic, were estimated by Goldstein and Nolan (1975) for a variety of systems. Even if moral benefits are ignored, economic benefits of security remain. These benefits are the losses avoided by reducing certain risks (see the discussion on opportunity costs in the preceding chapter) associated with industrial espionage for competing companies and with fraud by the company's own employees. Quantifying these economic benefits provides a challenge to operations researchers! Note that risk and risk attitudes are also discussed in Chapters Four and Seven.

RELIABILITY AND RECOVERY

Reliability or *availability* is measured by the probability that the system functions when the user wants to use it. The reliability of modern hardware has been drastically improved by more robust components based on Large Scale Integration (LSI), and by multiple components (see the discussion on reliability engineering in Chapter Three). The reliability of software has already been mentioned in the discussion on transformation errors. If, nevertheless, the computer system breaks down, *recovery* capability is needed. There may be a fail-soft capability: when one of the multiple components fails, the total system does not break down completely but works slower, a graceful degradation. If the system does not work at all, one may be able to switch temporarily to another computer. These two computers may be part of a computer network. In order to switch to a different computer, or to continue on the original computer after it has been repaired, one needs to know where and how to start. For instance, periodically the status of the database may be copied and stored. A number of techniques has been developed in computer science: grandfather–son tapes, logging, checkpoints, and so on; see the literature below.

In general, increased reliability and recovery capability require additional expenses for multiple components, logging overhead, and so on. Technological progress, however, provided increased reliability at lower cost: vacuum tubes were replaced by transistors, which in turn were replaced by LSI. In a DBMS one may again create redundancy of data in order to improve the reliability. The timeliness of data may be sacrificed by updating the database in batch mode; only retrieval is done on line.[41] The *benefits* of reliability and recovery consist of avoiding the dramatic expenses of the catastrophe that might occur without these facilities: opportunity loss. Because of the vital role information plays in an organization, recovery must be ensured at any price. The study of these facilities belongs primarily to the area of computer science, and will not be further discussed here. Note that in practice the attributes reliability, security, and integrity are closely related.[42]

The discussion on information attributes has gradually moved toward attributes associated not with an *individual* item of information but with the *ensemble* of information, the database.

SCOPE

The scope of the database determines whether particular data are recorded and stored in the database. For instance, one may decide, as supermarkets do, to record the sales volume but not the identity of the buyer. In this example the scope of the database is restricted to sales; data on buyers are unavailable. As the scope increases, so does the database size and hence its *cost*. As for the *value* of information, which data are needed is exactly known in computerized decision making but not in human decision-making; see the discussion on aggregation.[43]

In *decentralized* databases some information may be available to the "local" user but not to other users. For instance, in a large company with a multistage production process, a particular production phase (department) may have to base its production volume decisions only on the demand received from the next production phase, its immediate customer. Alternatively, the scope of the department's database can be widened to include information on demand exercised by the ultimate customers of the company. The latter information flows decrease internal business cycles. This aspect is investigated in various studies performed under the name IPSO at Philips Industries in the Netherlands.[44] Chapter Eight will return to these studies. Note that Welke (1977b) distinguishes between local and global data, local data being accessible with shorter delays. Trill (1977) reports on a case study in which the installation of a central database enabled all the various departments to be so well informed that they coordinated their actions; e.g., inferior deliveries rejected by the receiving department were not paid by the financial department.[45]

The attribute scope shows the following relationships with retention time, aggregation, and delay. The database size is controlled by aggregation, retention time, and scope. Lack of scope and detail, however, can be remedied only with a very large delay because data not contained in the database must be collected ad hoc. Some data may never be retrieved in such an ad hoc inquiry. Data on off-line storage media can be retrieved with a much shorter time delay.

USER-MACHINE MODES

The discussion of how information is further processed *after* it has been displayed to its user will be brief because this issue concerns the use of the information, not the quality of the information per se, and impinges on the area of operations research and management science. Refer to the Chapter Two discussion on the role of computers in number crunching versus EDP, and the relationships among the DP, the information, and the decision systems (see Fig. 2.1).

One may distinguish manual systems, batch computer systems, and conversational (interactive, on-line, user-machine) computer systems, plus combinations of these basic systems. The effects of the various system types on the information have already been discussed. For instance, on-line systems may improve both the timeliness and the accuracy of data; manual systems may show less scope, detail, and retention because of memory limitations. The *use* of information is definitely affected by the type of system. Manual systems afford fewer manipulations (calculations) of the data. Heuristic problem solving is easier in on-line systems than in batch systems because on-line systems provide fast feedback. The *costs* of computer systems might be higher than those of manual systems, but increasing wages will make manual systems more and more expensive. The *benefits* of computerized systems are the savings and gross revenues generated by more elaborate data manipulation, besides improved data quality. On-line systems may be more expensive than computer systems operating in batch mode, but on-line systems permit a more effective user-machine symbiosis. The utilization of data with the aid of computers is closely related to the application of models. Consider again briefly the role of computerized models.

The accuracy of a prediction for the future status of the organization depends on the accuracy and timeliness of the input data, on the length of the planning period, and on the forecast model. The forecast model may be a "black box" model based on exponential smoothing, it may be a more causal model using regression analysis, or it may be a detailed cause–effect model using operations research techniques. If one relies completely on computerized algorithms—either for decisions concerning the whole company or for decisions on a subsystem such as the inventory subsystem—one knows exactly which data are needed. The data's scope, degree of detail, and retention period are fixed. If reliance on the computer model were complete, no reports would be needed. Exception reports require that the computer perform internal screening based on some, possibly very simple model. In an interactive user-machine system, however, the kind of data required is not completely fixed because the human participant may base decisions on data required ad hoc. Note that a different strategy or model (world view) may be preferred not only for different user-machine modes, but also for different qualities of information. For instance, highly inaccurate data may require a conservative strategy or a crude model (see also the next chapter on information economics). Information may generate benefits by improving the decision maker's model of the world, i.e., by improving the structure of the model, not only the parameter values.[46] The study of the costs and benefits of modeling forms the subject of operation research, and will not be pursued here.

FLEXIBILITY

The desirable attributes of information *change over time* because both the organization and its environment change over time. The recency and accuracy of information may need improvement when the environment becomes more dynamic. The growing number of decisions in an expanding company tend to require more exception reports and query facilities so that the information burden is kept under control. Cheaper computer memories may permit longer retention periods and more detailed data. The growing awareness of privacy issues and security risks do ask for new provisions. The scope of a database can be extended by connecting the system with internal or external databases; e.g., service bureaus or governmental institutes may provide macroeconomic data. Developments in management science create new models that replace existing models and widen their scope. And so on.

The dynamics above imply that the information system should be *flexible*. Such flexibility can be realized by a modular construction of the information system. An outstanding module is the DBMS with its program and data independence, and multiple data views (subschemas). The flexibility may further be increased by splitting the database into several geographic modules to provide a distributed system.[47]

The immediate, short-run *costs* tend to increase with the flexibility of the information system as the advantages of specialization offered by a special-purpose system are sacrificed. (Specialization as one means for reducing costs was discussed in Chapter Five.) The *benefit* of flexibility is a decrease in costs if one considers the costs of several applications evolving over time. In such a long-run view additional applications or changes in existing applications can be realized at a lower cost if the system is flexible. Grindley and Humble (1973, p. 42) give a revealing example of the costs of inflexibility: including one additional piece of data in customers' records would require fifty user-years of work! Verhelst (1974) suggests that a proposed system change be cancelled if its benefits are small and it absorbs overcapacity that might be reserved for future, unforeseen system changes.[48] Note that the quantification of flexibility poses a particular problem: how can one specify (i.e., model) information requirements that by definition are unknown at present?

Note that flexibility of the IS is related to several characteristics relevant to computer selection: conversion effort, availability of additional hardware and software from the vendor, training facilities, and delivery date (see Chapter Four). Whereas flexibility concerns the *birth and death* of the system, the other information attributes discussed in the present chapter concern the daily operation of the system.

MULTIPLE USERS

Data may be used by more than one user especially when a DBMS is in use. Hence the effectiveness of a system depends not only on the controllable attributes, like timeliness and accuracy, of the information itself, but also on the uncontrollable characteristics of a multiplicity of users. Each user has individual attributes: criteria, cognitive style, and so on. The study of these aspects involves many *psychological* factors.[49] Furthermore the existence of a *hierarchy* among the users is related to the question of centralization versus decentralization.[50] Besides the users' characteristics, another class of uncontrollable attributes is formed by the characteristics of the *physical system* to be managed. These attributes vary with the function, say, marketing versus production, and with the environment, say, a monopolistic versus a highly competitive environment. For instance, Adams and Schroeder (1972) interviewed a number of managers and found that the financial department uses data that are more accurate and more aggregated than those used by the marketing department.

A previously mentioned advantage is that the multiplicity of users in a large, multinational company knows that the data used is the same apart from the accuracy. Another advantage is that reduced business cycles result from providing all users within the corporation with data on the ultimate demand for the company's product; see the section on scope. A disadvantage of a central database is that users may not access their data so fast as in local, distributed databases. A central database further involves privacy, security, and reliability risks as noted in the preceding sections. For a discussion on centralization versus decentralization see the next chapter on information economics, including "team theory."

MISCELLANEOUS ATTRIBUTES

Besides the information attributes above, some authors distinguish additional attributes. An example is the *source* of information. If the source is a department with a "bad record," the receiver may wish to ignore these data. Stamper (1975) and (1977) emphasizes the *meaning* and the *purpose* of information, and distinguishes between descriptive and prescriptive data. Actually these issues concern behavioral aspects of the information; see again note 49.

Sometimes the *relevance* of information is mentioned as an important attribute.[51] This characteristic was not included here because of the distinction between the information system and the decision system; see Chapter Two especially Fig. 2.1. Hence a piece of data is relevant if it is input into a decision rule, be it a formal or an informal rule or model. If a data item is required for a particular decision, that item will be obtained. However, obtaining it may involve a large delay because an ad hoc search has to be started, or a large inaccuracy because aggregated or out-of-date information is employed. Some authors, like Bonini (1963), claim to investigate information characteristics while merely investigating decision rules. Chapter Eight will return to this issue.

Other authors use terms that can easily be translated into the terms used in this book. For instance, the *amount of information* can be translated into "scope"; see Chapter Eight.

CONCLUSION

A problem completely neglected in the literature is how to characterize *a specific DBMS*—such as IBM's system IMS—by specifying its values for the various information attributes. The manufacturers do supply information on computer-oriented attributes, like the required amount of core, but do not specify user-oriented attributes. The reason may be twofold: a preoccupation with the computer itself; and the difficulty of specifying user-oriented data, which depend on the organization as well as on the computer. Moreover, some attributes, like flexibility, are hard to quantify.

The various characteristics of information can be mutually *related.* Smaller sampling errors may be obtained at the expense of an increased delay because, say, a larger market survey takes more time. A small update interval, however, tends to decrease measurement errors because on-line data entry provides fast feedback to the human operator once an error has been detected by the computer system. Accuracy can be improved also by error detecting and correcting techniques that increase the size of the database system. For a given database size, the retention period can be lengthened if older data are more aggregated. An alternative is to keep only a sample of the unaggregated data, but such sampling creates sampling error. On-line facilities improve timeliness but may endanger security, privacy, and reliability. When one emphasizes these relationships among the various information attributes of a particular computerized information system, the analysis is then aimed at the evaluation of various *specific* information systems. Verhelst (1974, pp. 216–224) investigates in detail the relationships among attributes. Chapter Eight refers to some studies, e.g., Kriebel (1969).

Alternatively, if one considers the several characteristics of information to be *independent*, one can then look for an *optimal* combination of characteristics, or at least determine the sensitivity of the organization's performance to the various characteristics. The assumption is that computer technology is so flexible, at least in the long run, that more desirable combinations of characteristics can be realized.

The present chapter provides a *framework* for evaluating the theories and techniques presented in the next two chapters. For instance, as already mentioned, Boyd and Krasnow (1963) simulated a system in which the processing delay P was *not* much smaller than the decision interval T. Information economics models are usually limited to periodic decision making without explicit representation of the components P, I, R and D. The other information attributes, too, can be utilized to evaluate information economics; see Chapter Seven. Moreover, this framework provides a common terminology useful when comparing studies by different authors, who employ a great variety of terms for the same concept. Finally, the present chapter might serve as a checklist so that relevant information attributes are not overlooked.

EXERCISES

1. The beginning of this chapter introduced the sequence of points of time t_0 through t_4. (a) Can you imagine how computers can reduce the time lag $t_3 - t_2$ in inventory management? (b) How can computers reduce this time lag in machine rescheduling?

2. Would you classify the time needed by a bank teller as P, I, R or D?

3. Gregory and Atwater (1957) use continuous functions to display the relationship between cost and update interval I. Please comment.

4. A total delay of, say, A can be "produced" by various combinations of the delays I and P. How would you interpret Fig. 4.4? Would you use Fig. 4.4(a) or 4.4(b)?

5. In their survey Grinyer and Batt (1974, p. 161) mention that corporate simulation models are used mainly for long-range planning. Do you expect these models to be run in batch mode or on-line?

6. a) Prove that sampling errors decrease only with the square root of the sample size. (b) If the variation coefficient of an individual item x_i is $v = \sigma/\mu$, what then is this coefficient for the aggregate, Σx_i? (c) If $x_t = \beta_0 + \beta_1 t + u_t$ for $t = 1, \ldots, n$, what then is the variance of the forecast for period $n + 1$? For which period does the estimator $\hat{x}_t$ have smallest variance?

7. What is the planning period in inventory control models?

8. Let sales be recorded in dollars. If a sale is recorded as \$36, how would you specify the actual sales figure statistically in the following cases: (a) cents are rounded towards the next dollar; (b) cents are truncated; (c) many causes may have disturbed the actual figure, but it is difficult to specify each of these causes.

9. The computer uses series expansion to evaluate functions like $\exp(x)$ and sinus (x). Such an approach becomes more accurate as more terms in the expansion are computed. Why it is useless to compute "very many" terms?

10. A number like 7.293 is more precise than 7.29. Give an example of alphanumeric precision.

11. Suppose total profit is reported in cents. Discuss the precision, accuracy, and arbitrariness of the reported figures.

12. A corporation has to decide between a single, centralized database and several, decentralized, divisional databases. Discuss the advantages and disadvantages of the decentralized solution.

13. Suppose the values of a variable show purely periodic behavior, say, $y_t = a + b$ if $t = 1, 3, 5,\ldots$, while $y_t = a - b$ if $t = 2, 4, 6,\ldots$. Is it wise to base a decision on the most recent information?

14. Data is captured at the source by an electronic device as in POS systems. How can such on-line data capture be combined with batch updating of the database?

15. A company carries one thousand different articles. After processing an error is discovered: ten units of article code 51, not of article code 15, were sold. Therefore the stock figure for article 15 is increased with ten units. Is this good enough?

16. How would you use this chapter's information attributes (P, I, sampling error, etc.) to specify the loss of a data item?

17. What kind of terminals can provide fail-soft capability?

NOTES

1. Adams and Schroeder (1972, p. 5), Brevoord (1971, pp. 14–15), Burch and Strater (1974, pp. 34–35), Feltham (1968), Frielink (1978), Graham (1976, pp. 97–109), Grünwald (1974), Hirshleifer (1973, pp. 32–33), King and Schrems (1978, p. 32), Rowe (1968, p. 71), C. V. Swanson (1971), van Belkum (1978), Verhelst (1974, pp. 20–28), Wallace and Boyd (1971, pp. 1215–1216), Welke (1975a, p. 6) and (1978), and Wheelwright and Makridakis (1973, pp. 146–147). See also section 9 in Welke (1977b).

2. For time-sharing, real-time, on-line systems see Martin (1967) and also Meadow (1970, pp. 78–111). For on-line systems with teleprocessing see Martin (1972) and also Eldin and Croft (1974, pp. 174–178, 193–197). For networks of computers refer to Abramson and Kuo (1973), Berg (1975), Canning (1976a), Farber (1972), and Stevens (1970c, p. 7). For minicomputers see Infotech (1976a) and Weitzman (1974). For an introduction to these various concepts refer to a number of contributions in Bassler and Joslin (1975, pp. 139–186).

3. Bassler and Logan (1976); Canning (1974b); Codasyl (1971); L. J. Cohen (1976); Date (1978); Davis (1975); Haseman and Whinston (1977); Infotech (1977b), (1977c), and (1978a); Jardine (1974); Kroenke (1977); Martin (1976) and (1977); Meadow (1976); Munson and Smith (1976); I. R. Palmer and

Curtice (1976); Schussel (1975); and Sundgren (1976). Recently Mohan (1978) published a bibliography with 415 references.

4. Barrif (1976), Couger and Knapp (1974), Taggart and Tharp (1977), and Welke (1978b).

5. See also Frielink (1978) and Welke (1975b, p. 4). This discussion of the timeliness of information is related to—yet different from—J. C. Emery (1971, pp. 33–37), Gregory and Atwater (1957), and Gregory and Van Horn (1963, pp. 576–580). The most detailed discussion can be found in Gregory and Atwater (1957), which, however, is completely batch-oriented. Delays are also discussed by Knutsen and Nolan (1974, p. 34), M. L. Smith et al. (1978), and Strassmann (1970). The effects of control frequency on DP costs and operating costs are studied by Braat (1973). Several additional references can be found in Bonney (1969, p. 122).

6. Canning (1974b, p. 3) and (1976).

7. Van Aken (1973, p. 89) and (1978, pp. 79–80, 160).

8. For instance, Welke (1975a, p. 2).

9. See also J. C. Emery (1971, pp. 36–37).

10. See also Gregory and Atwater (1957, p. 56).

11. J. C. Emery (1969, pp. 104–105) and (1971, pp. 36–37) discusses in some detail the relative costs of indexed sequential and random processing.

12. Brenner (1965). Gregory and Atwater (1957, p. 64) propose hill-shaped curves for value versus update interval I (not processing delay P).

13. Marschak (1971, pp. 201–202), and Wenzel (1975, pp. 149–154).

14. Gupta and Hasdorff (1970), Kuo (1963), and Truxal (1955).

15. Schroeder and Benbasat (1975).

16. For a different example see Mathusz (1977, p. 596).

17. See also Boehm and Bell (1975, pp. 18–20), J. C. Emery (1969, p. 100) and (1971, pp. 33–36), Rowe (1968, p. 69), and Verhelst (1974, pp. 28, 65).

18. Strassmann (1970, p. 144), Van Aken (1973, p. 89), and Wildermooth and Foote (1979, p. 43).

19. Van Aken et al. (1974, pp. 8–9); see also Braat (1977), and Grünwald (1973) for a mathematically oriented exposition.

20. For control theory see Truxal (1955), or the more recent references Gupta and Hasdorff (1970), and Kuo (1963). See also the concept of "sampling" in C. V. Swanson (1971, p. 12), and the discussion in Chapter Eight.

21. Wheelwright and Makridakis (1973, pp. 150–153) mention several other sources that are not relevant here, however.

22. See Votaw (1965, p. 23) for additional references on the necessity or efficiency of sampling.

23. Bassler and Joslin (1975, p. 235).

24. See Hoetink (1976) and the control engineering literature.

25. Easton (1973, pp. 93–97), and Suppes and Zinnes (1963).

26. See also Cardenas (1975), J. G. Carlson (1975), Chovanec (1976), Gregory and Van Horn (1963, pp. 562–563, 584), H. C. Lucas (1973, pp. 154–157), Miller (1976), Ortlieb (1976), M. L. Smith et al. (1978), Stevens (1970b, pp. 4, 41–42), and Thesen (1978, pp. 109–111). For database management systems see also Canning (1976a), Davis (1975, p. 56), Maynard (1974, p. 134), and the references of note 3. For modern data entry techniques refer to Benwell (1977), Stevens (1970a, pp. 12–13), and Weitzman (1974, pp. 265–267). Human error sources, such as fatigue, are discussed in London (1976, pp. 210–214). Certain data-capture techniques not only reduce errors but also increase labor productivity and hence reduce clerical costs; for data see Phister (1976, p. 141) and also Appendix 2.1.

27. For numerical mathematics see the classic book by Wilkinson (1965). For interactive programming including debugging see J. D. Aron (1974), Meadow (1970), and Stevens (1970c, pp. 29–30). For structured programming and correctness proofs see Dahl et al. (1972), Infotech (1976b), Jackson (1975), G. J. Myers (1976), and *Computing Surveys*, **6** (4), Dec. 1974. For hard software methodology see Coffman and Denning (1973), Freeman (1975), and the special issue of *Computing Surveys* edited by Yeh (1976). See also Dolotta et al. (1976, pp. 87–118), Fitzsimmons and Love (1978), and the survey papers by Leventhal (1978), Tanenbaum (1976), Van Amstel (1978), and Van Reeken (1975). Software development is also discussed by Phister (1976, pp. 210–221), who supplies many data on software costs and software errors. Phister (1976, pp. 532–534) further gives a bibliography.

28. See also J. C. Emery (1969, p. 106) and (1971, p. 39), Ferrara (1975), Gosden (1974), Gregory and Van Horn (1963, pp. 516–532), and Sibley (1974).

29. See also Verhelst (1974, pp. 26, 295).

30. See also Saaty (1977, pp. 257–261).

31. J. C. Emery (1969, pp. 98–99) and (1971, pp. 22–23, 26–28), Hax (1976), Lev (1968), Mertens and Griese (1972, p. 65), Rowe (1968, pp. 69, 71), and Stern (1970). Chapter Eight will return to Lev (1968).

32. See the IBM inventory management package called IMPACT; IBM (1967, p. 47).

33. See, for instance, IBM (1967), and Mertens and Griese (1972, p. 98) for the A, B, C classification. For a general discussion of exception reporting and information economics see J. C. Emery (1971, pp. 2–6, 26–31).

34. J. C. Emery, (1971, p. 29), and Senn (1974b, pp. 164–166).

35. Cuadra and Luke (1972), Lancaster and Fayen (1973), and R. W. Swanson (1975, pp. 70–71).

36. See also J. C. Emery (1971, pp. 26, 31–32), and Gregory and Van Horn (1963, pp. 566–570).

37. General references on report formats are Chervany (1972, p. 12), J. C. Emery (1971, p. 28), Mertens and Griese (1972, pp. 89–101), Nolan (1971, p. 5), Senn (1973), Stamper (1975, p. 116), Stevens (1970b), and Wooldridge (1975). References on behavioral problems in user-machine systems are given by H. T. Smith (1974); see also Lancaster and Fayen (1973, pp. 347–368), and Murron and Fife (1976, pp. 183–190). Human engineering for the design of terminal equipment is discussed in Stevens (1970c, pp. 10–13).

38. See also J. C. Emery (1971, pp. 23–25), Gregory and Van Horn (1963, pp. 561–562), and Stevens (1970c, pp. 39–40).

39. Recently a number of books on security and privacy has been published: Bequai (1978), Gerberick (1976), P. Hamilton (1972), L. J. Hoffman (1973) and (1977), Honeywell (1977), Katzan (1973), Krauss and MacGahan (1979), Martin (1973), Parker (1976), Sieghart (1976), and Turn (1974). See further J. M. Adams and Haden (1976, pp. 111–153), Allen (1973), Diroff (1978), Gosden (1974), Sibley (1974), and Tanenbaum (1976). These topics are also discussed in the general textbooks on DBMS; see note 3. Commercial services in "data processing risk management" are provided by Computer Resource Controls, Rockville, Maryland.

40. Graham (1976, pp. 132–142).

41. Canning (1976a, p. 7), Davis (1975, p. 38), and Sibley (1974, pp. 98–99).

42. Extensive surveys on reliability are Randell et al. (1978) and Verhofstad (1978). Infotech published a report of 829 pages; Infotech (1977a). Also refer to Gelenbe and Derochette (1978), and Gibbons (1976). Data on maintenance costs can be found in Phister (1976, pp. 226–333). Reliability is further discussed in general textbooks on DBMS; see note 3. General, not specifically computer-oriented discussions of reliability can be found in Barlow and Proschan (1975), Kapur and Lamberson (1977), and Kaufmann et al. (1977). Decision-theoretic approaches—see Chapter Seven—to "catastrophes" are discussed by Harrison (1977, p. 327).

43. See also J. C. Emery (1969, pp. 103–104), and (1971, p. 25).

44. Braat (1977), Grünwald (1974), Van Aken (1978, pp. 91–114), and Van Aken et al. (1974). See also Strassmann (1970).

45. For distributed systems see also Bucci and Streeter (1979), and J. C. Emery (1977).

46. For the relationships between information and decision systems see Boyd and Krasnow (1963, p. 9), Forrester (1968a, pp. 601–603), Kriebel (1969), Mock (1971), and C. V. Swanson (1971, p. 8). Refer also to Chapters Two, Seven, and Eight.

47. See the flexibility requirements for a DBMS in Davis (1975, p. 60); see also Canning (1976a).

48. Verhelst (1974, pp. 234–235). See also the discussions on flexibility in Blumenthal (1969), Brevoord (1971, pp. 20–21), J. C. Emery (1969, pp. 102, 106–107), Gregory and Van Horn (1963, pp. 572–573), W. R. King and Epstein (1976, p. 178), Ruisch (1978), Van Aken (1978), and Verhelst (1974, pp. 136–137).

49. Bariff (1974), Bariff and Lusk (1977), Barkin and Dickson (1977), Carlson (1979), Chervany (1972, pp. 7–10), Chervany and Dickson (1978), Dickson and Wynne (1973), Dickson et al. (1975), C. Edwards and Roxburgh (1977), Green et al. (1967), Hawgood (1975), Mason and Mitroff (1973), Stabell (1978), Stamper (1975), Stevens (1970c, p. 3), Taggart and Tharp (1977), Verrijn Stuart (1976, pp. 81, 96), and Zmud (1978). See also Pirsig (1974).

50. Hanken and Reuver (1977), and Mesarovic et al. (1970).

51. Streufert (1973) used a political game (see Chapter Eight) in a psychologically oriented study to examine information "relevance."

INFORMATION ECONOMICS: BAYESIAN DECISION THEORETIC APPROACH

CHAPTER SEVEN

INTRODUCTION

This chapter on information economics presents a methodology based on *statistical decision theory*, which goes back to Raiffa and Schlaifer.[1] Marschak pioneered its application to problems in economics under the name *information economics* (IE).[2] This is a quite sophisticated, mathematically oriented discipline. This chapter summarizes the major characteristics of IE and provides references for further study. The next section starts with an example illustrating the IE approach. First, however, note that J. C. Emery (1971) lists the following factors highlighted by the IE framework.

"Surprise content" of the information. Information already expected does not yield much value. An example would be the information that the oil crisis will diminish demand for big cars. Statistically the surprise content is shown by the difference between the prior and the posterior probabilities as the next section indicates. The more the posterior probabilities differ from the prior probabilities, the more effect the new information will have on the decision (in general but not always).

Effect of the information on the decision. If the same action is taken regardless of the information, additional information is worthless. For instance, regardless of the information to be provided by a market survey, auto manufacturers may decide to maintain production of big cars.

Effect of the decision on the performance or benefits. Even though the new information contains a surprise and changes the decision, the performance (say, profit) may be insensitive to this decision. For instance, a cost study may show that the inventory costs are quite different from what they were thought to be; as a result, the optimal reorder quantity computed by the well-known square-root formula is changed. The total inventory cost, however, is insensitive to the exact reorder quantity because this cost forms a rather flat curve in the neighborhood of the optimal reorder quantity.[3]

In IE a crucial role is played by *Bayes's theorem*, a statistical relationship. This theorem can be derived as follows. If there are two events A and B, the "conditional" probability satisfies

$$P(A|B) = \frac{P(AB)}{P(B)} \text{ if } P(B) > 0 \tag{7.1}$$

where $A|B$ means "A under the condition that B occurs" or briefly "A given B," and AB means "both A and B"; see also Fig. 7.1. Let B denote "black hair color" and A denote "child," where A can be split into its mutually exclusive and exhaustive subevents A_1 "boy" and A_2 "girl." Then

$$P(B) = P(B|A_1) \cdot P(A_1) + P(B|A_2) \cdot P(A_2). \qquad (7.2)$$

From the Eqs. (7.1) and (7.2) follows *Bayes's theorem:*

$$P(A_i|B) = \frac{P(A_i) \cdot P(B|A_i)}{P(B|A_1) \cdot P(A_1) + \cdots + P(B|A_n) \cdot P(A_n)}$$
$$(i = 1, \ldots, n) \qquad (7.3)$$

where $P(A_i|B)$ is called the *posterior* probability (computed after it is known that B occurred), and $P(A_i)$ is known as the *prior* probability.

Note that rules other than Bayes's theorem might be employed to combine old and new information. So Bamberg et al. (1976, p. 36) propose the general scheme

$$P(A_i|B) = \frac{P(A_i) \cdot [P(B|A_i)]^r}{\sum\limits_{i=1}^{n} P(A_i) \cdot [P(B|A_i)]^r}. \qquad (7.4)$$

Only if $r = 1$ are Eqs. (7.3) and (7.4) identical. If $r = 0$, the information on B is completely ignored. If $r = \infty$, the a priori distribution $P(A_i)$ is ignored. Whether people actually change their subjective probability assessments according to Bayes's theorem has been explored in a number of psychological studies. For references and results refer to Green et al. (1967). These authors found that "[subjects'] ability to manipulate probabilities in the manner prescribed by Bayesian statistics is quantitatively poor but qualitatively in the direction predicted by the model"[Green et al. (1967, p. 11)]. A later section on applications of IE will return to their study. The next section presents a detailed example of the decision theoretic calculus.

THE "NEWSBOY" EXAMPLE

The following example is known as the newsboy problem. Each day a retailer has to decide how many units (newspapers) to buy, say, a units; e units can be sold per day. Inventory keeping is not possible because old newspapers cannot be sold. A paper is bought at 6¢ and sold at 10¢ apiece; there are no stockout penalties.[4] This situation yields the *payoff matrix* shown in Table 7.1, which is based on the relationships

$$
\begin{aligned}
\text{PROFIT} &= 10e - 6a &&\text{if } e \leq a \\
&= 10a - 6a = 4a &&\text{if } e \geq a.
\end{aligned} \qquad (7.5)
$$

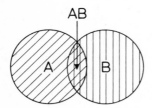

FIGURE 7-1.   The Events A, B, and AB.

TABLE 7.1.   *Payoff Matrix*

States of Nature: Demand e	Acts: Buy a			Prior Probability P(e)
	0	1	2	
0	0	− 6	− 12	0.10
1	0	+ 4	− 2	0.50
2	0	+ 4	+ 8	0.40

This table also shows the prior probability of demand, $P(e)$, which is based either on past experience or on subjective estimates. The payoff matrix might be interpreted as a *game against nature* played by the retailer.

From Table 7.1 one can compute the expected profit for each "strategy." For instance, if the retailer always buys $a = 2$, the corresponding column of Table 7.1 yields the expected profit (expectation denoted by $\mathcal{E}$):

$$\mathcal{E}\,(\text{PROFIT}|a = 2) = -12P(e = 0) - 2\,P(e = 1) + 8\,P(e = 2)$$
$$= -12(0.10) - 2\,(0.50) + 8\,(0.40)$$
$$= -1.2 - 1 + 3.2 = 1. \qquad (7.6)$$

In the same way one computes $\mathcal{E}\,(\text{PROFIT}|a = 0) = 0$ and $\mathcal{E}\,(\text{PROFIT}|a = 1) = 3$. Hence the optimal decision is to buy one unit.

The situation above can be graphically represented by a *decision tree.* In Fig. 7.2 a box denotes a decision, and a circle denotes a chance outcome. The result of a particular combination of decision and chance outcomes is displayed at the extreme

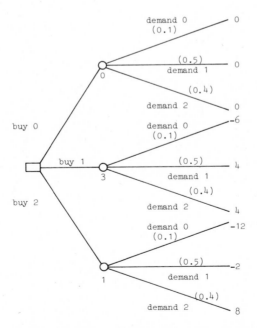

FIGURE 7–2.   *Decision Tree Corresponding to Table 7.1.*

right of the figure. Working backward (from right to left), one can compute expected values by using the probabilities shown in parentheses; this method is called a roll-up procedure.

In general, let the payoff table show payoffs w_{ij} corresponding to action a_j ($j = 1, \ldots, n$) and occurrence of event (state of nature) e_i ($i = 1, \ldots, m$). Then the optimal decision follows from finding the act j that maximizes the expected pay-off:

$$\max_j \left\{ \sum_{i=1}^{m} w_{ij} \cdot P(e_i) \right\}. \tag{7.7}$$

Next consider the value of installing an *information system* (IS). Suppose the retailer telephones customers to learn how much can be sold. Consider a perfect IS first and an imperfect IS next. In this example a *perfect* IS means that the messages y tell exactly what the states of nature will be; i.e., the posterior probabilities are specified by Table 7.2; or

$$P(e = i | y = k) = 1 \text{ for } i = k$$
$$= 0 \text{ for } i \neq k. \tag{7.8}$$

TABLE 7.2.   Posterior
Probabilities $P(e|y)$ of
Perfect IS

y	e		
	0	1	2
0	1	0	0
1	0	1	0
2	0	0	1

The perfect IS tells the retailer exactly which value of e will be experienced the next day. In other words, the retailer telephones *all* customers, who tell *exactly* how much they will buy. Hence the retailer selects the value of a that maximizes the pay-off; i.e., in the relevant row of Table 7.1 the retailer selects a^*, which maximizes the row element; see Table 7.3. The expected profit is

$$\mathcal{E} \text{ (PROFIT|perfect IS)} = 0(0.10) + 4(0.50) + 8(0.40)$$
$$= 5.2. \tag{7.9}$$

TABLE 7.3.   Perfect Information

y = e	a*	PROFIT	P(e)
0	0	0	0.10
1	1	4	0.50
2	2	8	0.40

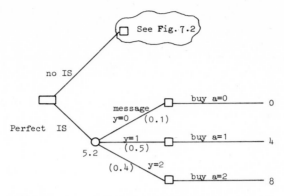

FIGURE 7–3.   A Perfect Information System.

The expected profit without any IS (but with the selection of an optimal policy $a^* = 1$) was 3. So the *gross benefits* of a perfect IS are $5.2 - 3 = 2.2$. The decision tree diagram is displayed in Fig. 7.3.

The *net benefits* of an IS are the gross benefits minus the cost of the IS. These costs may include data processing (DP) costs plus "decision-making" costs. The decision-making costs may be considerable when complex decision making is involved.

Consider next a more realistic *imperfect IS* where $P(e|y)$ deviates from Eq. (7.8). Usually one has to compute $P(e|y)$ from $P(y|e)$ by using Bayes's theorem, formulated in Eq. (7.3).[5] The next paragraph will demonstrate that indeed $P(y|e)$ can be the starting point for such a calculation.

In the example new information may be obtained by telephoning fifty customers from the whole customer population of a thousand. Suppose that the probability of each customer's buying one product unit is probability p, which is unknown and changes from day to day. If x denotes the quantity purchased by a single customer, then for a particular day

$$P(x = 1) = p$$
$$P(x = 0) = 1 - p. \tag{7.10}$$

Suppose that on a particular day twenty of the fifty customers will buy; i.e., that day the message y becomes

$$y = \sum_{j=1}^{50} x_j = 20. \tag{7.11}$$

Suppose further that in the past the retailer experienced, say, three values for p: $p = 0.25, 0.40, 0.45$. From Eqs. (7.10) and (7.11) it follows that for $p = 0.25$ one has the traditional binomial probability law:

$$P(y = 20|p = 0.25) = \binom{50}{20} (0.25)^{20} (0.75)^{30}. \tag{7.12}$$

Repeating Eq. (7.12) for other "states of nature," i.e., other p-values, yields $P(y_k|p_i)$. Applying Eq. (7.3) with $A_i = p_i$ and $B = y_k$ yields $P(p_i|y_k)$; see also the next paragraph. Note that the states of nature specified by the binomial probabilities p_i correspond with expected demand $\mathcal{E}(e) = 1000\,p$, which equals 250, 400, and 450 for the respective p_i-values. This paragraph serves to illustrate that $P(y\,|\,e)$, instead of $P(e\,|\,y)$, is usually given. Next forget this illustration and return to Table 7.2 in which the state of nature was identified by e, the total number of units demanded.

Let the imperfect IS be specified by the $P(y\,|\,e)$ of Table 7.4. Observe that the elements on the main diagonal no longer equal one as they do in Eq. (7.8). They do remain the maximum element in each column; i.e., it is not a "misleading" IS. For convenience of reference $P(e)$ is again displayed in Table 7.4.

TABLE 7.4. Conditional Probabilities
$P(y|e)$ of Imperfect IS

y	e		
	0	1	2
0	0.70	0.10	0.10
1	0.20	0.70	0.20
2	0.10	0.20	0.70
P(e)	0.10	0.50	0.40

This table shows $P(y\,|\,e)$, the conditional probability of certain messages, whereas one wishes to know the conditional probability of certain events, $P(e\,|\,y)$. To apply Bayes's theorem start by computing Eq. (7.2), the denominator of Eq. (7.3). For instance,

$$P(y = 0) = 0.7(0.1) + 0.1(0.5) + 0.1(0.4) = 0.16. \qquad (7.13)$$

Likewise $P(y = 1) = 0.45$ and $P(y = 2) = 0.39$. Bayes's theorem yields, for instance,

$$P(e = 0\,|\,y = 0) = \frac{(0.1)\,(0.7)}{0.16} = 0.07/0.16. \qquad (7.14)$$

This result produces Table 7.5. Observe that the prior probability was $P(e = 0) = 0.10$; but the posterior probability when $y = 0$ is much higher: $P(e = 0\,|\,y = 0) = 7/16 = 0.44$.

TABLE 7.5. Posterior Probabilities $P(e|y)$
of Imperfect IS

y	e		
	0	1	2
0	0.07/0.16	0.05/0.16	0.04/0.16
1	0.02/0.45	0.35/0.45	0.08/0.45
2	0.01/0.39	0.10/0.39	0.28/0.39

Combining the Tables 7.1 and 7.5 means that if the message is $y = 0$, and the retailer orders a units, the expected profits are

$$\mathcal{E}(\text{PROFIT} | a = 0, y = 0) = 0$$

$$\mathcal{E}(\text{PROFIT} | a = 1, y = 0) = -6(7/16) + 4(5/16) + 4(4/16) = -0.06/0.16$$

$$\mathcal{E}(\text{PROFIT} | a = 2, y = 0) = -12(7/16) - 2(5/16) + 8(4/16)$$
$$= -0.62/0.16. \tag{7.15}$$

So if $y = 0$, $a^* = 0$, and expected profit is zero. It is easy to compute that if $y = 1$, $a^* = 1$, and profit equals $1.60/0.45 = 3.56$. If $y = 2$, $a^* = 2$, and profit equals $1.92/0.39 = 4.92$. So the expected profit under an IS characterized by Table 7.4 can be computed using $P(y)$:

$$\mathcal{E}(\text{PROFIT} | \text{imperfect IS}) =$$
$$0(0.16) + (3.56)(0.45) + (4.92)(0.39) = 3.52. \tag{7.16}$$

The expected profit of an imperfect IS is 3.52 compared to 5.2 under a perfect IS; see Eq. (7.9). Hence the gross benefits are only $3.52 - 3 = 0.52$ compared to $5.2 - 3 = 2.2$ for a perfect IS.

In Fig. 7.4 the analysis above is represented graphically. An asterisk denotes the optimal path chosen at a decision node (square box). Hence the chance path leading to that decision node multiplies the expected payoff corresponding to this unique path. For instance, message $y = 2$ (with probability 0.39) leads to a decision node at which "$a = 2$" is selected. Hence 0.39 is multiplied by the corresponding expected payoff 4.92. To save space some paths are shown not in detail but by a "cloud."

Other pedagogical examples can be found in the literature on Bayesian decision analysis and information economics.[6]

MORE ABOUT INFORMATION ECONOMICS

Before one leaves the example of the preceding section, it can be used to illustrate the notion of a *coarse* versus a *fine* IS. This notion is the IE equivalent of the attribute "detail versus aggregation" discussed in the preceding chapter. In the example the IS would be coarser if it would not distinguish between, say, the events $e = 1$ and $e = 2$; a perfect but coarse IS would be characterized by

$$P(y = 0 | e = 0) = 1$$
$$P(\text{"}y\text{ is positive"} | e = 1 \text{ or } e = 2) = 1. \tag{7.17}$$

Obviously an imperfect IS in the sense of an inaccurate IS can be more or less coarse (detailed).

Before jumping to conclusions from the preceding section's demonstration of how an inaccurate IS generates smaller gross benefits than a perfect IS, consider a consistently wrong IS. Suppose this IS to be characterized by $P(e_1 | y_2) = 1$ and $P(e_2 | y_1) = 1$ whereas a more accurate IS would show $P(e_1 | y_2) = 0.50$ and $P(e_2 | y_1) = 0.50$. The consistently wrong IS permits one to make good decisions by simply taking the opposite of the action suggested by the IS! Nevertheless, such a degenerated IS is not typical for MIS. (See also Exercise 8.)

Another factor determining the gross benefits of the IS is formed by the *prior* probabilities. Limiting cases are prior probabilities approaching zero or one. In those cases additional information is worthless; see Exercises 1 through 4. More examples

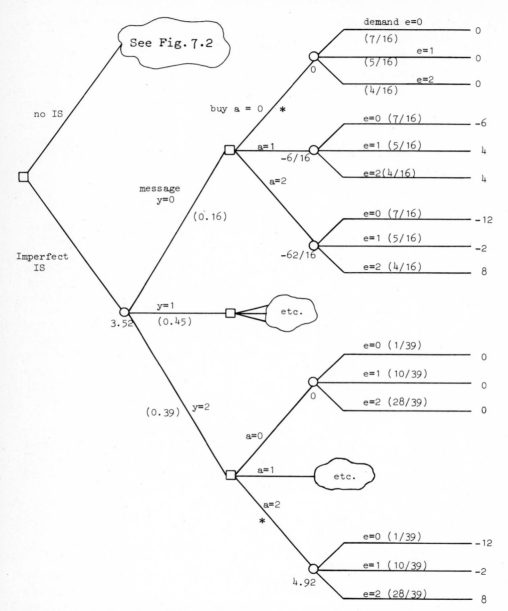

FIGURE 7-4.   An Imperfect Information System.

showing the effects of the prior probabilities and the accuracy of the IS can be found in the literature.[7]

An imperfect IS cannot have higher gross benefits than those of a perfect IS (see also the final section of this chapter). Hence the unrealistic assumption of *perfect* information yields a practical result: an *upper bound* for the gross benefits of a more realistic, imperfect IS. If the costs of an imperfect IS exceed the gross benefits of a perfect IS, the realistic IS can never be cost effective.[8]

The model (framework, world view) of information economics might be pictured as in Fig. 7.5. For a more elaborated model refer to the picture in Marschak (1971).

Note that graphical representation via decision trees can be found in various references.[9] For a more complicated situation Jewett (1972a) gives a network representation solved by dynamic programming.[10] Vazsonyi (1977a) discusses the use of Petri-networks to represent the kind of problems examined in this chapter.

Marschak and Radner (1972) extend the IE approach to an organization that comprises *multiple* decision-makers communicating with each other. In Marschak and Radner's *team theory* a team is a group of individuals (agents): each decides on his or her own acts, but all receive a common reward as the joint result of all their decisions. A team of *n* persons should be distinguished from a situation with *n* single-person systems because the team's result function involves interactions among the agents' actions. (For the concept "interaction" also refer to the two preceding chapters.) Without dwelling on the complicated mathematical representation of team theory, one can examine some simple applications of this theory (see the next section). Hanken and Reuver's (1977, pp. 168–178) survey of the research on multiperson systems does not concentrate on information systems. The survey includes multilevel, hierarchical system theory as developed by Mesarovic et al. (1970).

The newsboy example of the preceding section represented a *static* system. That is, the decision to buy *a* units for time period *t* had no effect on the next time periods. If in this simple example stock could be kept, such stockkeeping would connect the different periods. For example, if the retailer buys more than is sold in a particular period *t*, then the retailer can try to sell the surplus in the next period. Hence the performance of a period depends on the actions and events of preceding periods.

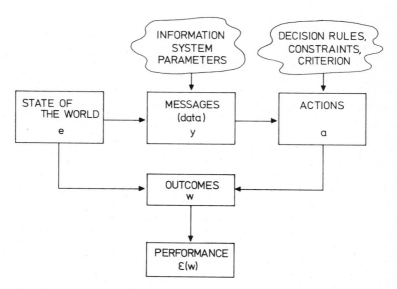

FIGURE 7–5. The Information Economics Model.

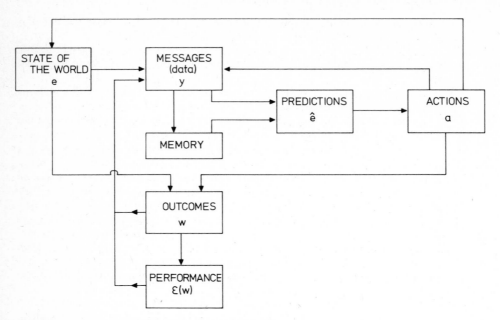

FIGURE 7–6.   Dynamic Information Economics Model.

It was Feltham (1968) who introduced a sequence of decisions over time. Figure 7.6 represents a dynamic information economics model: memory is updated through messages on the state of the world and also on actions and outcomes so that *learning and adaptive behavior* become possible. Actions affect not only the next outcome (performance) but also the future state of the world. Predictions of the environment for the "near" future (up to a planning horizon) are based on old and new messages. And so on. Ying (1977, pp. 16, 18) used a multiperiod model in which the system is supposed to remain stable during those multiple periods. Some of his interesting conclusions are that "each act he [the decision maker] takes in general has two values: (a) the present payoff value and (b) a future information value." Ying continues, "if we expect to learn rather rapidly about the decision environment through our experience [the consequences realized], then the value of an information system, while highly valuable initially, may decline drastically as time goes on." For more details on dynamic models refer to some of the applications in the next section, and to the literature.[11] Note that Fellingham et al. (1976, pp. 220–222) use a graphical representation related to Fig. 7.6, yet different from it.

Observe that the following approach is not truly dynamic. Action a_1 may denote "buy two units now and one unit next time"; and the event e_1 may be "one unit purchased now, and two units purchased yesterday"; and so on. Marschak (1971, p. 201) discusses such *semidynamic* definitions of the actions a, events e, and messages y. A realistic example, planning plant expansion, is discussed by Sullivan and Claycombe (1977, pp. 242–243).

A different dynamic aspect is the following. The information gathering activity may proceed in two or more steps; i.e., the outcome of step 1 (the first message) determines whether additional information will be collected before further action is taken. In such a *sequential information system* the decision may be either to collect additional information or to take action. Only the latter action affects the state of the world. In mathematical statistics such a stepwise approach is known as sequential sampling. A management-oriented example can be found in Green et al. (1967, p. 17): "purchase a survey which is 70 percent reliable in the first stage, but if a second stage is required, the reliability increases to 80 percent. . . ." Sequential information gathering complicates the decision tree but introduces no new principles. An example of such a decision tree appears in a figure in Green et al. (1967, p. 19). If successive observations are serially correlated, given a specific state of the world, the problem becomes further complicated.

In summary, information economics has been expanded toward team theory (multiperson situation) and toward dynamic systems. Vazsonyi (1977b) indicates relationships with *game theory* and *control theory*. Ho and Chu's (1974) survey from the control theoretic point of view includes nonzero sum games and stochastic (dynamic) control theory. (The latter survey article assumes a good knowledge of mathematics.) Static situations are essentially "open loop" control systems while dynamic structures demand "closed loop" solutions; see also Easton (1973, pp. 71–72). Game theory, including nonzero sum games, coalitions, and so on, is surveyed by Hanken and Reuver (1977, pp. 118–167).

APPLICATIONS

This section briefly describes some applications of information economics. Based on a literature search of moderate scope, this section does not cover the whole population but is reasonably representative of IE applications.

Beckmann's (1958) Airline Reservations

Airlines sell a highly perishable good, namely seats, and therefore are confronted with inventory control problems. If fewer tickets are sold than capacity permits, revenues are missed because the commodity is perishable. If too many tickets are sold, passengers must be turned down; and the stockout penalty is the loss of goodwill. Beckmann examines the optimal sales limit, i.e., how many seats should be sold given the capacity, and the probabilities of late cancellations and standby passengers. He also applies team theory to study the communication among the various sales agents and the central office. This issue involves the choice between a centralized and a decentralized organization. (Readers interested in reservation problems are referred also to Williams's (1977) article on motel reservation policy.)

McGuire's (1961) Wholesale Bakery Sales Organization

Theory of teams is applied to an inventory-type problem faced by a wholesale bakery. Bread is a perishable commodity: shelf-life is one or two days; stale bread sells at a lower price. The sales agent has to decide how much to deliver on consignment to the retail stores. Moreover, because several agents are needed to serve the many retail stores, the issues of communications among agents and the central office, and of centralized versus decentralized decision making arise. Supplying all agents plus the main office with all data may be too expensive. Hence one possibility is to limit an agent's knowledge to local data: decentralized decision making with local information only. McGuire's paper is an excellent demonstration of the serious mathematical problems arising in the solution of even simplified information economics models.

Kriebel's (1965) Inventory Supply Organization

The following simple logistics organization is studied. Goods are stored at two stocking locations, and controlled by a third location. The simple cost function consists of inventory carrying costs plus shortage costs, and is subject to a budget constraint. Team theory is applied because with three agents involved a centralized or a decentralized IS may be installed. Information may be delayed (see Kriebel, p. 150), and detailed or summarized (p. 151).

Tapiero's (1974) Dynamic Inventory Control System

Control theory can be applied to determine optimal measurement intervals (I in the symbols of the preceding chapter) in dynamic systems. In general this problem is extremely difficult to solve. Exact solutions requiring sophisticated control theory are possible if the system is linear with Gaussian noise terms. The second section of the next chapter discusses control theory in more detail. Tapiero applies his framework to inventory management systems. In the operations research literature attention is focused on ordering policies if inventory at hand is known. Tapiero's investigation of inventory monitoring policies recognizes that inventory status is measured imperfectly. Inventory measurement reduces the variability (variance σ^2) of inventory estimates. He assumes a simple quadratic cost function:

$$c(x_t - x^*)^2 \tag{7.18}$$

where x^* is the desired inventory level. (One could argue that in practice negative inventory may incur severe stockout penalties, and that positive inventory may lead to linear costs.) In his model the ordering (decision) subsystem could be separated from the information subsystem, and could be solved independently. The optimum measurement interval for the information subsystem is derived to be a square-root formula:

$$I = \sqrt{C_2/(C_1\sigma^2)} \tag{7.19}$$

where C_1 denotes inventory costs, C_2 measurement costs, and σ^2 the known variance of demand. He also examines a system with deteriorating inventory items, but this system is too complicated for an exact analytical solution.

Stohr's (1979) Information Systems for Observing Inventory Levels

This author investigates inventory systems based on physical stock taking versus "perpetual bookkeeping" (recording transactions and computing stock). Stocks are depleted not only through sales but also through pilferage and natural shrinkage. Errors can be made both in physical stock taking (counting errors) and in transaction recording. He investigates these problems in the context of a simple inventory problem.

More applications and references can be found in the literature; e.g., see Wenzel (1975, pp. 134–182). For inventory systems refer also to Odanaka (1972), who investigated accuracy in multiperiod inventory systems.

Green's et al. (1967) Bayesian Gaming Experiments

This final study has an orientation quite different from that of the applications above. A noncompetitive business game (i.e., a game against nature, not against human opponents), is constructed by the authors. (The next chapters will say more on gaming.) In this game players act as marketing managers, concerned with evaluating alternative advertising campaigns. This game serves as a controlled experiment to evaluate decision theory. The game is sufficiently simple to allow computation of an optimal Bayesian solution. The players involved, however, were inexperienced in Bayesian analysis. The player could buy additional information, namely marketing surveys, on the probabilities of alternative situations. Several options were available; i.e., more accurate information could be bought at a higher price. The question asked is whether the players studied behave according to the *normative* model of Bayesian decision analysis, and if not, how they deviate.[12] In *all* the experiments most players bought *too much* information, i.e., installed a more expensive (more accurate) IS than was optimal according to Bayesian decision theory! As predicted by the normative model, subjects tended to buy less additional information if the prior information was more certain. Variation among individuals was found to be significant.

Many more interesting but tentative results can be found in the original reference. Experiments were done varying the system's complexity, including perfect and various degrees of imperfect information, and varying prior probabilities, number of states and actions, and payoffs; the game was played by either students or marketing executives. As the complexity of the relatively simple model increased, "intuitive" behavior deviated more from the Bayesian solution.[13]

Note that the authors also try to construct a descriptive model of the actual behavior by players, besides the normative (prescriptive) Bayesian model. See the original reference for details on this tentative behavioral model. The authors also provide additional references to studies on actual decision behavior versus optimal Bayesian decision behavior.[14] Note that the authors apply full factorial designs (see Chapter Five) and analysis of variance including interactions.[15] Chesley (1975, p. 332) gives additional references to psychological studies on Bayes's Law.

LIMITATIONS OF THE IE APPROACH

The IE approach has five major limitations.

Large Amounts of Input Data

A lot of information is needed as input to the decision calculus. As Table 7.1 showed, one should know all possible actions a_j, all possible states of nature e_i, and the payoffs w_{ij} for each combination of actions and events. Hence there is no provision for developing a strategy as events call for action. Table 7.1 further shows that

m prior probabilities $P(e_i)$ must be specified, but these probabilities may be based on subjective estimates as well as on past experience. One also needs to specify the quality of the IS by means of conditional probabilities as in Table 7.4. The latter requirement, however, is not surprising; for a quantitative study of the IS effects on the gross benefits, one must specify the quality of the IS quantitatively. It is possible to formulate the IE model so that new actions, new states of nature, and new payoff values may be discovered as a result of additional information.[16]

One should investigate how sensitive the conclusions based on the IE model are to the assumed input data of the decision calculus. Such a sensitivity analysis may show that, say, the IS has positive net benefits provided the prior probabilities remain within a certain range; in that case the exact values of the prior probabilities are not needed. See the literature for additional details.[17] Note that such sensitivity studies are recommended also in a related area, that of utility theory (Chapter Four), in which subjective elements, namely preferences, are measured; e.g., see Keefer (1977, p. 17).

Purely Rational Decision Maker

The decision maker or makers are supposed to behave purely rationally. In the newsboy example the retailer wished to maximize expected profit. Statistical decision analysis, however, is more general in that it permits the maximization of expected utility rather than that of monetary payoffs. Of course this generalization presents many practical problems of utility specification; see Chapter Four. Other optimization criteria besides maximization of expected utility or monetary payoffs are possible. An example is the "maximin" rule: minimize the maximum loss. More optimization rules, such as Savage's minimax regret and the Hurwicz criterion, are discussed in the literature.[18]

In the views above the decision maker is supposed to optimize a unique criterion, not to satisfy one or more criteria. Satisficing behavior has been emphasized in behavioral organization theory à la Cyert and March (1963); remember the discussion in Chapter Four. Actual behavior of decision makers was studied and compared to the Bayesian norm by Green et al. (1967), as already mentioned in the preceding section. Mock and Vasarhelyi (1977) introduced behavioral variables in the information economics framework, but did not show how to solve the resulting model. Risk attitudes are the subject of Exercise 5.

Mathematical and Computational Problems

Even in static models, the computations may become tedious and pose difficult mathematical problems for certain statistical distributions. Examples can be found in any publication on decision analysis or information economics. In dynamic models the mathematical problems become tremendous; see for instance Huang et al. (1975). When the mathematical problems have been solved, the numerical evaluation can be greatly aided by means of computers. Interactive computer programs have been developed to elicit prior probabilities from users and to manipulate these estimates according to Bayes's theorem.[19] Ravin and Schatzoff (1977) develop an interactive graphics system, which displays decision trees and permits changing the structure of the decision tree diagram and computing the optimal strategy. Such a computer system greatly facilitates sensitivity analysis.[20]

Simplistic System Models

The system to be managed is modeled in extremely simple terms. Actual systems show interrelated processes, such as chains and networks of production processes, or production departments coupled with purchasing, selling, and finance departments, and so on. Decisions not only occur at prescheduled points of time but also are triggered, for instance, by a customer arrival or an out-of-bounds event; see the discussion on unscheduled decisions in the preceding chapter.[21] Moreover, systems are dynamic; i.e., a decision affects the future state of the world. In the newsboy example, inventories would create such a situation: buying "too much" creates an inventory that affects future payoffs. As mentioned in an earlier section, Feltham (1968) did indeed introduce a sequence of decisions over time. Marschak and Radner's (1972) theory of teams further extends the information economics approach to organizations that comprise several decision makers communicating with each other. Additional research was discussed in the two preceding sections. Unfortunately, these extensions remain quite abstract and complicated.

Limited Information Attributes

The IE framework, assuming purely rational decision makers, ignores behavioral attributes of information. Information attributes were discussed in the preceding chapter. Originally the IE framework concentrated on one information characteristic, namely inaccuracy, often called "garbling" in the IE jargon. Chapter Six discussed several inaccuracy sources: sampling, measurement, transcription, transformation, and logical errors. Accuracy adversely affected by sampling can be improved by taking additional observations. This aspect is highlighted in the original Bayesian textbooks by Raiffa and Schlaifer, and in most IE publications. Measurement errors are explicitly dealt with in a few papers, such as Stohr (1979) and Tapiero (1974). Transcription and transformation errors are typical computer-oriented attributes, and are not explicitly discussed in the IE literature. Logical errors conflict with the assumed rational behavior.

The timeliness attribute is discussed in a few IE references such as Feltham (1968). Usually scheduled, periodic decision making is assumed in such studies. The models are not so detailed as to allow the kind of analysis done in Chapter Six. The issue of aggregated versus detailed data is tackled under the heading "coarseness" of the IS in some IE models and in the team-theory extension of IE. In team theory a natural issue is the choice between a centralized organization (possibly with summarized data because detailed data would be too expensive and cumbersome) and decentralized decision making with local, detailed data. Refer back to the studies summarized earlier, especially Beckmann (1958), Kriebel (1975), and McGuire (1961).

Note that the use of local data implies a restriction on the scope of the database available to the individual user; see Chapter Six. The attribute "retention time" was translated by Marschak (1971) into the concept of a "coarser" IS.

A behavioral attribute of information discussed in the preceding chapter is the report mode, including periodic versus exception reporting (meant to reduce the information load of managers), queries versus standard reports, and—a purely behavioral aspect—report format (layout, graphs, precision, etc.). As mentioned such behavioral aspects do not fit in the IE framework.

Attributes like reliability and recovery are typically computer-oriented and are not explicitly discussed in the IE literature. These attributes can be introduced into the IE framework without great problems. Security, privacy, user-computer modes, and flexibility seem more difficult to translate into the IE model.

Consider one final comment on the attribute accuracy. Accuracy as defined in Chapter Six was limited to deviations between the true event and its image (data). Historical data (y) are needed to predict the future state of the system and its environment (e). The forecasting errors made in such predictions are represented by the conditional probabilities $P(e|y)$. Observe that there are two sources of random-ness: the variations in the states of nature $P(e)$; and the observation noise, i.e., varia-tions in the messages $P(y|e)$. Also note that a message y may be a historical datum such as "y units sold yesterday," or a prediction (based on historical data) such as "z units are expected to be sold tomorrow."

BENEFITS OF THE IE FRAMEWORK

The IE studies summarized in the applications section were quite drastic simplifica-tions of real-world situations; nevertheless such simplified models may give qualita-tive insight into basic aspects of a system. Furthermore the limitations discussed in the preceding section are less restrictive in decisions of a *nonrepetitive, one-shot* nature. Examples can be found at the tactical-strategic level: whether to introduce a new product (see Exercise 3), where to locate a new plant, and so on. See also the examples in House (1977, pp. 205–285) and Manne et al. (1979, pp. 22–31). These IE examples do not mean that no applications can be found at the operational level. For instance, in statistical quality control some sampling plans are based on statistical decision theory; however, this example concerns a very restricted information sys-tem; see Moskowitz and Berry (1976). Decision theoretic solutions for operational inventory control are surveyed by Zacks (1976, pp. 230–234). Notice that the application of IE to information evaluation at the strategic level typically concerns a noncomputerized IS, an area excluded in this book. Verhelst (1974, pp. 168–176) and Welke (1977) are strongly recommended, critical evaluations of information eco-nomics.

In the field of information systems many intuitive ideas (rules of thumb) are around. Using the IE model, one can prove some of these ideas to be true. Marschak (1971) proves the following lemmas:

A more accurate IS has higher expected utility if one neglects the costs of the IS and concentrates on gross benefits.

A "coarser" IS has lower gross value. As mentioned earlier a coarser IS is a less detailed IS. A coarser IS can also be an IS with shorter retention time so that fewer data are stored.

A timely but inaccurate IS *can* have less value than a delayed IS. The time-liness attribute was also studied by Feltham (1968) in his multiperiod model. In his quite rigid model more timely information has higher gross value.

More generally, information economics is a sophisticated, highly formalized theory based on purely rational behavior of the decision makers. The beginning of this chapter already emphasized the *conceptual framework* provided by this theory. In J. C. Emery's (1971) view the framework comprises the surprise content of information, its effect on the decision, and the effect of the decision on performance. Fellingham et al. (1976, p. 225) observe that information may have value even in an unchanged decision if the information decreases the riskiness associated with the decision; see the discussion on risk in Chapter Four. In Welke's (1977b) words IE provides "A model outline consisting of environment, observation, communication, decision, consequence (as a combination of act and state)." The IE theory emphasizes that observations (messages) might be in error (and proceeds by representing this error through conditional probabilities). A practical consequence is that the reports produced by an IS may include an explicit error estimate. Such a procedure is standard for sales forecasts, which are normally accompanied by an error prediction based on Mean Absolute Deviation or MAD. However, the data on "inventory at hand" are usually presented as perfectly accurate numbers. The decision calculus further shows that as the IS changes, the optimal decision must also change. For various ISs the value of the IS should be computed by comparing the gross benefits generated by the *optimal* combination of information quality and decision.

Information economics is a methodology that until now has been applied mainly by economists and not by computer and information scientists.[23] A case in point is that the "social" value of information (i.e. the value in a multiperson economy) is discussed at length by Demski (1974). It remains to be seen whether students of IS will be able to apply the IE framework and calculus to their systems. Some additional sources for further study of IE are provided in the references.[24] Note that IE is not well integrated into the classical economic theory discussed in Chapter Five because the classical theory assumes perfect knowledge.

Before proceeding to the next two chapters that include simulation (and gaming), one should examine the contrasts between *IE and simulation*. Simulation is an approach not restricted by the limitations discussed in the preceding section: purely rational behavior, mathematical sophistication, drastically simplified systems, and restricted informational attributes. Unfortunately, simulation is no more than a technique; simulation is not a theory. Chapter Nine studies an IBM management game that may be characterized in the terms of the present chapter.

> The IBM game is dynamic. Current decisions are affected by past results (feedbacks and feedforwards), and will in turn influence the future state of the system. Moreover, the structure and parameters of the system may change autonomously over time.

> It is nonlinear. The model shows various nonlinear functions, side conditions, and logical switches.

> It is stochastic (probabilistic, random).

> It is a nonzero sum game. Players compete for a market share while the total market may decline or grow.

> It is specified in implicit form. The outputs are a function of the inputs and state variables, but this function is so complicated that it can be expressed only by a complete computer (simulation) program.

> It is not played by a "homo economicus." Players are not supposed to optimize a single criterion, such as profit, but may satisfice several criteria. The players have imperfect knowledge about the structure and parameter values of the system they have to control.

EXERCISES

1. J. C. Emery (1971, pp. 2–6) gives the following example. The decision is whether to launch a new product ($a = 1$ or $a = 0$), and the event is acceptance or rejection by the public ($e = 1$ or $e = 0$). The payoff matrix is

	Acceptance	Rejection
Launch	100	-50
Cancel	0	0

(a) Let the prior probability be $P(e = 1) = 0.60$. What is the expected profit of launching the product? (b) What is the expected profit under perfect information? (c) Assume $P(y = 1|e = 1) = P(y = 0|e = 0) = 0.80$. Compute the posterior probability $P(e = 0|y = 0)$. (d) Compute the gross benefits of this imperfect information system. (e) How much do benefits increase if 0.80 in (c) is replaced by 0.85? (f) What are the gross benefits of any IS if the prior probability satisfies $P(e = 1) = 1$?

2. Assume that the quality of the IS is specified by the following $P(y|e)$:

y		e	
	0	1	2
0	0.4	0.2	0.2
1	0.4	0.4	0.4
2	0.2	0.4	0.4

Show that this IS does not generate any gross benefits for the newsboy example.

3. Assume $P(y|e)$ is given by the following matrix:

$$\begin{matrix} 0.2 & 0.7 & 0.1 \\ 0.7 & 0.2 & 0.7 \\ 0.1 & 0.1 & 0.2 \end{matrix}$$

Given a particular y message, what is the optimal action for the newsboy example?

4. Consider Bayes's theorem in Eq. (7.3) with $n = 2$. Compute the posterior probability $P(A_1|B)$ when $P(A_1) = 1$, and when $P(B|A_1) = 1$, respectively.

5. An individual is offered the following two bets on unbiased coin flips: (1) with one flip receive \$100,000 for heads or pay \$50,000 for tails; (2) with a thousand flips receive \$100 for each heads and pay \$50 for each tails. Which bet would be accepted by (a) an individual of modest wealth, (b) an individual of extreme wealth, (c) a gambler of modest wealth, (d) an individual minimizing the probability of a maximum loss?

6. If the payoffs are independent of the decision, what does the payoff matrix look like?

7. What would be a crude upper bound (requiring no calculations) for the expected value of perfect information in the example of Table 7.1?

8. Formulate the "worst possible" IS in terms of $P(y_k|e_i)$ with $i = 1, \ldots, m$. What would be the gross benefits of such a "diffuse" IS?

9. (a) When is action j "dominated" by action j'? (b) If one neglects its cost, when is an IS "too coarse"? (c) When is an IS "too fine"? (d) Compare a management-by-exception IS to a periodic IS. Will the former IS tend to be too coarse or too fine?

10. Consider the IS characterized by the following $P(y|e)$:

y	e		
	0	1	2
0	1/2	0	0
1	1/2	1/2	0
2	0	1/2	1/2
3	0	0	1/2

(a) Would you call this IS coarse or fine? (b) Assume you receive the message $y = 1$. Which state of nature is excluded?

11. (a) Which loss function is standard in regression analysis? (b) What other loss functions are used in some regression analysis techniques?

12. Stabell (1978a, p. 137), reporting on an empirical investigation, observes, "A reference to a source that is constantly changing in data content is not distinguished from reference to a source that is more stable." With which concept discussed in the present chapter would you associate Stabell's remark?

NOTES

1. Some general references on statistical decision analysis are Raiffa (1968) and Schlaifer (1967).

2. A reference is Marschak (1971); see also Radner (1978). Note that, its title notwithstanding, McDonough (1963) has nothing to do with the theory of this chapter.

3. See Churchman et al. (1957, p. 203), and also J. C. Emery (1969, pp. 91–98).

4. Except for some details, the numbers are taken from Verhelst (1974, pp. 160–165).

5. Bamberg et al. (1976), however, do not consider the two situations," $P(y|e)$ given "versus" $P(e|y)$ given," equivalent!

6. See the various contributions in House (1977, pp. 205–285), and also Pegels (1976, pp. 91–123), Rappaport (1970, pp. 182–190), and the literature references elsewhere in this chapter.

7. J. C. Emery (1971, p. 7), Stamper (1973, pp. 165–174), and Vazsonyi (1977b, p. 26) and (1979).

8. See also Firchau (1977).

9. See note 6, and also J. C. Emery (1971, p. 5), Verhelst (1974, pp. 158–159), and Wenzel (1975, pp. 104–115).

10. See also Feltham (1968).

11. Ho and Chu (1974), Jewett (1972a), Verhelst (1974, pp. 170–172), and Ying (1967). An informal summary of Ying (1967) is provided by Ying (1977).

12. Green et al. (1967, pp. 3–4).

13. Green et al. (1967, p. 63).

14. Green et al. (1967, pp. 8–9).

15. Green et al. (1967, p. 136).

16. See Wenzel (1975, pp. 119–127), and also Bamberg et al. (1976, p. 35), and Bemelmans (1976, pp. 175–176).

17. Hora (1977, p. 220), Howard (1971), Land (1976, pp. 8–9), Rappaport (1970, p. 186), and Vazsonyi (1977b, p. 27). For different approaches, see Charnetski (1977) and Rowe (1977, pp. 243–249).

18. Bamberg et al. (1976), Hanken and Reuver (1977, pp. 66–69), Verhelst (1974, pp. 166–167), and Wenzel (1975, pp. 66–103.

19. See W. Edwards (1966), Novick and Jackson (1974), and Wenzel (1975, pp. 36–51), and also some references listed in Chapter Four, especially Huber (1974a).

20. Concerning the magnitude of computations needed in IE, Verhelst (1974, p. 158) proves that for m states and n actions, no more than $n\,m$ strategies (not n^m) must be evaluated.

21. See further Welke (1975a, p. 7) and the mathematical treatise by Ho and Chu (1974).

22. See also J. C. Emery (1969, pp. 89–91) and (1971, p. 6), Welke (1975a, p. 7), and Wenzel (1975, pp. 53–55, 116).

23. See also Jewett (1972b).

24. Aykac and Brumat (1977), J. C. Emery (1969, pp. 67–88), Grum et al. (1977), Jagetia (1975), Kriebel (1968), MacCrimmon (1974), McGuire and Radner (1972), Merkhofer (1977), Mock (1971), Olsen (1971), Schoute (1978), and Vazsonyi (1976). Note that Huang et al. (1975) give a list with fifty-four references. References to the German literature can be found in Bamberg et al. (1976).

CHAPTER **EIGHT**

INTRODUCTION

Information economics (IE), discussed at length in the preceding chapter, is the only discipline explicitly focusing on the central issue of this book, the economic benefits of an information system (IS). Nevertheless several theories and techniques touch upon similar issues:

Control theory;

System dynamics (SD), which is related to control theory;

Simulation besides SD simulation studies;

Gaming, a simulation extension including human "players"; and

Ad hoc studies, which use linear programming (LP), the Shannon-Weaver entropy concept, empirical methods (field tests, prototypes) and so on.

In order to improve the continuity of the present chapter, each of these approaches will be illustrated by just a few examples in the main text; the appendices contain an exhaustive survey of additional examples. Moreover the chapter is restricted to brief summaries of the few examples that illustrate the great variety of relevant theories and techniques. In this way the reader, it is hoped, will get the flavor of the approach under discussion; for details consult the original publications.

CONTROL THEORY

Control theory focuses on the dynamic behavior of systems, and studies such phenomena as oscillations. Control theory highlights the role of feedback and feedforward information. *Negative feedback* means that information on a variable is compared to some desired goal value; and if a deviation exists between the actual and the goal value, corrective action is taken. *Feedforward* means that predictions or forecasts, such as sales forecasts, are made. The advantage of control theory over techniques like simulation is that control theory provides a framework and conclusions independent of specific numerical values. The disadvantage of control theory is that it must introduce drastic simplifications in order to keep the mathematical problems within limits. Hence its models are usually continuous; i.e., a very aggregated view of the world is maintained. The models are also linear in order to simplify analytical solutions (using Laplace transformations). Steady-state solutions are relatively easy to obtain so that transient behavior tends to be neglected. Deterministic models are simpler to solve than stochastic models. Hence bias but not stochastic noise is examined in the study by Politzer and Wilmès (1977), discussed in the next paragraph. Delays are modeled through, e.g., *first order exponential delay* functions. The effects of such delays are illustrated in Fig. 8.1: in the upper part the input shows a temporary increase (pulse), and in the lower part the input shows a permanent increase (ramp function). The reaction of the output depends on the order of the delay function as the figure illustrates. These delay concepts correspond to a *continuous* view of the world, like that maintained in electrical engineering. For a critical discussion of such delay functions (used also in system dynamics) see Riethmüller and Schreiber (1977). The various sources of delays presented in the framework of Chapter Six would require noncontinuous, nonlinear, stochastic models if one wished to remain close to real life. So control theory is far removed from the mental models used by system analysts and by most users in data processing: these people think in terms of transactions (say, orders), periodic reports, exception reporting, system flowcharts, and multiple copies of records. Possibly at higher levels of decision making a more aggregated view, as proposed by control theory, becomes more appropriate. A brief, nonmathematical discussion of control theory can be found in Van Aken (1978, p. 82). Remember that control theory was also briefly mentioned in the preceding chapter.

Politzer and Wilmès (1977) apply control theory to the evaluation of a MIS. They restrict their study to a classical model for planning inventories and production. Originated by Holt et al. (1960), this model, known as the HMMS model, assumes simple quadratic cost relationships.[1] (In practice, costs behave differently:

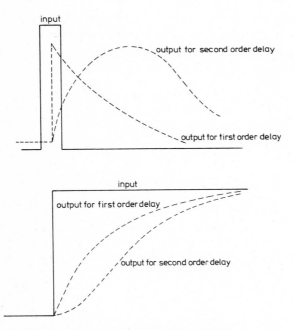

FIGURE 8-1.   Delays of First and Second Order.

negative inventory may incur severe stockout penalties, positive inventory may lead to linear costs, and production costs involve fixed set-up costs.) The authors derive a steady-state solution based on a continuous version of the HMMS model, and they study the effects of (exponential) "delay" and bias. Gross value reacts asymetrically to multiplicative bias; i.e., the effect of overestimation differs from that of under-estimation. Delay is found to have an optimal value larger than zero; i.e., on-line systems do not necessarily yield higher gross benefits. However, remember that these conclusions are derived under a number of restrictive assumptions.

If the control theoretic model cannot be solved analytically, one may resort to simulation, especially system dynamics simulation.

SYSTEM DYNAMICS

System dynamics (SD) was originally known as Forrester's industrial dynamics [see Forrester (1961)]. Its philosophy is that each sociotechnical system can be considered a dynamic system with (negative) *feedback*: if deviations are detected between the system output (response) and a normative value (such as a budget norm), one or more input variables are changed so that, it is hoped, the deviations diminish (see also the previous section). It takes time to collect and process data on the output, to compare the resulting information to the norm, and to adapt the decision variables (see also Chapter Six). These *time lags* make the model dynamic. Delays in information transmission may cause fluctuations within the company in contrast to externally caused business cycles.

The computer language that has been developed especially for the SD approach is DYNAMO, but other languages like FORTRAN or the simulation language CSMP can also be used.

There has been quite some controversy about the usefulness of the SD methodology. SD may tackle any problem, ranging from that of some subsystem within a company to world problems such as world energy resources. The approach does not pretend to give exact numerical predictions; but it does show the system's *dynamic properties*, e.g., oscillations.[2] Thissen (1978) examines a variety of techniques for improving the understanding of complex SD models. Nordhaus (1973) emphasizes that in SD, as opposed to traditional econometrics, relationships and variables are not based on empirical data, and that changing an assumption may drastically affect the model's outcome.[3]

As an evaluation tool, not as a framework, SD may be characterized as *simulation* based on a set of recursive (nonsimultaneous) difference equations with variable coefficients or "rates." Besides rates the framework distinguishes "levels": the levels represent the state of the system at a particular point of time; the rates specify the rate of flow between levels during a small time interval, DT. For instance, following the SD convention of representing the points of time t and $t + 1$ by J and K, respectively, with time unit DT, one obtains for the inventory level

$$INV.K = INV.J + DT. (PRODRATE.JK - SALERATE.JK) \qquad (8.1)$$

where PRODRATE.*JK* denotes the (known) production rate during the interval *JK*, and SALERATE.*JK* denotes the sales rate during that interval.

Rates and levels have data images that are inputs to decision functions. These decision functions can change rate values. A policy specifies which actual values are compared to which norms, and how corrective decisions are taken to diminish deviations between norm and realization. The SD framework distinguishes six inter-related networks of flows: materials, capital goods, personnel, money, orders, and information.

Compared to other simulation approaches, SD has the advantage of being more than a technique. However, the very advantage of SD's being a framework means that the modeler has to adopt a world view (with levels and rates) that is not spontaneous, but requires learning (or indoctrination?). For instance, a discrete-event simulation of a queuing system is a direct representation of the spontaneous, intuitive way such a system would be described by "anybody"; see Chapter Three. Unfortunately, such a discrete-event description is too detailed for "large" systems, which need a more aggregated view. A framework to realize this need is provided by SD. Note that even if one is willing to adopt the SD view of the world, mastering the SD technique takes quite some practicing. This is the *art* of model building. It is interesting to notice that Roberts (1978) reports how SD was taught to elementary school pupils.

Of special interest is the SD concept of *delay*, which is the SD analogue of the timeliness attribute discussed at length in Chapter Six. That chapter distinguished the update processing delay P, the update interval I, the retrieval delay R, and the decision delay D. These delays may have stochastic magnitudes, and play different roles in periodic as opposed to unscheduled decision making. Unfortunately, these delays are hard to translate into the SD framework. In SD there are delays of first order, second order, etc. as in the usual control engineering models; see Fig. 8.1. Riethmüller and Schreiber (1977) provide a critical discussion of such delay functions. These delay concepts correspond to a continuous world view like that in electrical engineering. A discrete view is more compatible with the MIS world view. More detailed summaries of SD from an MIS perspective can be found in Welke (1977b) and Verhelst (1974, pp. 176–190).[4]

Although a great many studies have been performed using the SD methodology, only a few of these studies concern the explicit study of information systems. Two SD studies in the area of information systems are summarized here. More SD studies are presented in Appendix 8.1. Included also is a series of studies performed at the Dutch Philips company because the series was strongly influenced by the SD framework.

Forrester (1961) employs a model for the following multiechelon production and inventory system. Customer orders are received by retailers, who reorder at "distributors" (wholesalers), who in turn place replenishment orders with the factory warehouse, which is supplied by the factory production department. One of the many topics studied by Forrester is a change in the delay of order processing. (Remember the comments on the nature of delays in the SD models.) Faster information processing results in smaller fluctuations of production at the factory in response to sales fluctuations. This positive benefit, however, is only small. Note that a second type of change is in the speed with which sections (echelons) of the model react to order fluctuations by adapting inventories, i.e., the speed of reaction to deviations between the desired and the actual inventories. The faster the inventories are adapted in response to a 10 percent increase in customer orders, the larger the factory production fluctuations are. This second type of change concerns not the timeliness dimension of information but the kind of decision rule. Whereas information economics assumes that the decision maker follows optimal decision rules, Forrester's work emphasizes that actual decision rules may amplify fluctuations in dynamic systems. The determination of optimal decision rules is a subject in itself:

control engineering. A truly optimal solution of a complicated system needs to acknowledge interdependencies between optimal IS design and optimal decision rules (see the preceding chapter). The relationship between information systems and decision systems is also briefly discussed in Forrester (1968a; pp. 601–603). More information attributes are studied in the following publication.

C. V. Swanson (1971) investigates the effects of "error" (variance in the terminology of Chapter Six), "distortion" (bias), "delay" (processing delay P), and "sampling" (update interval I). Personnel, production, and inventory are controlled by using information on sales and inventory. Swanson finds that delay has the largest effect and that error has the smallest effect. His conclusions, however, are not based on solid statistical methods: only two simulation runs per case; no interactions measured. For more detailed results refer to the original paper. The framework of Chapter Six allows translation of the terminologies used by different authors into a common terminology, which facilitates comparison of different studies.

At the Dutch *Philips* organization[5] under the acronym IPSO (Initiating Production by Sales Orders) a series of studies was performed on the effects of information delays (comparable to the processing delay P of Chapter Six). Moreover, the study examined the "scope" of the IS. In a chain or network of production processes, a process may be provided with information on the demand from the next process; or this information may be augmented with marketing information, the demand by the company's ultimate customers. Extending the scope of the database to make both "local" data and "global" data available dampens the oscillations in the company's inventories and activities; remember the discussion on scope in Chapter Six. Note that this series of studies combines a number of techniques and ideas ("models"), which were strongly influenced by system dynamics: the SD simulation experiments were combined with analytical results derived for simplified models, e.g., control theory models. Analysis suggested which SD models to simulate, and simulation results were used to test analytical approximations.

A major advantage of system dynamics is the usefulness of the SD framework in the derivation of optimal or satisficing *decision rules*. Especially when the MIS is integrated, relatively large systems, such as integrated production plus inventory systems, must be managed. Remember that the decision rules that Holt et al. (1960) derived for such integrated systems also comprised a "normative" value for inventories and production size. Moreover the HMMS model is strictly periodic just as SD models are.

In conclusion, SD is a method extremely popular with some people. It is much more than a technique; it is a world view. SD is best known for its study of large-scale systems: world dynamics, urban dynamics, etc. For such large systems an aggregated view seems necessary. At such high levels of aggregation ("the" pollution, "the" world consumption) continuous models may be adequate: flows, rates, exponential delays. At the level of MIS, however, more detailed models with discrete events, aperiodic decisions, and realistic representations of information attributes are preferable. A technique permitting such a level of detail is simulation—and its extension, gaming.

SIMULATION

This section surveys a number of simulation experiments with information systems. It is assumed that a basic knowledge of the simulation technique has been gained by the reader from one of the numerous textbooks on simulation.[7] Here the following terminology is used. *Simulation* means that a mathematical model of a system is solved by "experimentation." Hence, the mathematical model is solved not by mathematical analysis such as differential and integral calculus, nor by numerical methods such as linear programming. Instead numbers are substituted for the parameters and variables, and the model's response is computed, and so on. In this way the (dynamic) behavior of the system can be followed over time. If some of the input values are sampled by means of random numbers, the simulation is a *Monte Carlo* or stochastic simulation. An example is provided by the simulation of a queuing or waiting-line system; see Chapter Three. If some input variables of the simulation model are decided by human participants or "players," the simulation is a *gaming* or user-machine simulation in contrast to a pure machine (computer) simulation, in which all variables are determined by a computer program. Well-known gaming examples are business and military games meant for training. The section on gaming will present games played for research purposes.

The *structure* of simulation models can differ in the following respects. The system may be modeled by *difference equations* so that at *equispaced* points of time the state of the system is computed. An example is a *corporate simulation* model based on balance and profit and loss account relationships such as

$$\text{INVENTORY}_{t+1} = \text{INVENTORY}_t + \text{PURCHASES}_{\tau+1} - \text{SALES}_{\tau+1} \quad (8.2)$$

where $\tau + 1$ denotes the period of time between the points of time t and $(t + 1)$. Slightly more complicated difference equations are used in system dynamics: a set of recursive difference equations with variable coefficients (rates). In *discrete event* simulation the model represents the real-world system in great detail insofar as individual events are represented. An "event" is a change in the system's state, say, the arrival of a customer. Simulated time is not cut into slices; instead the program jumps from one event to the next, most imminent event. Many languages, e.g., GPSS and SIMSCRIPT, have been developed for this approach.

The simulation technique permits models that are much more realistic than the analytical models used in information economics and control theory. The models employed in simulation are also more realistic than "simulation" models of system dynamics. (In the present section the term simulation excludes SD models.) Moreover, the user—the client of the model builder—can understand a simulation model better. A disadvantage is that much effort is required to build and run a simulation model; but the responses are valid, strictly speaking, only for the specified values of the input variables and parameters. Chapter Five, however, explained how statistical techniques can be used to generalize simulation results.[7] In the simulation case study of the next chapter some of these problems will also be discussed. The various types of simulation have been discussed in more detail elsewhere.[8]

The following summary of some simulation experiments on the value of information includes such classical studies as Bonini (1963), and Boyd and Krasnow (1963), plus a recent simulation-oriented framework, developed by Welke (1975b), for the study of information systems. For fuller accounts the reader should consult the original publications.

Bonini's (1963) stochastic simulation model of a hypothetical company is based on the *behavioral theory of the firm*. In this approach the classical economic theory of the firm is extended with organizational and behavioral concepts. Bonini emphasizes the information and decision subsystems of the firm. In his model decisions are made not by a single, central decision maker but by *multiple*, decentralized decision makers. Decision makers do not optimize, but they try to satisfy aspiration levels by using heuristic decision rules.[9] In his model feedforward, as opposed to feedback, plays an important role: profit is forecast and if a nonsatisficing value is predicted, control variables such as prices are changed.[10] Bonini experiments with eight factors: two factors reflect the company's environment (the market), four factors reflect its decision rules (both parametric and structural changes), and two factors reflect its information system. Of the latter two factors one factor determines whether the general sales manager had information on the inventory status; the other factor concerns a change in the weights placed on past versus current information. In summary, Bonini (1963, p. 75) experiments with the following factors:

1. external environment: variability of demand;

2. external environment: growth pattern of demand;

3. decision rule 1: parametric change considered;

4. decision rule 2: parametric change;

5. decison rule 3: parametric change;

6. decision rule 4: last-in-first-out versus average cost valuation;

7. information "link": knowledge of inventory position by sales manager; and

8. information "content": emphasis on current versus past information.

Note that in the first part of his book Bonini (1963, pp. 23–24, 58) describes changes in his information system in much more sweeping terms:

"timing": update interval I in periodic decision making, and I plus processing delay in aperiodic decision making;

"content": scope, aggregation, report mode, format; and

"links": who receives what information in the decentralized decision system.

One could argue that Bonini's eight factors, including the factors 7 and 8, determine changes not in the IS but in the decision system; remember Fig. 2.1.

In his simulation Bonini considers not only main effects but also interactions among factors, plus the effects of the initial conditions.[11] (Remember that the concept "interaction" was explained in Fig. 5.10 and Eq. (5.22); see also Exercise 4 of the present chapter.) As output variables Bonini uses price, inventory, cost, sales, profit, and "pressure" exercised by a higher manager on a lower manager. These output variables are measured by their averages, standard deviations, and trends. Each simulation run extends over 108 periods (months). He analyzes these outputs through analysis of variance (ANOVA) and tests main effects and two-factor interactions for significance. This is one of the few simulation studies in which interactions among factors are statistically tested and if found to be significant, are explained on hindsight. It is hard to summarize Bonini's results in a few words because the output of the experiment consists of six variables (profit, etc.), each characterized by three measures (average, standard deviation, and trend) and evaluated for main effects, two-factor interactions, and starting conditions: in all there are eight main effects, twenty-eight interactions, and three "initialization" effects. Suffice it to say that Bonini's two so-called information factors, "knowledge of inventory" and "past versus current information," are not significant (considering all variables, measures, main effects, and interactions). The effects of Bonini's factor 6, last-in-first-out versus average cost valuation of inventory, are also analyzed by Bruns (1963) and Ijiri et al. (1970). Gilman (1973) extends Bonini's model and uses it to study the effects of information delays (see Appendix 8.2).

Boyd and Krasnow (1963) perform an interesting discrete-event simulation study on the timeliness of information in the context of a hypothetical manufacturing company. In the terminology of Chapter Six they investigate periodic decision making, the decision interval T being larger in tactical decisions than in operational decisions. The decision making delay D is included in T (smaller T values are combined with smaller D values). They also vary the update processing delay P. The delays affect the speed with which decisions can react to environmental changes, such as changes in demand. This delayed reaction leads to fluctuations in both profit and physical variables like inventory. Reductions in T (and D) and in P improve profit significantly. Note that if one varies the number of "sensors" in their model, the Boyd and Krasnow study can easily be extended to examine the "scope" of the information system.

Welke (1975b) criticizes the ad hoc character of simulation studies like those of Bonini (1963), and Boyd and Krasnow (1963). Welke proposes a general framework for the simulation modeling of information systems. This framework is provided by his system called CYSDEM. On the basis of Welke (1977b), CYSDEM can be described as a framework and methodology for information system description and evaluation from a user view rather than from a data processing (DP) view. The framework can be applied to a particular system, in order to generate a descriptive model, which can next be evaluated by using a (process-oriented) discrete-event simulation package.

The framework distinguishes

data,

processes, and

data links.

Data are further partitioned: periodic data are data accumulated over a time interval, several intervals becoming a file; transaction data are data images of events; and constant data include customer addresses and procedures. Events create transaction data, which move along specific paths and queue at various nodes or processes. Processes can be either user activities, such as decisions, or DP processes that process data of an activity, e.g., generate forecasts or monitor for exception reporting. User processes need data as input, e.g., data on machine breakdowns and on orders. User processes also create data images of their output, e.g., a production report. As far as the dynamics of the processes are concerned, a process may be periodic (say, weekly scheduling) or may be triggered by events such as the arrival of a transaction.[12] A DP process, called data link in CYSDEM, "massages" the data needed by user processes. For instance, DP may aggregate data or perform a forecast. Data links are the surrogates (models) for the more elaborate data processing sequences (such as collecting, recording, storing, and displaying) found in most information system descriptions. Different types of data links are used for the different types of data. These processes may show distortion and delay.

The model resulting from the application of the CYSDEM framework to a specific system is represented by special symbols adapted from the IBM flowcharting template. (Note that schematic representations are found also in GPSS and system dynamics.) The resulting schematic outline and a set of accompanying forms elicit the specification of all those details needed for the simulation of an information system.

As mentioned, CYSDEM is both a framework and a simulation package. The choice between using the simulation package or programming one's own simulator (in, say, GPSS or FORTRAN) reduces to the familiar problem of choosing among general purpose languages, simulation languages, and simulation packages: one must weigh the time to learn a language, flexibility of language, availability of compilers, core requirements, and so on. Like many other simulation packages, CYSDEM provides extensive error checking and output facilities (graphs and statistics such as averages). CYSDEM uses FORTRAN as its host language.

As an example of its use, CYSDEM was applied to a simple inventory system with delays and inaccuracies. The outputs—inventory and backorder levels—were subjected to a formal statistical analysis: ANOVA, followed by pairwise difference tests.[13] Delays showed significant average effects, but accuracy did not; inaccuracy did increase the variability of outputs.

GAMING

The previous section defined gaming or user-machine simulation as simulation in which one or more input variables are determined by human participants or "players." Several types of games may be distinguished:

Computerized versus noncomputerized games. Examples of noncomputerized games are entertaining games like Monopoly and chess, and also certain educational games used in urban planning and international policy evaluation. In the present chapter all games are computerized: the player gets input (information) from the computer, makes decisions that are next processed by the computer, and so on.

Competitive games versus games against nature. Many games have a competitive aspect: the outcomes (payoffs) depend not only on one's own decisions but also on other players' decisions. The players may engage in pure competition or may collude. In games against nature there are no opponents trying to counteract the player's actions. Nevertheless, the payoffs of an action remain uncertain or risky.

Dynamic versus static games. A static game may be played during more than a single period, but the payoffs do not depend on the state of the system in previous periods. Nevertheless, dynamic elements can creep into a static game as the player may learn during the game.

Training versus research games. Games may be used for training purposes as are most management or business games. In that case there is less interest in, say, the absolute value of the resulting total profit. The games discussed in the present section, however, are played mainly for the benefit of the researcher, not for that of the players.

Compare gaming to pure computer simulation including system dynamics simulation, which were discussed in the two preceding sections. The relative advantage of gaming is its *behavioral realism:* decision makers may have multiple—possibly vague—goals, may use heuristic—possibly inconsistent—decision rules, may form competing or colluding teams, and may show learning behavior or fatigue and boredom. The disadvantages of gaming, compared to pure machine simulation, are *lack of experimental control* and certain *practical nuisances:* if the purpose of the game is to reach general conclusions (rather than to train people), human participation creates much noise. For instance, players can show inferior performance even when they are supplied with good information because they lack "feeling," get bored, or are confronted with superior opponents. General conclusions require repeated runs with the game, but repeated runs are expensive and may even be impossible because of lack of players and of computer time. Moreover, repeated runs are not completely comparable because the players show learning or fatigue. This brief discussion is meant not to disqualify gaming as a useful research instrument, but to warn against possible pitfalls.[14] General references on gaming can be found in the references.[15] Consider next a number of gaming experiments aimed at the evaluation of information.

Mock (1969) and (1973a) studies the effects of timeliness, feedback, and behavioral factors in a sequence of experiments with a business game. (See also Fellingham et al. (1976) in Appendix 8.2 on simulation.) In this game the players' decision variables are production volume, advertising, and materials input. The players' goal is profit maximization. The system modeled by the game is very simple compared to many well-known games, such as the IBM game used in the next chapter: in Mock's game results per period are independent of previous periods (static system), and the exact structure and parameter values are communicated to the players (interwoven with verbal descriptions in the economics jargon). Consequently, a player with sufficient mathematical skills and time could compute the exact optimal solution yielding maximum profit.[16] Mock applies formal statistical tests to analyze main effects and interactions.[17] Mock (1973a) reports that *timely* information gives significantly more profit. As Jensen (1969) suggests, Mock actually investigates accuracy, not timeliness: under one information system the players know the price for the next period; under the other information system the players have only delayed information and must forecast the price, a situation that creates inaccuracy (see also Exercise 7). Mock's "feedback" attribute can be related to "exception reporting" discussed in Chapter Six. The effects of "timeliness" and "feedback" are of the same magnitudes. To prepare exception reporting budgets, players require significantly more decision-making time, a component discussed in Chapter Six.[18] In the delayed-information case players were expected to need more decision-making time because forecasts had to be prepared, but the effect is actually insignificant.[19] Observe that Uretsky (1969) raises a number of methodological questions regarding Mock's gaming experiment. This game is still in use for further studies concentrating on behavioral aspects; see Vasarhelyi and Mock (1977).

The *Minnesota experiments,* another group of gaming experiments, were performed at the University of Minnesota's MIS Research Center from 1970 to 1975. As an example Appendix 8.3 summarizes one of the most interesting experiments, Senn (1973). The Minnesota experiments investigate relationships among

the information system itself,

the decision maker (psychological characteristics, experience), and

the decision environment (operational versus strategic, etc.).

Dickson et al. (1977) summarize nine different gaming experiments. Part of their summary is reproduced and adapted in Table 8.1: decision quality reflects per-

TABLE 8.1.   The Minnesota Experiments. *

| Experi- menter(s) | Vehicle | Subjects | Independent Variables | | Dependent Variables Reference |
			Personal Characteristics	System Characteristics	
Chervany and Dickson (1974)	Production simulator	Graduate business students	Aptitude: quant. vs. verbal	Form: raw vs. summarized data	Decision quality Decision time Decision confidence
Kozar (1972)	Production simulator— CRT	Graduate business students	Aptitude: quant. vs. verbal	Medium: paper vs. CRT	Decision quality Decision time Decision confidence
Smith (1975)	Production simulator— CRT	Under- graduate business students	Attributes: high vs. low experience high vs. low knowledge of area	Form: database capability vs. none	Decision quality Decision time User evaluation
Barkin (1974)	Production simulator— timesharing	Under- graduate business students	Cognitive style	Form: information high- lighted vs. informa- tion distributed	Data selection
Senn (1973)	Procurement decision simulator— CRT	Purchas- ing agents	Attribute: large vs. small organization	Form: summary vs. detail data Medium: CRT vs. paper	System utilization Decision time Decision confidence Decision quality
Wynne and Dickson (1975)	Commodity simulator— timesharing	Middle managers	Individual differences: high vs. low defensiveness high vs. low need achievement high vs. low facilitat- ing anxiety cognitive style	Goal setting: presence vs. absence	Decision quality Computer perceptions
Benbasat and Schroeder (1975)	Inventory simulator— CRT	Graduate business students	Attribute: high vs. low knowledge of area	Form: tabular vs. graphic decision aids vs. no aids exception vs. full reports necessary reports vs. overload reports	Decision quality Decision time System utilization
Chervany and Sauter (1974)	Risk analysis simulator— timesharing	Middle managers and systems analysts	Attributes: manager vs. systems analyst experience risk preference computer/data attitudes	Decision aids: deterministic vs. probabilistic	Alternative selected Estimated outcomes Decision confidence User evaluation
Schroeder and Benbasat (1975)	Inventory simulator— CRT	Under- graduate business	Variability in the decision environment at levels: high, medium, and low		System utilization Decision confidence

*From Gary W. Dickson, James A. Senn, and Norman L. Chervany, 1977, Research in Management Information Systems: The Minnesota Experiments, *Management Science,* **23** (9): 918. Reprinted by permission.

formance criteria such as cost; decision time denotes the decision-making delay, also discussed in Chapter Six; decision confidence represents the players' confidence in their decisions; the risk analysis simulator, listed under vehicle, concerns a one-shot decision; and the other simulations concern repetitive decisions. For a discussion of all the experiments of Table 8.1, the reader is referred to the summaries in Dickson et al. (1977) or to the original reports listed in the references.[20] Taken together, the whole set of Minnesota experiments shows that effects do occur from changing the experimental factors, information system, decision maker, and environment. Unfortunately, no simple general relationships can be formulated. In general, such a lack of definitive conclusions might be explained by two basic causes:

> *Possible deficiencies in the experiments' design.* Design deficiency is a technical issue comprising runlength determination, randomization, and so on; see Kleijnen (1975b).

> *Too many relevant factors in the real-life systems.* Real-life systems may be affected by so many factors that no experimental design can control all factors in an experiment of practical scope. Hence, the experimental noise that remains makes final conclusions difficult to attain. See also the next chapter.

Appendix 8.3 surveys several more gaming experiments, including games performed at the RAND Corporation and at Philips.

LINEAR PROGRAMMING

Specific issues can be solved by specific techniques. For example, optimization under constraints can be approached by linear programming (LP).

Itami's (1972) interesting doctoral dissertation uses a linear programming framework in which uncertainty is reflected by the *stochastic* character of the LP parameters. He concentrates on an LP formulation for the "newsboy" inventory problem[21], presented in the preceding chapter; but Itami adds a production constraint and linear costs for shortage or inventory carrying. His model is dynamic: he assumes that *during* a period information on the true demand e becomes available so that the production a for the remainder of that period can be adapted. For this model the time at which information becomes available is considered a production factor (remember the discussion on production factors in Chapter Five).[22] Itami then derives various *laws of diminishing returns*. In other words, the faster the information becomes available, the better; however, the marginal benefits are decreasing; see Exercise 9. The benefits of information can also be realized by making the company more flexible. In Itami's simple model flexibility increases as the capacity constraint becomes less restrictive; i.e., in the restriction $a \leq d$, the parameter d increases. Itami derives a law of diminishing marginal rate of substitution between the two "production factors," information timing and production flexibility.[23] He extends these results from the simple newsboy problem to general LP models with stochastic parameters. Using an information economics framework, Itami examines the optimal values for the update intervals (called I in Chapter Six) of periodic reports and finds that the optimal intervals are not of constant lengths.[24] He further discovers a counterintuitive result concerning the degree of uncertainty in the LP parameters: depending on where in the LP model the parameters occur, increased uncertainty might increase the expected benefits.[25] Note that a revised edition of this dissertation is Itami (1977).

J.C. Emery (1969) discusses the effects of forecasting errors on machine scheduling costs. He formulates the scheduling problem as an LP model. As one knows, the optimal solution of an LP model changes only if the prices exceed a critical ratio.[26] More detailed LP examples can be found in Rappaport (1970, pp. 176–182). LP has the advantage of being a familiar technique, for which a variety of software packages are available. Postoptimal analysis provides interesting sensitivity results. Unfortunately, many MIS problems cannot be formulated as LP problems.

INVENTORY MODELS

Verhelst (1974) studies the benefits of better information in inventory management. He restricts his study to the time dimension of information within the context of a simplified inventory system: a single article, no stockouts, and constant lead times. He includes the data-processing costs of inventory control, and also considers "inventories of money."[27] Remember that Appendix 2.2 discussed in some detail the value of computers in inventory management.

J.C. Emery (1969) discusses the effects of forecasting errors on inventory costs (besides those effects on machine scheduling costs discussed in the preceding section). In the familiar square-root order-quantity model, inventory cost is highly insensitive to errors in the estimated parameters. More specifically, if forecasted demand is in error by a factor k, cost increases by a factor $(k^{1/2} + k^{-1/2})/2$. Like LP, inventory models are familiar to many MIS users, but not all their problems concern inventory management.

ENTROPY

The *entropy* concept can be found in the *Shannon-Weaver* communication theory. The entropy H of n events i occurring with probability p_i is defined as

$$H = - \sum_{i=1}^{n} p_i \log p_i \tag{8.3}$$

so that H measures the degree of uncertainty. For instance, uncertainty is at its maximum when each event is equally likely: p_i is a constant $1/n$. Uncertainty is at its minimum when one particular event, say j, is absolutely certain: $p_j = 1$ and $p_i = 0$ ($i \neq j$); see Ying (1977, pp. 2–3) and Exercise 11.

Lev (1968) uses the entropy concept to investigate *aggregation* of information in financial statements such as balance sheets. He argues intuitively—and then proceeds to use the entropy as criterion to prove this intuition—as follows: "First aggregation is regarded as more desirable when two items combined form a smaller fraction of a related total (e.g., total assets, total expenses, etc.) Second, aggregation is more desirable when the two items are less equal to each other."[28] The second rule may be phrased as follows: if an item is small relative to another item, the first item may be included in the second item.

A criticism of Lev's analysis is that the entropy approach, although related to the Bayesian approach used in information economics, neglects what can be done with the information: the actions and their consequences (as shown in a payoff table) are missing in the entropy analysis. For a critique on the Shannon-Weaver approach refer to Marschak (1971, p. 212) and Stamper (1971).

EMPIRICAL STUDIES

The studies above were theoretical studies (inspired, it is hoped, by practical problems). This section will summarize some empirical work.

Zani (1970) reports on an *empirical* investigation that compares six companies in the wholesale liquor industry. Three of these companies use real-time computer services. Contrary to expectations the real-time users show lower computer costs and no improvements in inventories, accounts receivable, and customer service. The explanation is that management did not use the real-time possibilities at all.

Lanahan (1973) discusses a practical application in steel manufacturing and demonstrates the importance of timely and accurate information. He feels that good quality information is more important than sophisticated modeling.

Kriebel (1969) studies "four commercially available computer systems" instead of such abstract attributes as timeliness and accuracy. He makes a study of the interactions between the decision and the information subsystems. Instead of investigating a real-life organization, he uses the model introduced by Holt et al. (1960) for planning production, inventories, and work force. Changing the IS changes the cost parameters, which in turn affect the decision parameters. Note that in this way only parametric changes, not structural changes, can result.

The empirical approach encompasses case studies, field tests, pilot projects, prototypes (small scale versions of the real information system), and sample surveys. More details can be found in the references.[29] The main disadvantage of these empirical methods is that lack of control over the experimental factors makes general conclusions hard to obtain. The usefulness of simulation and gaming, compared to empirical methods such as case studies and field tests, is discussed by Van Horn (1973) and Dickson et al. (1977). These authors strongly support gaming as a means for MIS research. [Remember that Uretsky (1969) raises a number of methological questions regarding the gaming experiments conducted by Mock (1969). Fisher (1971, pp. 286–301) discusses the pros and cons of gaming in the context of military systems analyses. Refer also to the discussion at the beginning of the section on gaming.]

EPILOGUE

Appendix 8.4 summarizes some studies that do not fit well into the framework of this chapter, but are nevertheless of interest. Several more studies on information systems can be found in the references.[30] Altogether, many studies on the economic benefits of information systems are presented in the present chapter. The selection was based on a thorough, but necessarily incomplete search of the literature. The selection was subjective: publications considered of less relevance were excluded. For instance, not presented was Gregory and Van Horn's very gross evaluation of accuracy and delay in information systems.[31]

The attempt has been to present the chaotic variety of studies in an organized way. The various theories and techniques were briefly evaluated in passing. An overall evaluation will be presented in the final chapter.

The next chapter combines a number of ideas contained in the preceding text. The chapter studies the economic effects of information accuracy in a system created by a well-known IBM *management game*. This game, however, is played not by human participants but by computerized "players" (robots); thus the game is a pure machine *simulation*. The decision rules of these robots include feedbacks and feedforwards as suggested by *control theory* and *system dynamics.* Some decisions are based on familiar *inventory models.* One will see that the different effects that the same magnitude of accuracy can have on the economic performance depend on whether the inaccuracy concerns the production cost or the sales information. *Information economics* emphasizes that decisions may indeed show different sensitivities to information. Remember further that Chapter Seven characterized the experiment of Chapter Nine in terms of concepts of information economics.

APPENDIX 8.1: SYSTEM DYNAMICS STUDIES

Wilmès (1973) examines the same information attributes that C.V. Swanson (1971) examined, plus the "quantity of information," which was called "scope" in Chapter Six. Wilmès simulates a transportation control system. No interactions among information attributes are examined. Wilmès uses both deterministic and stochastic system dynamics models.

    Millen (1972) studies the effects of combining the usual management information system with a "process control" information system, i.e., a system controlling a physical production process, such as that in a chemical plant or a steel mill. Besides this "scope," he examines information transmission delays, comparable to the update interval *I*. In the integrated system the response is "remarkably insensitive" to the delays.

    Weil (1971) also uses system dynamics, but actually he concentrates on the effects of decision rules, not on information quality.

APPENDIX 8.2: SIMULATION STUDIES

Note that more detailed summaries of many of the following studies can be found in Welke (1977b).

    Gilman (1973) extends *Bonini's* model and uses it to study the effects of delay in information. Gilman distinguishes three components in this delay:

delays in the receipt of information,

delays in the information dissemination throughout the organization, and

delays in the implementation of the resulting decisions.

As criterion he uses the effect on discounted profits over a time span of two years, a month being the basic period. The value of information decreases with delays in its receipt and implementation, at least for information on some events. This decrease is not a nicely behaving function of the magnitude of the delay. The dissemination of information has no significant effect.

    Verhelst (1974) also uses stochastic simulation of the time-slicing (difference equation) type to study the information processing delay (P in Chapter Six), update interval (I), accuracy, degree of exception reporting, and level of detail. The system studied is rather abstract, and models the detection of trends by a decision maker who could take corrective action. Verhelst finds that the update interval I has an optimum value, which, unlike the delay P, is not equal to the minimum value. His conclusions are based on detailed analyses of many simulation runs. Because no statistical design or analysis is performed, statistical errors of type I (type α) and type II (type β) are not controlled. The simulation results are summarized in Verhelst

(1974, pp. 349–350). The total voluminous (400 page!) study is summarized in Verhelst (1974, pp. 358–371).

Fellingham et al. (1976) reports on simulation experiments with a model extensively used by Mock et al. in a series of *gaming* experiments aimed at evaluating the benefits of different information systems (see the gaming section of the present chapter). The difference between Fellingham et al. and Mock et al. is that the former authors replace human decision makers with an optimizing algorithm. In both approaches managers—whether human or computerized—must decide on the quantity produced, the advertising amount, and the material input. Environmental factors, such as demand and input factor prices, fluctuate randomly. The model is exercised over fifteen time periods. The manager's goal is profit maximization. Two basic types of ISs are compared: systems with real-time error-free information versus systems with lagged information. Moreover, Fellingham et al. (1976) investigate the sensitivity of the model to its starting values (initial conditions). They find that the starting values of the simulation experiment have no significant effect on the gross value of a better IS. The better IS does have significant effects on the average profits. For comments on these experiments see the section on gaming because the major thrust of the research with this model is in the form of gaming rather than pure machine simulation. Refer also to Exercise 12.

APPENDIX 8.3: GAMING STUDIES

Senn (1973) uses a game in which players act as purchasers for a company. The criterion variables are purchasing cost, decision-making delay, and players' confidence in their solutions. The factors studied in the experiment are line printer versus CRT (cathode ray tube), level of detail, complexity of the decision, and organizational factors (see the next paragraph). Senn finds that in the line printer/batch mode, users ask for more reports just to ensure having all data that might ultimately be used. No effect, however, is found for the purchasing cost criterion. The decision-making delay is significantly affected by the two information attributes—detail versus summary, and printer versus CRT—because less time is needed in the case of summarized and CRT-displayed data.

The factor "line printer versus CRT" is confounded with (but not identical to) "batch versus on-line"; see Senn (1973, pp. 53–54, 83). The factors "complexity" and "organizational elements" are used as so-called blocking factors, a statistical design technique; Senn (1973, p. 109). The experiment's design might have been improved by introducing one factor "detail versus summary" and another factor "printer versus CRT"; but Senn (1973, p. 111) uses a different approach. Senn (1973, pp. 106–155) does apply analysis of variance, including an analysis of possible interactions.

I.K. Cohen and Van Horn (1965) give a detailed report on a practical study in which simulation, gaming, and field tests were used at the RAND Corporation. The purpose is to determine the effects of different sorts of information systems *and* decision rules in a job-shop-like system, namely, the maintenance of aircraft at an air force base. The quality of the information is not formally disaggregated into attributes like timeliness and accuracy. Refer also to Geisler and Ginsberg (1965).

Moskowitz and Miller (1975) use gaming to investigate the effects of sales forecast errors and the length of the forecast horizon in dynamic production scheduling. Their game is a noncompetitive game, a game against nature: human participants act in an environment provided by a simplified version of the Holt et al. (1960) model. The authors report that participants' performances improve with smaller forecast errors and longer planning horizons. Their study focuses not so much on IS attributes, like timeliness, as on behavioral aspects. The authors find that people's decisions tend to give more weight to variables with high forecast accuracy (possibly even if such a variable is not very relevant?).[32]

Grünwald (1977, p. 7) describes a gaming experiment at Philips in which a *chain* of production processes has to be managed (see the system dynamics section for background material). Each player is responsible for one link in the production chain. Players can be provided with global data besides their own local data. Such an integrated information system can drastically reduce production costs by reducing the internal business cycle. It is interesting to note that in this experiment, cost decreases from twenty-five to five units if players are willing to cooperate. OR optimalization would further reduce costs from five to one unit.

Wolff and Haines (1974) report on a series of experiments with a different, yet interesting focus. In their game players have access to an on-line database and a model bank, containing a set of simple interactive models. This "Toronto" game is based on the Harvard Management Game: four to seven companies; one to three products; decisions on advertising, pricing, and production scheduling; for details see McFarlan et al. (1970). A company (player) can buy information on its competitors. The accuracy of this information increases as more money is spent on it. Note that information on competitors is typically not the first candidate for a computerized MIS. The authors do not supply quantitative information about their experiments.

Rome and Rome (1971) report on very extensive gaming experiments—*Project Leviathan*— with a scope much wider than information systems evaluation. They investigate the total organizational system, including indeed an informal IS and a formal, computerized IS. The laboratory provided by their game is extremely flexible: groups of players can choose their own goals, their formal organizational structure (a strict hierarchy, coordinating committees, etc.), procedures (trial and error versus algorithms), and so on. Rome and Rome's *sociodrama* includes major decision-making elements: participants play the role of decision makers at various levels of a complex organization. The study is mainly a behavioral, sociological analysis of how an organization grows and matures over time. Nevertheless, the authors do include certain aspects that are of direct interest in IS evaluation: higher levels of management receive more aggregated information; exception reporting is introduced; and the update interval (called I in Chapter Six) is manipulated; see Rome and Rome (1971, pp. 57–59, 132, 142, 181, 187–188).

A few more experiments in an information context can be found in Welke (1977b) and in the references.[33]

APPENDIX 8.4: MORE STUDIES

Ackoff (1967) in his famous article emphasizes that operations research models and techniques might be used to determine which data to collect and how to use them. Refer further to the discussion in Chapter Six on scope, aggregation, exception reports, and user-machine modes; see also Kleijnen (1978a).

Ackoff and Beer (1969) report on a two-group experiment: one group solves a problem with sophisticated operations research techniques but inaccurate data; the other group using simple techniques with accurate data performs better. Note that this result may not be generalized to all situations; other unpublished experiments have had opposite results.

Ijiri and Itami (1973) make a study of timeliness and accuracy in a "production department," characterized by a quadratic cost-volume relationship. (Remember that such relationships were discussed in Chapter Five; see Fig. 5.2 and Fig. 5.7.) These authors study a very abstract and simple system; their assumptions concerning the role of inventories seem quite unrealistic.[34] Production for the next month is started but information on total demand for that month becomes available with a delay. Marginal loss is derived to increase as the delay increases. Assuming that more timely information could be obtained with less accuracy, they find that the optimum delay is not zero. Note that Chapter Six distinguished several components of timeliness and accuracy. The components P (processing delay) and I (update interval) can be reduced by an on-line computer system. On-line systems can reduce not only these delays but also some inaccuracies, namely measurement and transcription errors, but not sampling errors, the type of errors Ijiri and Itami have in mind. The authors briefly mention the possibility of delays with stochastic lengths.[35]

Seppälä (1979) examines the role of information accuracy and delay in both strategic and operational information systems. However, Seppälä uses a very abstract model.

Meddaugh (1976) investigates the effects of the update interval I, i.e., weekly versus monthly reports. A stream of artificial reports, supposed to cover weekly and monthly periods respectively, is presented to subjects (students) who must judge the performance of the (artificial) process generating these reports. (Notice that this process is not a simulation.) He finds that the update interval does affect the subjects' judgments.

EXERCISES

1. A production plan is prepared at time t for τ periods ahead. At time $t + 1$ the same procedure is repeated, a procedure called revolving planning.[36] Is such planning based on feedback and/or feedforward?

2. a) In which sciences are systems modeled not by difference equations but primarily by differential equations (continuous time)? (b) How can differential equations be solved on a digital computer?

3. How can computers dampen internal business cycles?

4. Bonini (1963) assumes that the initial conditions of his simulation show no interaction with his other eight factors. If you are interested in the effect of factor 3 only, do you need to run your simulation for one or two sets of initial conditions?

5. Give examples of simulation with physical (not mathematical) models that satisfy the other elements of the definition of simulation.

6. Suppose that a simulation model has seven parameters. (a) At least how many parameter combinations can be distinguished? (b) If the model represents a queuing system, how many customers should be simulated? (c) If the congestion (traffic) in a specific system variant is high, should more or fewer customers be simulated?

7. In the gaming section Mock (1969) was said to investigate accuracy not time-liness in his gaming experiments. How would you introduce various degrees of timeliness for the forecasting of prices in Mock's game?

8. You wish to study the effects of "budget variance" information; i.e., managers are supplied with information on the deviation between budgeted, normative expenditures and actual, realized expenditures. Which approach would be more appropriate: information economics modeling or gaming? Why do you think so?

9. Assume that for the recency of information a law of decreasing returns applies. What does this law imply for the marginal loss when the update interval increases?

10. If an iterative method is defined as one in which each "step" in the procedure gives a better solution, which of these qualifies as an iterative method: simulation, linear programming, and/or differential calculus?

11. Compute the entropy of a fair coin and a fair die respectively.

12. Fellingham et al. (1976, pp. 227–229) report the following responses ("average expected profits") with the standard deviations shown in parentheses:

high starting conditions:	$152,964 (31,022)
medium starting conditions:	189,000 (28,813)
low starting conditions:	229,957 (30,499)

(a) The authors use an F-test with degrees of freedom 2 and 27. Do you approve when you know that each of the three alternative conditions was replicated forty times? (b) Fellingham et al. (1976, p. 229) make the following claim: "The null hypothesis is that different starting conditions yield results drawn from the same population. This hypothesis was rejected with high confidence. . . ." Do you agree when you study the maximum pairwise difference between responses?

13. Use the list of information attributes in Chapter Six to categorize the publications of the present chapter. Which publications examine response time (R), sampling error, etc.?

NOTES

1. The HMMS model is discussed in many publications; e.g., see L.B. Schwartz and Johnson (1977), and Van Aken (1978, pp. 89–91).

2. Ansoff and Slevin (1968), and Senge (1973).

3. SD is also compared to econometric methods by Goankar (1977). A critical discussion and overview are further given by DeGreene (1977).

4. The continuous world view is also discussed by Van Aken (1978, p. 79).

5. Braat (1973) and (1977), Grünwald (1974) and (1977), and Van Aken (1978); see also Bos (1978) and Magee and Boodman (1967, pp. 208–214).

6. Meier et al. (1969), Naylor et al. (1966), Shannon (1975), and so on. See Kleijnen (1975b, p. 28) for more references.

7. Kleijnen (1975b) and (1977a) give more details.

8. Kleijnen (1976b).

9. Bonini (1963, p. 21).

10. Bonini (1963, pp. 39–45).

11. Technically this was realized in a 2^{8-4} design in four blocks (viz., the initial conditions), altogether sixty-four observations; see Bonini (1963, pp. 85–96). The use of the initial conditions as a blocking factor implies the assumption that these conditions have no interactions with the other eight factors.

12. Note that Frielink (1978) also discusses triggers. The constant data, which Welke (1975b) distinguishes besides periodic and transaction data, may be compared to the "descriptive" data that Frielink (1978) distinguishes besides "status" information.

13. After ANOVA rejects the hypothesis of equal means (H_0: $\mu_1 = \mu_2 = \ldots = \mu_k$), pairwise differences $\mu_i - \mu_j$ ($i < j$) can be tested, together $k(k-1)/2$ differences; see also Kleijnen (1975b, pp. 542–546).

14. See also Bruns (1963) and Green et al. (1967, pp. 133–134).

15. Grooms (1974), Remus (1978, pp. 828–829), and Shubik (1975).

16. See Mock (1969, pp. 151–152) and also Jensen (1969, p. 176).

17. His report on the analysis of variance is too limited to determine exactly how he conducted his tests; see Mock (1973b, p. 532). The statistical analysis of the first experiments in the sequence are criticized by Jensen (1969, pp. 173–175).

18. Mock (1973b, p. 524).

19. Mock et al. (1972, pp. 134–138).

20. See also the summaries in Welke (1977b). In addition to the references in Dickson et al. (1977), Dickson and Wynne (1973) study personality effects in a gaming experiment.

21. Itami (1972, p. 21).

22. Itami (1972, pp. 30, 105).

23. Itami (1972, p. 45).

24. Itami (1972, p. 108).

25. Itami (1972, p. 76).

26. For more details see J.C. Emery (1969, pp. 91–98) and also Bradley et al. (1977, pp. 91–156). For a related real-life study involving sensitivity testing refer to Wildermooth and Foote (1979).

27. See Verhelst (1974, pp. 238–278).

28. Lev (1968, p. 42).

29. For case studies and field tests see Dickson et al. (1977), and Van Horn (1973). For pilot projects see London (1976, p. 196). For prototypes see Bally et al. (1977), and Van Aken (1978, pp. 176–187). Famous surveys on computer systems are the Booz-Allen and the Diebold reports: see Chapter Two. For empirical studies, refer also to Section 8 in Welke (1977b).

30. See Amphlett Lewis (1966), Mock (1973a, p. 41), and Verhelst (1974, pp. 15–19).

31. The Gregory-Van Horn model has been summarized and criticized by Boutell (1968, pp. 113–125).

32. See also Lee and Khumawala (1974).

33. See Lucas (1979), Muller and De Samblanckx (1977), Segal and O'Neal (1979), Verver (1978), and Wilmer and Berry (1976).

34. For their assumptions on inventory see Ijiri and Itami (1973, pp. 727, 730).

35. See also Call (1975), and Ijiri and Itami (1975).

36. Baker and Peterson (1977), and Van Aken (1978, p. 162).

SIMULATION WITH AN IBM MANAGEMENT GAME[1]

CHAPTER **NINE**

INTRODUCTION

The preceding chapter was restricted to brief summaries of a number of simulation and gaming experiments (besides other studies). The present chapter is a highly detailed report on a simulation experiment carried out by the author himself. This report will demonstrate how one can cope with the many technical issues that have to be resolved in a scientifically planned and analyzed experiment; i.e., the present chapter illustrates a general methodology useful in ad hoc simulation and real-life (empirical) experiments. The experiment's results may be interesting in themselves insofar as they corroborate or conflict with the reader's intuitive ideas (rules of thumb) about the economic effects of information accuracy.

Compared to the simulation experiments discussed in Chapter Eight, this simulation model emphasizes competitive elements. The experimental control is greater that that of the gaming experiments of Chapter Eight because computerized players (robots) replace human players. These robots show behavioral realism insofar as they have multiple goals and heuristic decision rules, but unfortunately the robots do not show behavioral aspects like fatigue and "inspiration." Chapter Eight already indicated the different world view of system dynamics and control theory: a high level of aggregation, and exponential delays. However, the concepts of feedbacks and feedforwards do influence some of the decision rules used by the robot players. Inventory models, also discussed in Chapter Eight, inspired the robots' production decision rule. Finally Chapter Seven on information economics characterized this experiment: dynamic, nonlinear, stochastic, nonzero sum game, complicated, not played by "homo economicus"; refer also to Exercise 26 of the present chapter.

The present simulation experiment is based on a well-known IBM business game, IBM Management Decision-Making Laboratory,[2] which has been played by many people since the early sixties. Its extensive use suggests that the game is not too unrealistic a model, and in this sense the game has been "validated." This IBM game has fostered several other games, e.g., NIMEX by ICL (1973). A similar game has been used in national management competitions in Belgium and the Netherlands.[3] For more details on simulation and gaming refer back to the preceding chapter.

Management decisions in the IBM game are based on imperfect information on both the environment and the company itself. The results of these decisions depend on the quality of the information input into the decision rules;

the decision rules themselves; and

the system into which the decisions are fed, i.e., the company itself and its environment.

Whereas operations research concentrates on the decision rules, this study concentrates on the effects of the information quality. The present chapter will examine a single information attribute—accuracy—from the many relevant attributes discussed in Chapter Six. From the manifold criteria for judging the effectiveness of decisions, the following criteria have been chosen: return on investment (ROI), market share, and balance sheet total (total assets).

Because this chapter is quite lengthy and includes a number of technical issues, an initial synopsis may help the reader follow the main line of thought. The next section will present the IBM game, which is a dynamic simulation model requiring strategic and tactical decisions, based on imperfect knowledge. The game provides a model for three companies and the environment (market) in which these companies compete with each other. Although the IBM model was developed as a game, i.e., a simulation model accepting decisions made by human participants, the decision was made to use computerized players (robots). The third section derives the computer program, called DUMMY, that makes the decisions that provide the input for the IBM game. This DUMMY, like human players, does not know the exact structure and parameter values of the game. The DUMMY does not try to derive an optimal solution but uses heuristics instead. The fourth section discusses an experiment with inaccurate information on production unit cost. Statistical methodology shows that this inaccurate information has a significant linear effect on the growth of total assets, and on the average ROI and market share. The fifth section repeats the experiment for inaccurate information not on production, but on sales. The final section summarizes the results.

THE IBM MANAGEMENT GAME

The IBM Management Decision-Making Laboratory is a model of a hypothetical, oligopolistic situation with three companies. At the start of the competition each company has the same means (assets): inventory, productive capacity, and cash. For each quarter management has to make a number of strategic–tactical decisions on production and sales. The economic consequences of these decisions, computed by the IBM model, determine the situation at the beginning of the next quarter, in which the same type of decisions must again be made. Note that a company's results depend not only on its own decisions but also on the competitors' decisions, and on external variables and parameters such as the market's sensitivity and general economic growth.

The market consists of four geographical segments: each of the three companies has its home market, for which transportation costs are minimal; for the open market transportation costs are higher. Transportation to a competitor's home market requires the highest expenses.

The following *decisions* in dollars have to be made:

Product prices charged in each of the four market segments.

Marketing per segment.

Plant expansion. Productive capacity decreases 2 percent per quarter. This depreciation can be overcompensated through plant expansion. There is a time lag because the money spent on expansion at the beginning of a quarter will affect productive capacity only at the beginning of the next quarter.

Production. How much physical production is made possible by a production budget depends on the production unit cost. The presence of fixed costs means that the unit cost decreases as capacity utilization increases; see also Exercise 1.

Research and Development (R&D). These expenses decrease the production unit cost and stimulate the market potential. A (highly unrealistic) rule of the game stipulates that a company cannot spend more per quarter than the cash available at the beginning of that quarter. (In newer versions of this game, loans can be obtained, and several other more realistic possibilities have been introduced.[4])

The *information* on which the decisions above can be based comprises confidential, internal data and public data known to all companies. The public data consist of aggregated balance sheets and profit and loss accounts per company. The confidential data comprise a detailed balance sheet and profit and loss account, cash-flow statement, marketing survey, and production report (including unit cost). As more periods are played, the database expands.

The game is dynamic: the results depend not only on decisions of the current period but also on the results and decisions of previous periods. For instance, marketing and R&D exercise effects during several quarters; overproduction generates inventory that can be sold in the next quarter. The model is quite complicated. For example, unit cost depends on capacity size, capacity utilization, and R&D. Moreover, the game is characterized by imperfect knowledge: the participants do not know the exact structure and parameter values of the market, their own company, and their competitors' companies. For instance, the cost–volume relationship in the production department is not known exactly; the competitors' R&D remains unknown. The players, whether human or computerized, do have qualitative economic knowledge. For example, unit cost is known to decrease as capacity utilization or R&D increases. (Moreover, the production report supplies the unit cost for a few alternative degrees of utilization.) Altogether, the model consists of fifteen reaction equations plus eighteen accounting identities, and more than thirty parameters; see Naylor et al. (1966, pp. 209–213).

THE DUMMY PLAYER

As mentioned above, the decision was made to use not real people but *computerized players* for the IBM game. In principle the resulting computer program DUMMY could serve the following purposes:

Elimination of human players. Human participants add behavioral realism to the simulation but reduce the control over the experiment. As pointed out in the preceding chapter, players may show bad performance when supplied with better information simply because they have no feeling for the game. Moreover, using real people creates several practical problems including unavailability of human participants and long executing times.

Creation of a control, dummy player against whom human players can compete.[5]

Creation of a decision aid for the human player. The DUMMY may assist the players in their decision making; the players make the final decision. Various works offer more details on the use of computers and operations research in game playing.[6]

Pilot studies before actual gaming. The use of the DUMMY transforms the game into a pure machine simulation. Simulation experiments can be executed much faster than gaming experiments. Hence, the pure computer simulation with the DUMMY can be utilized for preliminary testing of certain ideas whereas the final testing is based on subsequent gaming experiments. Moreover, pure computer simulation can be employed to perform sensitivity analysis on the environmental parameters. In this way the parameter values of the gaming experiment might be fixed.[7]

Business games are usually played by *teams* of players. The DUMMY program may be interpreted as representing not a single player but a team of players, one player being responsible for the production department, another player being in charge of marketing, etc. The program does reflect interactions among these decisions; but it does not represent organizational factors like delays and inaccuracies caused by communication links among departments, or behavioral aspects like pressure exercised by superiors in the organizational hierarchy. Such organizational factors can indeed be included in either a simulation or a gaming experiment: Bonini (1963) programs behavioral aspects into his pure machine simulation; see the discussion in the preceding chapter. To investigate the effects of a hierarchical organization, Haines (1971) suggests using gaming augmented with pure computer simulation of *lower* managers, who can be hired and fired.[8] Rome and Rome's (1971) investigation of hierarchical organizations in an intensive series of gaming experiments—Project Leviathan—includes multiple decision makers, either human or computerized. However, the focus is on the behavioral analysis of organizational performance in general although formal and informal information systems are included; see Appendix 8.3.

During the development of the computerized player, related research was unknown. After completion of the work, a few, more or less related efforts became known. As mentioned in the preceding chapter, for Mock's (1973a) very simple, static game an optimal solution, assuming perfect knowledge of the game's structure and parameter values, was derived; see also Fellingham et al. (1976). Hoggatt (1967), Shubik et al. (1971), and Wolf (1972), too, use games for which optimal decision rules can be derived. However, even if the structure of the IBM game had been known to the players, optimal decision rules would have been impossible to derive because the game is too complicated. Actually the DUMMY player does not know the exact structure, let alone the parameter values. The DUMMY player is supplied with the same data that the human players receive: confidential data on the player's own company and public aggregated data on the competitors. The DUMMY uses qualitative knowledge of economic systems; e.g., it is known that the sales volume decreases as the price increases if other variables like marketing are kept constant. The DUMMY tries to realize its goals by using such economic "common sense," simple heuristic rules, and not sophisticated operations research models. Only after the completion of his research did the author become aware of Hoffman's computerized player for the same IBM game. Actually T.R. Hoffmann (1965) uses quite different heuristics (and research goals).

The DUMMY's *goal* variables or criteria are these:

Return on investment (ROI): profit divided by total assets. In the IBM game total assets equal cash plus inventory plus plant value. See also Exercise 3.

Market share: own sales revenues divided by total sales revenues of all companies taken together.

The aim of the DUMMY is to have these two variables not decrease over time. This aim is a very realistic goal formulation according to various publications.[9]

The previous section has already introduced the five types of decision variables. The *decision rules* used by the DUMMY follow. The first discussion, on the production budget, is quite elaborate because this decision needs information for which accuracy will be varied in the next section. The other decisions will be discussed only briefly; details are given in Appendix 9.1.

Production Budget

The four following steps use the notation illustrated by Fig. 9.1.

1. For the next quarter denoted by $(\tau + 1)$, DUMMY wants to produce enough so that production, together with the inventory available at the beginning t of that quarter, can satisfy demand. However, the actual demand in the next quarter is not known yet, but will deviate from the forecasted, expected demand. (Forecasts are made by exponential smoothing; see Eq. (9.7) below.) If actual demand exceeds forecasted demand, demand is lost because no backordering is possible in this game. Both profit and sales are then lost so that the two goal variables are negatively affected. If actual demand is smaller than forecasted demand, production is added to inventory. Then ROI decreases because total assets, including inventory, increase. In a following quarter, however, inventory can be adjusted. Therefore this case has less serious consequences. (In other games like ICL's NIMEX, an excess of demand creates loss of goodwill, and inventories deteriorate so that the analysis becomes more complicated.) Because of these considerations DUMMY adds a safety margin to expected demand:

    $$\text{Production}_{\tau + 1} + \text{inventory}_t = \text{expected}$$
    $$\text{demand}_{\tau + 1} + \text{safety}_{\tau + 1}. \tag{9.1}$$

    In Eq. (9.1) inventory is known from the balance sheet; i.e., inventory is an item in DUMMY's database. Expected demand is forecast from

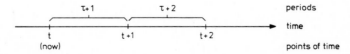

FIGURE 9-1. *Definition of Time Dimension.*

demand data in the past periods by use of exponential smoothing. Safety is based on the forecast errors made in the past:

$$\text{Safety}_{\tau + 1} = k \cdot \hat{\sigma}_{\tau + 1} \qquad (9.2)$$

where k is a constant and $\hat{\sigma}$ is a *forecast* of the forecast error σ. To be precise, $\sigma_{\tau + 1}$ is forecast by applying exponential smoothing to the observations σ_1 through σ_τ where

$$\sigma_\tau = \left\{ \sum_{i = 1}^{\tau} (\text{forecasted demand}_i - \text{actual demand}_i)^2 / \tau \right\}^{1/2}. \qquad (9.3)$$

Selecting $k = 2$ means that it is hoped that in 97.7 percent of all periods no stockouts occur; see Exercise 4. Equation (9.2) is traditional in inventory control; Eq. (9.3) deviates from the traditional formulas.[10]

2.   Underutilization of plant capacity increases the unit cost dramatically. Hence the production resulting from Eq. (9.1) may be too small. Therefore a side condition is introduced:

$$0.50 \, \text{capacity}_{\tau + 1} \leq \text{production}_{\tau + 1} \leq 1.00 \, \text{capacity}_{\tau + 1}. \qquad (9.4)$$

Observe that cutting off at 50 percent utilization is arbitrary.

3.   Production should be specified not in volume units but in dollars. DUMMY does not know the exact unit cost, say y, for the next quarter. It is known that unit costs vary over time because of R&D and capacity expansion besides capacity utilization. The production report displays the unit cost in the past period for four alternative utilization degrees: actual utilization, 10 percent more, 10 percent less, and full utilization. DUMMY's estimate of the unit cost for the next quarter uses the following model:

$$\text{Total production} = \text{fixed cost} + \text{variable unit}$$
$$\text{cost} \times \text{production}$$
$$= a + b \cdot x \qquad (9.5)$$

so that the unit cost y satisfies

$$y = a/x + b. \qquad (9.6)$$

To estimate a and b, DUMMY fits a least-squares line to the four observations on x and y.[11]

4.   The production budget is simply the product of the unit cost y in Eq. (9.6) and the production volume x following from Eqs. (9.1) through (9.4). Note that in this game no production smoothing over time is needed; an issue on which much research has been done is eliminated.[12]

Plant Expansion

Remember the definition of the time dimension shown in Fig. 9.1. The desired plant capacity at point of time $t + 1$ must be decided on and paid for at time t. With the inventory at time $t + 1$, capacity should be high enough to satisfy demand over period $\tau + 2$. Demand is taken as an average of expected demand and "desirable" demand. Desirable orders are determined by the desired market share, which is in turn calculated by exponential smoothing of the past actual market shares. In this way *feedback* with DUMMY's goal variables is created. The resulting desirable plant expansion is not realized (paid) within one period because it may turn out that desired plant expansion is based on too optimistic a prediction of demand. To reduce the chance that DUMMY will be stuck with overcapacity, the actual plant expansion is smoothed. Appendix 9.1 gives details on this decision variable and on those discussed in the remainder of this section.

Marketing

It is very difficult to determine an economic basis for a reasonable marketing budget.[13] The following heuristics are introduced:

1. How much cash is available?

2. How much did competitors spend on marketing in the "recent past"? DUMMY takes into account that a marketing expenditure remains effective over several periods.

3. The first two components are weighted. The larger component— whether the first or the second—gets a higher weight whenever the desired market share or capacity utilization shows deterioration; see Appendix 9.1.

4. In order to reduce drastic fluctuations in marketing expenditures, DUMMY restricts changes to 50 percent of marketing in the previous period. (In such business games as ICL's NIMEX and IBM's newer version, all decision variables must remain within prespecified ranges when decided upon by human players.)

Research and Development

Like marketing, an economically justifiable R&D budget is difficult to determine.[14] The approach used is the same as that for marketing. A difference is that the competitors' R&D is unknown. Therefore DUMMY assumes that R&D equals a particular fraction of the competitors' available cash, which is known indeed. For more details refer to Appendix 9.1.

Prices

From the start the preference was to base prices on the indirect and direct price elasticities, i.e., on the reaction of the sales volume to changes in the competitors' prices and in the DUMMY's own prices, respectively; see also Exercise 8. To keep the DUMMY program simple, the following heuristics, which with hindsight could even be related to some real life practices, were chosen.[15]

1. Which price would yield the desired ROI (goal 1)? The desired ROI is set to 15 percent per year before taxes. This ROI determines the desired profit and hence, allowing for costs, the desired sales revenues, pro-

vided DUMMY assumes the actual sales equal the predicted sales volume. Because sales revenues are equal to the product of sales volume times price, the "ROI price" can be computed.

2. DUMMY forecasts the competitors' prices because the sales volume in 1 will be realized only if competitors do not charge a much lower price; see DUMMY's goals 1 and 2.

3. The prices resulting from 1 and 2 are weighted. The higher price gets the higher weight if the company does well (full capacity used, market share maintained).

4. Prices are differentiated over market areas because transportation costs differ.

5. Price changes are restricted to 50 percent. See also Exercises 9 and 10.

Cash Restriction

If the total of planned expenditures exceeds available cash, budgets need revision. The following priority scheme is used. Plant expansion is reduced to zero while production, marketing, and R&D are maintained in the proportion 100:75:25. The resulting production volume is recomputed; and because this lower volume may imply "too many" orders, prices may be adjusted; see Appendix 9.1.

Forecasting

The decisions above use as inputs the forecasts on demand, competitors' prices, and so on. These forecasts are based on historical data contained in DUMMY's database. (This database further comprises data describing the company's current status and past history, specified by such items as inventories and market shares, which also affect DUMMY's decisions.) Forecasting uses exponential smoothing:

$$\text{New forecast} = \text{old forecast} + \alpha \cdot (\text{new value} - \text{old forecast}). \tag{9.7}$$

Competitors' prices are predicted using Eq. (9.7) with $\alpha = 0.50$. Such a high α-value is applied to cause the DUMMY to place much weight on the opponents' most recent move. The other variables are predicted with a possible trend taken into account: second order model. The growth is then predicted by Eq. (9.7) with $\alpha = 0.20$; see Appendix 9.1 and Exercises 11 and 12.

The relationships among DUMMY's decision variables and the information in the database are summarized in Fig. 9.2. This figure is meant to demonstrate that although DUMMY uses simple decision rules, the overall decision system becomes quite complicated. The relationships between DUMMY and the environment are summarized in Fig. 9.3.

How good is the resulting DUMMY player? DUMMY is based on qualitative knowledge of economics and on heuristic decision rules. In this investigation three DUMMYs, representing three companies, use the same decision rules to compete only with each other. Because each of the DUMMYs uses different information, their decisions differ and the results diverge; this divergence is input into their decision rules, and so on. It is reassuring that bankruptcy seldom occurs, and that information quality has effects that on hindsight are reasonable as the next section will show.

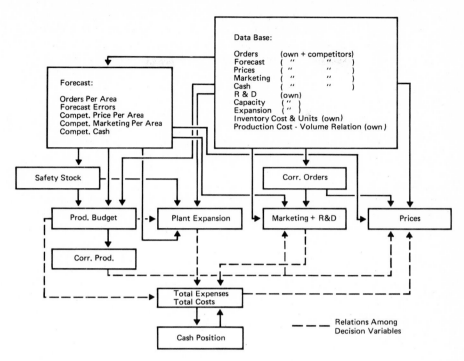

FIGURE 9–2.   Interactions among Database and
Decision Variables.

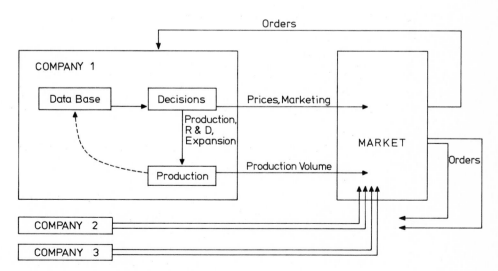

FIGURE 9–3.   The DUMMY and Its Environment.

It would be nice to have DUMMY compete with human players in the IBM game; see also Shubik et al. (1971, pp. 29, 42). A program closely related to DUMMY did play against human teams in ICL's NIMEX game. The results show that DUMMY behaves satisfactorily except for its (most important) price strategy: human participants knowing they competed with a computer program could beat the DUMMY because DUMMY priced itself out of the market; see also Exercise 10. The DUMMY program (model) seems reasonably validated.

INACCURATE PRODUCTION INFORMATION

Chapter Six discussed a variety of information quality characteristics or attributes: timeliness, accuracy, aggregation, report mode (exception reports, queries, formats including precision), retention time, privacy and security, reliability and recovery, scope, user-computer modes, flexibility, and multiple users. Scientific analysis requires avoidance of the use of "accuracy" as a catch-all: using outdated information might be said to create inaccuracy; aggregated data are inaccurate when detailed data are required, etc. Instead one should reserve the term *inaccuracy* for the following types of errors:

Sampling errors created when not the whole population but only a sample from it is measured; think of marketing surveys.

Measurement errors caused by incorrect observation; for instance, counting errors in physical stock taking.

Transcription errors made when recording from one medium to another medium; for instance, hand-written documents may be key-punched incorrectly.

Transformation errors created when the computer processes (transforms) input data into intermediate or final output data. Such errors may be truncation, programming, or computer hardware errors.

Logical errors caused by the use of incorrect formulas or models.

The IBM game gives so aggregated a view of the company that a detailed model of the data processing in the company would be incompatible. The inaccuracies resulting from data processing are therefore modeled by simply adding a stochastic noise component to the true values. In the present section assume that the production unit cost y of Eq. (9.6) shows additive inaccuracies e around its true value η; or

$$y_i = \eta_i + e_i \qquad (i = 1, \ldots, 4) \tag{9.8}$$

where y is displayed in the production report for four values of the production volume x in the past period. Assume that the inaccuracies e are normally distributed because many factors can contribute to the inaccuracies and therefore the central limit theorem applies. The inaccuracies are supposed to have zero expectation: no systematic errors. (Statistically speaking, the errors are further assumed to be independent.) Assume that the error variances σ_i^2 depend on the *quality of the information system* (IS); see Fig. 9.4. In this figure the better IS (corresponding to I) is characterized by the Gaussian curve with the smaller spread, measured by σ^2. There is a 1 percent chance that the relative errors e/η are larger than some upper level C;

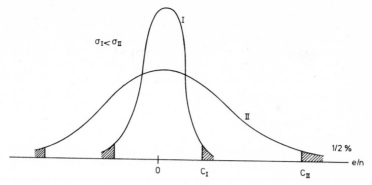

FIGURE 9–4.   The Distribution of the Relative Errors e/n.

see the shaded areas. This formulation seems quite realistic; compare the discussion by Jordan (1975, p. 193) on the accuracy of inventory records.

Statistically σ_i^2 is so high that the relative errors e_i/η_i remain below an upper limit C (which depends on the IS) with 99 percent probability; or

$$P\left\{\frac{|y_i - \eta_i|}{\eta_i} \le C\right\} = 0.99 \qquad\qquad (i = 1, \ldots, 4). \qquad\qquad (9.9)$$

Hence the variances σ_i^2 should satisfy the condition

$$\text{var } (e_i) \equiv \sigma_i^2 = C \cdot \eta_i/2.56 \qquad\qquad (9.10)$$

where the constant 2.56 corresponds with the 99 percent point in the tables for the Gaussian (normal) distribution; see Exercise 13. The assumptions concerning e are summarized by

$$e_i \sim \text{NID } (0, \sigma_i^2) \qquad\qquad (9.11)$$

where NID means that the e_i are normally (N), independently distributed (ID) with mean zero and variance σ_i^2, specified by Eq. (9.10). To be more realistic, in the simulation when errors larger than C are sampled, they are cut off at C; see Exercise 14. As mentioned after Eq. (9.6), a least-squares curve is fitted to the four observations on the production value x and the observed unit cost y (not η). Only the four observations from the most recent period are used because R&D and plant expansion change the unit cost over time.

As in any simulation experiment the experimenter must fix many parameters, variables, and initial conditions: an *experimental design* problem. The constant C in Eq. (9.10) is fixed at the value zero for company 1: this company has a perfect IS for production costs. For company 3 arbitrarily $C = 20$ percent: production cost errors may be as large as 20 percent. The focus is on company 2 and on the effects of changing C over the range from 0 to 20 percent: C can be 0, 4, 8, 12, 16 or 20 percent. For each of these six C-values, twenty periods (quarters) are simulated because a five-year period, common in business planning practice, should permit realization of possible benefits of a more accurate IS.[16] Because inaccuracies e are just samples, repetition (replication) of each twenty-period simulation run serves to reduce chance effects. Ten replicated runs per C-value indeed permit reliable conclusions as the analysis will show. (All six-times-ten time paths are statistically independent because they use different random numbers.) As responses (outputs, criteria) of the simulation experiment, the following variables are measured for company 2[17]: ROI, market share, and total assets. Note that two of these variables are also DUMMY's goal variables. The three response variables are computed per period. A time path of twenty periods is then characterized by either its average or its trend over twenty periods. The initial conditions for each time path are generated by taking the end conditions obtained after simulating forty periods starting from conditions based on the example in IBM (1963b); see also Exercise 15.

Consider whether the time paths should be characterized by a simple *average* or by a *trend*. If a response (ROI, market share, or assets) in period t is denoted by the general symbol r_t, the average is

$$\bar{r} = \sum_{t=1}^{20} r_t/20; \tag{9.12}$$

and the *linear trend* model is

$$r_t = \beta_0 + \beta_1 t + u_t \qquad (t = 1, \ldots, 20) \tag{9.13}$$

where u is a noise or disturbance term (for which no statistical assumptions such as normality are made). The coefficients β_0 and β_1 (growth) are estimated by least squares; see Figs. 9.5 and 9.6 for illustrations. Appendix 9.2 shows that total assets, one response variable, can be characterized by the linear trend model of Eq. (9.13).

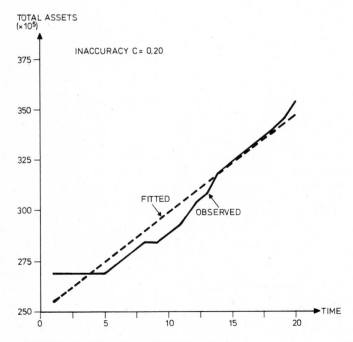

FIGURE 9–5.   *Time Path of Total Assets.*

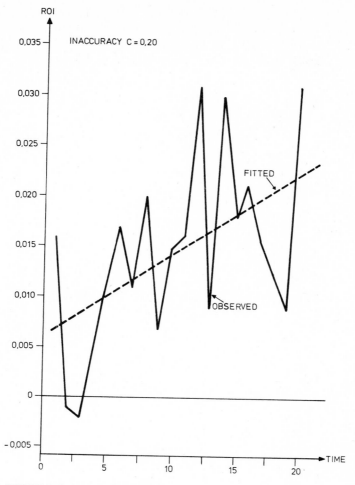

FIGURE 9–6.   The Path of ROI.

(Statistically R^2 varies between 94.5 percent and 99.9 percent.) The other responses, ROI and market share, can be better characterized by the simple average of Eq. (9.12) (because R^2 remains lower than 41 percent). See also Exercise 17.

Each time path (characterized by either its estimated growth $\hat{\beta}_1$ or its estimated average $\hat{\bar{r}}$) is replicated with different random numbers. For each of the six C-values ten such replicates are obtained. For growth ($\hat{\beta}_1$) of total assets the results are shown in Fig. 9.7; see the little circles. Per C-value (accuracy of the information system) the average of these ten replicates is computed, e.g., $\bar{\hat{\beta}}$ (estimated growth of total assets, averaged over ten replicates) or $\bar{\hat{r}}$ (estimated average ROI over twenty periods, averaged over ten replicates). To simplify the notation, let the general symbol $\bar{\beta}$ denote the averaged responses $\hat{\beta}_1$ and $\hat{\bar{r}}$. One wishes to know whether the response variables $\bar{\beta}$ decrease for increasing inaccuracy of the information system measured by C; see

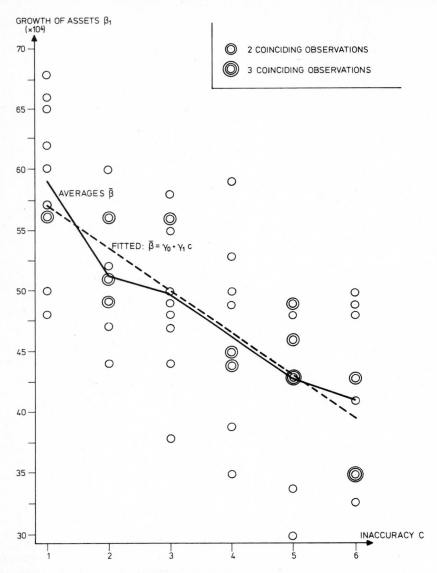

FIGURE 9–7.   *Growth of Assets versus Inaccuracy.*

the solid line in Fig. 9.7. One hypothesizes that the inaccuracy level C has a *linear* effect on the average response $\bar{\beta}$; see the dashed line in Fig. 9.7. Therefore the model for the effect of the IS accuracy on the company's performance is

$$\bar{\beta}_i = \gamma_0 + \gamma_1 C_i + v_i \qquad (i = 1, \ldots, 6) \tag{9.14}$$

where v is a noise term. Appendix 9.3 proves statistically that one can confidently accept the hypothesis that the linear model of Eq. (9.14) gives a good explanation of the effect of inaccurate production cost information, measured by C, on the growth of the time path of the total assets response variable, and on the average ROI and market share. (R^2 is 0.95 for total assets, 0.86 for market share, and 0.97 for ROI. Appendix 9.3 also discusses the F-test for lack of fit.)

The *linear* model of Eq. (9.14) does not exclude the possibility of a *zero* (or approximately zero) coefficient γ_1, the effect of accuracy. Appendix 9.3 explains that the intervals of Table 9.1 cover the true value γ_1 with (approximately) 90 percent probability. Because these intervals do not cover the value zero, one may conclude with 90 percent confidence that inaccurate production cost information has a *negative* effect on the growth of total assets, and on the average ROI and market share. (Results not displayed in Table 9.1 show that the y-intercept or β_0 of the trend model for total assets is not significantly affected by inaccuracy.)

If one has to specify a best estimate for the (negative) effect of inaccurate production cost information, Table 9.1 gives the following "point" estimates:

Total assets: when the inaccuracy level C decreases with 0.04 units, quarterly growth increases with \$33,500, i.e., roughly 7 percent (because growth is \$485,767 at the midpoint, $C = 3.5$).

Market share: when C decreases with 0.04 units, market share (averaged over twenty quarters) increases with 0.269 points or only 0.8 percent of the "normal" share of 33 percent.

ROI: when C decreases with 0.04 units, ROI per quarter (averaged over twenty quarters) increases with 0.08 points or 5 percent of the normal ROI of 1.5 percent per quarter.

As mentioned before, trend and averages are linearly affected by accuracy over the *whole* experimental area; this linear effect is unlike the S-shaped effects conjectured by some authors; see J. C. Emery (1971) and Chapter Five.

The experiment is repeated for *less favorable initial conditions:* an initial situation in which the companies show losses that seem to increase steadily. In this new experiment some time paths lead to bankruptcy; the probability of bankruptcy is estimated to be roughly 5.8 percent (because seven out of one hundred twenty time paths resulted in bankruptcy; see Exercise 21). If bankruptcy occurs, the simulation is repeated with new random numbers. Hence the analysis and conclusions are restricted to situations without bankruptcies. As above, the trend model of Eq. (9.13) does not explain the ROI and market share time paths very well. For total assets the trend model behaves much better (but not as well as in the previous experiment[18]); therefore the decision is to use the trend model for total assets. After the linear model of Eq. (9.14) is postulated for the effect of inaccuracy on the responses, analysis shows that stochastic fluctuations (noise) are dominant in Eq. (9.14).[19] In order to reduce the influence of stochastic noise, ten more replications per c-value are added.

TABLE 9.1.   *Effects of Inaccurate Production Cost Information (Including 90 Percent Confidence Limits)*

Effect of Inaccuracy	Growth Total Assets	Average Market Share	Average ROI
Average $\hat{\gamma}_1$	$- 335 \times 10^2$	$- 269 \times 10^{-5}$	$- 843 \times 10^{-6}$
Lower limit	$- 422 \times 10^2$	$- 391 \times 10^{-5}$	$- 1031 \times 10^{-6}$
Upper limit	$- 247 \times 10^2$	$- 146 \times 10^{-5}$	$- 654 \times 10^{-6}$

The twenty replicates taken together give better results: the linear model of Eq. (9.14) need not be rejected in favor of a more complicated model. (The F-statistics explained in Appendix 9.3 remain below one.) Its R^2 is reasonably high for assets (67 percent) and ROI (62 percent), but not for market share (9 percent). In agreement with these R^2-values, Table 9.2 shows significant effects for assets and ROI but not for market share. Table 9.2 gives *smaller* effects for accuracy than Table 9.1

TABLE 9.2. Effects of Inaccurate Production Cost Information
(Unfavorable Initial Conditions)

Effect of Inaccuracy	Average Assets	Average Market Share	Average ROI
Average $\hat{\gamma}_1$	$- 102 \times 10^2$	69×10^{-5}	$- 370 \times 10^{-6}$
Lower limit	$- 177 \times 10^2$	$- 143 \times 10^{-5}$	$- 711 \times 10^{-6}$
Upper limit	$- 26 \times 10^2$	282×10^{-5}	$- 29 \times 10^{-6}$

INACCURATE SALES INFORMATION

The next experiment investigates the effects of inaccurate information about the sales volume. In practice the exact sales volume is rarely known, but computers can dramatically increase the accuracy of sales information. One example is the use of point-of-sale terminals in self-service retail stores such as grocery and department stores, and tax-free shops at airports; see Appendix 2.1.

Sales figures affect a number of other variables. In the IBM game, data on the sales volume affect data on sales revenues, sales costs, inventory (value and volume), profit, taxes, cash, and total assets; see for instance the relationship

$$\text{New inventory} = \text{old inventory} + \text{production} - \text{sales volume}. \quad (9.15)$$

The relationships for the other variables are specified in Appendix 9.4.

Because the original IBM game does not provide for inaccurate sales data, the following submodel is developed. If administrative inventory (contained in the database) is zero, orders are not accepted even if physical inventory is positive. On the other side, if administrative inventory is positive, but physical inventory is zero, accepting an order triggers a signal from the company's warehouse so that the order will be cancelled after all. Hence

$$\text{Sales volume} = \text{orders}$$

if

$$\text{Orders} \leq \text{production} + \min \, (\text{old inventory}, \text{administrative inventory}). \quad (9.16)$$

For the inaccurate IS on sales figures, assume a model analogous to the model for the inaccurate IS on production unit cost as specified in Eq. (9.8.) Hence

$$\text{Administrative sales} = \text{sales volume} + \text{inaccuracy}. \quad (9.17)$$

DUMMY uses the inaccurate data of Eq. (9.17) in its bookkeeping. [In Eqs. (A9.4.2) through (A9.4.9), sales volume has to be replaced by administrative sales.] In two cases, however, corrections are needed:

If administrative inventory becomes negative, it is set at zero [see Eq. (A9.4.10)].

Because DUMMY's database may show too much cash, DUMMY may decide on total expenses such that the actually available cash is exceeded. In that case total expenditures are cut off at available cash.

Note that DUMMY forecasts its orders from the data on sales, not those on orders [demand may exceed sales; see also Eq. (A9.4.1)]. Such a procedure is standard in self-service stores where sales, not demand, is known. Inaccuracy in Eq. (9.17) is statistically specified in the same way as with production cost information; see Eqs. (9.9) through (9.11) in which the index i now denotes the market segment.

This simulation uses the same initial conditions (the "favorable" conditions) as those in the first part of the production cost experiment. Again ten replicates using new random number streams are generated. The three response variables are measured without inaccuracies, i.e., independent of DUMMY's bookkeeping. The time paths might again be characterized by the linear trend of Eq. (9.13). The resulting R^2-values show that more complicated trend models [Eq. (A9.2.3)] are no better than the simple linear trend model. It is not clear whether a simple average, as in Eq. (9.12), gives a better explanation (R^2 is smaller than 50 percent in eleven out of sixty cases for assets, fourteen times for market share, and forty-five times for ROI). Therefore both trends and averages are analyzed.

The simple linear model of Eq. (9.14) is used to explain the effects of inaccuracy on the responses. This linear model need not be rejected in favor of a more complicated model.[20] The R^2-values are displayed in Table 9.3.

TABLE 9.3. R^2 for Trends and Averages versus Accuracy

Response	Assets	Market Share	ROI
Growth β_1	87%	77%	80%
Intercept β_0	82%	67%	76%
Average $\bar{r}$	90%	79%	82%

If the R^2-values of Table 9.3 are "small," one concludes that accuracy has no effect [flat line instead of sloped line in Eq. (9.14)]. Statistical confidence can be realized by means of the 90 percent confidence bands as used before in Table 9.1. Tables 9.4 and 9.5 show that all responses are significantly affected by inaccuracy: if one characterizes the time paths by a linear trend (Table 9.4), this line is "tilted"; i.e., the slope (growth) decreases with inaccuracy while the y-intercept (β_0) increases. If one

TABLE 9.4.   Effects of Inaccurate Sales Data on Trends

Effect of Inaccuracy γ_1	Assets		Market Share		ROI	
	Growth β_1	Intercept β_0	Growth β_1	Intercept β_0	Growth β_1	Intercept β_0
Average $\hat{\gamma}_1$	-674×10^2	3186×10^2	-12429×10^{-7}	373×10^{-5}	-3255×10^{-7}	158×10^{-5}
Lower limit	-968×10^2	1546×10^2	-18219×10^{-7}	164×10^{-5}	-4741×10^{-7}	98×10^{-5}
Upper limit	-378×10^2	4827×10^2	-6638×10^{-7}	583×10^{-5}	-1768×10^{-7}	217×10^{-5}

TABLE 9.5. *Effects of Inaccurate Sales Data on Averages*

Effect of Inaccuracy	Average Assets	Average Market Share	Average ROI
Average $\hat{\gamma}_1$	$- 3889 \times 10^2$	$- 932 \times 10^{-5}$	$- 1840 \times 10^{-6}$
Lower limit	$- 5383 \times 10^2$	$- 1354 \times 10^{-5}$	$- 2880 \times 10^{-6}$
Upper limit	$- 2395 \times 10^2$	$- 510 \times 10^{-5}$	$- 800 \times 10^{-6}$

characterizes the time paths by their averages $\bar{r}$ (Table 9.5), these averages decrease significantly. Comparison of Tables 9.4 and 9.5 with Table 9.1 shows that in general, sales data accuracy has *larger* effects than those of the accuracy of production cost data. On hindsight, this result is not surprising because sales are the driving force of a company.

CONCLUSION

This chapter has presented a number of experiments with a simulation model of a company engaged in a competition with two other companies. The decisions are made by the computer program DUMMY, and the results of these decisions are computed by the IBM management game. In experiments with different degrees of accuracy for the information that DUMMY uses for its decision making, both information on production cost and information on sales were found to have significant, linear effects on the time paths of the three criterion variables: total assets, market share, and ROI.

How reliable are the conclusions above? The analysis of the stochastic simulation guarantees statistical confidence; but strictly speaking, the conclusions are valid only for the specific structure and for the specific parameter values of the IBM game, the DUMMY, and the information system model. Hence future experiments can follow two directions:

Sensitivity analysis. Change the structure and parameters to see how the changes affect the conclusions and to find some results that apply in general: rules of thumb, heuristics.

Methodology. Consider this chapter as an illustration of a methodology. Next apply this methodology to a specific real-life system; i.e., replace the IBM game by a model of the actual organization, say, a corporate simulation model. Obviously the DUMMY decision rules need to be adjusted, too. Another problem is the specification of the quality of the actual information system; in this specification an approach like that of Eqs. (9.9) through (9.11) might be followed. Other attributes besides accuracy may then also be modeled; see Chapter Six.

APPENDIX 9.1: DETAILS ON THE DUMMY PLAYER

Plant Expansion

Capacity depreciates at 2 percent per period. Expansion paid at t becomes available at $t + 1$. Hence

$$\text{Capacity}_{\tau + 2} = 0.98 \, \text{capacity}_{\tau + 1} + \text{expansion}_t. \tag{A9.1.1}$$

The desired capacity follows from

$$\text{Desired capacity}_{\tau+2} + \text{inventory}_{t+1} = \text{demand}_{\tau+2} \qquad \text{(A9.1.2)}$$

with

$$\text{Demand}_{\tau+2} = (\text{expected demand}_{\tau+2} + \text{desired demand}_{\tau+2})/2 \qquad \text{(A9.1.3)}$$

where expected demand is forecast by exponential smoothing. Desired demand is introduced so that DUMMY does not slavishly follow the historical development of orders, but tries to realize its goals. Desired demand is based on desired market share, which is a smoothed average of all historical shares (with smoothing constant $\alpha = 0.2$). Inventory in Eq. (A9.1.2) is not forecast from past inventories but is set equal to the safety stock of Eq. (9.2). [If Eq. (9.4) shows that the desired production exceeds capacity, this safety stock cannot be realized; therefore inventory in Eq. (A9.1.2) is corrected downwards for the difference between actual and desired production.] Next solve Eq. (A9.1.2) for desired capacity, substitute this amount for capacity$_{\tau+2}$ in Eq. (A9.1.1), and solve Eq. (A9.1.1) for expansion. Negative values are cut off at zero because excess capacity cannot be sold in this IBM game (unlike ICL's NIMEX game). Positive values may be based on a too optimistic demand$_{\tau+2}$, which can be revised at $t+1$. Therefore at time t DUMMY spends

$$\text{Improvement}_t = \alpha \cdot \text{expansion}_{t-1} + (1-\alpha] \cdot \text{expansion}_t \qquad \text{(A9.1.4)}$$

where $\alpha = 0.50$.

Marketing

1. How much cash does DUMMY wish to spend? Take

    $$\text{Marketing}_{\tau+1} = a \cdot \text{cash}_t \qquad \text{(A9.1.5)}$$

    where the constant a equals the fraction of cash spent on marketing during $\tau = 0$. Marketing is allocated per area i by using

    $$\text{Area weight}_i = \frac{\text{demand area } i}{\text{total demand}} \qquad (i = 1, \ldots, 4) \quad \text{(A9.1.6)}$$

    where demand equals demand in units in the most recent period, τ.

2. How much should be spent to keep up with competitors? Let competitors$_i$ denote marketing in area i, averaged over (two) competitors. DUMMY assumes that the marketing effect declines over time. The following "time weights" are used: 10, 9, 5, 3, 0. Let own denote DUMMY's own marketing. Then the following equation needs to be solved for own$_{i(\tau+1)}$:

    $$\sum_{j=\tau-2}^{\tau+1} (\text{time weight}_j) \cdot (\text{competitors}_{ij}) =$$

    $$\sum_{j=\tau-2}^{\tau+1} (\text{time weight}_j) \cdot (\text{own}_{ij}) \qquad \text{(A9.1.7)}$$

    where the variables competitors and own are known for $j = \tau - 2$, $\tau - 1$, τ, and competitors$_{\tau+1}$ is forecast by exponential smoothing using a trend model with $\alpha = 0.2$.

3. Take an average of the components 1 and 2; weigh the higher compo-nent with ω_3, derived as follows. (For simplicity of notation the indices i and τ of the ω factors are dropped.)

$$\omega_1 = \max\left\{\frac{\text{desired demand}_{i\tau}}{\text{actual demand}_{i\tau}}, 1\right\} \tag{A9.1.8}$$

$$\omega_2 = \frac{\text{capacity}_{\tau+1}}{\text{desired production}_{\tau+1}} \tag{A9.1.9}$$

where desired production is the result of Eqs. (9.1) and (9.2) so that it is possible that $\omega_2 < 1$. The two correction factors are combined into ω_3:

$$\omega_3 = \frac{(\omega_1 \cdot \omega_2)^2}{1 + (\omega_1 \cdot \omega_2)^2}. \tag{A9.1.10}$$

Refer also to Exercise 22.

Research and Development

The heuristic is the same as that used with marketing except for the following changes.

The competitors' R&D, which is unknown, is set equal to a fraction of their cash; see step 1 in marketing.

R&D has two effects: it increases the attractiveness of the product and hence the orders; and R&D stimulates productivity. The second effect is ignored [$\omega_2 = 1$ in Eq. (A9.1.9)].

R&D is not specified "per area." Therefore ω_1 in Eq. (A9.1.8) is collapsed into a single value, weighing each ω_1 with the desired market share per area.

Prices

The following steps are used. (The step numbers do not correspond with those of the main text.)

1. By definition

$$\text{Desired profit}_{\tau+1} = (\text{desired ROI}_{\tau+1}) \cdot (\text{assets}_\tau) \tag{A9.1.11}$$

where assets are known from the balance sheet, and the desired ROI equals $(15/4)$ percent per quarter. Actual profit equals

$$\begin{aligned}
\text{Profit}_{\tau+1} &= \text{revenues}_{\tau+1} - \text{costs}_{\tau+1} \\
&= (\text{sales volume}_{\tau+1}) \cdot (\text{price}_{\tau+1}) + \\
&\quad - (\text{marketing}_{\tau+1} + \text{R\&D}_{\tau+1} + \\
&\quad + \text{depreciation}_{\tau+1} + \text{transportation}_{\tau+1} + \\
&\quad + \text{production costs}_{\tau+1})
\end{aligned} \tag{A9.1.12}$$

where marketing and R&D (decision variables) are known, and depre-ciation is fixed at 2 percent. If the orders are assumed to be given, transportation can be computed from the transportation unit cost. "Production costs" comprise old inventory (known from balance sheet) plus new production [see the production budget, especially Eq. (9.6)]. Notice that the fixed costs in the production budget do not comprise depreciation; see also Exercise 1. Replacing profit in Eq. (A9.1.12) by desired profit of Eq. (A9.1.11), and setting sales volume equal to its forecast, Eq. (A9.1.12) can be solved for price. However, before Eq. (A9.1.12) is solved, the following price differentiation is introduced.

2. Transportation charges are \$2 for the competitors' markets, \$1 for the open market, and zero for the home market. DUMMY decides to lower its price on the home market with 75 percent of the \$2 competitive advantage. On the open market DUMMY can afford to charge \$1 less than on the competitors' markets. Hence if the time index is ignored, revenues in Eq. (A9.1.12) become

$$\text{Revenues} = \sum_{i=1}^{4} (\text{sales volume}_i) \cdot (\text{price}_i) \qquad \text{(A9.1.13)}$$

with the following price structure:

$$\text{Price}_2 = \text{price}_3 = P \qquad \text{(competitors' market)}, \qquad \text{(A9.1.14)}$$
$$\text{Price}_1 = P - (0.75)2 \qquad \text{(home market)}, \qquad \text{(A9.1.15)}$$
$$\text{Price}_4 = P - 1 \qquad \text{(open market)}. \qquad \text{(A9.1.16)}$$

3. Predict the competitors' average price per area by exponential smoothing ($\alpha = 0.50$). If this price is much lower than the "ROI price" resulting from steps (1) and (2), the predicted sales volume will not be realized. Whether a higher or a lower price than the competitors' will be charged depends on whether there are "too many" or "too few" orders. Too many orders mean that forecasted orders exceed current inventory plus production (limited by capacity). Therefore Table 9.6 is used, in which ω_3 was defined in Eq. (A9.1.10). Notice that "too many" orders might actually not be realized if DUMMY charges P_1 with $P_1 > P_2$. Therefore the weight ω_3 is used: if in the past period desired orders were realized and capacity was fully utilized, $\omega_3 \leq 0.50$. In the case of too few orders, $\omega_3 > 0.50$ so that the low P_2 gets the higher weight.

TABLE 9.6.   *Price Determination*

	ROI Price (P_1) versus Competitors' Price (P_2)	
Orders	$P_1 < P_2$	$P_1 > P_2$
Too many	$\max (P_1, P_2) = P_2$	$\omega_3 \cdot P_2 + (1 - \omega_3) \cdot P_1$
Too few	$\min (P_1, P_2) = P_1$	$\omega_3 \cdot P_2 + (1 - \omega_3) \cdot P_1$

Cash Restriction

The cash restriction policy is shown in Fig. 9.8. A cash deficit has consequences not taken into account by DUMMY: the ROI price changes; a decrease in marketing and R&D leads to fewer orders; and so on.

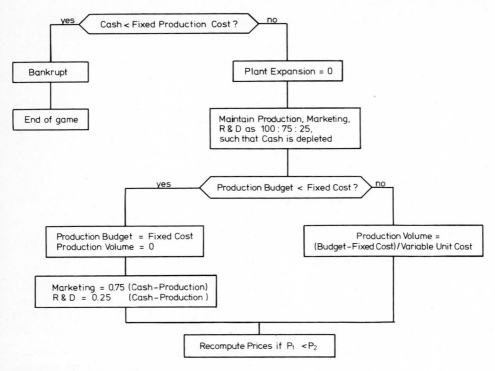

FIGURE 9-8.   *Cash Deficit Policy*

Forecasting

Forecasts are needed for DUMMY's own demand and forecast errors, and for the competitors' prices, marketing, and cash. The competitors' prices are forecast by simple exponential smoothing; see Eq. (9.7). Own demand is predicted allowing for a trend: a linear trend $(a + b \cdot t)$ is fitted, and the slope b is updated by

$$\text{New slope} = \text{old slope} + \alpha \cdot (\text{new demand} - \text{old forecast}) \qquad \text{(A9.1.17)}$$

so that

$$\text{New forecast} = \text{old forecast} + (\text{new slope}) \cdot (\Delta\tau) \qquad \text{(A9.1.18)}$$

where $\Delta\tau = 1$ for a forecast one period ahead. Forecast errors for demand (needed in the safety stock computation) are predicted by Eqs. (A9.1.17) and (A9.1.18) with new "observation" σ defined in Eq. (9.3). Competitors' marketing and cash are also based on the trend model with $\alpha = 0.20$. Note that players know that orders show no seasonality.

APPENDIX 9.2: THE R^2 STATISTIC

To see how well a fitted trend such as Eq. (9.13) explains the observed time path, compute R^2, well-known from statistics:

$$R^2 = \frac{\sum\limits_{t=1}^{20} (\hat{r}_t - \bar{r})^2}{\sum\limits_{t=1}^{20} (r_t - \bar{r})^2} = 1 - \frac{\sum\limits_{t=1}^{20} (r_t - \hat{r}_t)^2}{\sum\limits_{t=1}^{20} (r_t - \bar{r})^2} \qquad (A9.2.1)$$

where $\hat{r}$ follows from the least-square estimates $\hat{\beta}_0$ and $\hat{\beta}_1$,

$$\hat{r}_t = \hat{\beta}_0 + \hat{\beta}_1 \cdot t, \qquad (A9.2.2)$$

and $\bar{r}$ is the average, defined by Eq. (9.12). The rightmost side of Eq. (A9.2.1) follows from the least-squares properties, and shows that the trend model of Eq. (9.13) gives an adequate explanation whenever R^2 approaches the value one. For all sixty time paths, one computes R^2 corresponding to Eq. (9.13). Moreover, one computes R^2 corresponding to polynomials of degrees 2 and 3, i.e., trend models specified by

$$r_t = \sum\limits_{i=0}^{n} \beta_i \cdot t^i + u_t \qquad (n = 2 \text{ or } 3). \qquad (A9.2.3)$$

These R^2-values yield the following conclusions (see also Figs. 9.5 and 9.6): *Total assets* are well characterized by the *linear trend* model of Eq. (9.13) because R^2 varies between 94.5 percent and 99.9 percent. *ROI* and *market share* are better characterized by the simple *average* of Eq. (9.12). R^2 for the linear trend varies between 0 percent and 41 percent. Using the second and third degree polynomials of Eq. (A9.2.3) does not increase R^2 drastically; for instance, R^2 increases from 27.5 percent to 31.2 percent and 31.7 percent, respectively.

APPENDIX 9.3: F-TESTS AND t-TESTS

In order to have a prespecified confidence in the conclusions based on the model of Eq. (9.14), statistical techniques based on statistical assumptions regarding the noise v are used. Theoretically the classical assumptions of regression and analysis of variance are required:

$$v_i \sim \text{NID}(0, \sigma_v^2). \qquad (A9.3.1)$$

To test whether the model of Eq. (9.14) is adequate, compare the following two variances with each other.

Consider a particular C-value, C_i, with its ten replicated observations on, say, total assets growth $\hat{\beta}_{ij}$ where $i = 1, \ldots, 6$ and $j = 1, \ldots, 10$. The ten observations $\hat{\beta}_{ij}$ show a variance around their average $\bar{\beta}_i$:

$$\text{vâr}(\hat{\beta}_i) \equiv \hat{\sigma}_i^2 = \sum\limits_{j=1}^{10} (\hat{\beta}_{ij} - \bar{\beta}_i)^2/(10 - 1). \qquad (A9.3.2)$$

This estimated variance $\hat{\sigma}_i^2$ does *not* depend on the specification of a model such as the linear model of Eq. (9.14). Each C-value gives such a $\hat{\sigma}_i^2$; and the average is computed:

$$\bar{\hat{\sigma}}^2 = \sum\limits_{i=1}^{6} \hat{\sigma}_i^2/6. \qquad (A9.3.3)$$

Hence the variance of $\bar{\beta}_1$, an average, is estimated by

$$\hat{var}\,(\bar{\beta}_i) = \bar{\hat{\sigma}}^2/10. \tag{A9.3.4}$$

From the theory on regression analysis one knows that *if* the fitted model is correct, the "residuals" provide an estimate of "the" variance. More precisely, Eq. (9.14) is fitted to the observations $\bar{\beta}_i$ and yields model predictions $\hat{\bar{\beta}}_i$:

$$\hat{\bar{\beta}}_i = \hat{\gamma}_0 + \hat{\gamma}_1 \cdot C_i. \tag{A9.3.5}$$

Hence the mean squared residual is given by

$$\text{MSR} = \sum_{i=1}^{6} (\hat{\bar{\beta}}_i - \bar{\beta}_i)^2/(6-2). \tag{A9.3.6}$$

MSR does depend on the fitted model: if the model is inadequate, systematic deviations occur between the observations $\bar{\beta}_i$ and the model predictions $\hat{\bar{\beta}}_i$, and inflate MSR.

Statistically, the two estimates of var $(\bar{\beta}_i)$ in Eqs. (A9.3.4) and (A9.3.6) can be compared through the *F*-statistic:

$$F_{4,54} = \frac{\displaystyle\sum_{1}^{6} (\bar{\beta}_i - \hat{\bar{\beta}})^2/(6-2)}{\dfrac{1}{10} \displaystyle\sum_{i=1}^{6} \sum_{j=1}^{10} (\beta_{ij} - \bar{\beta}_i)^2/\{6(10-1)\}}. \tag{A9.3.7}$$

Kleijnen (1975b, p. 367) gives more details and reports on some experiments suggesting that this *F*-test is not "very" sensitive to violations of normality and common variance as assumed in Eq. (A9.3.1). Remember that independence of observations is realized because independent random number streams are used.

If the *F*-statistic in Eq. (A9.3.7) were significantly larger than one, one would have to reject the linear model of Eq. (9.14). In this experiment all *F*-values turn out to be smaller than one. [Values smaller than one are quite possible: tables for the *F*-statistic show that $P(F_{4,54} < 0.85) = 0.50$ and $P(F_{4,54} < 1.4) = 0.75$.] Because the *F*-statistics are not significant, a higher degree polynomial need not be used; possibly a lower degree polynomial is adequate; i.e., in Eq. (9.14) γ_1 becomes zero. This possibility can be tested statistically by means of the Student *t*-statistic:

$$t_d = \frac{\hat{\gamma}_1 - \mathcal{E}(\hat{\gamma}_1)}{\{\hat{var}(\hat{\gamma}_1)\}^{1/2}} = \frac{\hat{\gamma}_1 - \gamma_1}{s(\gamma_1)}. \tag{A9.3.8}$$

Under the standard assumptions of Eq. (A9.3.1), the expression in Eq. (A9.3.8) has indeed a *t*-distribution; see Draper and Smith (1966). The actual finding was that $\max(\hat{\sigma}_i^2)/\min(\hat{\sigma}_i^2) = 1.98$ for the total assets growth, 3.24 for the ROI average, and 4.17 for the market share average. [In the second experiment with bad initial conditions $\max(\hat{\sigma}_i^2)/\min(\hat{\sigma}_i^2)$ is 15.6, 12.9, and 3.6, respectively; in the experiment on sales data these numbers vary between 9.9 for average market share and 336.0 for assets growth.] Therefore one estimates var$(\hat{\gamma}_1)$ using

$$\text{var}(\hat{\gamma}_1) = \sum_{i=1}^{6} \frac{\sigma_i^2}{10} \tilde{C}_i^2 \bigg/ \left(\sum_{1}^{6} \tilde{C}_i^2\right)^2 \tag{A9.3.9}$$

where var $(v_i) = \sigma_v^2 = \sigma_i^2/10$, and $\tilde{C}_i$ is a shorthand notation for $C_i - \bar{C}$ with $\bar{C} = \Sigma C_i/6$. The degrees of freedom d of the t-statistic in Eq. (A9.3.8) are set to nine because each component $\hat{\sigma}_i^2$ in Eq. (A9.3.9) has nine degrees of freedom; see Eq. (A9.3.2). Hence taking $d = 9$ is conservative; i.e., the actual α-error (type I error) is smaller than the nominal α-error of 10 percent; see also Kleijnen (1975b, pp. 471–473). Nonnormality is no problem because the t-statistic is insensitive in this respect.

Above was shown how one can confidently accept (literally not reject) the hypothesis that the linear model of Eq. (9.14) gives a good explanation of the effect of inaccurate production cost information. One can also compute R^2 for Eq. (9.14). This R^2 is not restricted by the statistical assumptions of Eq. (A9.3.1), but does not give conclusions with prespecified confidence. The R^2-computations give the following results (which are in line with the results of the above statistical tests):

Market share and ROI show an *average* $\bar{r}$ that is well characterized by a *linear* model because R^2 is 86 percent and 97 percent respectively. Had the trend model of Eq. (9.13) been used, the growth $\hat{\beta}_1$ would have been found not well explained by the linear model of Eq. (9.14); but the intercept $\hat{\beta}_0$ is indeed well explained.

Total assets show a *growth* $\hat{\beta}_1$ that is well characterized by the *linear* model of Eq. (9.14) because R^2 is 95 percent. Its y-intercept β_0 (the start of the trend) is not affected by the inaccuracy C: if β in Eq. (9.14) denotes the y-intercept $\hat{\beta}_0$ of total assets, $R^2 = 0.50$. A second degree polynomial makes R^2 increase to only 0.77. (The F-test does not suggest either a second or a higher degree polynominal.) Hence the noise v in Eq. (9.14) is so big that a simple "horizontal" model suffices; i.e., inaccuracy C does not affect the intercept $\hat{\beta}_0$. See also Exercises 18 through 20.

APPENDIX 9.4: A MODEL FOR INACCURATE SALES DATA

Sales figures affect a number of other variables because the original IBM game shows that the following relationships hold:

$$\text{Sales volume} = \text{orders (if orders} \leq \text{old inventory} + \text{production)}$$
$$= \text{old inventory} + \text{production (if orders} \geq \text{old inventory} + \text{production),} \qquad \text{(A9.4.1)}$$

and

$$\text{New inventory} = \text{old inventory} + \text{production} - \text{sales volume.} \qquad \text{(A9.4.2)}$$

Not only the inventory volume but also its value is affected; but the value is not shown in Eq. (A9.4.2); see also Eq. (A9.4.4). Further relationships include

$$\text{Sales revenues} = \text{sales volume} \times \text{price} \qquad \text{(A9.4.3)}$$

and

$$\text{Sales costs} = \text{old inventory costs} + \text{(sales volume} + {} $$
$$- \text{ old inventory)} \times \text{unit cost} \qquad \text{(A9.4.4)}$$

where Eq. (A9.4.4) holds if

$$\text{Old inventory} + \text{production} > \text{sales volume} \geq \text{old inventory.} \qquad \text{(A9.4.5)}$$

If the condition in Eq. (A9.4.5) is not satisfied, Eq. (A9.4.4) needs some adjustment. Further effects of sales volume are shown by the following relationships:

$$\text{Transportation cost} = \text{sales volume} \times \text{transportation unit cost} \qquad \text{(A9.4.6)}$$

$$\text{Taxes} = 0.50\,(\text{sales revenues} - \text{total cost}) \qquad \text{(A9.4.7)}$$

$$\text{Cash} = \text{old cash} + \text{sales revenues} - \text{expenses} \qquad \text{(A9.4.8)}$$

$$\text{Assets} = \text{cash} + \text{inventory} + \text{capacity.} \qquad \text{(A9.4.9)}$$

Note that if administrative inventory becomes negative, it is set at zero; or

$$\text{Administrative sales} = \min\,(\text{administrative sales,}$$
$$\text{production} + \text{administrative inventory}). \quad \text{(A9.4.10)}$$

EXERCISES

1. Total production costs can be split into fixed and variable costs. An example of such fixed cost is depreciation. Explain why this depreciation has no effect on the physical production volume permitted by the dollar amount of the production budget. Can you think of fixed production costs that do affect this production volume? (Hint: cost vs. expense)

2. On which market segment might a company wish to concentrate?

3. Why is the definition ROI = profit/total assets incomplete? (Hint: time dimension)

4. a) Why does $k = 2$ in Eq. (9.2) yield only approximately 97.7 percent service? (Hint: consider σ.) (b) Service is defined here as the quotient of number of periods with no stockout, divided by the total number of periods. Give an alternative definition. (c) What effect does this new definition have on k?

5. How could the forecast-routine monitor its own performance? [Hint: See IBM (1967).]

6. Demand is forecast *per* geographic area. How can these forecasts be used to determine the safety stock?

7. The unit cost forecast is based on the most recent period; see Eq. (9.6). How could all past periods be utilized?

8. How might DUMMY base its price on price elasticities? (Hint: regression)

9. Define price discrimination as price differentiation not based on a difference in costs but based on different demand structures. (a) Is the price differentiation by the DUMMY (primarily) price discrimination? (b) How about the lower price a computer center charges for nighttime as opposed to daytime usage?

10. In a confrontation between the DUMMY and human players, the human players could quite accurately predict the future price of the DUMMY (and then set their own prices). How could the DUMMY change the transparency of its price setting?

11. Show that exponential smoothing is a weighted average.

12. In light of the commentary after Eq. (9.7), consider an inventory management system, in which some articles may have a trend; and other articles may show purely erratic fluctuations. For which articles would you apply the highest α-value?

13. Derive the formula for inaccuracies displayed in Eq. (9.10).

14. Inaccuracies e larger than C are cut off at C. Compare the resulting distribution to the following distribution: if an error exceeds C, then sample again.

15. The initial conditions of the simulation experiment are generated by starting from given initial conditions (identical for the three companies) and then simulating forty periods. The three companies are represented by DUMMYs with identical decision rules. Let D_{it} denote a DUMMY i decision variable in period t. Which is correct: $D_{it} = D_{i,t+1}$ or $D_{it} = D_{i't}$ $(i \neq i')$? What if $t > 40$?

16. Consider Eq. (9.14). Prove that var $(\bar{\beta}_i) = \sigma_v^2$.

17. The linear trend model of Eq. (9.13) is fitted to the twenty observations of a single time path. This procedure is repeated ten times. What would be wrong with fitting a single line to the two hundred observations?

18. Derive the relationship between the sample average $\hat{r}$ and the trend model parameters $\hat{\beta}_0$ and $\hat{\beta}_1$.

19. Why should the F-test, shown in Eq. (A9.3.7), for lack of fit be a one-sided test and not a two-sided test?

20. Derive var $(\hat{\gamma}_1)$ shown in Eq. (A9.3.9).

21. In the experiment with less favorable initial conditions, bankruptcy probability was estimated to be $7/120 = 0.058$. Why can one not claim that this estimate is based on 120 observations with an *equal* chance of bankruptcy?

22. Consider the correction factor ω_3 used in the marketing decision, as specified by Eq. (A9.1.10). (a) Compute ω_3 for $\omega_1 = 1$, $\omega_2 = 2$, and for $\omega_1 = 0.5$, $\omega_2 = 0.5$; and comment. (b) Comment on the function ω_3 in general.

23. DUMMY estimates a and b in the production unit cost curve of Eq. (9.6). Which obvious side conditions would you impose on a and b?

24. In the IBM game cash does not earn interest, and inventory does not incur a carrying cost. How would you change the DUMMY's decision rules to take advantage of this (unrealistic) property?

25. If the company can operate on the capital market, which goal would you add to DUMMY's two goal variables?

26. Information economics, explained in Chapter Seven, emphasizes the following factors determining the value of information: surprise content, effect of information on decision, and effect of decision on performance. With which factor would you associate the following experiments: (a) monopolistic versus competitive market, (b) static versus dynamic economy, and (c) changing the factor k in the safety stock computation of Eq. (9.2)?

27. The introduction mentioned that the IBM game has been played by many people and that this extensive use might indicate that the game is indeed a valid model. Can you think of a different explanation for the game's extensive use?

NOTES

1. This chapter is based on Kleijnen (1976a). Most references of this chapter were discovered only after the actual simulation experiment was completed.

2. For a complete description see IBM (1963a) and (1963b). An extensive summary can be found in Naylor et al. (1966); see also Bruns (1963, pp. 97–103).

3. See Vandepitte and Corthouts (1974). Such management competitions have been organized in other countries also. In England, for instance, approximately one thousand teams registered for the 1976 National Management Championship (source: *Computer Weekly*, January 15, 1976).

4. In NIMEX, developed by ICL (1973), penalties are incurred if orders cannot be fulfilled because of too low production or transportation budgets. Expenses can be financed from cash on hand, loans, and revenues from sale of plant. Hence additional decisions are needed on transportation budgets, loans accepted and repaid, and sale of plant. Cash surpluses earn a specific interest rate; cash deficits are financed by (expensive) emergency loans. Inventories deteriorate over time and are evaluated using a procedure different from that of the IBM game. Taxes are treated more realistically.

   In a newer IBM game, called the IBM Management Decision-Making Exercise, players can buy market information on the competitors' market shares, the quality index of competitors' products, etc. Additional decisions are needed on dividends, loans, and plant scrapping. Production smoothing over time decreases the unit production cost. Minimum production cost occurs when capacity utilization is 95 percent instead of 100 percent. Stockouts create loss of goodwill in the next four periods. Inventories lead to inventory carrying cost. Credit facilities depend on profits, the rating of the company on the stock exchange, and inventories. See IBM (1971b). Even more elaborated is IBM's IBGS, Interactive Business Game Simulation; see IBM (1971a).

5. See Hoffman (1965), Hoggatt (1967), and G. Wolf (1972) and (1976).

6. After finishing the study, the author became aware of Haines's (1971) experiment with a marketing game (called MATE) in which players could utilize a computer program for data handling and decision making; see also R. N. Wolff and Haines (1974). This computer program used both heuristic and operations research techniques. The application of operations research techniques and computer technology in modern management games is also discussed by Fisher (1971, pp. 286–287), and Muller and de Samblanckx (1977). Within IBM's IBGS game, APL routines are made available for regression analysis, linear programming, etc.; see IBM (1971a, pp. 32–35). A management game was used by Courtney et al. (1978) to teach the design and evaluation of information systems. This game is closely related to the IBM game of the present chapter. Decisions are supported by an on-line information system developed by the players themselves; see also Courtney and Jensen (1978). A noncompetitive game was employed by Boe (1977) to teach the role of models and information in a production and inventory control situation.

7. See also Geisler and Ginsberg (1965, p. 21). Remember that the preceding chapter reported on a series of gaming experiments by Mock et al. and on a pure computer simulation experiment by Fellingham et al. (1976). In the latter experiment human decision makers were replaced by an optimal algorithm.

Among other things, the sensitivity of the model to its starting values was investigated. Note that these simulation experiments, however, were not done to pretest the gaming experiments; the simulation experiments were performed *after* the majority of the gaming experiments had been executed.

8. See also Wolff and Haines (1974, p. 215).

9. Diebold (1977, p. 10), Naylor and Vernon (1969, pp. 4–9), Schendel and Patton (1978, pp. 1612–1615), Schoeffler et al. (1974), and Van Dam et al. (1976). Profit maximization was the major criterion of management game players in an extensive experiment by J. Wolfe (1975). See also Muller and de Samblanckx (1977, p. 350).

10. The traditional approach is as follows: $\sigma = 1.25$ MAD for normal probability distributions; $\text{MAD}_\tau = |\text{forecast}_\tau - \text{actual}_\tau|$; $\hat{\text{MAD}}_{\tau+1} = \hat{\text{MAD}}_\tau + \alpha(\text{MAD}_\tau - \hat{\text{MAD}}_\tau)$; see IBM (1967). Equation (9.3) does not pretend to be better than the traditional approach but was born "spontaneously." On hindsight the traditional approach is preferred; see also Exercise 5.

11. One or more data points may coincide. For instance, x_3 and x_4 coincide if 110 percent of actual production exceeds full capacity and hence is cut off at 100 percent utilization. In that case the two observations y_3 and y_4 have identical expectations $\eta_3 = \eta_4$. Note that production costs should be called production expense; see also Eq. (A9.1.12), in which depreciation is displayed besides production costs.

12. Ebert (1976), Eilon (1972), Elmaleh and Eilon (1974), Goodman (1974), Kleindorfer et al. (1975), Lee and Khumawala (1974), and Yuan et al. (1975). See also the IPSO studies at Philips in the preceding chapter. Damon and Schramm (1977) discuss simultaneous decision making on production, marketing, and finance; see also L.B. Schwartz and Johnson (1977). A recent survey paper is Mellichamp and Love (1978).

13. This may be explained partly by the author's relative ignorance regarding this particular scientific discipline, partly by the lack of solid guidelines in the literature (which was retrieved *after* the experiment was finished); e.g., see Clarke (1978), Damon and Schramm (1977), Forrester (1968b), Haines (1971), Little (1975), Mann (1975), Oomens (1979), Simon (1978), and Tapiero (1975) and (1978). For a collection of abstracts of mathematical models in marketing refer to Funke (1976).

14. For a general discussion of R&D and for references see N. Baker and Freeland (1975), Bemelmans (1976), Chase and Aquilano (1973, pp. 592–617), Keefer (1977), Rubinstein and Schröder (1977), and Schwartz and Vertinsky (1977). Note that the IBM model computes the company's market share by relating $\text{R\&D}$ to $\text{sales}_{\tau-1}$; see IBM (1963a, p. 7). It seems hard to justify this computation.

15. See Farley et al. (1971).

16. See Diebold (1977, pp. 18, 30), Grinyer and Batt (1974, p. 160), Land (1976, p. 2), Van de Wouw (1977, pp. 74, 79), and also Baker and Peterson (1977).

17. See also Hand and Sims (1975).

18. For large inaccuracy ($C = 0.20$) four replicates have R^2 lower than 80 percent: 79 percent, 68 percent, 43 percent, and 41 percent. The other replicates and C-values give much better R^2 values, up to 98 percent.

19. R^2 is very low: 5 percent for assets and 17 percent for ROI, but 82 percent for market share. The confidence intervals for the linear effect γ_1 in Eq. (9.14) are so wide that no significant effects can be established. ROI and market share even show an insignificant *positive* effect of inaccuracy.

20. All but one of the F-statistics of Appendix 9.3 are smaller than one; the exception has an F-value of 1.26, which is not significant either.

CONCLUSION

CHAPTER **TEN**

INTRODUCTION

This final chapter seeks to achieve three things:

Indicate some research and publications not covered in the preceding chapters, and yet related to the topic of this book.

Summarize the preceding chapters in order to provide an overview.

Evaluate the role of the various theories and techniques covered in this book.

RELATED RESEARCH

The preceding chapters have discussed a rather large variety of techniques and theories for the economic evaluation of information systems. Methods for such benefit evaluation are critically reviewed in an interesting article by E.D. Carlson (1974). See further the article by King and Epstein (1976).

R.W. Swanson (1975, pp. 53–60) surveys the following techniques for the evaluation of information systems, including not only management information systems but also library systems and the like: systems analysis, operations research, benefit–cost analysis, planning-programming-budgeting (PPB), value analysis, management audit, and evaluation. She emphasizes that library information scientists should get involved in management information systems. For a survey on the economic analysis of library systems refer further to Hindle and Raper (1976).

To control the efficiency and effectiveness of data processing and information systems, the use of *ratios* such as "company's output/number of DP personnel" is suggested by Baumgarten et al. (1975, pp. 58–65).

Chervany and Dickson (1970) provide a *logical framework* for the cost/effectiveness analysis of MIS. They distinguish between the *analysis* decisions in MIS development and the *design* decisions. The analysis decisions concern the question of "Which requirements?", and comprise the specification of the system's scope, the information requirements, and the data requirements. The design decisions concern the question of "Which technology?" and comprise the processing system, the installation, and the operations requirements. The Scandinavian literature emphasizes the distinction between *infological* (user-oriented) and *datalogical* (computer-oriented) design and analysis; see, e.g., Langefors (1969).

Verhelst (1974, pp. 111–136) discusses the construction of general models of information systems. These models are intended as frameworks to speed up the sound construction of specific (integrated) information systems for a particular company. The models are not meant for the evaluation of the economic benefits of an IS. Refer further to the proceedings of a conference on strategic planning for MIS; see McLean and Soden (1977). Evaluating economic benefits is only part of such a more comprehensive planning system.[1]

Van de Wouw (1977, p. 25) provides the following framework for the study of information systems. "In all we distinguish seven strata:

1.   The (meta)stratum of the organization as a system.

2.   The stratum of the goal-task hierarchy.

3.   The stratum of the control structure with decisions as the chief components.

4.   The communication stratum: how communication occurs within the organizational units for the purpose of decisions.

5.   The stratum of messages from the automated information system. A proportion of the messages are obtained from automated information systems. That proportion is the chief component in this stratum.

6.   The stratum of files and programmes. The automated messages are generated from these components.

7.   The stratum of data elements and elementary operations. These are the components of the files and programs."

Van de Wouw summarizes a variety of models and concepts for each stratum.

Stamper (1975), to whom brief reference was made in Chapter Six, bases his proposed framework for the study of information system design on the discipline of *semiotics*. Semiotics, the theory of signs, can be subdivided into

Pragmatics: signs in relation to human behaviour;

Semantics: how signs are related to the "real" things they signify,

Syntactics: the formal relations among signs;

Empirics: the statistical relations among sets of signs.[Stamper (1975, p. 109)]

The application of *general systems theory* (GST) to information systems has been advocated by several authors.[2] GST has been pioneered in various disciplines by researchers such as Boulding (economics) and von Bertalanffy (biology). Much has been published on this new discipline.[3] GST does indeed provide a useful frame of reference for the study of problems in the management of sociotechnical systems. GST emphasizes useful concepts such as open versus closed systems, and black box systems. However, specific techniques and methods in GST are either missing or borrowed from other disciplines such as control theory and operations research.

Nurminen (1976) tries to apply fuzzy set theory—pioneered by Zadeh (1975)—to information systems.

The fuzziness of the information system originates from the judgment of the degree of necessity or the information which the system is supposed to produce.[Nurminen (1976, p. 11)]

OVERVIEW OF PRECEDING CHAPTERS

Chapter One limited the scope of this study to the quantification of the financial benefits of computerized (or "computerizable") information. Thereby the fuzzy problems of nonfinancial benefits like job satisfaction, and of informal information systems were eliminated. Notwithstanding the limited scope of this study a very nasty problem area was exposed in subsequent chapters.

As sketched in Chapter Two, information is an "immaterial product" deriving its benefits from its effects on managerial decision making. To make predictions regarding information benefits, one needs some kind of model relating data (information), decisions, and results. At the operational management level, formal models are readily available and well accepted.[4] Well-known examples are provided by inventory systems. At the strategic–tactical level things become much more difficult. The fundamental cause of this difficulty is that strategic decisions cross the boundary between the organization to be controlled, and the "infinite" environment with its many customers, competitors, labor unions, and government agencies. Another dimension that creates problems, even in a purely financial analysis, is the "human" dimension: human processors do not react as automata, do not yield reproducible results.

Several approaches to the benefit problem were surveyed in the Chapters Three through Eight. Chapter Three discussed the technical performance of computers, i.e., performance measured by turnaround time, CPU utilization, etc. Relevant techniques are benchmark programs, queuing theory, simulation, and so on. One bibliography, E.F. Miller (1973), lists seven hundred papers, but very few of them concern the economic performance directly. Indirectly economic performance is indeed affected by technical performance; e.g., bad response times deteriorate the timeliness of information (Chapter Four) or impair the effectiveness of a decision support system.

Chapter Four emphasized computer users' growing awareness of relevant factors other than technical attributes such as response time. Examples include costs, delivery dates, and flexibility. Scoring methods, introduced to combine different factors (criteria) in computer system selection, can be used also to combine multiple criteria in the financial and economic evaluation of information systems. Scoring models are special cases of more general utility models used in economics. A related approach is represented by multiple-criteria decision making in management science. Actually a computer system forms only a part of the information system (IS), and derives its economic benefits from that IS. The focus of this book is not on prescriptive choice models, but on causal models explaining the relationships between IS economic benefits (such as the company's profit) and information attributes (such as accuracy and timeliness); the latter attributes are affected by the introduction of computers.

Chapter Five provided an economic framework for the discussion of the financial benefits of computerized information systems. A central issue in economic theory is the price and market mechanism; i.e., market prices are determined by the supply and demand functions. The limitations of the market mechanism, especially for computers and information products, were examined: external effects, monopolies, etc. The substitution mechanism between capital (computers) and labor was also presented. A different issue is the price charged by the data processing department to its clients within the company. Various microeconomic costing principles were surveyed: cost versus loss, variable versus fixed costs, and marginal versus integral costing. Costing and pricing can be used for efficiency control and allocation of scarce resources. A final topic was the investment aspects of computer and MIS projects: net present value techniques, purchase versus lease, risk analysis (uncertain cash flows), and sensitivity analysis (using a regression metamodel and such experimental designs as fractional factorials).

Chapter Six gave a checklist of the many attributes that determine "the" quality of information: timeliness, accuracy, aggregation, etc. The costs and benefits of these information characteristics were analyzed in rather qualitative terms. Quantitative analysis techniques were presented in the following chapters.

Chapter Seven summarized information economics (IE), based on Bayesian decision theory. IE calculus and its graphical representation by means of decision trees were demonstrated by the newsboy example. Also indicated were some extensions of the basic theory: team theory (multiple-person organization) and dynamic systems (multiple-period decisions). Several applications of this approach were summarized. The limitations of the IE models were discussed, but the conceptual framework provided by this school was also mentioned.

Chapter Eight contained a number of miscellaneous approaches. Control theory focuses on the dynamic behavior of systems, and studies phenomena such as oscillations. If its models—usually continuous, linear, steady-state, and deterministic—cannot be solved analytically, one may resort to simulation, especially system dynamics (SD) simulation. SD, like control theory, concentrates on the dynamic system behavior. SD can be useful in the derivation of optimal or satisficing decision rules, especially for large, integrated systems. More realistic, detailed models are made possible by applying (discrete-event) simulation and gaming. The ad hoc character of simulation models might be mitigated by applying the framework CYSDEM, developed by Welke (1977b). Behavioral aspects can be introduced into simulation models by resorting to management games. The price paid for this behavioral realism is the lack of experimental control (presence of noise and learning effects) and certain practical nuisances (lack of players, high cost). Specific issues can be handled by specific techniques and models: optimization under constraints can be approached by linear programming; inventory problems can be modeled using classic inventory models. This chapter also included a survey of empirical work: case studies, prototypes, and sample surveys. Unfortunately the empirical approach suffers from a lack of experimental control so that general conclusions are hard to obtain.

Chapter Nine gave a detailed demonstration of a simulation experiment with an IBM management game. This study illustrated a general methodology for designing and analyzing simulation, gaming, and real-life experiments. The experiment concentrated on the role of accurate information in tactical and strategic decisions. A computer program (model), called DUMMY, was constructed to play the IBM business game. Accuracy of sales data and production cost data was found to have a linear effect on the economic performance, measured by such criteria as return on investment and market share.

Note that a much more detailed summary of this book is available as a separate paper; Kleijnen (1978b).

FINAL EVALUATION

It is the tenet of this book that as more effort is spent, more so-called intangible factors can be quantified and can be quantified more accurately. (This quantification creates the problem of the cost–benefit analysis of the analysis itself.) Without a quantitative analysis the intangible factors still play a role, but in a "mystic" way. Any MIS design rests on some model, be it a mental, intuitive, informal model or a formal, mathematical model.[5] As emphasized in Chapter One, *formal models* have certain advantages: precise statement of the problems, discovery of alternatives, communication with other people, and so on. Moreover, formal models give reproducible results so that scientific methods become relevant: controlled experiments and mathematical calculus can aid the user and the expert's intuition. A new management style, fostered by more scientifically trained managers, might stimulate the acceptance of formal models. [Several surveys on the actual usage of operations research techniques can be found in Ledbetter and Cox (1977).] A disadvantage of formal models is the temptation to forget that the model is merely a model; the model is not the real system itself with its richness of aspects and relationships.

In order to make progress in the quantification of the financial benefits of information, one needs *theory plus tools*. Theories provide frameworks, clues, guidelines, and ideas. Tools provide numerical results. In the context of MIS relevant theories seem to be Bayesian information economics, control theory, and system dynamics. Useful tools are simulation, gaming, and—more generally—mathematical modeling and statistics. These theories and techniques require more specific evaluation.

Information economics (IE) is the only theory explicitly dedicated to the economic evaluation of information. Its model seems adequate enough for nonrepetitive, one-shot decisions, occurring mainly at the strategic level, e.g., where to locate a new plant. Unfortunately, information systems are built for repetitive use so that the IE model becomes too restrictive. The model is useful insofar as it provides general concepts like surprise content of information, effect of information on the decision and on the performance, and observation error. The IE framework was illustrated by Fig. 7.6: environment, observation, communication, decision, and consequence as determined by act and state of nature. As the information quality changes, the optimal decision may also change. (See Chapter Seven and the introduction to Chapter Nine.)

As mentioned, if the decision is not a one-shot decision, *dynamic* aspects become highly relevant. Although Feltham (1968) and others try to expand IE to dynamic situations, a more adequate theory is provided by *control theory*. Dynamic phenomena such as oscillations and "exploding" time paths can be studied using this theory. Important general concepts are feedback and feedforward, delay functions, and sampling intervals. This theory provides an excellent framework for the evaluation of different control policies in dynamic systems. Unfortunately control theory conceptual models are quite restrictive in the eyes of most MIS practitioners: the models are continuous (aggregated), linear, steady-state, and deterministic. More realistic models are possible through *system dynamics* simulation. System dynamics (SD) uses the same concepts as control theory. However, since SD uses simulation instead of analytical solution techniques, SD can cope with nonlinearities. Transient and stochastic analysis is missing in most SD studies. Its world view remains highly aggregated. (See Chapter Eight.)

More *detailed* studies on the behavior of dynamic systems are possible through *simulation* as developed in operations research: discrete-event simulations, and corporate simulation models. Because these models are more detailed, they tend to have a more restricted scope than SD simulations. Moreover, simulation is only a technique; its models and experiments must be based on relevant theories, such as those listed above. To mitigate the ad hoc character of simulation, Welke (1977b) proposes a general framework called CYSDEM. To generalize the numerical results of simulation, the use of regression metamodels and experimental designs was proposed in Chapters Eight, Five, and Three.

Some information attributes such as report mode have important *behavioral* aspects; no longer is the decision maker assumed to be purely rational. Behavioral aspects can be investigated in the laboratory provided by a user-machine simulation or a *business game*. For instance, a prototype information system may be evaluated in this way. A game can also be used to sell and train prospective users. Unfortunately general conclusions are hard to reach because human players create much noise in gaming experiments. Note that although most games are played in an academic environment, some gaming experiments have been performed at Philips and RAND. (See Chapter Eight and note 6 of Chapter Nine.)

Specific situations may take advantage of specific techniques. For example, if the IS is developed to support an inventory system, a traditional inventory model may provide a good vehicle for the scientific study of the IS. If the system focuses on optimization with side conditions, a linear proramming model is a natural candidate. (See Chapter Eight.)

Empirical studies are needed to provide the data for developing a useful model. The implementation of the model again requires empirical work such as field tests and prototypes. However, empirical work by itself will not form an adequate science of information systems. (See Chapter Eight.)

The various theories and case studies employing specific techniques provide some *rules of thumb:* "surprise" information is more effective (source: IE); different information quality requires different decision rules (IE); dynamic stabilization may require counterintuitive decision rules (SD); more timely and accurate information may have important economic consequences (simulation and gaming experiments); the IS (together with the characteristics of the decision makers themselves and of the environment) may influence the time decision makers need to reach a decision and the confidence they have in their decision (gaming).

One way to regard the results of the studies discussed in this book is as sources of heuristics or rules of thumb. Another way is to consider results contrary to one's intuition as a warning against jumping to conclusions.

In summary, this survey included various formal theories, models, and techniques that have direct or indirect relevance to the economic evaluation of an IS. (Compare, e.g., information economics to technical computer performance models.) For a *practical* situation in a specific firm, no simple recipe will serve. Instead this book provides the reader who believes in the value of formal modeling with a box of tools and specifications on their strengths and weaknesses. Developing an adequate model, however, remains an *art!* Many theories and tools may play a conscious or unconscious role in such a practical study. (See, e.g., the Philips study, called IPSO, in Chapter Eight.) A parallel is provided by inventory management: a textbook may cover models, such as s,S inventory models, and techniques, such as simulation and dynamic programming. Practice, however, requires an artful application of these tools.

It is hoped that readers have gained awareness of the various aspects of the benefit issue, and have acquired new ideas and tools. The many references in this book should facilitate further study of those aspects of particular interest.

NOTES

1. See also Colombatto and Omurtag (1976), Sundgren (1978), and Van de Wouw (1977). Sundgren's article is in Dutch, but it contains references to publications in English on the Scandinavian school including Langefor's work.

2. De Blasis (1976), Van Aken (1978), and Van de Wouw (1977).

3. A recent survey is provided by Hanken and Reuver (1977). See also Ackoff (1971), and F. E. Emery (1969).

4. Hall and Lincoln (1976) report extensively on a case study at British Aircraft Corporation, in which benefits were restricted to reductions in operating costs.

5. See also Pounds (1969), Weil (1971, pp. 1202–1203), and Welke (1977b).

SOLUTIONS TO EXERCISES

The following answers do not give the unique perfect solutions, but indicate the direction of the author's thinking.

CHAPTER ONE

1. Sales revenues increase profit, return on investment, market share, and balance sheet total. Expenses decrease profit, return on investment, and balance sheet total.

2. Cost savings: replacement of clerks, reduced inventory. Gross benefits: sales increase through airline reservation system. See Chapter Two.

3. No. Financial model, sociological model, etc.

CHAPTER TWO

1. Operational: daily detailed planning, purchasing. Tactical: price changes, project selection within budget constraints. Strategic: merger, market selection. See also any textbook on management.

2. Developments in modeling, management style, and costs of computers.

3. No practical optimizing algorithm available for this combinatorial problem.

4. Interactive worker-computer systems for planning, personnel assignment, etc.

5. Tactical-strategic, unstructured.

6. Capital budgeting simulation with subjective probabilities. See Chapter Five.

7. Fast, accurate, detailed data.

8. Depends on situation. See also Chapter Eight.

9. Provide links with other records. See also Chapter Six.

10. DBMS, security, reliability.

11. Availability of appropriate models.

12. Measured demand $= \mu + e + m$ where μ denotes average, e the deviation of true demand from average, and m measurement error. Hence $\sigma_d^2 = \sigma_e^2 + \sigma_m^2$ so that SS $= k\,\sigma_d$ increases if σ_m^2 increases.

13. Decreased safety stock and working stock. See Appendix 2.2.

14. Unfavorable reaction, protest.

15. Pilferage, shrinkage, etc.

16. Half a week.

17. The order size might be reduced to permit utilization of a more frequently revised forecast.

18. POS equipment registers the identity of cashier and the number of transactions.

CHAPTER THREE

1. Mean queuing (waiting) time. The 90 percent quantile is exceeded by 10 percent of jobs.

2. $\bar{r} = \Sigma(c_i - a_i)/n$. $T = n/(\max c_i - \min a_i)$.

3. a) Small jobs first. (b) Same throughput. (c) Small jobs first.

4. User: $\bar{r}$. Computer center: throughput, utilization.

5. $1 - (1 - r_1)(1 - r_2)$ with probability of working r_i. Series: $r_1 r_2 \ldots r_n$.

6. System 1 has highest reliability; see Exercise 5. System 2 has best response time; see Hellerman and Conroy (1975, p. 111).

7. Needed: representative sample of future workload.

8. No.

9. a) $C'D' = \frac{1}{2}CD = 14$; $B'C' = \frac{1}{2}BC = 20$; $A'B' = AC - B'C' = 72 - 20 = 52$. (b) $A'B' = AB/4 = 8$; $B'D' = BD/2 = 34$; total $= 42$; $B'C' = 40/4 = 10$; see also Drummond (1973, pp. 110–111). (c) Instruction times, kernel, etc.

10. Round-robin.

11. Working set size 1.9, 2.6, 2.9, respectively.

12. 2^n different addresses yield 2^{n-s} pages.

13. More time than hardware monitors.

14. Priority for I/O jobs. During their "wait," CPU jobs can execute.

15. Storage space and retrieval time.

16. No. Example: $\text{START}_1 = 10.00$, $\text{END}_1 = 10.04$ (TS $= 0.04$), $\text{START}_2 = 10.04$, $\text{END}_2 = 10.08$, $\text{AT}_3 = 10.05$. Job 1 has priority over job 3.

17. See, e.g., Drummond (1973) or Hellerman and Conroy (1975).

CHAPTER FOUR

1. Category 2, performance data.

2. $w_i = 0$ means characteristic i is irrelevant.
   $w_i = 1$ means only characteristic i is relevant.

3. s can be measured by benchmarks, etc., and does not then depend on personal preference. However, w measures a manager's personal preference.

4. Criteria: speed, safety, cost, esthetics.
   Inputs: number of cylinders, type of paint, etc.

5. Move solid line downward.

6. Make angle of budget line steeper.

7. Draw picture.

8. Locally, a linear function can be a good (Taylor) approximation to a nonlinear function.

9. $w_0 + w_1 s_1 + w_2 s_2 + w_{12} s_1 s_2 + w_{11} s_1^2 + w_{22} s_2^2$.

10. $10 \times 9/2 = 45$.

11. Response time, availability.

12. Disadvantage.

13. Profit, market share, etc.

14. $P = \Sigma w_i \log s_i = \Sigma \log s_i^{w_i} = \log \pi(s_i^{w_i})$ so that $P' = \exp(P) = \pi s_i^{w_i}$.

15. Response time.

16. No; interpersonal utility comparison required.

17. a) $$P_j = \sum_{i=1}^{n} w_i (s_{ij} - s_i^0) \text{ or}$$

   $$P_j = \Sigma w_i (s_{ij} - s_i^0)^2$$

   b)   Usually s_i^0 is zero or infinite.

18. Adding a "crazy" but feasible alternative may change s_i^0 and hence P_j.

19. a) $P = w_1 \cdot Q_1 + w_2 \cdot Q_2 + w_3 \cdot Q_3$ where Q_i denotes average queuing time in class i ($i = 1, 2, 3$), and w_i = number of class i jobs divided by total number of jobs. (b) 90 percent quantile of class i divided by mean service time of class i. (c) Lower borderline means fewer small jobs and more medium jobs ($w_1 -$, $w_2 +$). Hence Q_1 decreases (fewer competitors) and Q_2 increases.

20. Cost minimization, LP.

21. If $d(XP)/dX = 0$; and if $d(XP)/dX = dC/dX$. See also Chapter Five.

22. —

CHAPTER FIVE

1. No: company–government, company–community interface, etc.

2. Changes in total national income, income distribution, tastes (preferences), and price changes of other products.

3. Higher prices may be thought to express better quality so that more is demanded. Examples: fashion products, technically sophisticated products (computers?), but also fountain-pen ink.

4. a) $s = a + bp$ (price = p). (b) Higher coefficient a means positive shift. (c) Lower price, higher market volume.

5. Proprietary software besides raw computer power.

6. a) $(dx/dp) \cdot (p/x) = b \cdot p/(a + bp)$. (b) For $x = p^b$ the elasticity is $(bp^{b-1}) (p/p^b) = b$ (constant!). (c) Regression parameters become constant price elasticity coefficients.

7. Monopolistic; see lower half of Fig. 5.1.

8. $x_0 = (B - a)/(2b)$.

9. No.

10. $A' < 2A$ (A' and A: fixed cost for $x > x_1$, and $x \leq x_1$, respectively).

11. Suppose $\Delta u/\Delta x_1 > \Delta u/\Delta x_2$. Put $\Delta x_1 = +1$; $\Delta x_2 = -1$. Hence u increases.

12. a) $\partial x/\partial y = 0$ (vertical dashed line in upper part of Fig. 5.6). (b) $p_z/p_y = (\alpha_1 - \alpha_2)/(\beta_2 - \beta_1)$. Hence $\alpha_1 = \alpha_2 + (\beta_2 - \beta_1) p_z/p_y$. So $\gamma_1 = \alpha_1 p_y + \beta_1 p_z = \alpha_2 \cdot p_y + \beta_2 \cdot p_z \equiv \gamma_2$. (c) $\gamma_1/\gamma_2 < \beta_1/\beta_2 (< \alpha_1/\alpha_2)$.

13. Substituting $\partial x/\partial y = \alpha \cdot y^{\alpha-1} \cdot z^\beta$ and $x = y^\alpha \cdot z^\beta$ results in α.

14. Cost reduction, plus no other technical alternative (high volume of checks to be processed with reasonable turnaround time).

15. a) U-shaped. (b) Third degree polynomial $c = a + bx + cx^2 + dx^3$. (c) Too high costs; i.e., actual costs at x exceed $c(x)$, the efficiency frontier. (d) No; *minimum* net value also corresponds to $dr/dx = dc/dx$.

16. Agricultural products like wheat and sugar.

17. Fixed relative to cards. Variable relative to CPU.

18. Replacement cost in inflation countries.

19. a) $dc/dx = B$, $c/x = (A/x) + B$. (b) No; loss versus cost.

20. Joint costs.

21. Wait can be caused by interruptions from other jobs (demurrage).

22. a) No long-run cost. (b) Low price stimulates use.

23. Fixed cost, possibly joint.

24. Software: more unusual product.

25. a) Marginal cost. (b) Different demand function: price discrimination.

26. Student ID required.

27. a) Reliability (accuracy) of estimated regression coefficients decreases with number of variables. (b) Own price, competitors' price, national income.

28. Fixed cost and low use create high unit "cost"; hence fewer jobs; hence less use, etc.

29. Deduct preventive maintenance, downtime, idle time (100 percent utilization gives infinite waiting times), rerun time (nonchargeable to user), multiprogramming degradation (demurrage).

30. Cost: necessary for increased overall efficiency.

31. If programming assistance remains a "free" good, users will minimize computer use by having "efficient" programs developed.

32. a) Lower charges. (b) Longer waiting times: spillover. (c) Preemptive higher priority for old customers. (d) Overhead for administering such a priority scheme.

33. University: charge resources used.

34. Simultaneous arrival of cars from each of four directions.

35. Cash flow = profit + depreciation.

36. Polynomial of degree n has n solutions; some may coincide or be imaginary.

37. No. Use discounted cash flows.

38. a) Project 1 by all criteria. (b) Project 1 by payback and rate of return criteria.

39. Correlation between C_i.

CHAPTER SIX

1. a) Delivery lag can be reduced through a teleprocessing DP system connected to the supplier's system. (b) Numerically controlled machines.

2. Input time P.

3. Unrealistic because the organization will consider for I only a few discrete values such as weeks versus months.

4. Figure 6.4a with straight line for producing delay A from various combinations of I and P, and dashed curve U for buying combinations of I and P. See also Gregory and Atwater (1957, p. 60).

5. Batch unless interactive manipulation is desired.

6. a) For independent x_i with common variance $\sigma^2(x)$, var $(\Sigma x_i/n) = n^{-2}$ var $(\Sigma x_i) = n^{-1}$ var (x). Hence $\sigma(\bar{x}) = \sigma(x)/\sqrt{n}$. (b) var $(\Sigma x_i) = n\sigma^2$. Hence $(\sigma\sqrt{n})/(\mu n) = v/\sqrt{n}$. (c) var $(\hat{x} \mid t = n + 1) = \sigma_u^2 \{1/n + (n + 1 - \bar{t})^2 / \sum_{t=1}^{n} (t - \bar{t})^2\}$. Smallest var $(\hat{x}|t)$ if $t = \bar{t}$. See any book on regression analysis.

7. Planning period = review time + lead time (+ record keeping lag); see Appendix 2.2.

8. a) Uniform distribution between $35.50 and $36.49. (b) Uniform between $36.00 and $36.99. (c) Normal distribution with mean $36.00 and unknown variance (central limit theorem).

9. Limited word length of registers.

10. Smith is less precise than John P. Smith.

11. Precision: report in, say, thousands of dollars (depending on size of company). Accuracy: wrong sales figures, pilferage. Arbitrariness: LIFO versus FIFO costs, depreciation scheme. See Chapter Five.

12. Pros: reliability and recovery, security and privacy, communication cost. Cons: duplicated records (synchronization), processing cost (economies of scale plus specialization).

13. No; use information of period 5 (not 6) to forecast period 7.

14. Daily update by processing of, say, POS diskette. See Appendix 2.1.

15. No; also decrease article 51 with ten units.

16. R is infinite.

17. Intelligent terminals.

CHAPTER SEVEN

1. a) $0.60 \times 100 + 0.40 \times (-50) = 40$.

   b) $0.60 \times 100 + 0.40 \times (0) = 60$

   c) $P(y = 0) = P(y = 0|e = 0) \cdot P(e = 0) + P(y = 0|e = 1) \cdot P(e = 1)$
   $$= (0.8)(0.4) + (1 - 0.8)(0.6) = 0.44$$

   where $P(y = 0|e = 1) = 1 - P(y = 1|e = 1)$.
   $$P(e = 0|y = 0) = P(y = 0|e = 0) \cdot P(e = 0)/P(y = 0).$$
   $$= (0.8)(0.4)/0.44 \approx 0.73.$$

   d) $\mathcal{E}(w|y = 1) = P(e = 1|y = 1) \cdot (100) + P(e = 0|y = 1) \cdot (-50)$
   $$= 0.86 \,(100) + (0.14)(-50) = 79$$
   $\mathcal{E}(w|y = 0) = 0.27(100) + (0.73)(-50) = -9.5$. Hence $a^* = 0$,
   $\mathcal{E}(w|y = 0, a^*) = 0$.
   $\mathcal{E}(w|\text{IS}) = 79(1 - 0.44) + 0(0.44) = 44$.
   $\mathcal{E}(w|\text{IS}) - \mathcal{E}(w|\text{no IS}) = 44 - 40 = 4$.

   e) 4.

   f) zero.

2. $a^* = 1$, and expected profit $= 3$, independent of message y.

3. For $y = 0$ or $y = 2$, $a^* = 1$; for $y = 1$, $a^* = 2$.

4. $P(A_1|B) = \dfrac{1 \cdot P(B|A_1)}{P(B|A_1) \cdot 1 + P(B|A_2) \cdot 0} = 1$

   and

   $P(A_1|B) = \dfrac{P(A_1) \cdot 1}{1 \cdot P(A_1) + P(B|A_2) \cdot P(A_2)} < 1$.

5. a) Bet 2. (b) Indifferent, same expected value. (c) Bet 1. (d) Bet 2; same maximum loss, but probability is 0.50 in bet 1. See also Chapter Four.

6. Identical columns.

7. $\underset{i,j}{\text{Max}} \,(w_{ij}) = 8$.

8. Diffuse IS: $P(y_k|e_i) = 1/m$ with $i = 1, \ldots, m$. Zero value because $P(e|y) = P(e)$.

9. a) Payoffs satisfy $w_{ij} \leq w_{ij}$, for all i. (b) Identical messages are generated by "different" events, i.e., events with different payoffs. (c) Same event may generate different messages; think of different degrees of precision. (d) Too coarse.

10. a) Coarse. (b) State $e = 2$.

11. a) Sum of squared residuals (standard least squares algorithm). (b) Sum of absolute or relative residuals. Bayesian loss functions depending on decision problem in which regression analysis is used.

CHAPTER EIGHT

1. Feedback plus feedforward.

2. a) Electrical engineering, physics, chemistry, etc. (b) Difference-equation approximation; see such languages as CSMP and CSSL.

3. Real-time, on-line computer systems, plus central database; see discussions on IPSO system.

4. One set of initial conditions suffices.

5. Physical scale models of ships and airplanes in wind tunnels. Worker-machine simulation: link trainers for pilots, automobile test tracks.

6. a) $2^7 = 128$. (b) Depends on desired statistical accuracy. See Kleijnen (1975b). (c) More customers in more congested system (higher autocorrelation).

7. All players receive delayed information, but some delays are longer than others.

8. Gaming because IE assumes purely rational behavior; no behavioral effects.

9. Increasing marginal losses.

10. Linear programming.

11. Coin: log 2. Die: log 6.

12. a) No: degrees of freedom $(3 - 1) = 2$ and $3(40 - 1) = 117$. (b) Maximum difference: $229,957 - 152,964 = 76,993$. Standard deviation (in thousands): $\{31^2 + 30.5^2\}^{1/2} = \{1,891.25\}^{1/2} = 43.5$. The ratio is $77/43.5 = 1.77$ whereas $P(|t_{39}| \geq 1.77) < 10$ percent. So agree with Fellingham et al. (1976).

13. See the subject index under accuracy, etc.

CHAPTER NINE

1. Depreciation is a cost item but involves no out-of-pocket expenses. Fixed costs involving expenses: indirect labor expenses like production planning personnel expenses.

2. Home market: lowest cost.

3. $\text{ROI}_r = \text{profit}_r/\text{assets}_t$ (or assets_{t+1} or $\frac{1}{2} \text{assets}_t + \frac{1}{2} \text{assets}_{t+1}$).

4. a) σ is only estimated. (b) Service = total demand fulfilled/demand over all periods. (c) Replace k by "service function" $g(k)$; see IBM (1967).

5. Wrong forecasts if too large errors or too many errors of same sign occur; increase α. (Too large error if $|\text{demand} - \text{forecast}| \geq 4$ MAD.)

6. $\text{MAD} = | (\sum_{1}^{4} x_i) - (\sum_{1}^{4} \hat{x}_i) |$ where x_i (or $\hat{x}_i$) denotes demand (or forecast) in area i.

7. Estimate a and b per (past) period, applying least squares. Use exponential smoothing to forecast a and b.

8. As more periods are played, data become available for regression analysis; e.g., $\ln x = a + b \ln p + c \ln \tilde{p}$ with own price p, competitors' price $\tilde{p}$, and sales x.

9. a) DUMMY: no price discrimination. (b) Computer center: price discrimination.

10. Augment with a random component; e.g., multiply by r uniformly distributed over the interval 0.9–1.10.

11. $\hat{x}_{\tau+1} = \alpha \cdot x_\tau + (1 - \alpha) \cdot \hat{x}_\tau$. Also $\hat{x}_{\tau+1} = \Sigma \beta_i \cdot x_i$ with $\beta_i = \alpha \cdot (1 - \alpha)^{i-1}$ and $\Sigma \beta_i = 1$ so that β_i are weights indeed.

12. Trend: higher α-value.

13. From Eq. (9.9) it follows that $0.99 = P(-C\eta \le y - \eta \le C\eta) =$
$= P(-C\eta/\sigma \le (y - \eta)/\sigma \le C\eta/\sigma) = P(-C\eta/\sigma \le z \le C\eta/\sigma)$ with
$z \sim NID(0, 1)$. Hence $C\eta/\sigma = 2.56$ or $\sigma = C\eta/2.56$.

14. Distribution has jump at $e = C$ if e is cut off.

15. Correct $D_{it} = D_{i't}$. For $t > 40$ $D_{it} \ne D_{i't}$ (different inaccurate input data).

16. In Eq. (9.14) $\gamma_0 + \gamma_1 c$ is a constant term so that var $(\bar{\beta}_i) =$ var(v_i). Note that var $(\bar{\beta}_i) \ne$ var(β_i).

17. It is possible that points on, say, time path 1 cannot be reached from a point on time path 2.

18. $\hat{\bar{r}} = \hat{\beta}_0 + \hat{\beta}_1 \cdot \bar{t} = \hat{\beta}_0 + 10.5\hat{\beta}_1$ since $\hat{\beta}_0 = \hat{\bar{r}} - \hat{\beta}_1 \cdot \bar{t}$.

19. H_1: $\mathcal{E}$ (MSR) $> \sigma^2$, not $\mathcal{E}$ (MSR) $\ne \sigma^2$.

20. In general, if $Y = X\beta$, then $\hat{\beta} = (X'X)^{-1}X'Y$ so that $\Omega_\beta = W \cdot \Omega_y \cdot W'$ with $W \equiv (X'X)^{-1}X'$. Here Ω_y has elements $\omega_{ij} = 0(i \ne j)$ and $\omega_{ij} = \sigma_i^2/10$. See Appendix 5.1.

21. Last observation cannot be a bankruptcy observation because the experiment would then continue. Compare Pascal distributions in statistics literature.

22. a) If $\omega_1 = 1$ and $\omega_2 = 2$, then $\omega_3 = 4/(1 + 4) = 0.8$ (high weight). If $\omega_1 = 0.5$ and $\omega_2 = 0.5$, then $\omega_3 = (1/16)/(1 + 1/16) = 1/17$ (ω_2 shows too small capacity; hence no marketing desired). (b) Monotonously increasing; $0 \le \omega_3 \le 1$.

23. $a \ge 0$ and $b \ge 0$.

24. Spend all remaining cash on production; unsold production does not generate inventory cost.

25. Goal 3: Stabilize (dividend/share price).

26. a) Effect of decision on performance. (b) Surprise content. (c) Effect of information on decision.

27. High usage just because game is IBM supported.

Abramson, N., and F. Kuo (eds.), 1973. *Computer–Communications Networks.* Englewood Cliffs, N.J.: Prentice-Hall.

Ackoff, R.L., 1967. Management misinformation systems. *Management Science,* 14(4):B147–B156.

––––––, and S. Beer, 1969. In conclusion: some beginnings. In J.S. Aronofsky (ed.), *Progress in Operations Research, Relationship between Operations Research and the Computer,* vol. 3. New York: Wiley.

––––––, 1971. Towards a system of systems concepts. *Management Science,* 17(11):661–671.

ACM, 1974. Scanning UPC: its impact on computing, the supermarket and you. SIGBDP, San Francisco Golden Gate Chapter Meeting, Nov. 7.

Adams, C.R., 1975. How management users view information systems. *Decision Sciences,* 6(2):337–345.

––––––, and R.G. Schroeder, 1972. *Current and Desired Characteristics of Information Used by Middle Managers: A Survey.* MISRC-WP-72-01. Minneapolis: Management Information Systems Research Center, Graduate School of Business Administration, University of Minnesota.

Adams, J.M., and D.H. Haden, 1976. *Social Effects of Computer Use and Misuse.* New York: Wiley.

Agajanian, A.H., 1976. A bibliography on system performance evaluation. *Performance Evaluation Review,* 5(1):53–64.

Agrawala, A.K., and J.M. Mohr, 1978. *The Relationship between the Pattern Recognition Problem and the Workload Characterization Problem.* College Park, Md.: Department of Computer Science, University of Maryland.

Allen, B.R., 1973. Computer security. In S. Teglovic and R. Lynch (eds.), *Topics in Management Information Systems.* New York: MSS Information.

Amphlett Lewis, W.A., 1966. *Communications and Organizations.* Occasional paper no. 2. Birmingham, England: Department of Operational Research, University of Lancaster.

Ansoff, H.I., 1971. Managerial problem solving. *Journal of Business Policy,* 2(1):3–20.

––––––, and D.P. Slevin, 1968. An appreciation of industrial dynamics. *Management Science,* 14(7):383–397.

Anthony, R.N., 1965. *Planning and Control Systems: A Framework for Analysis.* Boston: Harvard University Graduate School of Business Administration.

APICS, 1974. State-of-the-art survey: a preliminary analysis. *Production and Inventory Management,* 15(4):1–11.

Aron, J., 1969. Estimating resources for large programming systems. *Software Engineering Techniques,* Report on a Conference sponsored by the NATO Science Committee.

Aron, J.D., 1974. *The Program Development Process: The Individual Programmer.* Reading, Mass.: Addison-Wesley.

Ashenhurst, R.L., (ed.), 1972. Curriculum recommendations for graduate professional programs in information systems. *Communications ACM,* 15(5):363–398.

Auerbach, 1975. *Guide to Computer Performance Evaluation.* Philadelphia: Auerbach.

Avolio, L.C., 1975. Computer economics in Italy. In A.B. Frielink (ed.), *Economics of Informatics,* Proceedings of the IBI-ICC International Symposium. Amsterdam: North Holland.

Aykac, A., and C. Brumat (eds.), 1977. *New Developments in the Applications of Bayesian Methods.* Amsterdam: North Holland.

Baker, K.R., 1974. *Introduction to Sequencing and Scheduling.* New York: Wiley.

_____, and D.W. Peterson, 1977. *An Analytic Framework for Evaluating Rolling Schedules.* GSBA Paper 177. Durham: Graduate School of Business, Duke University.

Baker, N., and J. Freeland, 1975. Recent advances in R&D benefit measurement and project selection methods. *Management Science,* 21(10):1164–1175.

Balanchandran, V., and E.A. Stohr, 1977. *Optimal Pricing of Computer Resources in a Competitive Environment.* Discussion Paper no. 268. Evanston: Graduate School of Management, Northwestern University.

Bally, L., J. Brittan, and K.H. Wagner, 1977. A prototype approach to information system design and development. *Information and Management,* 1(1):21–26.

Bamberg, G., A.G. Coenenberg, and R. Kleine-Doepke, 1976. Zur entscheidungsorientierten Bewertung von Informationen (On the decision theoretic evaluation of information). *Zeitschrift für Betriebswirtschaftliche Forschung,* 28(1): 30–42.

Barber, B., and W. Abbott, 1972. *Computing and Operational Research at the London Hospital.* London: Butterworth.

Bariff, M.L., 1974. An operational framework for the design of management information systems. *Proceedings Sixth Annual Meeting American Institute for Decision Sciences,* Atlanta, Oct. 30–Nov. 2.

_____, 1976. *Information Requirements Analysis: A Methodological Review.* W.P. 76-08-02. Philadelphia: Decision Sciences Department, Wharton School, University of Pennsylvania.

_____, and E.J. Lusk, 1977. Cognitive and personality tests for the design of management information systems. *Management Science,* 23(8):820–829.

Barkin, S.R., 1974. An Investigation into Some Factors Affecting Information System Utilization. Unpublished Ph.D. Thesis. Minneapolis: University of Minnesota.

_____, and G.W. Dickson, 1977. An investigation of information system utilization. *Information and Management*, 1(1):35–45.

Barlow, R.E., and F. Proschan, 1975. *Statistical Theory of Reliability and Life Testing; Probability Models.* New York: Holt, Rinehart and Winston.

Bassler, R.A., and E.O. Joslin (eds.), 1975. *An Introduction to Computer Systems.* 3rd ed. Arlington, Virginia: College Readings.

_____, and J.J. Logan, 1976. *The Technology of Data Base Management Systems.* 3rd ed. Alexandria, Virginia: College Readings.

Baugut, G., 1973. *Modelle zur Auswahl von Datenverarbeitungsanlagen* (Models for the selection of computers). Köln-Braunsfeld, Germany: Verlagsgesellschaft Rudolf Müller.

Baumgarten, A., C. Brevoord, R.W. Dunning, J. Th. Geilenkirchen, and M.A. Van Hoepen, 1975. *Beïnvloeding van de Productiviteit van het Administreren* (Affecting the productivity of clerical workers). (With an English abstract, pp. 174–184.) Leiden, Netherlands: H.E. Stenfert Kroese N.V.

Beckmann, M.J., 1958. Decision and team problems in airline reservations. *Econometrica*, 26(1):134–145.

Beilner, H., and E. Gelenbe (eds.), 1978. *Measuring, Modelling, and Evaluating Computer Systems.* Amsterdam: North Holland.

Bell, D.E., R.L. Keeney, and H. Raiffa (eds.), 1977. *Conflicting Objectives in Decisions.* Chicester: Wiley.

Bell, T.E., 1971. *Computer Performance Analysis: Measurement Objectives and Tools.* R-584-NASA/PR. Santa Monica: RAND.

_____, 1972. Objectives and problems in simulating computers. *Proceeding AFIPS 1972 Fall Joint Computer Conference.* Montvale: AFIPS.

Bemelmans, T.M.A., 1976. *Research Planning in de Onderneming* (Research planning in the company). Doctoral dissertation. Tilburg, Netherlands: Katholieke Hogeschool. (English edition. Hague: Martinus Nijhoff, 1980.)

Bénay, J., 1965. General considerations on the economics of A.D.P. In A.B. Frielink (ed.), *Economics of Automatic Data Processing.* Amsterdam: North Holland.

Benbasat, I., and R.G. Schroeder, 1975. *An Experimental Investigation of Some MIS Design Variables.* Management Information Systems Working Paper Series, MISRC-WP-75-01. Minneapolis: University of Minnesota.

Benwell, N., (ed.), 1977. *Data Preparation Techniques.* London: Advance Publications.

Bequai, A., 1978. *Computer Crime.* Farnborough, U.K.: Lexington Books.

Berg, S.V., 1975. Planning for computer networks: the trade analogy. *Management Science*, 21(12):1458–1465.

Bernard, D., J.C. Emery, R.L. Nolan, and R.H. Scott, 1977. *Charging for Computer Services: Principles and Guidelines.* New York: Petrocelli.

Bernhard, R.H., 1977. State preference synthesis of utility and interest with critical implications for discounting under risk. *Engineering Economist*, 22(3):203–217.

Bhat, U.N., 1969. Sixty years of queuing theory. *Management Science*, 15(6):B280–B294.

Blumenthal, S.C., 1969. *Management Information Systems: A Framework for Planning and Development*. Englewood Cliffs, N.J.: Prentice-Hall.

Boe, W.J., 1977. *Introducing Students to a Manufacturing Information System*. Iowa City: College of Business Administration, University of Iowa.

Boehm, B.W., and T.E. Bell, 1975. Issues in computer performance evaluation: some consensus, some divergence. *Performance Evaluation Review*, 4(3):4–39.

Bonini, C.P., 1963. *Simulation of Information and Decision Systems in the Firm*. Englewood Cliffs, N.J.: Prentice Hall. (Reprinted Chicago: Markham Publishers, 1967.)

Bonney, M.C., 1969. Some considerations of the cost and value of information. *Computer Journal*, 12:118–123.

Boodman, D.M., 1977. *Risk Management and Risk Management Science, an Overview*. Cambridge, Mass.: Arthur D. Little.

Borovits, I., and P. Ein-Dor, 1977. Cost/utilization: a measure of system performance. *Communications ACM*, 20(3):185–191.

Bos, H., 1978. Logistieke systemen in een industrie (Logistic systems in an industry). In L.C. Van Zutphen (ed.), *Aspecten van Logistieke Informatiesystemen* (Aspects of Logistic Information Systems). Alphen aan den Rijn, Netherlands: Samsom Uitgeverij.

Bosman, A., 1976. *What Are Information Systems? An Introduction*. Groningen, Netherlands: Department of Management Science, Economic Faculty, University of Groningen.

Bottler, J., P. Horváth, and H. Kargl, 1972. Methoden der Wirtschaftlichkeitsrechnung für die Datenverarbeitung (Methods for the computation of the effectiveness of data processing). Munich: Verlag Moderne Industrie.

Boutell, W.S., 1968. *Computer-oriented Business Systems*. Englewood Cliffs, N.J.: Prentice-Hall.

Bovet, D.P., 1972. On the use of models employing both simulation and analytical solutions for scheduling computing centers. *Computer Simulation versus Analytical Solutions for Business and Economic Models*. Gothenburg, Sweden: University of Gothenburg.

Boyd, D.F., and H.S. Krasnow, 1963. Economic evaluation of management information systems. *IBM Systems Journal*, 2(March):2–23.

Braat, J.J.M., 1973. The IPSO control system. *International Journal of Production Research*, 11(4):417–436.

————, 1977. *Integrale Goederenstroombesturing* (Integrated materials management). Deventer, Netherlands: Uitgeverij Kluwer, B.V.

Bradley, S.P., A.C. Hax, and T.L. Magnanti, 1977. *Applied Mathematical Programming*. Reading, Mass.: Addison-Wesley.

Brandon, D.H., and S. Segelstein, 1976. *Data Processing Contracts—Structure, Contents, and Negotiations*. New York: Van Nostrand Reinhold.

Brenner, J.R., 1965. Toward a value theory of information. In A.B. Frielink (ed.), *Economics of Automatic Data Processing*. Amsterdam: North Holland.

Brevoord, C., 1971. *Informatiebeleid* (Information management). Leiden, Netherlands: H.E. Stenfert Kroese N.V.

Brigham, E.F., 1976. Hurdle rates for screening capital expenditure proposals. *Financial Management*, **5**:17–25.

Britney, R.R., 1976. Bayesian point estimates and the PERT scheduling of stochastic activities. *Management Science*, **22**(9):938–948.

Brittan, J.N.G., (ed.), 1974. *An International Curriculum for Information Systems Designers*. Rome: IBIICC, Intergovernmental Bureau for Informatics.

Brocato, L.J., 1971. Getting the best computer system for your money. *Computer Decisions*, **13**(Sept.): 12–16.

Brock, G.W., 1975. *The United States Computer Industry: A Study of Market Power*. Cambridge, Mass.: Ballinger.

Bromley, A.C., 1965. Choosing a set of computers. *Datamation:* **11**(8):37–40.

Brooks, F.P., 1974. The mythical man-month. *Datamation:* **20**(12):44–52.

Brown, R.G., 1977. *Materials Management Systems: A Modular Library*. New York: Wiley.

Bruns, W.J., 1963. *A Simulation Study of Alternative Methods of Inventory Valuation*. Ph.D. dissertation, University of California, Berkeley. No. 63-5491. Ann Arbor: University Microfilms.

Bucci, G., and D.N. Streeter, 1979. A methodology for the design of distributed information systems. *Communications ACM*, **22**(4):233–245.

Buchholz, W., 1969. A selected bibliography on computer system performance evaluation. *Computer Group News*, **2**(8):21–22.

Burch, J.G., and F.R. Strater, 1974. *Information Systems: Theory and Practice*. Santa Barbara: Hamilton.

Burpo, C.W., 1973. Is the post audit necessary? *Data Management*, **11**(12):14–17.

Burt, J.M., 1977. Planning and dynamic control of projects under uncertainty. *Management Science*, **24**(3):249–258.

Bussey, L.E., 1978. *The Economic Analysis of Industrial Projects*. Englewood Cliffs, N.J.: Prentice-Hall.

———, and G.T. Stevens, 1972. Formulating correlated cash flow streams. *Engineering Economist*, **18**(1):1–30.

Butterworth, J.E., and W.T. Ziemba, 1978. Teaching the foundations for the economic analysis and evaluation of information systems. *Interfaces*, **8**(4):76–81.

Cale, E.G., L.L. Gremillion, and J. L. McKenney, 1979. Price/performance patterns of U.S. computer systems. *Communications ACM*, **22**(4):225–233.

Call, W.L., 1975. Quadratic cost-volume relationship and timing of demand information; a comment. *Accounting Review*, **50**(1):133–137.

Campbell, E.J., 1971. Economics of regional computing centers. In B.E. Squires (ed.), *Economic Considerations in Managing the Computer Installation*, SIGCOSIM Proceedings. New York: ACM.

Campise, J.A., 1973. Computer aided data processing management. *Data Management*, **11**(11):12–17.

Canning, R.G., 1966. Equipment selection. *Data Processing Digest*, **12**(6):1–9.

———, 1973. The effects of charge-back policies. *EDP Analyzer*, **11**(11):1–14.

———, 1974a. Charging for computer services. *EDP Analyzer*, **12**(7):1–13.

_____, 1974b. The current status of data management. *EDP Analyzer*, **12**(2):1–14.

_____, 1976a. Distributed data systems. *EDP Analyzer*, **14**(6):1–13.

_____, 1976b. Over het doorberekenen van computer service-werkzaamheden (On charging computer services). EDP Analyzer Special Report, *Informatie*, **18**(12): 680–688.

Cardenas, A.F., 1975. Data entry: a cost giant. In R.A. Bassler and E.O. Joslin (eds.), *An Introduction to Computer Systems*. Arlington, Va.: College Readings.

Carlson, E.D., 1974. Evaluating the impact of information systems. *Management Informatics*, **3**(2):57–67.

_____, 1979. An approach for designing decision support systems. *Data Base*, **10**(3):3–15.

Carlson, J.G., 1975. Interactive systems for the physical control of material. *Eighteenth Annual Conference Proceedings*. Washington: American Production and Inventory Control Society.

Carter, C., 1974. *Guide to Reference Sources in the Computer Sciences*. New York: Macmillan Information.

Cetron, M., 1969. Technological Resource Management—Quantitative Methods. Cambridge, Mass.: M.I.T. Press.

Chandy, M.K., 1977. Operations research models of recovery in database systems. *On-line Data Bases*. Maidenhead: Infotech.

_____, and M. Reiser (eds.), 1978. *Computer Performance*. Amsterdam: North Holland.

Chanson, S.T., and C.D. Bishop, 1977. A simulation study of adaptive scheduling policies in interactive computer systems. *Performance Evaluation Review*, **6**(3):33–39.

Chaplin, J.E., 1969. A feasibility study guide. *Journal of Systems Management*, **20**(7):20–26.

Charnes, A., and W.W. Cooper, 1977. Goal programming and multiple objective optimizations. *European Journal of Operational Research*, **1**(1):39–54.

Charnetski, J.R., 1977. Bayesian decision making with ordinal information. *Operations Research*, **25**(5):889–892.

Chase, R.B., and N.J. Aquilano, 1973. *Production and Operations Management*. Homewood: Irwin.

Chervany, N.L., and G.W. Dickson, 1970. Economic evaluation of management information systems: an analytical framework. *Decision Sciences*, **1**(3 and 4): 296–308.

_____, 1972. *Management Information Systems: Design Questions from a User's Perspective*. MISRC-WP-71-11. Minneapolis: Management Information Systems Research Center, Graduate School of Business Administration, University of Minnesota.

_____, and G.W. Dickson, 1974. An experimental evaluation of information overload in a production environment. *Management Science*, **20**(10):1335–1344.

_____, and R.F. Sauter, 1974. *Analysis and Design of Computer-based Management Information Systems: An Evaluation of Risk Analysis Decision Aids.*

Monograph 5. Minneapolis: Management Information Systems Research Center, University of Minnesota.

_____, and G.W. Dickson, 1978. On the validity of the analytic-heuristic instrument utilized in "the Minnesota experiments": a reply. *Management Science,* **24**(10):1091–1092.

Chesley, G.R., 1975. Elicitation of subjective probabilities: a review. *Accounting Review,* **50**(2):325–337.

Chovanec, R.J., 1976. Attacking the data accuracy problem. *Nineteenth Annual Conference Proceedings.* Washington: American Production and Inventory Control Society.

Chow, G.C., 1967. Technological change and the demand for computers. *American Economic Review,* **57**:117–130.

Chrysler, E., 1978. Some basic determinants of computer programming productivity. *Communications ACM,* **21**(6):472–483.

_____, 1979. *A Methodology for Improved Management of Information Systems Development.* Sacramento: School of Business and Public Administration, California State University.

Churchman, C.W., R.L. Ackoff, and E.L. Arnoff, 1957. *Introduction to Operations Research.* New York: Wiley.

_____, 1971. *The Design of Inquiring Systems: Basic Concepts of Systems and Organization.* New York: Basic Books.

_____, 1972. Management and planning problems. In H. Sackman and H. Borko (eds.), *Computers and the Problems of Society.* Montvale, N.J.: AFIPS.

Cichetti, C.J., and V.K. Smith, 1976. The measurement of individual congestion costs: an economic application to wilderness recreation. In S.A.Y. Lin (ed.), *Theory and Measurement of Economic Externalities.* New York: Academic.

Clarke, D.G., 1978. Strategic advertising planning: Merging multidimensional scaling and econometric analysis. *Management Science,* **24**(16):1687–1699.

Codasyl, 1971. *Data Base Task Group April 71 Report.* New York: ACM.

Coffman, E.G. (ed.), 1976. *Computer and Job Shop Scheduling Theory.* New York: Wiley.

_____, and P.J. Denning, 1973. *Operating System Theory.* Englewood Cliffs, N.J.: Prentice-Hall.

Cohen, I.K., and R.L. Van Horn, 1965. A laboratory exercise for information system evaluation. In J. Spiegel and D. Walker (eds.), *Information System Sciences,* Proceeding of the Second Congress. Washington: Spartan.

Cohen, L.J., 1976. *Data Base Management Systems.* Rev. ed. Dublin: CACI, Ireland.

Colombatto, P.J., and Y. Omurtag, 1976. *An Interactive Planning Model for the Development of Information Systems.* Rolla, Mo.: Engineering Management Department, University of Missouri.

Conrath, D.W., 1973. From statistical decision theory to practice: some problems with the transition. *Management Science,* **19**(9): 873–883.

Constable, C.J., 1972. Managerial problems associated with process control computer installations. *International Journal Production Research*, 10(2):129–139.

Conway, R.W., W.L. Maxwell, and L.W. Miller, 1967. *Theory of Scheduling.* Reading, Mass.: Addison-Wesley.

Cook, T.M., 1974. Schedule-constrained job scheduling in a multiprogrammed computer system. *Winter Simulation Conference*, 2(Jan. 14–16):674–685.

Cooper, M.D., 1973. The economics of information. In C.A. Cuadra and A.A. Luke (eds.), *Annual Review of Information Science and Technology*, vol. 8. Washington: American Society for Information Science.

Coppus, G.W.J., M.P.F.M. Van Dongen, and J.P.C. Kleijnen, 1976. Quantile estimation in regenerative simulation: a case study. *Performance Evaluation Review*, 5(3):5–15.

Corum, W., 1975. Evaluation purchase/lease/rent alternatives. In F.W. McFarlan and R.L. Nolan (eds.), *The Information Systems Handbook.* Homewood: Dow Jones-Irwin.

Cotton, I.W., 1975. Microeconomics and the market for computer services. *Computing Surveys*, 7(2):95–111.

Couger, J.D., and R.K. Knapp (eds.), 1974. *Systems Analysis Techniques.* New York: Wiley.

Courtney, J.F., J.M. Bierer, T.G. Luckew, and J.J. Kabbes, 1978. Using management games as an aid in teaching MIS design. *Decision Sciences*, 9(3):496–509.

_____, and R. Jensen, 1978. *Business Management Laboratory Data Management System (BLM-DMS); User Manual.* Atlanta: College of Industrial Management, Georgia Institute of Technology.

Courtois, P.J., 1977. *Decomposability: Queueing and Computer System Applications.* New York: Academic.

Crabill, T.B., D. Gross, and M.J. Magazine, 1977. A classified bibliography of research on optimal design and control of queues. *Operations Research*, 25(2): 219–232.

Crozier, M., 1976. Sociologische aspecten van de informatica (Sociological aspects of informatics). *Informatie*, 18(9):526–532. (Translated from Aspects sociologiques de l'informatique. In N. Manson (ed.), *Traité Pratique d'Informatique.* Paris: Techniques de l'Ingénieur, 1972.)

Cuadra, C.A., and A.W. Luke, 1972. *Annual Review of Information and Technology.* New York: Wiley-Interscience.

Cuninghame-Green, R.A., 1973. Assessing the success of the computer. *Computing Economics.* Maidenhead: Infotech.

Cyert, R.M., and J.G. March, 1963. *A Behavioral Theory of the Firm.* Englewood Cliffs, N.J.: Prentice Hall.

Dahl, O.J., E.W. Dijkstra, and C.A.R. Hoare, 1972. *Structured Programming.* London: Academic.

Damon, W.W., and R. Schramm, 1977. On a simultaneous decision model for marketing, production, and finance: a rejoinder. *Management Science*, 23(9): 1010–1011.

Date, C.J., 1978. *An Introduction to Database Systems.* 2nd ed. Reading, Mass.: Addison-Wesley.

Davis, B., 1975. *Data Base Management Systems: User Experience in the U.S.A.* Manchester: National Computer Centre Limited.

Dean, N.J., 1968. The computer comes of age. *Harvard Business Review,* **46**(1): 83–91.

Dearden, J., 1972. MIS is a mirage. *Harvard Business Review,* **50**(1):90–99.

————, J.W. McFarlan, and W.M. Zani, 1971. *Managing Computer-based Information Systems.* Homewood: Irwin.

De Blasis, J., 1976. *Systems Approach as a Tool for Information Systems Design: Illustrations and Comments,* Report 76-02-03. Rocquencourt, France: Institut de Recherche d'Informatique et d'Automatique (IRIA).

Debons, A., (ed.), 1974. *Information Science, Search for Identity.* New York: Marcel Dekker.

De Bruijn, W.K., 1965. The choice between renting and buying computers. In A.B. Frielink (ed.), *Economics of Automatic Data Processing.* Amsterdam: North Holland.

De Coster, M.A., 1975. Cost allocation in a multi-user environment. In A.B. Frielink (ed.), *Economics of Informatics.* Amsterdam: North Holland.

De Greene, K.B., 1977. Problems of modeling emergent phenomena in complex societal systems. In M.H. Hamza (ed.), *Simulation '77,* Proceedings of the International Symposium. Anaheim: Acta.

De Lutis, T.G., 1977. *A Methodology for the Performance Evaluation of Information Processing Systems.* Columbus: Department of Computer and Information Science, Ohio State University. (Available from NTIS, Springfield, Virginia 22161.)

Demski, J.S., 1974. *The Value of Financial Accounting.* Palo Alto: Graduate School of Business, Stanford University.

Denning, P.J., 1970. Virtual memory. *Computing Surveys,* **2**(3):153–189.

Dewhurst, R.F.J., 1972. *Business Cost–Benefit Analysis.* Maidenhead: McGraw-Hill (UK).

Dickson, G., and B. Wynne, 1973. *Managers and Man-Machine Information Systems.* MIS RC-WP-72-04. Minneapolis: Management Information Systems Research Center, Graduate School of Business Administration, University of Minnesota.

Dickson, G.W., J.A. Senn, and N.L. Chervany, 1977. Research in management information systems: The Minnesota experiments. *Management Science,* **23**(9): 913–923.

Diebold, 1973. *Investments in Management Information Systems.* Document no. M 28, Diebold Research Program.

————, 1977. *Key Management Indicators of ADP Performance.* E Report no. 153, Document no. S25, Diebold Research Program.

Diebold, J., 1969. Bad decisions on computer use. *Harvard Business Review,* **47**(1):14.

Diroff, T.E., 1978. The protection of computer facilities and equipment: physical security. *Data Base,* **10**(1):15–24.

Dolotta, T.A., M.I. Bernstein, R.S. Dickson, N.A. France, B.A. Rosenblatt, D.M. Smith, and T.B. Steel, 1976. *Data Processing in 1980–1985: A Study of Potential Limitations to Progress.* New York: Wiley-Interscience.

Dorn, P.H., 1979. DP budget survey. *Datamation,* 25(1):162–170.

Dowkont, A.J., W.A. Morris, and T.D. Buettell, 1967. *A Methodology for Comparison of Generalized Data Management Systems: PEGS (Parametric Evaluation of Generalized Systems).* AD 811 682. Springfield, Virginia: National Technical Information Service.

Draper, N.R., and H. Smith, 1966. *Applied Regression Analysis.* New York: Wiley.

Dreesmann, A.C.R., 1978. Artikelcoderingssystemen (Article coding systems). Presented at the symposium "De ontwikkeling van de automatisering in de detailhandel" (Developments in retail trade automation), organized by NOVI, Feb. 21. (Author's address: Vroom and Dreesmann, P.O. Box 276, Amsterdam.)

Drummond, M.E., 1973. *Evaluation and Measurement Techniques for Digital Computer Systems.* Englewood Cliffs, N.J.: Prentice-Hall.

Dujmovic, J.J., 1975. Extended continuous logic and the theory of complex criteria. *Publicaije Elektrotehnickog Fakulteta,* pp. 197–216. Belgrade: University of Belgrade.

————, 1976. Evaluation, comparison, and optimization of hybrid computers using the theory of complex criteria. In L. Dekker (ed.), *Simulation of Systems.* Amsterdam: North Holland.

————, 1977a. The preference scoring method for decision making—survey, classification and annotated bibliography. *Informatica,* (2):26–34.

————, 1977b. *Professional Evaluation and Selection of Computer Systems.* Belgrade: Department of Electrical Engineering, University of Belgrade.

————, 1978. *Criteria for Computer Performance Evaluation.* Belgrade: Department of Electrical Engineering, University of Belgrade.

Dutton, W.H., and K.L. Kraemer, 1978. Management utilization of computers in American local governments. *Communications ACM,* 21(3):206–218.

Easton, A., 1973. *Complex Managerial Decisions Involving Multiple Objectives.* New York: Wiley.

Ebert, R.J., 1976. Aggregate planning with learning curve productivity. *Management Science,* 23(2):171–182.

Edwards, C., and K. Roxburgh, 1977. Analysis and implications of management uses of information. *Operational Research Quarterly,* 28(2):243–249.

Edwards, W., (ed.), 1966. Revision of opinions by men and man-machine systems. *IEEE Transactions on Human Factors in Electronics,* HFE-7(1):1–64.

Eilon, S., 1972. The production smoothing problem. *Production Engineer,* 51(4):123–129.

Ein-Dor, P., and E. Segev, 1978a. Organizational context and the success of management information systems. *Management Science,* 24(10):1064–1077.

————, and E. Segev, 1978b. Strategic planning for management information systems. *Management Science,* 24(15):1631–1641.

Eldin, H.K., and F.M. Croft, 1974. *Information Systems—A Management Science Approach.* New York: Petrocelli.

Elmaghraby, S., 1977. *Activity Networks; Project Planning and Control by Network Models.* New York: Wiley.

Elmaleh, J., and S. Eilon, 1974. A new approach to production smoothing. *International Journal of Production Research,* 12(6):673–681.

Elnicki, R.A., 1977. *Pricing in a University Computer Utility.* Gainesville: Department of Management, College of Business Administration, University of Florida.

Emery, F.E., (ed.), 1969. *Systems Thinking.* Harmondsworth: Penguin.

Emery, J.C., 1969. *Organizational Planning and Control Systems.* New York: Macmillan.

_____, 1971. *Cost-Benefit Analysis of Information Systems.* SMIS Workshop Report no. 1, The Society for Management Information Systems. (Second printing, March 1973.)

_____, 1972. Can we develop cost-effective information systems? *Management Informatics,* 1(6):243–249.

_____, and H.L. Morgan, 1973. *Management and Economics of Data Base Management Systems.* Prepared for SHARE Working Conference on Database Management Systems, Montreal, July.

_____, and H. L. Morgan, 1974. Management and economics of data base management systems. In D.A. Jardine (ed.), *Data Base Management Systems.* Amsterdam: North Holland.

_____, 1977. *Managerial and Economic Issues in Distributed Computing.* Princeton: EDUCOM.

Estes, N., 1969. Step-by-step costing of information systems. *Journal of System Management,* 20(8):31–35; 20(10):20–28.

Estrin, G., and L. Kleinrock, 1967. Measures, models, and measurements for time-shared computer utilities. *Proceedings ACM 1967 National Conference.* Washington: Thomson.

Etz, D.V., 1965. The marginal utility of information. *Datamation,* 11(8):41–44.

Evans, R.W., 1972. EDP system simulators. *EDP In-depth Reports,* 1(12). Downsview, Ontario: R.W. Evans.

Farber, D.J., 1972. Networks: an introduction. *Datamation,* 18(4):36–39.

Farley, J.U., J.A. Howard, and J. Hulbert, 1971. An organizational approach to an industrial marketing information system. *Sloan Management Review,* 13(1):35–54.

Farquhar, P.H., 1975. A fractional hypercube decomposition theorem for multi-attribute utility functions. *Operations Research,* 23(5):941–967.

Fellingham, J.C., T.J. Mock, and M.A. Vasarhelyi, 1976. Simulation of information choice. *Decision Sciences,* 7(2):219–234.

Feltham, G.A., 1968. The value of information. *Accounting Review,* 43(4):684–696.

Ferrara, R., 1975. Organization and control of the data acquisition function. In F.W. McFarlan and R.L. Nolan (eds.), *The Information Systems Handbook.* Homewood, Ill.: Dow Jones-Irwin.

Ferrari, D., 1978. *Computer Systems Performance Evaluation.* Englewood Cliffs, N.J.: Prentice-Hall.

Fife, D.W., 1968. *Alternatives in Evaluation of Computer Systems.* ESD-TR-67-380, MTR-413. Bedford, Mass.: MITRE Corporation.

Firchau, V., 1977. *Wieviel Sind Informationen Maximal Wert* (What is the maximum value of information)? Doctoral dissertation. Augsburg, Germany: Department of Economics, University of Augsburg.

Fishburn, P.C., 1970. *Utility Theory for Decision Making.* New York: Wiley.

_____, 1977. Multicriteria choice functions based on binary relations. *Operations Research,* **25**(6):989–1012.

Fisher, G.H., 1971. *Cost Considerations in Systems Analysis.* New York: American Elsevier.

Fitzsimmons, A., and T. Love, 1978. A review and evaluation of software science. *Computing Surveys,* **10**(1):3–18.

Flowerdew, A.D.J., and C.M.E. Whitehead, 1975. Problems in measuring the benefits of scientific and technical information. In A.B. Frielink (ed.), *Economics of Informatics.* Amsterdam: North Holland.

Forrester, J.W., 1961. *Industrial Dynamics.* Cambridge, Mass.: M.I.T. Press.

_____, 1968a. Industrial dynamics—a response to Ansoff and Slevin. *Management Science,* **14**(9):601–618.

_____, 1968b. Market growth as influenced by capital investment. *Industrial Management Review,* **9**(2):83–105.

Frane, J.E., (ed.), 1975. *Proceedings of the Computer Science and Statistics Eighth Annual Symposium.* Los Angeles: Health Sciences Computing Facility, University of California.

Freeman, P., 1975. *Software Systems Principles: A Survey.* Chicago: Science Research Associates.

Freiberger, W., (ed.), 1972. *Statistical Computer Performance Evaluation.* New York: Academic.

Fried, L., 1969. Estimating the cost of system implementation. *Data Processing,* **11**(3):32–35; **11**(4):24–28.

_____, 1971. How to analyse computer project costs. *Computer Decisions,* **13**(August):22–26.

Frielink, A.B., (ed.), 1965. *Economics of Automatic Data Processing.* Proceedings of the IBI-ICC International Symposium. Amsterdam: North Holland.

_____, 1978. Informatie en communicatie bij logistieke systemen (Information and communication in logistic systems). In L.C. Van Zutphen (ed.), *Aspecten van Logistieke Informatiesystemen* (Aspects of logistic information systems). Alphen aan den Rijn, Netherlands: Samsom Uitgeverij.

Funke, U.H., 1976. *Mathematical Models in Marketing: A Collection of Abstracts.* Berlin: Springer-Verlag.

GAO Task Group, 1976. *Selected Literature on Cost Accounting and Cost Control for Automatic Data Processing—A Bibliography.* Washington: United States General Accounting Office.

_____, 1978a. *Accounting for Automatic Data Processing Costs Needs Improvement.* Report FGMSD 78-14. Washington: United States General Accounting Office.

_____, 1978b. *Illustrative Accounting Procedures for Federal Agencies.* Washington: United States General Accounting Office.

Gayle, J.B., 1971. Multiple regression techniques for estimating computer programming costs. *Journal Systems Management,* **22**(2):13–16.

Geisler, M.A., and A.S. Ginsberg, 1965. *Man–Machine Simulation Experience.* Report P-3214. Santa Monica: RAND.

Gelenbe, E., (ed.), 1976. *Proceedings Second International Workshop on Modelling and Performance Evaluation of Computer Systems.* Amsterdam: North Holland.

_____, and D. Derochette, 1978. Performance of rollback recovery systems under intermittent failures. *Communications ACM,* **21**(6):493–499.

Geoffrion, A.M., 1976. The purpose of mathematical programming is insight, not numbers. *Interfaces,* **7**(1):81–92.

Gerberick, D.A., chairman, 1976. *Privacy, Security, and the Information Processing Industry.* A Report of the Ombudsman Committee on Privacy, Los Angeles Chapter. New York: ACM.

Giauque, W.C., and T.C. Peebles, 1976. Application of multidimensional utility theory in determining optimal test-treatment strategies for streptococcal sore throat and rheumatic fever. *Operations Research,* **24**(5):933–950.

Gibbons, T.K., 1976. *Integrity and Recovery in Computer Systems.* Rochelle Park, N.J.: NCC Publications, Manchester/Hayden.

Gilb, T., and G.M. Weinberg, 1977. *Humanized Input; Techniques for Reliable Keyed Input.* Cambridge, Mass.: Winthrop.

Gilchrist, B., and R.E. Weber, (eds.), 1973. *The State of the Computer Industry in the United States.* Montvale, N.J.: AFIPS.

Gilman, R., 1973. *Cost Benefit Analysis in the Design of Management Decision Systems: The Time Value of Information.* Dissertation. Los Angeles: Graduate School of Business Administration, University of Southern California.

Gitman, L.J., and J.R. Forrester, 1977. A survey of capital budgeting techniques used by major United States firms. *Financial Management,* **6**(3):66–71.

Goankar, R., 1977. Comparative analysis of systems dynamics modeling and econometric modeling. In M.H. Hamza (ed.), *Simulation '77,* Proceedings of the International Symposium. Anaheim: Acta.

Goddard, W.E., (ed.), 1977. *Master Production Scheduling Reprints.* Washington: American Production and Inventory Control Society.

Goldstein, R.C., and R.L. Nolan, 1975. Individual privacy and the corporate computer. In F.W. McFarlan and R.L. Nolan (eds.), *The Information Systems Handbook.* Homewood, Ill.: Dow Jones-Irwin.

Goodman, D.A., 1974. A sectioning search approach to aggregate planning of production and work force. *Decision Science,* **5**(4):545–563.

Goodwin, P.G., 1972. A method for evaluation of subsystem alternate designs. *IEEE Transactions on Engineering Management,* **EM-19**(1):12–21.

Gorry, G.A., and M.S. Scott Morton, 1971. A framework for management information systems. *Sloan Management Review,* **12**(1):55–70.

Gosden, J.A., 1974. Current deficiencies and user requirements. In D.A. Jardine (ed.), *Data Base Management Systems.* Amsterdam: North Holland.

Gotlieb, C.C., 1973. Pricing mechanisms. In F.L. Bauer (ed.), *Advanced Course on Software Engineering.* Berlin: Springer Verlag.

Gould, I.H., (ed.), 1971. *IFIP Guide to Concepts and Terms in Data Processing.* Amsterdam: North Holland.

Graham, G.S., (ed.), 1978. Queueing network models of computer system performance. (Special issue.) *Computing Surveys,* 10(3):219–359.

Graham, J., 1976. *Making Computers Pay.* London: Allen and Unwin.

Green, P.E., P.J. Robinson, and P.T. Fitzroy, 1967. *Experiments on the Value of Information in Simulated Marketing Environments.* Boston: Allyn and Bacon.

_____, and F.J. Carmone, 1974. Evaluation of multiattribute alternatives: additive versus configural utility measurement. *Decision Sciences,* 5(2):164–181.

Greenberg, H.J., D. Heyman, and R. Van Slyke, (eds.), 1978. Operations research/computer science interface. *Operations Research,* 26(5):625–935.

Gregory, R.H., and T.V.V. Atwater, 1957. Cost and value of management information as functions of age. *Accounting Research,* 8(1):42–70.

_____, and R.L. Van Horn, 1963. *Automatic Data-Processing Systems.* 2nd. ed. Belmont: Wadsworth.

Grindley, K., and J. Humble, 1973. *The Effective Computer: A Management by Objectives Approach.* Maidenhead, England: McGraw-Hill (UK).

Grinyer, P.H., and C.D. Batt, 1974. Some tentative findings on corporate financial simulation models. *Operational Research Quarterly,* 25(1):149–167.

Gritten, R.A., 1975. Computer options: in-house capability, computer utilities, time-sharing, facilities management. In F.W. McFarlan and R.L. Nolan (eds.), *The Information Systems Handbook.* Homewood, Ill.: Dow Jones–Irwin.

Grochla, E., 1970. Grundfragen der Wirtschaftlichkeit automatisierter Datenverarbeitung (Fundamental economic problems in automated data processing). *Zeitschrift für Organisation,* 30(8):329–336.

Grochow, J.M., 1972. A utility theoretic approach to evaluation of a time-sharing system. In W. Freiberger (ed.), *Statistical Computer Performance Evaluation.* New York: Academic.

Grooms, D.W., 1974. *Management Games—A Bibliography with Abstracts.* NTIS/PS-74/112. Springfield, Va.: National Technical Information Service.

Gross, D., and A. Soriano, 1972. On the economic application of airlift to product distribution and its impact on inventory levels. *Naval Research Logistics Quarterly,* 19(3):501–507.

Grum, A.F., D.R.E. Hale, and T.A. Bresnick, 1977. *The Value of Information in Combat Decision Making.* West Point: Department of Engineering, United States Military Academy.

Grünwald, H., 1973. *Analyse van het Ketensimulatiemodel, voor Drie Manieren van Informatieverstrekking* (Analysis of the chain simulation model for three ways of information supply). Notitie Nr. 5. Eindhoven, Netherlands: Systeemtheorie Philips.

_____, 1974. *Impact of the Way of Information Supply on the Internal Business Cycle.* Eindhoven, Netherlands: Information Systems and Operations Research Department, Philips.

_____, 1977. *Analyse der Internen Konjunktur* (Analysis of internal business cycles). ISA–R. Eindhoven, Netherlands: Philips.

Grupp, B., 1974. *Elektronische Einkaufsorganisation* (Electronic purchasing organization). Berlin: Walter de Gruyter.

Gupta, S.C., and L. Hasdorff, 1970. *Fundamentals of Automatic Control.* New York: Wiley.

Habermann, W.F., 1975. *Pricing and the Allocation of Data Processing Resources,* Monterey, Calif.: Naval Postgraduate School. (Distributed by NTIS, Springfield, Virginia; Order no. AD–A012–413.)

Hackathorn, R.D., 1977. Modeling unstructured decision making. In E.D. Carlson (ed.), *Proceedings of a Conference on Decision Support Systems. Data Base,* 8(2):41–42.

Haines, G.H., 1971. A simulation of a management information system with embedded decision making. *Proceedings 1971 Summer Computer Simulation Conference.* Reprint Series No. R–78. Rochester, N.Y.: Graduate School of Management, University of Rochester.

Hall, P.G., and T.J. Lincoln, 1976. A cost effectiveness study of production and engineering systems within a tightly integrated manufacturing environment. *Management Datamatics,* 5(6):261–273.

Hamilton, K.L., 1977. *On Pricing of Computer Services: A Bibliography with Annotations and Categorical Listings.* Working Paper MS–77–2. Atlanta: College of Industrial Management, Georgia Institute of Technology.

_____, 1978. *Problems in the Choice of a System for Costing and Pricing of Computer Services.* Working Paper MS–78–2. Atlanta: College of Industrial Management, Georgia Institute of Technology.

Hamilton, P., 1972. *Computer Security.* London: Cassell/Associated Business Programmes.

Hand, H.H., and H.P. Sims, 1975. Statistical evaluation of complex gaming performance. *Management Science,* 21(6):708–717.

Hanken, A.F.G., and H.A. Reuver, 1977. *Sociale Systemen en Lerende Systemen* (Social systems and learning systems). Leiden: H.E. Stenfert Kroese B.V.

Hanssmann, F., (ed.), 1971. *Operational Research in the Design of Electronic Data Processing Systems.* London: English University Press.

Harman, A., 1971. *The International Computer Industry.* Cambridge, Mass.: Harvard University.

Harris, W.I., 1971. Project scheduling. *Data Management,* 9(9):40–43.

Harrison, J.M., 1977. Independence and calibration in decision analysis. *Management Science,* 24(3):320–328.

Hart, L.E., 1970. The user's guide to evaluate products. *Datamation,* 16(17):32–35.

Harubi, N., M. Shechter, and A. Subotnik, 1977. A pricing policy for a computer facility with congestion externalities. *European Journal of Operational Research,* 3(4):296–307.

Haseman, W.D., and A.B. Whinston, 1977. *Introduction to Data Management.* Homewood, Ill.: Irwin.

Hauser, J.R., 1978. Consumer preference axioms: behavioral postulates for describing and predicting stochastic choice. *Management Science,* **24**(13):1331–1341.

Hawgood, J., 1975. Quinquevalent quantification of computer benefits. In A.B. Frielink (ed.), *Economics of Informatics.* Amsterdam: North Holland.

Hax, A.C., 1976. The design of large scale logistics systems: a survey and an approach. In W.H. Marlow (ed.), *Modern Trends in Logistics Research.* Cambridge, Mass.: M.I.T.

Hayes, R.L., and R. Radosevich, 1974. Designing information systems for strategic decisions. *Long Range Planning,* **7**(4):45–48.

Head, J.G., 1975. Estimating the costs and benefits and monitoring the effectiveness of large government installations. In A.B. Frielink (ed.), *Economics of Informatics.* Amsterdam: North Holland.

Head, R., 1970. The elusive MIS. *Datamation,* **16**(10):22–27.

Heijn, A., 1978. (No title.) Presented at the symposium "De ontwikkeling van de automatisering in de detailhandel" (Developments in retail trade automation), organized by NOVI, Feb. 21. (Author's address: Ahold, Zaandam, Netherlands.)

Hekman, R.J., 1972. The best time to purchase your computer. *Datamation,* **18**(12):59–62.

Hellerman, H., and H.J. Smith, 1970. Throughout analysis of some idealized input, output, and compute overlap configurations. *Computing Surveys,* **2**(2):111–118.

_____, and T.F. Conroy, 1975. *Computer System Performance.* New York: McGraw-Hill.

Hertz, D.B., 1964. Risk analysis in capital investments. *Harvard Business Review,* **42**(2):95–106.

_____, 1969. *New Power for Management: Computer Systems and Management Science.* New York: McGraw-Hill.

Hespos, R.F., and P.A. Strassmann, 1970. Stochastic decision trees for the analysis of investment decisions. In A. Rappaport (ed.), *Information for Decision Making.* Englewood Cliffs, N.J.: Prentice-Hall.

Highland, H.J., (ed.), 1973 through 1976. *Proceedings of Symposium on Simulations of Computer Systems.* (Obtainable from Dr. H. Highland, New York State University, Technical College, Farmingdale, N.Y. 11735.)

_____, T.J. Schriber, and R.G. Sargent, 1976. *Proceedings of the 1976 Bicentennial Winter Simulation Conference.* New York: ACM.

Hindle, A., and D. Raper, 1976. The economics of information. In M.E. Williams (ed.), *Annual Review of Information Science and Technology,* vol. 11. Washington: American Society for Information Science.

Hirshleifer, J., 1973. Where are we in the theory of information? *American Economic Review,* **63**(2):31–39.

Ho, Y.C., and K.C. Chu, 1974. Information structure in dynamic multiperson control problems. *Automatica,* **10**(4):341–351.

Hoetink, B.J. 1976. Besturingseffektiviteit van informatiesystemen (Control effectiveness of information systems). *Informatie,* **18**(9):520–525.

Hofer, C.W., 1970. Emerging EDP pattern. *Harvard Business Review,* **48**(2):16–31, 169–171.

Hoffman, L.J., (ed), 1973. *Security and Privacy in Computer Systems.* Los Angeles: Melville.

————, 1977. *Modern Methods for Computer Security and Privacy.* Englewood Cliffs, N.J.: Prentice-Hall.

Hoffmann, G.M., 1975. *The World of the Industrial Practitioner.* (Paper prepared for TIMS XXII, Kyoto, July 1975.) Standard Oil Company (Indiana), 200 East Randolph Drive, Chicago, Illinois 60601.

Hoffmann, T.R., 1965. Programmed heuristics and the concept of par in business games. *Behavioral Science,* **10**:169–172.

Hogarth, R.M., 1977. Cognitive processes and the assessment of subjective probability distributions. In A. Aykac and C. Brumat (eds.), *New Developments in the Applications of Bayesian Methods.* Amsterdam: North Holland.

Hoggatt, A.C., 1967. Measuring the cooperativeness of behavior in quantity variation duopoly games. *Behavioral Science,* **12**(2):109–121.

Holden, G.K., 1976. *Production Control Packages and Services.* (A survey of computer application packages and services for production control in the UK.) 2nd. ed. Manchester: National Computing Centre.

Hollingworth, F.D., 1971. Evaluating computer system projects. *Canadian Chartered Accountant,* May, pp. 331–333.

Holt, C.C., F. Modigliani, J.F. Muth, and H.A. Simon, 1960. *Planning Production, Inventories, and Work Force.* Englewood Cliffs, N.J.: Prentice-Hall.

Honeywell, 1977. *Computer Security and Privacy Symposium.* Waltham, Mass.: Honeywell Information Systems.

Hootman, J.T., 1977. Basic considerations in developing computer charging mechanisms. *Data Base,* **8**(4):4–9.

Hopkins, D.S.P., J. Larréché, and W.F. Massy, 1977. Constrained optimization of a unversity administrator's preference function. *Management Science,* **24**(4):365–377.

Hora, S.C., 1977. A path to better decision making. In W.C. House, (ed.), *Interactive Decision-Oriented Data Base Systems.* New York: Petrocelli/Charter.

House, W.C., (ed.), 1977. *Interactive Decision-Oriented Data Base Systems.* New York: Petrocelli/Charter.

Howard, P.C., (ed.), 1977. Fifth annual survey of performance-related software packages. *EDP Performance Review,* **15**(2):1–42.

Howard, R.A., 1971. Proximal decision analysis. *Management Science,* **17**(9):507–541.

Hoyt, G.S., 1975. (Part of) the art of buying software. *Conference Proceedings.* Washington: American Production and Inventory Control Society.

Hsu, J.I.S., 1968. An empirical study of computer maintenance policies. *Management Science,* **15**(4):B180–B195.

Huang, C.C., I. Vertinsky, and W.T. Ziemba, 1975. *Sharp Bounds on the Value of Perfect Information.* Working Paper no. 293. Vancouver: Faculty of Commerce and Business Administration, University of British Columbia. (An abbreviated version appeared in *Operations Research,* **25**(1):128–139.)

Huber, G.P., 1974a. Methods for quantifying subjective probabilities and multiattribute utilities. *Decision Sciences*, 5(3):430–458.

_____, 1974b. Multiattribute utility models: a review of field and field-like studies. *Management Science*, 20(10):1393–1402.

Huesmann, L.R., and R.P. Goldberg, 1967. Evaluating computer systems through simulation. *Computer Journal*, 10(2):150–155.

Hultén, C., and L. Söderlund, 1977. *A Simulation Model for Performance Analysis of Large Shared Data Bases*. Research Group CADIS. Stockholm: Department of Information Processing, University of Stockholm.

IBM, 1963a. *IBM Management Decision-Making Laboratory: Administrator's Reference Manual*. GB20–8099–0. White Plains: IBM.

_____, 1963b. *IBM Management Decision-Making Laboratory: Instructions for Participants*. SE20–8098–0. White Plains: IBM.

_____, 1967. *Basic Principles of Wholesale Impact-Inventory Management Program and Control Techniques*. Rev. ed. E20–8105–1. White Plains: IBM.

_____, 1971a. *IBGS—Interactive Business Game Simulation: A General Business Simulation for APL/360*. SB21–0394–0. White Plains: IBM.

_____, 1971b. *IBM Management Decision-Making Exercise: Deelnemershandleiding*. (IBM Management Decision-making Exercise: Participants' manual). Report GE14–5015–01. Amsterdam: IBM Nederland.

_____, 1974. *Customer Online Order Processing (COOP) with IMS/360–Douglas Aircraft*. Application brief, GK20–0640. White Plains: IBM.

ICL, 1973. *Business Management Exercise NIMEX: Participants' Manual*. London: International Computers Limited.

Iglehart, D.L., and R.C. Morey, 1972. Inventory systems with imperfect asset information. *Management Science*, 18(8):B 388–B 394.

Ignizio, J.P., and D.E. Satterfield, 1977. *Multicriteria Optimization in Ballistic Missile Defense System Design*. University Park, Pa.: Pennsylvania State University.

Ijiri, Y., R.K. Jaedicke, and K.E. Knight, 1970. The effects of accounting alternatives on management decisions. In A. Rappaport (ed.), *Information for Decision Making: Quantitative and Behavioral Dimensions*. Englewood Cliffs, N.J.: Prentice-Hall.

_____, and H. Itami, 1973. Quadratic cost–volume relationship and timing of demand information. *Accounting Review*, 48(4):724–737.

_____, and H. Itami, 1975. Quadratic cost–volume relationship and timing of demand information: a reply. *Accounting Review*, 50(1):138–139.

Infotech, 1973. *Computing Economics*. Maidenhead, England: Infotech International.

_____, 1976a. *Microprocessors*, Maidenhead, England: Infotech International.

_____, 1976b. *Structured Programming*. Maidenhead, England: Infotech International.

_____, 1977a. *Computer Systems Reliability*. Maidenhead, England: Infotech International.

_____, 1977b. *Data Base Systems*. Maidenhead, England: Infotech International.

_____, 1977c. *On-Line Data Bases*. Maidenhead, England: Infotech International.

_____, 1977d. *Performance Modelling and Prediction.* Maidenhead, England: Infotech International.

_____, 1978a. *Data Base Technology.* (In two volumes.) Maidenhead, England: Infotech International.

_____, 1978b. *System Tuning.* Maidenhead, England: Infotech International.

Itami, H., 1972. *Evaluation of Adaptive Behavior and Information Timing in Management Control.* Ph.D Dissertation. Pittsburgh: Graduate School of Industrial Administration, Carnegie-Mellon University. Order No. 73–26, 958. Ann Arbor: University Microfilms.

_____, 1977. *Adaptive Behavior: Management Control and Information Analysis.* Studies in Accounting Research, No. 15. Sarasota: American Accounting Association.

Jackson, M.A., 1975. *Principles of Program Design.* London: Academic.

Jacquin, J.L., and P. Mevellec, 1978. *A Critical Analysis of Information Cost and Utility Appraisal Methods.* Working paper no. 1, UER Sciences Economiques. Rennes, France: University of Rennes.

Jagetia, L.C., 1975. *Statistical Decision Theory in Cost Analysis.* Cleveland: College of Business Administration, Cleveland State University.

Jain, A.K., 1977. *Statistical Approaches in Computer Performance Evaluation Studies: A Tutorial.* Holmdel, N.J.: Bell Telephone Laboratories.

Jardine, D.A., (ed.), 1974. *Data Base Management Systems.* Amsterdam: North Holland.

Jarvis, J.J., V.E. Unger, C.C. Schimpeler, and J.C. Corradino, 1972. *Application of Multi-Criteria Decision Analysis and Citizen Involvement in New Airport Site Selection.* Louisville: Schimpeler–Corradino Associates.

Jensen, R.E., 1969. Discussion of comparative values of information structures. *Journal of Accounting Research.* 7(2, supplement):168–181.

Jewett, J.E., 1972a. *The Economics of Information: A Probabilistic Network Framework.* Working Paper Series, no. 7209. Rochester, N.Y.: Graduate School of Management, University of Rochester.

_____, 1972b. *Research in Information Science.* Working Paper Series, no. 7216. Rochester, N.Y.: Graduate School of Management, University of Rochester.

_____, 1973. *Methodological Framework for Estimating the Information Impact to Decision Makers.* Working Papers Series, no. 7316. Rochester, N.Y.: Graduate School of Management, University of Rochester.

Johnson, R.W., and W.G. Lewellen, 1972. Analysis of the lease-or-buy decision. *Journal of Finance,* 27(4):815–823. (See also the Comments in 28(4):1015–1028.)

Johnston, J., 1963. *Econometric Methods.* New York: McGraw-Hill.

Jones, G.T., 1977. *Data Capture in the Retail Environment.* Manchester, England: National Computing Centre (NCC).

Jordan, C.M.C., 1975. How to start a cycle counting program. *APICS Conference Proceedings.* Washington: American Production and Inventory Control Society.

Joslin, E.O., 1968. *Computer Selection.* Reading, Mass.: Addison-Wesley.

_____, 1977. *Computer Selection; Augmented Edition.* Fairfax Station, Virginia: Technology.

Joyce, J.D., J.T. Murray, and M.R. Ward, 1974. Data management system requirements. In D.A. Jardine (ed.), *Data Base Management Systems*. Amsterdam: North
Holland.

Kapur, K.C., and L.R. Lamberson, 1977. *Reliability in Engineering Design*. New
York: Wiley.

Katzan, H., 1973. *Computer Data Security*. New York: Van Nostrand Reinhold.

Kaufmann, A., D. Grouchko, and R. Cruon, 1977. *Mathematical Models for the
Study of the Reliability of Systems*. New York: Academic.

Keefer, D.L., 1978. Allocation planning for R&D with uncertainty and multiple
objectives. *IEEE Transactions on Engineering Management*, **EM-25**(1):8–14.

Keen, P.G.W., and M.S. Scott Morton, 1978. *Decision Support Systems: An Organizational Perspective*. Reading, Mass.: Addison-Wesley.

Keeney, R.L., 1976. A group preference axiomatization with cardinal utility.
Management Science, **23**(2):140–145.

_____, and H. Raiffa, 1976. *Decisions with Multiple Objectives: Preferences and
Value Tradeoffs*. New York: Wiley.

Keller, R.F., and C.R. Denham, 1968. Computer selection procedures. *Proceedings
23rd ACM National Conference*. ACM Publication 8-68. Princeton:
Brandom/Systems.

Kendall, M.G., and A. Stuart, 1963. *The Advanced Theory of Statistics*, Vol. 1.,
2nd ed. London: Charles Griffin.

Kimbleton, S.R., 1972. Performance evaluation; a structured approach. *Proceedings
AFIPS 1972 Spring Joint Computer Conference*. Montvale: AFIPS.

_____, 1975. *Considerations in Pricing Distributed Computing*. Marina del Rey:
USC/Information Sciences Institute.

King, J.L., 1975. *Cost–Benefit Analysis: A Problematic Exercise in Local Government Computing*. Report WP-75-08, Urban Information Systems Research Group
(URBIS), Public Policy Research Organization. Irvine: University of California.

_____, and E.L. Schrems, 1978. Cost–benefit analysis in information systems devel-
opment and operation. *Computing Surveys*, **10**(1):19–34.

King, W.R., and B.J. Epstein, 1976. Assessing the value of information. *Management Datamatics*, **5**(4):171–180.

_____, 1977. *Information for Strategic Planning: An Analysis*. Pittsburgh:
Graduate School of Business, University of Pittsburgh.

Kirkwood, C.W., 1976. Parametrically dependent preferences for multiattributed
consequences. *Operations Research*, **24**(1):92–103.

Kleijnen, J.P.C., 1975a. Computers en werkgelegenheid: poging tot economische
analyse (Computers and employment: a preliminary economic analysis). *Informatie*,
17(6):327–331.

_____, 1975b. *Statistical Techniques in Simulation*. (In two volumes). New York:
Marcel Dekker.

_____, 1976a. Het economisch nut van nauwkeurige informatie: simulatie van
ondernemingsbeslissingen en informatie (The economic benefits of accurate information: simulation of management decisions and information). *Maandblad voor Accountancy en Bedrijfshuishoudkunde*, **50**(8):453–470.

_____, 1976b. Discrete-simulation: types, applications, and problems. In L. Dekker (ed.), *Simulation of Systems.* Amsterdam: North Holland.

_____, 1976c. Computers and operations research: a survey. *Computers and Operations Research,* 3(4):327–335.

_____, 1977. Design and analysis of simulation: practical statistical techniques. *Simulation,* 28(3):81–90.

_____, 1978a. Operations research and computers. In J. Belzer, A.G. Holzman, and A. Kent (eds.), *Encyclopedia of Computer Science and Technology.* New York: Marcel Dekker.

_____, 1978b. *Quantifying Financial Benefits of Information: An Overview and Evaluation.* Tilburg, Netherlands: Department of Business and Economics, Katholieke Hogeschool.

_____, and P.J. Rens, 1978. IMPACT revisited: a critical analysis of IBM's inventory package "IMPACT." *Production and Inventory Management,* 14(1):71–90.

_____, 1979a. Regression metamodels for generalizing simulation results. *IEEE Transactions on Systems, Man, and Cybernetics,* SMC-9(2):93–95.

_____, 1979b. The role of statistical methodology in simulation. In B. Zeigler et al. (eds.), *Methodology in Systems Modelling and Simulation.* Amsterdam: North Holland.

_____, A.J. Van den Burg, and R.T. Van der Ham, 1979. Generalization of simulation results: practicality of statistical methods. *European Journal of Operational Research.* 3(1):50–54.

Kleindorfer, P.R., C.H. Kriebel, G.L. Thompson, and G.B. Kleindorfer, 1975. Discrete optimal control of production plans. *Management Science,* 22(3):261–272

Kleinrock, L., 1976. *Queueing Systems.* (In two volumes.) New York: Wiley.

Kling, R., 1978. Value conflicts and social choice in electronic funds transfer system developments. *Communications ACM,* 21(8):642–657.

Knight, K.E., 1968. Evolving computer performance, 1963–1967. *Datamation,* 14(1):31–35.

Knutsen, K.E., and R.L. Nolan, 1974. Assessing computer costs and benefits. *Journal of Systems Management,* 25(2):28–34.

Kobayashi, H., 1978. *Modeling and Analysis: An Introduction to System Performance Evaluation Methodology.* Reading, Mass.: Addison-Wesley.

Korteweg, W.H., 1978. Automatiseren met beleid (Management automation). *Informatie,* 20(12):763–774.

Kozar, K.A., 1972. *Decision Making in a Simulated Environment: A Comparative Analysis of Computer Display Media.* Unpublished Ph.D. Thesis. Minneapolis: University of Minnesota.

Kraemer, K.L., H.C. Lucas, R.D. Hackathorn, and R.C. Emrey, 1973. *Computer Utilization in Local Governments: A Critical Review and Synthesis of Research.* Irvine: Urban Information Systems Research Group (URBIS), Public Policy Research Organization, University of California.

Krauss, L.E., and A. MacGahan, 1979. *Computer Fraud and Countermeasures.* Englewood Cliffs, N.J.: Prentice-Hall.

Kreutzer, W., 1976. Comparison and evaluation of discrete event simulation programming languages for management decision making. In L. Dekker (ed.), *Simulation of Systems*. Amsterdam: North Holland.

Kriebel, C.H., 1965. Team decision models of an inventory supply organization. *Naval Research Logistics Quarterly*, **12**(2):139–154.

————, 1967. Operations research in the design of management information systems. In J.F. Pierce (ed.), *Operations Research and the Design of Management Information Systems*. New York: Technical Association of the Pulp and Paper Industry.

————, 1968. Quadratic teams, information economics, and aggregate planning decisions. *Econometrica*, **36**(3–4):530–543.

————, 1969. Information processing and programmed decision systems. *Management Science*, **16**(3):149–164.

————, A.A. Atkinson, and H.W.H. Zia, 1974. *Optimal Investment, Pricing, and Replacement of Computer Resources*. W.P. No. 16–74–75. Pittsburgh: Graduate School of Industrial Administration, Carnegie-Mellon University.

————, and O. Mikhail, 1975. Dynamic pricing of resources in computer networks. In M.A. Geisler (ed.), *Logistics*. Amsterdam: North Holland.

Krishnan, K.S., 1979. Incorporating thresholds of indifference in probabilistic choice models. *Management Science*, **23**(11):1224–1233.

Kroenke, D., 1977. *Database Processing; Fundamentals, Modelling, Applications*. Chicago: Science Research Associates.

Kumar, B., and E.S. Davidson, 1978. Performance evaluation of highly concurrent computers by deterministic simulation. *Communications ACM*, **21**(11):904–913.

Kuo, B., 1963. *Analysis and Synthesis of Sampled Data Control Systems*. Englewood Cliffs, N.J.: Prentice-Hall.

Lamberton, D.M., (ed.), 1971. *Economics of Information and Knowledge*. Harmondsworth: Penguin.

Lanahan, J., 1973. Data base applications at Inland Steel. *Data Base*, **5**(2, 3, and 4):87–94.

Lancaster, F.W., and E.G. Fayen, 1973. *Information Retrieval On-line*. Los Angeles: Melville.

Land, F.F., 1976. *Economic Analysis of Information Systems*. London: London School of Economics.

Langefors, B., 1969. *Theoretical Analysis of Information Systems*, Vols. 1 and 2. New York: Barnes and Noble.

Layton, R.A., 1965. Some aspects of the economics of a system study from the point of view of the equipment supplier. In A.B. Frielink (ed.), *Economics of Automatic Data Processing*. Amsterdam: North Holland.

Ledbetter, W.N., and J.F. Cox, 1977. Operations research in production management: an investigation of past and present utilization. *Production and Inventory Management*, **18**(3):84–92.

Lee, W.B., and B.M. Khumawala, 1974. Simulation testing of aggregate production planning models in an implementation methodology. *Management Science*, **20**(6):903–911.

Le Moigne, J., 1974. The "manager–terminal–model" system is also a model (toward a theory of managerial metamodels). *Information Processing 74, Systems for Management and Administration,* IFIP Congress 1974. Amsterdam: North Holland.

_____, 1975. The four flows model: a tool for designing the information system of an organization. In E. Grochla and W. Szyperski (eds.), *Information Systems and Organizational Structure.* Berlin: De Gruyter.

Le Moine, A.J., 1977. Networks of queues—a survey of equilibrium analysis. *Management Science,* **24**(4):464–481.

Leroudier, J., and M. Parent, 1976. *Discrete Event Simulation Modelling of Computer System for Performance Evaluation.* Report No. 177. Rocquencourt, Le Chesnay, France: Institute de Recherche d'Informatique et d'Automatique (IRIA).

Lesourne, J., 1973. *Modèles de Croissance des Entreprises* (Growth models for the firm). Paris: Dunod.

Lev, B., 1968. The aggregation problem in financial statements: an informational approach. *Journal of Accounting Research,* **6**(2):247–261.

Leventhal, L.A., 1977. Microprogramming and simulation. *Simulation Today,* Society for Computer Simulation, (52): 205–208. [Also published in *Simulation,* **28** (6).]

_____, 1978. Program design methods. *Simulation Today,* (57): 125–128. [Also published in *Simulation,* **30** (1).]

Levy, H., and M. Sarnat, 1978. *Capital Investment and Financial Decisions.* Englewood Cliffs, N.J.: Prentice-Hall.

Lieber, Z., and Y.E. Orgler, 1975. An integrated model for accounts receivable management. *Management Science,* **22**(2):212–219.

Lin, S.A.Y., (ed.), 1976. *Theory and Measurement of Economic Externalities.* New York: Academic.

Lincoln, T.J., 1977. *Management Implications of Cost-effectiveness Studies.* La Hulpe, Belgium: European Systems Research Institute, IBM.

Little, J.D.C., 1975. BRANDAID: A marketing-mix model (part 1: structure; part 2: implementation, calibration, and case study). *Operations Research,* **23**(4):628–673.

_____, and J.F. Shapiro, 1977. *A Theory for Pricing Nonfeatured Products in Supermarkets.* Working Paper 931-77. Cambridge, Mass.: Alfred P. Sloan School of Management, M.I.T.

London, K., 1976. *The People Side of Systems: The Human Aspects of Computer Systems.* Maidenhead, England: McGraw-Hill (UK).

Loomis, M.E.S., 1976. Simulation to study effects of pricing computer services. In H.J. Highland, T.J. Schriber, and R.G. Sargent (eds.), *Winter Simulation Conference,* Vol. 2. New York: ACM.

Lucas, H.C., 1971. Performance evaluation and monitoring. *Computing Surveys,* **3**(3):79–91.

_____, 1973. *Computer Based Information Systems in Organizations.* Chicago: Science Research Associates.

_____, K.W. Clowes, and R.B. Kaplan, 1974. Framework for information systems. *Infor,* **12**(3):245–260.

_____, 1979. Some speculation on simulation and information systems. *Simuletter*, **10**(3):83–85.

Lyons, N.R., 1978. Systems design education: a gaming approach. *Communications ACM*, **21**(11):889–895.

MacCrimmon, K.R., 1974. Descriptive aspects of team theory: observations, communication and decision heuristics in information systems. *Management Science*, **20**(10):1323–1334.

McDonough, A.M., 1963. *Information Economics and Management Systems*. New York: McGraw-Hill.

MacDougall, M.H., 1970. Computer systems simulation: an introduction. *Computing Surveys*, **2**(3):191–209.

McFarlan, F.W., J.L. McKenney, and J.A. Sieler, 1970. *The Management Game: Simulated Decision Making*. Toronto: Macmillan.

_____, and R.L. Nolan, 1975. *The Information Systems Handbook*. Homewood, Ill.: Dow Jones-Irwin.

McGuire, C.B., 1961. Some team models of a sales organization. *Management Science*, **7**(2):101–130.

_____, and R. Radner, (eds.), 1972. *Decision and Organization*. New York: American Elsevier.

McIntyre, E.V., 1977. Cost–volume–profit analysis adjusted for learning. *Management Science*, **24**(2):149–160.

McKinney, J.M., 1969. A survey of analytical time-sharing models. *Computing Surveys*, **1**(2):105–116.

McLean, E.R., 1973. Assessing returns from the data processing investment. In F. Gruenberger (ed.), *Effective vs. Efficient Computing*. Englewood Cliffs, N.J.: Prentice-Hall.

_____, 1976. *The Human Side of Systems: The User's Perspective*. Information System Working Paper 2–77, Center for Information Studies. Los Angeles: Graduate School of Management, University of California.

_____, and J.V. Soden, 1977. *Strategic Planning for MIS*. New York: Wiley–Interscience.

Magee, J.F., and D.M. Boodman, 1967. *Production Planning and Inventory Control*. 2nd ed. New York: McGraw-Hill.

Maguire, J.N., 1972. Discrete computer simulation—technology and applications—the next ten years. *Proceeding AFIPS 1972 Spring Joint Computer Conference*. Montvale: AFIPS.

Maisel, H., and G. Gnugnoli, 1972. *Simulation*. Chicago: Science Research Associates.

Mann, D.H., 1975. Optimal theoretic advertising stock models: a generalization incorporating the effects of delayed response from promotional expenditure. *Management Science*, **21**(7):823–832.

Manne, A.S., R.G. Richels, and J.P. Weyant, 1979. Energy policy modeling: a survey. *Operations Research*, **27**(1):1–36.

Mantey, P.E., J.A. Sutton, and C.A. Holloway, 1977. Computer support for management decision making. *Computer-assisted Corporate Planning*, SRA Lectures and Tutorials. San Jose: IBM Research Laboratory.

Marron, B., and D. Fife, 1976. Online systems—techniques and services. In M.E. Williams (ed.), *Annual Review of Information Science and Technology*. Washington: American Society for Information Science.

Marschak, J., 1971. Economics of information systems. *Journal American Statistical Association,* **66**(333):192–219.

———, 1972. Optimal systems for information and decision. *Techniques of Optimization*. New York: Academic.

———, and R. Radner, 1972. *Economic Theory of Teams*. New Haven: Yale University.

Martin, J., 1967. *Design of Real-time Computer Systems*. Englewood Cliffs, N.J.: Prentice-Hall.

———, 1972. *Introduction to Teleprocessing*. Englewood Cliffs, N.J.: Prentice-Hall.

———, 1973. *Security, Accuracy, and Privacy in Computer Systems*. Englewood Cliffs, N.J.: Prentice-Hall.

———, 1976. *Principles of Data-base Management*. Englewood Cliffs, N.J.: Prentice-Hall.

———, 1977. *Computer Data-base Organization*. 2nd ed. Englewood Cliffs, N.J.: Prentice-Hall.

Mason, R.O., and I.I. Mitroff, 1973. A program for research on management information systems. *Management Science,* **19**(5):475–487.

Matheson, J.E., and R.L. Winkler, 1976. Scoring rules for continuous probability distributions. *Management Science,* **22**(10):1087–1096.

Mathusz, D.V., 1977. The value of information concept applied to data systems. *Omega,* **5**(5):593–604.

Maynard, H.S., 1974. User requirements for data base management systems (DBMS). In D.A. Jardine (ed.), *Data Base Management Systems*. Amsterdam: North Holland.

Meadow, C.T., 1970. *Man–Machine Communication*. New York: Wiley-Interscience.

———, 1976. *Applied Data Management*. New York: Wiley-Interscience.

Meddaugh, E.J., 1976. Report frequency and management decisions. *Decision Sciences,* **7**(4):813–828.

Meier, R.C., W.T. Newell, and H.L. Pazer, 1969 *Simulation in Business and Economics*. Englewood Cliffs, N.J.: Prentice-Hall.

Mellichamp, J.M., and R.M. Love, 1978. Production switching heuristics for the aggregate planning problem. *Management Science,* **24**(12):1242–1251.

Mendelssohn, R.C., 1976. *Data Processing at BLS*. Report 471. Bureau of Labor Statistics, United States Department of Labor.

Menkhaus, E.J., 1969. E.D.P.: What's it worth? *Business Automation,* **16**(11):49–54.

Merkhofer, H.W., 1977. The value of information given decision flexibility. *Management Science,* **23**(7):716–727.

Mertens, P., 1972. *Industrielle Datenverarbeitung,* Band 1: *Administrations—und Dispositionssysteme* (Industrial data processing, vol. 1: administrative and operational systems). 2nd rev. ed. Wiesbaden: Betriebswirtschaftlicher Verlag Dr. Th. Gabler.

_____, and J. Griese, 1972. *Industrielle Datenverarbeitung,* Band 2: *Informations—und Planungssysteme* (Industrial data processing, vol. 2: information and planning systems). Wiesbaden: Verlag Dr. Gabler.

Mesarovic, M.D., D. Macko, and Y. Takahara, 1970. *Theory of Hierarchical Multilevel Systems.* New York: Academic.

Millen, R.N., 1972. An industrial dynamics simulation of the process control/business control interfaces of a large firm. *IEEE Transactions on Engineering Management,* **EM-19**(4):118–124.

Miller, E.F., 1973. *Bibliography and KWIC Index on Computer Performance Measurement.* Report R.M.–1809. Santa Barbara: General Research Corporation.

Miller, G.A., 1956. The magical number seven plus or minus two: some limits on our capacity for processing information. *Psychological Review,* **63** (March): 81–97.

Miller, W.D., 1976. Data accuracy—what, why, and how. *Nineteenth Annual Conference Proceedings.* Washington: American Production and Inventory Control Society.

Miller, W.G., 1969. Selection criteria for computer system adoption. *Educational Technology,* **9**(10):71–75.

Minsky, H., 1975. The manager's job: folklore and fact. *Harvard Business Review,* (4):49–61.

Mintzberg, H., D. Raisinghani, and A. Théorêt, 1976. The structure of "unstructured" decision processes. *Administrative Science Quarterly,* **21**(2):246–275.

Mishan, E.J., 1971. The postwar literature on externalities: an interpretative essay. *Journal of Economic Literature,* **9**(1):1–28.

Mock, T.J., 1969. Comparative values of information structures. *Journal of Accounting Research,* **7**(supplement):124–159.

_____, 1971. Concepts of information value and accounting. *Accounting Review,* **46**(4):765–778.

_____, T.L. Estrin, and M.A. Vasarhelyi, 1972. Learning patterns, decision approach, and value of information. *Journal of Accounting Research,* **10**(1):129–153.

_____, 1973a. A longitudinal study of some information structure alternatives. *Data Base,* **5**(2, 3, and 4):40–49.

_____, 1973b. The value of budget information. *Accounting Review,* **48**(3):520–534.

_____, and M.A. Vasarhelyi, 1977. *A Synthesis of the Information Economics and Lens Models.* Los Angeles: Department of Accounting, School of Business Administration, University of Southern California.

Mohan, C., 1978. An overview of recent data base research, *Data Base,* **10**(2):3–24.

Molnar, T.P., 1965. Advanced applications for computers: the economic justification for further expansion in A.D.P. In A.B. Frielink (ed.), *Economics of Automatic Data Processing.* Amsterdam: North Holland.

Moneta, J., 1965. Hire or purchase of A.D.P. equipment. In A.B. Frielink (ed.), *Economics of Automatic Data Processing.* Amsterdam: North Holland.

Montgomery, D.C., and V.M. Bettencourt, 1977. Multiple response surface methods in computer simulation. *Simulation,* **29**(4):113–121.

Moore, J.B., 1973. Optimal control of the job input rate to a computing facility. In F. Hanssmann (ed.), *Operational Research in the Design of Electronic Dataprocessing Systems.* London: English University.

Moore, J.R., and N.R. Baker, 1969. An analytical approach to scoring model design—application to research and development project selection. *IEEE Transactions on Engineering Management,* **EM-16**(3):90–98.

Morris, P.A., 1977. Combining expert judgments: a Bayesian approach. *Management Science,* **23**(7):679–693.

Morse, J.N., 1976a. *Human Choice Theory: Implications for Multicriteria Optimization.* Newark: Department of Business Administration, University of Delaware.

_____, 1976b. *Multiple Objective Situations in Capital Budgeting.* Newark: Department of Business Administration, University of Delaware.

Morton, M.S. Scott, 1971. *Management Decision Systems.* Boston: Harvard University.

Moskowitz, H., and W.L. Berry, 1976. A Bayesian algorithm for determining optimal single sample acceptance plans for product attributes. *Management Science,* **22**(11):1238–1250.

Moskowitz, H., and J.M. Miller, 1975. Information and decision systems for production planning. *Management Science,* **22**(3):359–370.

Muller, H., and S. De Samblanckx, 1977. An automated multicriteria evaluation procedure for a multimedia laboratory on decision sciences and systems management: concepts and results. In M.H. Hamza (ed.), *Simulation '77,* Proceedings of the International Symposium. Anaheim: Acta.

Mumford, E., (ed.), 1979. *The Impact of Data Processing on the Working Conditions of Nonmanual Workers.* EEC Study, European Economic Community. (Editor at Manchester Business School, England).

Munro, M.C., and G.B. Davis, 1974. *Determining Management Information Needs: A Comparison of Methods.* MISRC-WP-75-04, Management Information Systems Research Center. Minneapolis: Graduate School of Business Administration, University of Minnesota.

Munson, B.R., and C.M. Smith, 1976. The study of data base management systems with bibliography. In L. Berg (ed.), *Data Base Directions. Data Base,* **8** (2).

Myers, E. 1972. Supermarkets seek systems solutions to profit squeeze. *Datamation,* **18**(11):142–148.

Myers, G.J., 1976. *Software Reliability: Principles and Practices.* New York: Wiley.

Nahmias, S., 1978. Inventory Models. In J. Belzer, A. Holzman, and A. Kent (eds.), *Encyclopedia of Computer Science and Technology,* Vol. 9. New York: Marcel Dekker.

Naylor, T.H., J.L. Balintfy, D.S. Burdick, and K. Chu, 1966. *Computer Simulation Techniques.* New York: Wiley.

_____, and J.M. Vernon, 1969. *Microeconomics and Decision Models of the Firm.* New York: Harcourt Brace & World.

_____, and C. Jeffress, 1975. Corporate simulation models: a survey. *Simulation,* 24(6):171–197.

_____, and H. Schauland, 1976. A survey of users of corporate planning models. *Management Science,* 22(9):927–937.

Nielen, G.C., 1972. *Information Systems in a Management Structure.* Tilburg: Tilburg University.

_____, 1976. *De Bedoeling van Informatie voor Mens en Organisatie* (The meaning of information for man and organization). Alphen aan den Rijn, Netherlands: Samsom Uitgeverij.

Nielsen, N.R., 1970. The allocation of computer resources—Is pricing the answer? *Communications ACM,* 13(8):467–474.

Nijkamp, P., and P. Rietveld, 1978. Methoden voor de selectie van economische activiteiten (Methods for the selection of economic activities). *Intermediair,* 14(25):39–47.

Nolan, R.L., 1971. Systems analysis for computer-based information systems design. *Data Base,* 3(4):1–10.

_____, 1973. Systems analysis for computer-based information systems design. In H.L. Morgan (ed.), *Proceedings of the Wharton Conference on Research on Computers in Organizations,* Special Report no. 2. Chicago: Society for Management Information Systems. (Also published in *Data Base,* 5(2–3–4),1973.)

_____, 1977. Controlling the costs of data services. *Harvard Business Review,* 55 (4):114–214.

Nordhaus, W.D., 1973. World dynamics: measurement without data. *Economic Journal,* 83(Dec.):1156–1183.

Novick, M.R., and P.H. Jackson, 1974. *Statistical Methods for Educational and Psychological Research.* New York: McGraw-Hill.

Nunamaker, J.F., B.R. Konsynski, T. Ho, and C. Singer, 1976. Computer-aided analysis and design of information systems. *Communications ACM,* 19(12):674–687.

Nurminen, M.I., 1976. *About the Fuzziness in the Analysis of Information Systems.* Turku, Finland: Turku School of Economics.

Nutt, G.J., 1973. *Computer System Monitoring Techniques.* PB–233 372/2. Springfield, Va.: National Technical Information Service (NTIS).

Odanaka, T., 1972. *Information and Decision in Optimal Inventory Processes.* Tokyo: Metropolitan College of Technology.

Olsen, H.A., 1971. *The Economics of Information: Bibliography and Commentary on the Literature.* Washington: ERIC Clearinghouse on Library and Information Sciences.

Oomens, W.J., 1979. *Vertragingsverdelingen van het Overloopeffect van Marketing*

Uitgaven (Lag distributions for the carry-over effects of marketing expenditures). Tilburg, Netherlands: Department of Economics, Katholieke Hogeschool.

Oppenheimer, K.R., 1978. A proxy approach to multiattribute decision making. *Management Science,* 24(6):675–689.

Orlovsky, S.A., 1978. Decision making with a fuzzy preference relation. *Fuzzy Sets and Systems,* 1(3):155–167.

Ortlieb, T.A., 1976. On-line systems—managing the data. *Nineteenth Annual Conference Proceedings.* Washington: American Production and Inventory Control Society.

Osswald, B., 1973. *Leistungsvermögensanalyse von Datenverarbeitungsanlagen* (Performance analysis of computers). Darmstadt, Germany: S. Toeche-Mittler Verlag.

Palmer, C.R., (ed.), 1975. *Management Guidelines for Cost Accounting and Cost Control for Automatic Data Processing Activities and Systems.* Washington: Financial and General Management Studies Division, U.S. General Accounting Office.

Palmer, I.R., and R.M. Curtice, 1976. *Data Base Systems: A Practical Reference.* Dublin: CACI, Ireland.

Parker, B.R., and V. Srinivasan, 1976. A consumer preference approach to the planning of rural primary health-care facilities. *Operations Research,* 24(5): 991–1025.

Parker, D.B., 1976. *Crime by Computer.* New York: Scribner.

Parkin, A., 1977. The probable outcomes of a data processing project. *Computer Journal,* 20(2):98–101.

————, 1978. Critique on multicriteria assessment applied to alternative data processing systems. *Computer Journal,* 21(2):188–190.

Parks, G.M., 1972. Policy analysis in retail inventory and distribution systems. *Conference Proceedings, APICS.* International Meeting of the American Production and Inventory Control Society, Oct. 1972, Toronto, Canada.

Pegels, C.C., 1976. *Systems Analysis for Production Operations.* New York: Gordon and Breach.

Penniman, D., A. Butrimenko, and J. Page, 1978. *International Data Exchange and the Application of Informatics Technology—Critical Research Needs.* Research Memorandum RM–78–43, Laxenburg, Austria: International Institute for Applied Systems Analysis.

Perrakis, S., and I. Sahin, 1976. On risky investments with random timing of cash returns and fixed planning horizon. *Management Science,* 22(7):799–809.

Peterson, R.E., 1977. The components of information. *Interfaces,* 7(4):87–91.

Phister, M., 1976. *Data Processing Technology and Economics.* Rev. ed. Santa Monica: Santa Monica Publishing.

Pirsig, R.M., 1974. *Zen and the Art of Motorcycle Maintenance: An Inquiry into Values.* London: Bodley Head.

Plagman, B.K., and G.P. Altschuler, 1972. A data dictionary system/directory system within the context of an integrated corporate data base. *Proceedings AFIPS 1972, Fall Joint Computer Conference,* 41, Part II. Montvale, N.J.: AFIPS.

Politzer, J.P., and P. Wilmès, 1977. *Optimal Design of Management Information Systems through Control Theory.* Working paper no. 77–5. Sherbrooke, Quebec: Faculté d'Administration, University of Sherbrooke.

Popadic, R.P., 1975. Design of chargeout control systems for computer services. In F.W. McFarlan and R.L. Nolan (eds.), *The Information Systems Handbook.* Homewood: Dow Jones-Irwin.

Pope, D.J.M., 1975. Estimating the resources needed for ADP systems. In A.B. Frielink (ed.), *Economics of Information.* Amsterdam: North Holland.

Pounds, W.F., 1969. The process of problem finding. *Industrial Management Review,* **11**(1):1–19.

Power, W.D., 1971. Retail terminals . . . a POS survey. *Datamation,* **17**(13):22–31.

Pritchard, J.A.T., 1976. *Quantitative Methods in On-line Systems.* Manchester: National Computing Centre.

Proceedings of the International Symposium on Computer Performance Modeling, Measurement, and Evaluation. 1976. Harvard University, Cambridge, March 29–31. (Obtainable from ACM, Inc., PO Box 12105, Church Street Station, New York, N.Y. 10249.)

Radford, K.J., 1973. *Information Systems in Management.* Reston, Virginia: Reston.

Radner, R., 1978. Jacob Marschak. *Behavioral Science,* **23**(2):63–66.

Raiffa, H., 1968. *Decision Analysis: Introductory Lectures on Choices under Uncertainty.* Reading, Mass.: Addison-Wesley.

Ramer, S., 1973. *Konfigurations—und Anwendungsplanung von E.D.V. Systemen* (Configuration and application planning of EDP systems). Berlin: De Gruyter.

Randell, B., P.A. Lee, and P.C. Treleaven, 1978. Reliability issues in computing system design. *Computing Surveys,* **10**(2):123–165.

Rappaport, A., 1970. Sensitivity analysis in decision making. In A. Rappaport (ed.), *Information for Decision Making: Quantitative and Behavioral Dimensions.* Englewood Cliffs, N.J.: Prentice-Hall.

Ravin, J., and M. Schatzoff, 1977. An interactive graphics system for analysis of business decisions. In W.C. House (ed.), *Interactive Decision-oriented Data Base Systems.* New York: Petrocelli/Charter.

Reichardt, K.E., 1974. Capitalizing costs of information systems. *Management Accounting,* **52**(4):39–43.

Remus, W.E., 1978. Testing Bowman's managerial coefficient theory using a competitive gaming environment. *Management Science,* **24**(8):827–835.

Rettus, R.C., and R.A. Smith, 1972. Accounting control of data processing. *IBM Systems Journal,* **11**(1):74–92.

Ricker, H.S., and H.F. Krueckeberg, 1971. *Computerized Checkout Systems for Retail Food Stores.* Terre Haute: Bureau of Business Research, School of Business, Indiana State University.

Rietmüller, C.E., and B.D. Schreiber, 1977. Delays in socio-economical systems dynamics models. In M.H. Hamza (ed.), *Simulation '77,* Proceedings of the International Symposium. Anaheim: Acta.

Roberts, N., 1978. Teaching dynamic feedback systems thinking: an elementary view. *Management Science,* **24**(8):836–843.

Rogers, F.A., and R.L. Van Horn, 1976. *Goal-oriented Resource Allocation for University Management.* Pittsburgh: Carnegie-Mellon University.

Rome, B.K., and S.C. Rome, 1971. *Organizational Growth through Decisionmaking: A Computer-based Experiment in Eductive Method.* New York: American Elsevier.

Rose, C.A., 1978. A measurement procedure for queuing network models of computer systems. *Computing Surveys,* 10(3):263–280.

Rosenblatt, M.J., and J.V. Jucker, 1979. Capital expenditure decision making: some tools and trends. *Interfaces,* 9(2, part 1):63–69. [Also 9(3):100–105.]

Rosenkranz, F., and S. Pellegrini, 1976. Corporate modelling: methodology and computer-based model design procedure. *Angewandte Informatik,* 6:259–267.

Rowe, A.J., 1968. Coming to terms with computer management systems. *Financial Executive,* 36(4):64–73.

Rowe, W.D., 1977. *An Anatomy of Risk.* New York: Wiley-Interscience.

Rubinstein, A.B., and H. Schröder, 1977. Managerial differences in assessing probabilities of technical success for R&D projects. *Management Science,* 24(2):137–148.

Ruisch, R., 1978. Groei in de automatisering binnen een bedrijf (Growth in computerization within a company). *Informatie,* 20(3):151–157.

Rullo, T.A., 1970. Understanding the software package market. *Data Processing,* 12(7):35–38.

Ruschitzka, M., and R.S. Fabry, 1977. A unifying approach to scheduling. *Communications ACM,* 20(7):469–477.

Saaty, T.L., 1977. A scaling method for priorities in hierarchical structures. *Journal Mathematical Psychology,* 15:234–281.

Sassone, P.G., and W.A. Schaffer, 1978. *Cost–Benefit Analysis: A Handbook.* New York: Academic.

Sauer, C.H., and K.M. Chandy, 1979. The impact of distributions and disciplines on multiple processor systems. *Communications ACM,* 22(1):25–34.

Savas, E.S., 1978. On equity in providing public services. *Management Science,* 24(8):800–808.

Schaller, C., 1974. Survey of computer cost allocation techniques. *Journal of Accountancy,* 137(6):41–46.

Scharf, T.G., 1969. How not to choose an EDP system. *Datamation,* 15(4):73–74.

Schendel, D., and G.R. Patton, 1978. A simultaneous equation model of corporate strategy. *Management Science,* 24(15):1611–1621.

Scherr, A.L., 1967. *An Analysis of Time-shared Computer Systems.* Cambridge, Mass.: M.I.T.

Schlaifer, R.O., 1967. *Analysis of Decisions under Uncertainty.* New York: McGraw-Hill.

Schneidewind, N.F., 1967. The practice of computer selection. *Datamation,* 13(2):22–25.

Schoeffler, S., R.D. Buzzel, and D.F. Heany, 1974. Impact of strategic planning on profit performance. *Harvard Business Review,* 52(2):137–145.

Schonberger, R.J., 1977. *MIS Design: A Contingency Approach.* Lincoln: Department of Management, University of Nebraska.

Schoute, F.C., 1978. Decentralized control in packet-switched satellite communication. *IEEE Transactions on Automatic Control,* **AC-23**(2):362–371.

Schrieber, A.N., (ed.), 1970. *Corporate Simulation Models.* Seattle: Graduate School of Business Administration, University of Washington.

Schroeder, R.G., and I. Benbasat, 1975. An experimental evaluation of the relationship of uncertainty in the environment to information used by decision makers. *Decision Sciences,* **6**(3):556–567.

Schussel, G., 1974. Scoring DP performance. *Infosystems,* **21**(7):59–60.

_____, 1975. Data bases. In F.W. McFarlan and R.L. Nolan (eds.), *The Information Systems Handbook.* Homewood, Ill.: Dow Jones-Irwin.

Schuster, E.G., 1969. *Selective Demand Determinants in the Computer Acquisition Process.* Ph.D. Dissertation, The American University. Ann Arbor: University Microfilms.

Schwartz, E.S., 1968. Computer evaluation and selection. *Journal Data Management,* **6**(6):58–62.

Schwartz, L.B., and R.E. Johnson, 1977. *An Appraisal of the Empirical Performance of the Linear Decision Rule.* Paper no. 641. Lafayette, Indiana: Krannert Graduate School of Management, Purdue University.

Schwartz, M.H., 1969. Computer project selection in the business enterprise. *Journal of Accountancy,* **127**(4):35–43.

Schwartz, S.L., and I. Vertinsky, 1977. Multiattribute investment decisions: a study of R&D project selection. *Management Science,* **24**(3):285–301.

Schwetman, H.D., 1978. Hybrid simulation models of computer systems. *Communications ACM,* **21**(9):718–723.

Scott, J.E., and P. Wright, 1976. Modeling an organizational buyer's product evaluation strategy: validity and procedural considerations. *Journal Marketing Research,* **13**(August):211–224.

Scull, J.A., (ed.), 1973. Performance evaluation bibliography. *Performance Evaluation Review,* **2**(2):37–49.

SDC, 1975. *IMSIM: System Capabilities.* Santa Monica: System Development Corporation.

Segal, R., and B. O'Neal, 1979. Dynamic simulation of a national resource sharing computer network. *Simuletter,* **10**(3):67–74.

Seiler, K., 1969. *Introduction to Systems Cost-effectiveness.* New York: Wiley-Interscience.

Selwyn, L.L., 1971a. Competition and structure in the computer service industry. In B.E. Squires (ed.), *Economic Considerations in Managing the Computer Installation,* SIGCOSIM Proceedings. New York: ACM.

_____, 1971b. Computer resource accounting and pricing. In B.E. Squires (ed.), *Economic Considerations in Managing the Computer Installation,* SIGCOSIM Proceedings. New York: ACM.

Senge, P.M., 1973. *Tests for Building Confidence in System Dynamics Models.* D-2760 System Dynamics Group. Cambridge, Mass.: Alfred P. Sloan School of Management, M.I.T.

Senn, J.A., 1973. *Information System Structure and Purchasing Decision Effectiveness: An Experimental Study.* Ph.D. Thesis. Minneapolis: University of Minnesota. (Ann Arbor: University Microfilms, 1974.)

————, 1974. Economic evaluation of management information decision systems (MIDS). In M.W. Hopfe (ed.), *Proceedings of the Sixth Annual Meeting of the American Institute for Decision Sciences.* Atlanta: American Institute for Decision Sciences.

Seppälä, Y., 1979. *The Relative Value of a Management Information System; A Simulation Study.* Helsinki: Department of Computer Science, University of Helsinki.

Severance, D.G., and J.V. Carlis, 1977. A practical approach to selecting record access paths. *Computing Surveys,* 9(4):259–272.

Shaftel, T.L., and R.W. Zmud, 1973. *Allocation of Computer Resources through Flexible Pricing.* Tucson: College of Business and Public Administration, University of Arizona.

Shannon, R.E., 1975. *Systems Simulation: The Art and Science.* Englewood Cliffs, N.J.: Prentice-Hall.

Sharpe, W.F., 1965. Computer pricing policies from an economist's point of view. In A.B. Frielink, (ed.), *Economics of Automatic Data Processing.* Amsterdam: North Holland.

————, 1969. *The Economics of Computers.* New York: Columbia University.

Shaul, D.R., 1964. What's really ahead for middle management? *Personnel,* 31(6):6–16.

Shephard, R.W., 1976. Cost and production functions: a survey. In W.H. Marlowe (ed.), *Modern Trends in Logistics Research.* Cambridge, Mass: M.I.T.

Sherman, S.W., 1976. Trace-driven modeling: an update. *Simuletter,* 7(4):87–91.

Shubik, M., 1975. *The Uses and Methods of Gaming.* New York: Elsevier Scientific.

————, G. Wolf, and S. Lockhart, 1971. An artificial player for a business market game. *Simulation and Games,* 2(1):27–43.

Sibley, E.H., 1974. Data management systems—user requirements. In D.A. Jardine (ed.), *Data Base Management Systems.* Amsterdam: North Holland.

Sieghart, P., 1976. *Privacy and Computers.* London: Latimer New Dimensions.

SIGMETRICS, 1976. Technical meeting on pricing computer services proceedings. Palm Springs, November 20–21, 1975. *Performance Evaluation Review,* 50(1).

Silver, E.A., A.L. Loss, and F. Black, 1971. A quantitative rule for the use of resources in a multiprogrammed computer system. *Infor,* 9(2):96–110.

Simon, H., 1978. An analytical investigation of Kotler's competitive simulation model. *Management Science,* 24(14):1462–1473.

Simon, H.A., 1960. *The New Science of Management Decision.* New York: Harper & Row.

_____, and A. Ando, 1961. Aggregation of variables in dynamic systems. *Econometrica*, **29**(2):111–138.

Singer, N.M., H. Kanter, and A. Moore, 1968. Prices and the allocation of computer time. Fall Joint Computer Conference, *AFIPS Conference Proceedings*, **33**, part 1.

SMI, 1972. *Report on the Migross/Zellweger Field Test of the APOSS*. Chicago: Super Market Institute.

Smidt, S., 1968. The use of hard and soft money budgets and prices to limit demand for centralized computer facility. Joint Computer Conference, *AFIPS Conference Proceedings*, **33**(Fall), part 1.

Smith, H.R., 1975. *Experimental Comparison of Database Inquiry Techniques*. Unpublished Ph.D. thesis. Minneapolis: University of Minnesota.

Smith, H.T., 1974. Human decision making in a sequential task. In A. Debons (ed.), *Information Science: Search for Identity*. New York: Marcel Dekker.

Smith, M.L., H.E. Metzner, and W.A. Brooks, 1978. Computerized costing model for inland waterways barge transportation. *Interfaces*, **8**(4):31–37.

Snyders, J., 1973. Software: the make or buy decision. *Infosystems*, **21**(7):38–40.

Sollenberger, H.M., and A.A. Arens, 1973. Systems control and post-completion audit. *Internal Auditor*, **30**(2):22–33.

Spetzler, C.S., and C.S. Staël von Holstein, 1975. Probability encoding in decision analysis. *Management Science*, **22**(3):340–358.

Squires, B.E., (ed.), 1971. *Economic Considerations in Managing the Computer Installation*. Proceedings Second Annual SIGCOSIM Symposium. New York: SIGCOSIM, ACM.

Stabell, C.B., 1978a. Integrative complexity of information environment perception and information use: an empirical investigation. *Organizational Behavior and Human Performance*, **22**:116–142.

_____, 1978b. *On Defining and Improving Decision Making Effectiveness*. Stanford: Graduate School of Business, Stanford University.

Stamper, R.K., 1971. Some ways of measuring information. *Computer Bulletin*, **15**(12):432–436.

_____, 1973. *Information in Business and Administrative Systems*. London: B.T. Batsford.

_____, 1975. Information science for systems analysis. In E. Mumford and H. Sackman (eds.), *Human Choice and the Computers*. Amsterdam: North Holland. (Reprint available from the author at London School of Economics.)

_____, 1977. *Physical Objects, Human Discourse, and Formal Systems*. London: London School of Economics.

Starr, M.K., and M. Zeleny, (eds.), 1977. *Multiple Criteria Decision Making*. Amsterdam: North Holland.

Statland, N., (ed.), 1977. Guidelines for cost accounting practices for data processing. *Data Base*, **8** (3 Supplement): 2–20.

Sterling, T.D., 1979. Consumer difficulties with computerized transactions: an empirical investigation. *Communications ACM*, **22**(5):283–289.

Stern, H., 1970. Information systems in management science. *Management Science,* 17(2):B119–123.

Stevens, M.E., 1970a. *Research and Development in the Computer and Information Sciences,* Vol. 1, *Information Acquisition, Sensing, and Input: A Selective Literature Review.* Monograph 113, vol. 1. Washington: National Bureau of Standards.

_____, 1970b. *Research and Development in the Computer and Information Sciences,* Vol. 2, *Processing, Storage, and Output Requirements in Information-Processing Systems; A Selective Literature Review.* Monograph 113, vol. 2. Washington: National Bureau of Standards.

_____, 1970c. *Research and Development in the Computer and Information Sciences,* Vol. 3, *Overall System Design Considerations: A Selective Literature Review.* Monograph 113, vol. 3. Washington: National Bureau of Standards.

Stohr, E.A., 1979. Information systems for observing inventory levels. *Operations Research,* 27(2):242–259.

Stone, B.K., 1978. *Computer-assisted Cash Flow Generation and Sensitivity Analysis for Major Capital Investment Projects.* Working Paper no. MS–78–5. Atlanta: College of Industrial Management, Georgia Institute of Technology.

Strassmann, P.A., 1970. Forecasting considerations in design of management information systems. In A. Rappaport (ed.), *Information for Decisionmaking: Quantitative and Behavioral Dimensions.* Englewood Cliffs, N.J.: Prentice Hall.

Streufert, S.C., 1973. Effects of information relevance on decision making in complex environments. *Memory and Cognition,* 1(3):224–228.

Sullivan, W.G., and W.W. Claycombe, 1977. The use of decision trees in planning plant expansion. In W.C. House (ed.), *Interactive Decision-oriented Data Base Systems.* New York: Petrocelli/Charter.

Sundgren, B., 1976. *The Theory of Data Bases.* New York: Petrocelli/Charter.

_____, 1978. Een raamwerk voor het ontwerpen van informatiesystemen (A framework for the design of information systems). *Informatie,* 20(1):33–39.

Suppes, P., and J.L. Zinnes., 1963. Basic measurement theory. In R.D. Luce, R.R. Bush, and E. Galanter (eds.), *Handbook of Mathematical Psychology,* Vol. 1. New York: Wiley.

Svobodova, L., 1976. *Computer Performance Measurement and Evaluation Methods: Analysis and Applications.* New York: American Elsevier.

Swanson, C.V., 1971. *Evaluating the Quality of Management Information.* Working paper. Cambridge, Mass.: Alfred P. Sloan School of Management.

Swanson, R.W., 1975. Design and evaluation of information systems. In C.A. Cuadra, A.W. Luke, and J.L. Harris (eds.), *Annual Review of Information Science and Technology,* Vol. 10. Washington: American Society for Information Science.

Sweeney, D.J., E.P. Winkofsky, P. Roy, and N.R. Baker, 1978. Composition vs. decomposition: two approaches to modeling organizational decision processes. *Management Science,* 24(14):1491–1499.

Taggart, W.M., and M.O. Tharp, 1977. A survey of information requirements analysis techniques. *Computing Surveys,* 9(4):273–290.

Tanenbaum, A.S., 1976. A survey of operating systems. *Informatie*, 18(12):689–698.

Tapiero, C.S., 1974. *Optimization of Information Measurements with Inventory Applications.* Research Paper No. 57. New York: Graduate School of Business, Columbia University.

_____, 1975. On-line and adaptive optimum advertising control by a diffusion approximation. *Operations Research*, 23(5):890–907.

_____, 1978. Optimum advertising and goodwill under uncertainty. *Operations Research*, 26(3):450–463.

Taylor, S., 1979. Production and inventory management in the process industry: a state of the art survey. *Production and Inventory Management*, 20(1):1–16.

Tenenbein, A., and M. Gargano., 1978. *Generation of Bivariate Distributions with Fixed Marginals and Correlation Structure.* New York: Graduate School of Business Administration, New York University.

Ter Linde, W., 1978. Het doorberekeningsprincipe bij de Stichting Academisch Rekencentrum Amsterdam (The principle of charging at the Academic Computing Center Amsterdam Foundation). *Informatie*, 20(2):105–107.

Thesen, A., 1978. *Computer Methods in Operations Research.* New York: Academic.

Thiriez, H., and S. Zionts, (eds.), 1976. *Multiple Criteria Decision Making.* Berlin: Springer-Verlag.

Thissen, W.A.H., 1978. *Investigations into the Club of Rome's World3 Model: Lessons for Understanding Complicated Models.* Doctoral dissertation. Eindhoven, Netherlands: Technical University.

Timmreck, E.M., 1973. Computer selection methodology. *Computing Surveys*, 5(4):199–222.

Treille, J.M., 1978. *New Strategies for Business Informations.* Working paper. Joue-en-Josas, France: GAPSET.

Trill, G.P., 1977. PAYPUR, a complete CRT on-line, real-time procurement system. *Production and Inventory Management*, 18(3):63–83.

Truxal, J.G., 1955. *Automatic Feedback Control System Synthesis.* New York: McGraw-Hill.

Turban, E., and M.L. Metersky, 1971. Utility theory applied to multivariable system effectiveness evaluation. *Management Science*, 17(12):B817–828.

Turn, R., 1974. *Privacy and Security in Personal Information Databank Systems.* Santa Monica: Rand.

Unger, B.W., 1978. Programming languages for computer system simulation. *Simulation*, 30(4):101–110.

Uretsky, M., 1969. Discussion of comparative values of information structures. *Journal of Accounting Research*, 7(supplement):160–167.

Van Aken, J.E., 1973. Enige micro-economische beschouwingen over conjunctuur (Some microeconomic reflections on business cycles). *Maandblad voor Bedrijfsadministratie en Organisatie*, 77(912):88–94.

_____, P. Van Beek, and G.L. Polderman, 1974. *Prospect, A Prototype-distributed MIS for Operational Control of a Network of Factories and Sales Organizations.* Eindhoven, Netherlands: Information Systems and Operations Research Department, Philips.

_____, 1978. *On the Control of Complex Industrial Organizations.* Leiden, Netherlands: Martinus Nijhoff Social Sciences Division.

Van Amstel, J.J., 1978. Software engineering. *Informatie,* 20(10):593–600.

Van Belkum, J.W., 1978. Het ontwerpen van logistieke informatiesystemen (The design of logistic information systems). In L.C. Van Zutphen (ed.), *Aspecten van Logistieke Informatiesystemen* (Aspects of logistic information systems). Alphen aan den Rijn, Netherlands: Samsom Uitgeverij.

Van Dam, C., P.J. Hesp, P.F.M. Koeleman, and T. de Wit, 1976. *Planning Capital Budgeting and Valuation—A Study within 33 Dutch Firms.* Breukelen, Netherlands: Netherlands School of Business "Nijenrode."

Vandepitte, G., and L. Corthouts, 1974. De ontwikkeling van simulatiespelen en toepassingen in België (The development of simulation games and their applications in Belgium). *Informatie,* 16(1):38–42.

Van de Wouw, C.J.M., 1977. *Information System Planning,* part 1, *An Attempt to Synthesize Models and Methods.* Eindhoven, Netherlands: ISA-Research, Philips.

Van Dinten, W.L., 1978. De evolutie van de automatisering in het bankbedrijf (The evolution of automation in the banking industry). In *De Betekenis van de Automatisering voor de Ontwikkeling van het Nederlands Bankbedrijf* (The significance of automation for the development of the Dutch banking industry). Pre-adviezen, NIBE-jaardag. Amsterdam: Nederlands Instituut voor het Bank- en Effectenbedrijf.

Van Horn, R.L., 1973. Empirical studies of management information systems. *Data Base,* 5(2, 3, and 4):172–182.

Van Lommel, E.M., 1968. *De Beoordeling en Selectie van Investeringsprojecten* (The evaluation and selection of investment projects). Antwerp: Standaard Wetenschappelijke Uitgeverij.

Van Loon, P.J.J.M., 1975. Beslissingsmethoden bij meer doelstellingen (Decision methods for multiple goals). *Economie,* 39(8):383–416.

Van Raaij, W.F., 1978. *Het Gebruik van de Conjuncte Meettechniek* (The use of the conjoint measurement technique). Tilburg, Netherlands: Department of Psychology, Katholieke Hogeschool.

Van Reeken, A.J., *On Programming Methodology: A Tutorial.* Tilburg, Netherlands: Computer Center, Katholieke Hogeschool.

Van Zanten, J.H., 1975. Economische aspecten, kosten versus baten (Economic aspects, costs versus benefits). Presented at *Het Gebruik van Terminals,* organized by NOVI, Stadhouderskade 6, Amsterdam, Nov. 18–19.

Van Zutphen, L.C., 1976. Informatiegebruikers: Enkele problemen van het geautomatiseerde informatiesysteem, gezien door de optiek van de gebruiker (Information users: some problems of computerized information systems as seen by its user). *Managers en Computers.* Alphen aan den Rijn, Netherlands: Samsom Uitgeverij.

Vasarhelyi, M.A., and T.J. Mock, 1977. *An Information-processing Analysis of Budget Variance Information.* Los Angeles: Department of Accounting, Graduate School of Business Administration, University of Southern California.

Vasicek, O.A., 1977. An inequality for the variance of waiting time under a general queuing discipline. *Operations Research,* **25**(5):879–884.

Vazsonyi, A., 1975. *Formal Techniques of Analysis and Evaluation of Information Systems.* Working Paper 7526. Rochester: Graduate School of Management, University of Rochester.

———, 1976. The decision to inquire. *Interfaces,* **7**(1):73–80.

———, 1977a. *Geometry of Information Systems.* Working Paper no. 7727. Rochester, N.Y.: Graduate School of Management, University of Rochester.

———, 1977b. *Mathematical Models of Information Systems,* part 1, *The Mathematical Paradigm.* Working Paper Series no. 7703. Rochester, N.Y.: Graduate School of Management, University of Rochester.

———, 1978. Geometry of information systems, part 2. *Interfaces,* **8**(2):88–94.

———, 1979. Concerning the dangers of little knowledge. *Interfaces,* **9**(3):78–86.

Verhelst, M., 1974. *Contribution to the Analysis of Organizational Information Systems and Their Financial Benefits.* Louvain: Department of Economics, University of Louvain.

Verhofstad, J.S.M., 1978. Recovery techniques for database systems. *Computing Surveys,* **10**(2):167–195.

Verrijn Stuart, A.A., 1976. *Kwantitatieve Aspecten van Informatiesystemen* (Quantitative aspects of information systems). Alphen aan den Rijn, Netherlands: Samsom Uitgeverij. (An English translation will be published by NCC, London.)

Verver, J.M., 1978. Simulation with human players as a technique for transfer of knowledge and as a tool for system specification. *Proceedings of "Modelling in Business,"* a seminar organized by NIAG (Netherlands IFIP Applied Information Processing Group), Amsterdam, Jan. 12–13.

Votaw, D.F., 1965. Statistical science and information technology. In J. Spiegel and D.E. Walker (eds.), *Second Congress on the Information System Sciences.* Washington: Spartan.

Walkowicz, J.L., 1974. *Benchmarking and Workload Definition: A Selected Bibliography with Abstracts.* Special Publication 405 (SD Catalog no. C13.10:405). Washington: National Bureau of Standards.

Wallace, J.B., 1975. An experimental evaluation of simulation techniques for analysing costs and benefits of information systems. In A.B. Frielink (ed.), *Economics of Informatics,* Amsterdam: North Holland.

———, and E.W. Boyd, 1971. Simulation of information system design decisions. *Proceedings 1971 Summer Computer Simulation Conference,* pp. 1210–1218. New York: Board of Simulation Conferences, ACM.

Walsh, D.S., 1976. *Computerized Point-of-Sale Systems: A Revolution in Supermarket Checkout Concepts.* Woodbridge, N.J.: Supermarkets General Corporation.

Walston, C.E., and C.P. Felix, 1977. A method of programming measurement and estimation. *IBM Systems Journal,* **16**(1):54–73.

Wehrung, D.A., 1978. Interactive identification and optimization using a binary preference relation. *Operations Research,* 26(2): 322–332.

Weil, H.B., 1971. Industrial dynamics and MIS. *Proceedings Computer Simulation Conference,* Boston. New York: ACM.

Weitzman, C., 1974. *Minicomputers Systems: Structure, Implementation, and Application.* Englewood Cliffs, N.J.: Prentice-Hall.

Welke, R.J., 1975a. *Information System Evaluation—A "Non-Bayesian" Approach, Part 1.* Hamilton, Ontario: Faculty of Business, McMaster University.

———, 1975b. *Information System Evaluation—A "Non-Bayesian" Approach, Part 2.* Hamilton, Ontario: Faculty of Business, McMaster University.

———, 1977a. *The "Economic" Evaluation of Information Systems—Issues and Outlooks.* Hamilton, Canada: Faculty of Business, McMaster University.

———, 1977b. *Management Information Systems Description and Evaluation.* Seminar presented at the Katholieke Hogeschool Tilburg. (Papers available from the author at the Faculty of Business, McMaster University, Hamilton, Ontario, Canada.)

———, 1978a. *Bibliography on Information System Effectiveness Evaluation.* Hamilton, Ontario: McMaster University.

———, 1978b. *Lecture Notes on Information Requirements Analysis.* Hamilton, Ontario: Faculty of Business, McMaster University.

Wenzel, F., 1975. Entscheidungsorientierte Informationsbewertung (Decision-oriented information evaluation). Opladen, Germany: Westdeutscher Verlag.

Wessel, C.J., and K.L. Moore, 1969. *Criteria For Evaluating the Effectiveness of Library Operations and Services,* Report no. 21. Washington: Army Technical Library Improvement Studies.

Wheelwright, S.C., and S. Makridakis, 1973. *Forecasting Methods for Management.* New York: Wiley-Interscience.

White, D.R.J., D.L. Scott, and R.N. Schulz, 1963. POED—a method of evaluating system performance. *IEEE Transactions on Engineering Management,* EM–10 (4):177–182.

Wiest, J.D., and F.K. Levy, 1977. *A Management Guide to PERT/CPM: with GERT/PDM/CPM and Other Networks.* Englewood Cliffs, N.J.: Prentice-Hall.

Wildermooth, B.L., and B.L. Foote, 1979. Evaluation of the maintenance management information systems of the United States postal service. *Interfaces,* 9(2, part 1):42–49.

Wilkes, F.M., 1977. *Capital Budgeting Techniques.* London: Wiley.

Wilkinson, J.H., 1965. *The Algebraic Eigenvalue Problem.* Oxford: Clarendon.

Williams, F.E., 1977. Decision theory and the innkeeper: an approach for setting hotel reservation policy. *Interfaces,* 7(4):18–30.

Willoughby, T.C., 1975. Pricing of computer services. In A.B. Frielink (ed.), *Economics of Informatics.* Amsterdam: North Holland.

Wilmer, M.A.P., and A. Berry, 1976. *Managerial Performance and System Uncertainty.* Manchester: Manchester Business School.

Wilmès, P., 1973. *Un Modèle de Transport Multi-resources: Application de la Dynamique des Systemes* (A multiresource transportation model: application of systems dynamics). Louvain, Belgium: Department of Economic, Social, and Political Sciences, University of Louvain.

Wimbrow, J.H., 1971. A large-scale interactive administrative system. *IBM Systems Journal*, 10(4):260–282.

Wind, Y., and L.K. Spitz, 1976. Analytical approach to marketing decisions in health-care organisations. *Operations Research*, 24(5):973–990.

Wiorkowski, G.K., and J.J. Wiorkowski, 1973. A cost allocation model. *Datamation*, 19(8):60–65.

Wissema, J.G., 1978. Waarschuwingssignalen voor ondernemer: managementinformatie ten dienste van de strategische beleidsvorming en beleidsbeheersing (Warning signals for managers: management information serving strategic management and control). *Intermediair*, 14(9):29–37.

Wolf, G., 1972. Some research and teaching with an on-line oligopoly game using an artificial player. *Decision Sciences*, 3(3):101–114.

_____, 1976. *Market Structure, Opponent Behavior and Information in a Market Game*. Report M–76–11. Atlanta: College of Industrial Management, Georgia Institute of Technology.

Wolfe, J., 1975. Effective performance behaviors in a simulated policy and decision-making environment. *Management Science*, 21(8):872–882.

Wolfe, J.N., 1974. *The Economics of Technical Information Systems*. New York: Praeger.

Wolff, R.N., and G.H. Haines, 1974. The executive education experience using the Toronto management game. *Proceedings of the First National ABSEL Conference*, Oklahoma City, April 26–27. (Available in Reprint Series, Faculty of Management Studies, University of Toronto.)

Wooldridge, S., 1975. *Computer Output Design*. New York: Petrocelli/Charter.

Wyatt, J.B., 1975. Computer systems: simulation. In F.W. McFarlan and R.L. Nolan (eds.), *The Information Systems Handbook*. Homewood, Ill.: Dow Jones-Irwin.

Wynne, B., and G.W. Dickson, 1975. Experienced managers' performance in experimental man-machine decision system simulation. *Academy of Management Journal*, 18(1):25–40.

Yearsley, R.B., and G.M.R. Graham, 1973. *Handbook of Computer Management*. New York: Halsted.

Yeh, R.T., (ed.), 1976. Special issue: reliable software 1: software validation. *Computing Surveys*, 8(3):301–353.

Ying, C.C., 1967. Learning by doing—an adaptive approach to multiperiod decisions. *Operations Research*, 15(5):797–812.

_____, 1977. *Information, Decision, and Adaptation*. Newark: Graduate School of Business Administration, Rutgers University.

Yuan, J.S.C., J.H. Horen, and H.M. Wagner, 1975. Optimal multiproduct production scheduling and employment smoothing with deterministic demands. *Management Science*, 21(11):1250–1262.

Zacks, S., 1976. Review of statistical problems and methods in logistics research. In W.H. Marlow (ed.), *Modern Trends in Logistics Research.* Cambridge, Mass: M.I.T.

Zadeh, L.A., 1975. Fuzzy sets and their applications to cognitive and decision processes. In L.A. Zadeh, K. Fu, and K. Tanaka (eds.), *Proceedings of the United States–Japan Seminar on Fuzzy Sets and Their Applications.* New York: Academic.

Zangemeister, C., 1975. Measurement of effectiveness of computerized information systems from a management point of view through utility analysis. In A.B. Frielink (ed.), *Economics of Informatics.* Amsterdam: North Holland.

Zani, W.M., 1970. Real-time information systems: a comparative economic analysis. *Management Science,* 16(6):350–355.

Zeigler, B.P., 1976. *Theory of Modelling and Simulation.* New York: Wiley.

Zeleny, M., 1976a. The attribute-dynamic attitude model (ADAM). *Management Science,* 23(1):12–26.

———, (ed.),1976b. *Multiple Criteria Decision Making.* Berlin: Springer-Verlag.

Zelkowitz, M.V., 1978. Perspectives on software engineering. *Computing Surveys,* 10(2):197–216.

Zijlker, A.W., 1974. Unit informatiesystemen (Unit information systems). *Intermediair,* 10(7):57–65.

Zionts, S., and J. Wallenius, 1976. An interactive programming method for solving the multiple criteria problem. *Management Science,* 22(6):652–663.

Zmud, R.W., 1978. On the validity of the analytic-heuristic instrument in "the Minnesota experiments." *Management Science,* 24(10):1088–1090.

This index includes references implicit in the et al. construction. Organizations, like IBM, acting as author, can be found in the Subject Index.

Abbott, W., 47
Abramson, N., 111
Ackoff, R. L., 87, 133, 151, 193
Adams, C. R., 16, 108, 111
Adams, J. M., 114
Agajanian, A. H., 19, 30
Agrawala, A. K., 31
Allen, B. R., 114
Altshuler, G. P., 17
Amphlett Lewis, W. A., 114
Ando, A., 102
Ansoff, H. I., 16, 153
Anthony, R. N., 6
Aquilano, N. J., 185
Arens, A. A., 3
Arnoff, E. L., 87, 133
Aron, J. D., 113
Ashenhurst, R. L., 3
Atkinson, A. A., 61
Atwater, T. V. V., 95, 110, 112, 199
Avolio, L. C., 17
Aykac, A., 134

Baker, K. R., 84, 155, 185
Baker, N., 49, 185
Baker, N. R., 47, 65
Balanchandran, V., 69, 85
Balintfy, J. L., 153, 159, 184
Bally, J. L., 154
Bamberg, G., 116, 133, 134
Barber, B., 47
Bariff, M. L., 112–114
Barkin, S. R., 114, 145

Barlow, R. E., 30, 144
Bassler, R. A., 111, 112
Batt, C. D., 110, 185
Baugut, G., 30
Baumgarten, A., 2, 3, 10, 17, 60, 67, 85, 107
Beckmann, M. J., 125, 129
Beer, S., 151
Beilner, H., 30
Bell, D. E., 43, 47, 48
Bell, T. E., 2, 31, 84, 112
Bemelmans, T. M. A., 40, 47, 48, 49, 134, 185
Bénay, J., 17
Benbasat, I., 112, 145
Benwell, N., 113
Bequai, A., 114
Berg, S. V., 69, 111
Bernard, D., 85–87
Bernhard, R. H., 48, 69
Bernstein, M. I., 113
Berry, W. L., 130, 155
Bettencourt, V. M., 48
Bhat, U. N., 30
Bierer, J. M., 184
Bishop, C. D., 31
Black, F., 30
Blumenthal, S. C., 16, 17, 92, 114
Boe, W. J., 184
Boehm, B. W., 2, 31, 112
Bonini, C. P., 44, 109, 140, 142, 149, 152, 154, 160

Bonney, M. C., 16, 17, 85, 112
Boodman, D. M., 87, 153
Borovits, J., 47
Bos, H., 153
Bosman, A., 3, 16–17
Bottler, J., 3, 47–49, 85–87
Boutell, W. S., 7, 86, 154
Bovet, D. P., 84
Boyd, D. F., 87, 98, 110–111, 114, 140, 142
Boyd, E. W., 111
Braat, J. J. M., 112, 114, 153
Bradley, S. P., 154
Brandon, D. H., 45, 47
Brenner, J. R., 95, 112
Bresnick, T. A., 134
Brevoord, C., 2, 3, 10, 16, 17, 60, 67, 85, 111, 114, 187
Brigham, E. F., 86
Britney, R. R., 86
Brittan, J. N. G., 3, 154
Brocato, L. J., 35, 47
Brock, G. W., 52–54, 85
Bromley, A. C., 46, 48
Brooks, F. P., 54, 86, 112–113
Brooks, W. A., 112–113
Brown, R. G., 14
Brumat, C., 134
Bruns, W. J., 152, 154, 184
Bucci, G., 84, 114
Buchholz, W., 30
Buettel, T. D., 47
Burch, J. G., 111
Burdick, D. S., 153, 159, 184
Burpo, C. W., 3
Burt, J. M., 86
Bussey, L. E., 86, 87
Butrimenko, A., 16
Butterworth, J. E., 3, 49
Buzzel, R. D., 185

Cale, E. G., 84
Call, W. L., 155
Campbell, E. J., 84
Campise, J. A., 85
Canning, R. G., 47, 69, 86, 111, 112, 113, 114
Cardenas, A. F., 113
Carlis, J. V., 30

Carlson, E. D., 2, 31, 49, 87
Carlson, J. G., 113
Carmone, F. J., 48, 49, 114, 116, 125, 127, 128
Carter, C., 17
Cetron, M., 40
Chandy, M. K., 29, 30
Chanson, S. T., 31
Chaplin, J. E., 86
Charnes, A., 48
Charnetski, J. R., 134
Chase, R. B., 185
Chervany, N. L., 17, 113, 114, 144–145, 148, 154, 187
Chesley, G. R., 86, 127
Chovanec, R. J., 113
Chow, C. C., 85
Chrysler, E., 86
Chu, K. C., 125, 134, 153, 159, 184
Churchman, C. W., 3, 10, 87, 133
Cichetti, C. J., 85
Clarke, D. G., 185
Claycombe, W. W., 124
Clowes, K. W., 6
Coenenberg, A. G., 116, 133, 134
Coffman, E. G., 84, 113
Cohen, I. K., 150
Cohen, L. J., 111
Colombatto, P. J., 193
Conrath, D. W., 86
Conroy, T. F., 21, 22, 29, 30, 31, 85, 196
Constable, C. J., 2
Conway, R. W., 84
Cook, T. M., 84
Cooper, M. D., 48, 84, 85
Cooper, W. W., 48
Coppus, G. W. J., 31, 46
Corradino, J. C., 48
Corthouts, L., 184
Corum, W., 86
Cotton, I. W., 69, 69, 84, 85
Couger, J. D., 84, 112
Courtney, J. F., 184
Courtois, P. J., 102
Cox, J. F., 191
Crabill, T. B., 30
Croft, F. M., 16, 17, 30, 47, 48, 86, 111

Crozier, M., 2
Cruon, R., 114
Cuadra, C. A., 113
Cunninghame-Green, R. A., 85
Curtice, R. M., 112
Cyert, R. M., 44, 128

Dahl, O. J., 113
Damon, W. W., 185
Date, C. J., 111
Davidson, E. S., 27
Davis, B., 2, 3, 7, 84, 111, 113, 114
Dean, N. J., 17, 71
Dearden, J., 16, 31
De Blasis, J., 10, 102, 193
Debons, A., 17
De Bruijn, W. K., 86
De Coster, M. A., 86
De Greene, K. B., 153
De Lutis, T. C., 30, 31
Demski, J. S., 131
Denham, C. R., 47
Denning, P. J., 30, 113
Derochette, D., 114
De Samblanckx, S., 155, 184, 185
Dewhurst, R. F. J., 84
Dickson, G. W., 17, 113–114, 144–145, 148, 154, 187
Diebold, J., 17
Dijkstra, E. W., 113
Diroff, T. E., 114
Dolotta, T. A., 113
Dorn, P. H., 60
Dowkont, A. J., 47
Draper, N. R., 180
Dreesmann, A. C. R., 17
Drummond, M. E., 21, 27, 30, 31, 196
Dujmovic, J. J., 31, 39, 45, 47, 48
Dunning, R. W., 2, 3, 10, 17, 60, 67, 85, 107
Dutton, W. H., 16

Easton, A., 2, 42, 43, 44, 48, 84, 87, 112, 125
Ebert, R. J., 56, 185
Edwards, C., 114
Edwards, W., 134
Eilon, S., 185
Ein-Dor, P., 16, 47, 76, 87

Eldin, H. K., 16, 17, 30, 47, 48, 86, 111
Elmaghraby, S., 86
Elmaleh, J., 185
Elnicki, R. A., 68
Emery, F. E., 193
Emery, J. C., 16–17, 55, 60, 69, 76, 82, 84–86, 112–115, 130, 132–134, 147, 154, 171
Emrey, R. C., 1
Epstein, B. J., 114, 187
Estes, N., 86, 87
Estrin, G., 31, 150, 154, 184
Etz, D. V., 16
Evans, R. W., 31

Fabry, R. S., 22
Farber, D. J., 111
Farley, J. U., 185
Farquhar, P. H., 41
Fayen, E. G., 113
Felix, C. P., 86
Fellingham, J. C., 124, 131, 144, 150, 153, 160, 184, 201
Feltham, G. A., 111, 124, 129, 130, 133, 191
Ferrara, R., 113
Ferrari, D., 30
Fife, D. W., 47, 49, 113
Firchau, V., 133
Fishburn, P. C., 49
Fisher, G. H., 1, 48, 65, 69, 72, 75, 84–87, 148, 184
Fitzroy, P. T., 134, 154
Fitzsimmons, A., 113
Flowerdew, A. D. J., 84
Foote, B. L., 112, 154
Forrester, J. W., 86, 87, 114, 137, 138, 185
France, N. A., 113
Frane, J. E., 31
Freeland, J., 49, 185
Freeman, P., 113
Freiberger, W., 31
Fried, L., 86, 87
Frielink, A. B., 16, 111, 112, 154
Funke, U. H., 185

Gargano, M., 87
Gayle, J. B., 86

Geilenkirchen, J. Th., 2, 3, 10, 17, 60, 67, 85, 187
Geisler, M. A., 150, 184
Gelenbe, E., 30, 36, 114
Geoffrion, A. M., 78
Gerberick, D. A., 114
Giauque, W. C., 49
Gibbons, T. K., 114
Gilb, T., 101
Gilchrist, B., 11
Gilman, R., 142, 149
Ginsberg, A. S., 150, 184
Gitman, L. J., 86, 87
Gnugnoli, G., 31
Goankar, R., 153
Goddard, W. E., 16
Goldberg, R. P., 31
Goldstein, R. C., 105
Goodman, D. A., 185
Goodwin, P. G., 49
Gorry, G. A., 6, 16
Gosden, J. A., 113, 114
Gotleib, C. C., 86
Gould, I. H., 17, 31
Graham, G. M. R., 47, 86
Graham, G. S., 30
Graham, J., 86, 111, 114
Green, P. E., 48, 49, 114, 116, 125, 127, 128, 134, 154
Greenberg, H. J., 30
Gregory, R. H., 17, 47, 85, 95, 110, 112–114, 148, 154, 199
Gremillion, L. L., 84
Greise, J., 16, 113
Grindley, K., 2, 5, 16, 17, 72, 84, 86, 108
Grinver, P. H., 110, 185
Gritten, R. A., 47, 49
Grochla, E., 16, 49
Grochow, J. M., 42, 48
Grooms, D. W., 154
Gross, D., 14
Grouchko, D, 114
Grum, A. F., 134
Grünwald, H., 111–112, 114, 151, 153
Grupp, B., 17
Gupta, S. C., 112

Habermann, W. F., 69, 85

Hackathorn, R. D., 1, 6
Haden, D. H., 114
Haines, G. H., 151, 160, 184, 185
Hale, D. R. E., 134
Hall, P. G., 71, 193
Hamilton, K. L., 69, 85
Hamilton, P., 114
Hand, H. H., 185
Hanken, A. F. G., 48, 49, 114, 123, 125, 134, 193
Hanssmann, F., 30, 31
Harman, A., 85
Harris, W. I., 86
Harrison, J. M., 72, 114
Hart, L. E., 31
Harubi, N., 85
Hasdorf, L., 112
Haseman, W. D., 111
Hauser, J. R., 49
Hawgood, J., 2, 44, 114
Hax, A. C., 14, 16, 17, 113
Hayes, R. L., 16
Head, J. G., 71
Head, R., 17
Heany, D. F., 185
Heijn, A., 12, 17
Hellerman, H., 21, 22, 29, 30, 31, 85, 196
Hertz, D. B., 17, 75
Hesp, P. J., 185
Hespos, R. F., 87
Heyman, D., 30
Highland, H. J., 16, 28, 30, 31
Hindle, A., 187
Hirshleifer, J., 84, 111
Ho, Y. C., 31, 125, 134
Hoare, C. A. R., 113
Hoetink, B. J., 112
Hofer, C. W., 16
Hoffman, G. M., 16
Hoffman, L. J., 114
Hoffman, T. R., 161, 184
Hogarth, R. M., 86
Hoggatt, A. C., 184
Holden, G. K., 16
Hollingworth, F. D., 85, 86
Holloway, C. A., 16
Holt, C. C., 136, 139, 148, 151
Hootman, J. T., 69

Hopkins, D. S. P., 48
Hora, S. C., 134
Horen, J. H., 185
Horvath, P., 3, 47–49, 85–87
House, W. C., 16, 130, 153
Howard, J. A., 185
Howard, P. C., 31, 69, 84
Howard, R. A., 134
Hoyt, G. S., 84, 86
Hsu, J. I. S., 30
Huang, C. C., 128, 134
Huber, C. P., 41–43, 48–49, 86, 134
Huesmann, L. R., 31
Hulbert, J., 185
Hultén, C., 31
Humble, J., 2, 5, 16, 17, 72, 84, 86, 108

Iglehart, D. L., 15
Ignizio, J. P., 48
Ijiri, Y., 142, 152, 155
Itami, H., 67, 142, 146, 152, 154, 155

Jackson, M. A., 113, 134
Jacob, J. P., 84
Jacquin, J. L., 3
Jagetia, L. C., 134
Jain, A. K., 31
Jardine, D. A., 111
Jarvis, J. J., 47, 48
Jeffress, C., 16
Jensen, R. E., 144, 154, 184
Jewett, J. E., 3, 48, 123, 134
Johnson, R. E., 153, 185
Johnson, R. W., 86–87
Johnston, J., 80
Jones, G. T., 13, 16, 17
Jordan, C. M. C., 167
Joslin, E. O., 2, 30, 31, 45, 47, 49, 86, 111, 112
Joyce, J. D., 30
Jucker, J. V., 86, 87

Kabbes, J. J., 184
Kanter, H., 86
Kaplan, R. B., 6
Kapur, K. C., 114

Kargl, H., 3, 47–49, 85–87
Katzan, H., 114
Kaufmann, A., 114
Keefer, D. L., 43, 49, 128, 185
Keen, P. G. W., 16
Keeney, R. L., 1, 40–43, 45, 47–49, 70, 73, 84, 86
Keller, R. F., 47
Kendall, M. G., 81
Khumawala, B. M., 155, 185
Kimbleton, S. R., 30, 69
King, J. L., 84–86, 111
King, W. R., 16, 114, 187
Kirkwood, C. W., 49
Kleijnen, J. P. C., 10, 15, 16, 31, 46, 48, 60, 75–76, 78–79, 87, 151, 153–154, 180–181, 190, 201
Kleindorfer, P. R., 185
Kleinedoepke, R., 116, 133, 134
Kleinrock, L., 30, 31
Kling, R., 17
Knapp, R. K., 84, 112
Knight, K. E., 54
Knutsen, K. E., 16, 17, 112
Kobayashi, H., 30
Koeleman, P. F. M., 185
Konsynski, B. R., 31
Korteweg, W. H., 16
Kozar, K. A., 145
Kraemer, K. L., 1, 16
Krasnow, H. S., 98, 110, 114, 140, 142
Krauss, L. E., 114
Kreutzer, W., 31
Kreibel, C. H., 30, 55, 61, 69, 84, 85, 110, 114, 126, 129, 134, 148, 185
Krishnan, K. S., 49
Kroenke, D., 111
Krueckeberg, H. F., 12, 13, 17
Kumar, B., 27
Kuo, B., 111, 112

Lamberson, L. R., 114
Lamberton, D. M., 84
Lanahan, J., 148
Lancaster, F. W., 113
Land, F. F., 2, 47, 48, 86, 134, 185
Langefors, B., 187
Larréché, J., 48
Layton, R. A., 85

Ledbetter, W. N., 191
Lee, W. B., 114, 155, 185
LeMoigne, J., 11, 16
Le Moine, A. J., 30
Leroudier, J., 31
Lesourne, J., 86
Lev, B., 113, 147, 154
Leventhal, L. A., 31, 113
Levy, H., 86
Lewellen, W. G., 86, 87
Leiber, Z., 16
Lin, S. A. Y., 62
Lincoln, T. J., 17, 71, 87, 193
Little, J. D. C., 17, 185
Lockhart, S., 166
Logan, J. J., 111
London, K., 113, 154
Loomis, M. E. S., 69
Loss, A. L., 30
Love, T., 113, 185
Love, R. M., 185
Lucas, H. C., 1, 6, 16, 30, 31, 47, 113, 155
Luckew, T. G., 184
Luke, A. W., 113
Lusk, E. J., 114
Lyons, N. R., 28

MacCrimmon, K. R., 134
McDonough, A. M., 3, 133
MacDougall, M. H., 31
McFarlan, F. W., 30, 31, 84, 86, 151
MacGahan, A., 114
McGuire, C. B., 125, 129, 134
McIntyre, E. V., 56
McKenney, J. L., 84
McKinney, J. M., 30
Macko, D., 123
McLean, E. R., 2, 16, 17, 188
Magee, J. F., 153
Magnanti, T. L., 154
Maguire, J. N., 31
Maisel, H., 31
Makridakis, S., 111, 112
Mann, D. H., 185
Manne, A. S., 130
Mantey, P. E., 16
March, J. G., 44, 128

Marschak, J., 102, 112, 115, 123, 124, 129, 130, 133, 147
Martin, J., 111, 114
Mason, R. O., 7, 87, 114
Massy, W. F., 48
Matheson, J. E., 86
Mathusz, D. V., 112
Maxwell, W. L., 84
Maynard, H. S., 31, 113
Meadow, C. T., 31, 111, 113
Meddaugh, E. J., 152
Meier, R. C., 153
Mellichamp, J. M., 185
Mendelssohn, R. C., 10
Menkhaus, E. J., 86
Merkhofer, H. W., 134
Mertens, P., 16, 17, 113
Mesarovic, M. D., 114, 123
Metersky, M. L., 42, 47
Metzner, H. E., 112, 113
Mevellec, P., 3
Mikhail, O., 55, 69, 84, 85
Millen, R. N., 149
Miller, E. F., 19, 30–31, 189
Miller, G. A., 47
Miller, J. M., 150
Miller, L. W., 84
Miller, W. D., 113
Miller, W. G., 33–34, 45, 48–49
Minsky, H., 6
Mintzberg, H., 6, 44
Mishan, E. J., 62, 85
Mitroff, I. I., 7, 87, 114
Mock, T. J., 114, 124, 128, 131, 134, 144, 148, 150, 153, 154, 160, 184, 201
Modigliani, F., 139, 148, 151
Mohan, C., 112
Mohr, J. M., 31
Molnar, T. P., 85
Moneta, J., 86
Montgomery, D. C., 48
Moore, A.,, 86
Moore, J. B., 69
Moore, J. R., 47
Moore, K. L., 84
Morey, R. C., 15
Morgan, H. L., 85
Morris, P. A., 47, 86

Morse, J. N., 47, 48
Morton, M. S. Scott, 6, 16, 94
Moskowitz, H., 130, 150
Muller, H., 155, 184, 185
Mumford, E., 2
Munro, M. C., 7
Munson, B. R., 111
Murray, J. T., 30
Murron, B., 113
Muth, J. F., 136, 139, 148, 151
Myers, E., 17
Myers, G. J., 113

Nahmias, S., 14
Naylor, T. H., 16, 153, 159, 184, 185
Newell, W. T., 153
Nielen, G. C., 3, 17, 90
Nielsen, N. R., 86
Nijkamp, P., 48, 84
Nolan, R. L., 16, 17, 30, 69, 84–86,
    105, 112, 113, 151
Nordhaus, W. D., 137
Novick, M. R., 134
Nunamaker, J. F., 31
Nurminen, M. I., 188
Nutt, G. J., 31

Odanaka, T., 127
Olsen, H. A., 84, 134
Omurtag, Y., 193
O'Neil, B., 155
Oomens, W. J., 185
Oppenheimer, K. R., 48
Orgler, Y. E., 16
Orlovsky, S. A., 48
Ortlieb, T. A., 113
Osswald, B., 30

Page, J., 16
Palmer, C. R., 69, 71
Palmer, I. R., 111
Parent, M., 31
Parker, B. R., 48–49
Parker, D. B., 114
Parkin, A. 47, 87
Parks, G. M., 17
Patton, G. R., 185
Pazer, H. L., 153
Peebles, T. C., 49

Pegels, C. C., 133
Pelligrini, S., 86
Penniman, D., 16
Perrakis, S., 87
Peterson, R. E., 17, 155, 185
Phister, M., 12, 17, 19, 31, 53, 60, 84,
    85, 91, 113, 114
Pirsig, R. M., 114
Plagman, B. K., 17
Polderman, G. L., 112, 114
Politzer, J. P., 136
Popadic, R. P., 69
Pope, D. J. M., 86
Pounds, W. F., 6, 193
Power, W. D., 17
Pritchard, J. A. T., 30
Proschan, F., 30, 114

Radford, K. J., 3
Radner, R., 123, 129, 133, 134
Radosevich, R., 16
Raiffa, H., 1, 40–43, 45, 47–49, 70, 73,
    84, 86, 115, 129, 133
Raisinghani, D., 6, 44
Ramer, S., 48
Randell, B., 114
Raper, D., 187
Rappaport, A., 76, 133, 134, 147
Ravin, J., 128
Reichardt, K. E., 86
Reiser, M., 30
Remus, W. E., 154
Rens, P. J., 15
Rettus, R. C., 86
Reuver, H. A., 48, 49, 114, 123, 125,
    134, 193
Richels, R. G., 130
Ricker, H. S., 12, 13, 17
Reitmüller, C. E., 136, 138
Reitveld, P., 48, 84
Roberts, N., 138
Robinson, P. J., 134, 154
Rogers, F. A., 85
Rome, B. K., 151, 160
Rome, S. C., 151, 160
Rose, C. A., 31
Rosenblatt, M. J., 86, 87, 113
Rosenkranz, F., 86
Rowe, A. J., 103, 111–113

Rowe, W. D., 48–49, 134
Roxburgh, K., 114
Rubenstein, A. B., 86, 185
Ruisch, R., 114
Rullo, T. A., 84, 86
Ruschitzka, M., 22

Saaty, T. L., 47–48, 113
Sahin, I., 87
Sargent, R. G., 16, 28
Sarnat, M., 86
Sassone, P. G., 84
Satterfield, D. E., 84
Sauer, C. H., 29
Sauter, R. F., 145
Savas, E. S., 85
Schaffer, W. A., 84
Schaller, C., 86
Scharf, T. G., 47
Schatzoff, M., 128
Schauland, H., 16
Schendel, D., 185
Scheer, A. L., 22, 31
Schimpeler, C. C., 48
Schlaifer, R. O., 115, 129, 133
Schneidewind, N. F., 28
Schoeffler, S., 185
Schonberger, R. J., 6
Schoute, F. C., 134
Schramm, R., 185
Schreiber, B. D., 136, 138
Schrems, E. L., 85–86, 111
Schriber, T. J., 16, 28, 30–31
Schrieber, A. N., 16
Schröder, H., 86, 185
Schroeder, R. G., 108, 111–112, 145
Schulz, R. N., 39–40, 47, 49
Schussel, G., 47, 112
Schwartz, L. B., 153, 185
Schwartz, M. H., 86
Schwartz, S. L., 48–49, 185
Schwetman, H. D., 31
Scott, D. L., 49
Scott, J. E., 39–40, 47–49, 69, 85–86
Scott Morton, see Morton, M. S. Scott
Scott, R. H., 85, 86, 87
Scull, J. A., 30
Segal, R., 155
Segelstein, S., 45, 47

Seger, E., 16, 76, 87
Seiler, K., 30, 48, 84, 86
Selwyn, L. L., 84–85
Senge, P. M., 153
Senn, J. A., 48, 113–114, 144–145,
    148, 150, 154
Seppälä, Y., 152
Severance, D. G., 30
Shaftel, T. L., 86
Shapiro, J. F., 17
Shannon, R. E., 62, 153
Sharpe, W. F., 17, 30, 47–49, 53, 57,
    59, 65, 67, 69, 71, 84–87
Shaul, D. R., 16
Shephard, R. W., 84
Sherman, S. W., 27
Shubik, M., 154, 166
Sibley, E. H., 84, 113–114
Sieghart, P., 114
Silver, E. A., 30
Simon, H., 185
Simon, H. A., 6, 102, 136, 139, 148,
    151
Sims, H. P., 185
Singer, N. M., 31, 86
Smidt, S., 87
Smith, C. M., 111
Smith, D. M., 113
Smith, H., 180
Smith, H. J., 30
Smith, H. R., 145
Smith, H. T., 113
Smith, M. L., 112–113
Smith, R. A., 86
Smith, V. K., 85
Snyders, J., 84, 86
Soden, J. V., 188
Söderland, L., 31
Sollenberger, H. M., 3
Soriano, A., 14
Spetzler, C. S., 86
Spitz, L. K., 48
Squires, B. E., 69
Srinivasan, V., 48–49
Stabell, C. B., 3, 16, 114, 133
Staël von Holstein, C. S., 86
Stamper, R. K., 109, 113–114, 133,
    147, 188
Starr, M. K., 48

Statland, N., 67–69, 85
Steel, T. B., 113
Sterling, T. D., 101
Stern, H., 16, 113
Stevens, M. E., 86–87, 111, 113–114
Stohr, E. A., 69, 85, 126, 129
Stone, B. K., 87
Strassmann, P. A., 87, 112, 114
Strater, F. R., 111
Streeter, D. N., 84, 114
Streufert, S. C., 114
Stuart, A., 81
Subotnik, A., 85
Sullivan, W. G., 124
Sundgren, B., 112, 193
Suppes, P., 112
Sutton, J. A., 16
Svobodova, L., 30
Swanson, C. V., 111–112, 114, 139, 149
Swanson, R. W., 113, 187
Sweeney, D. J., 65

Taggart, W. M., 16, 112, 114
Takahara, Y., 123
Tanenbaum, A. S., 113–114
Tapiero, C. S., 126, 129, 185
Taylor, S., 14
Tenenbein, A., 87
Ter Linde, W., 86
Tharp, M. O., 16, 112, 114
Théorêta, A., 6, 44
Thesen, A., 16, 86, 113
Thiriez, H., 48
Thissen, W. A. H., 137
Thompson, G. L., 185
Timmreck, E. M., 30–31, 48, 86–87
Treille, J. M., 7, 85
Treleaven, P. C., 114
Trill, G. P., 8, 10, 86, 106
Truxal, J. G., 112
Turban, E., 42, 47
Turn, R., 114

Unger, B. W., 31, 48
Uretsky, M., 144, 148

Van Aken, J. E., 10–11, 16, 90, 112, 114, 136, 153–155, 193
Van Amstel, J. J., 113
Van Beek, P., 112, 114
Van Belkum, J. W., 17, 111
Van Dam, C., 185
Van den Burg, A. J., 87
Vandepitte, G., 184
Van der Ham, R. T., 87
Van de Wouw, C. J. M., 3, 16, 185, 188, 193
Van Dinten, W. L., 17
Van Dongen, M. P. F. M., 46
Van Hoepen, M. A., 2–3, 10, 60, 67, 85, 187
Van Horn, R. L., 17, 47, 85, 95, 112–114, 148, 150, 154
Van Lommel, E. M., 48
Van Loon, P. J. J. M., 48–49
Van Raaij, W. F., 48
Van Reeken, A. J., 113
Van Zanten, J. H., 16, 85
Van Zutphen, L. C., 10
Vasarhelyi, M. A., 124, 128, 131, 144, 150, 153–154, 160, 184, 201
Vasicek, O. A., 29
Vazsonyi, A., 3, 123, 125, 133–134
Verhelst, M., 16–17, 86, 97, 108, 110–114, 130, 133–134, 138, 147, 149, 154, 187
Verhofstad, J. S. M., 114
Vernon, J. M., 185
Verrijn Stuart, A. A., 3, 114
Verver, J. M., 155
Vertinsky, I., 48–49, 128, 134, 185
Votaw, D. F., 112

Wagner, K. H., 154, 185
Walkowicz, J. L., 30
Wallace, J. B., 9, 87, 111
Wallenius, J., 48
Walsh, D. S., 12, 17
Walston, C. E., 86
Ward, M. R., 30
Weber, R. E., 11
Wehrung, D. A., 48
Weil, H. B., 69, 149, 193
Weinberg, G. M., 101
Weitzman, C., 111, 113

Welke, R. J., 2–3, 17, 49, 65, 84, 111–112, 130–131, 134, 138, 140, 142, 149, 151, 190, 192–193
Wenzel, F., 112, 127, 133–134
Wessel, C. J., 84
Weyant, J. P., 130
Wheelwright, S. C., 111–112
Whinston, A. B., 111
White, D. R. J., 39–40, 47, 49
Whitehead, C. M. E., 84
Wiest, J. D., 86
Wildermooth, B. L., 112, 154
Wilkes, F. M., 86–87
Wilkinson, J. H., 113
Williams, F. E., 125
Willoughby, T. C., 69, 84–85
Wilmer, M. A. P., 130, 155
Wilmès, P., 136, 149
Wimbrow, J. H., 8
Wind, Y., 48
Winkler, R. L., 86
Winkofsky, E. P., 65
Wiorkowski, G. K., 86
Wiorkowski, J. J., 86
Wissema, J. G., 16
Wolf, G., 166, 184

Wolfe, J., 185
Wolfe, J. N., 47
Wolff, R. N., 151, 184–185
Wooldridge, S., 113
Wright, P., 48
Wyatt, J. B., 31
Wynne, B., 114, 145, 154

Yearsley, R. B., 47, 86
Yeh, R. T., 113
Ying, C. C., 124, 134, 147
Yuan, J. S. C., 185

Zacks, S., 130
Zadeh, L. A., 44, 188
Zangemeister, C., 48–49
Zani, W. M., 31, 148
Zeigler, B. P., 31
Zeleny, M., 42, 46–48
Zelkowitz, M. V., 56, 86
Zia, H. W. H., 61
Ziemba, W. T., 3, 49, 128, 134
Zijlker, A. W., 6, 16
Zinnes, J. L., 112
Zionts, S., 48
Zmud, R. W., 86, 114

SUBJECT INDEX

A, B, and C classification, 103, 113
Accuracy, 12, 14–15, 45, 89, 96,
    98–101, 103–104, 107–110, 113,
    121, 126–127, 129–131, 136, 139,
    142, 144, 147–153, 157–158, 160,
    162, 166, 169, 190–192, 195,
    198–199, 201–202
Adaptive behavior, 124
Adequate knowledge, 96
Advertising, 144, 150
Age, see Delay
Aggregation, 12–13, 89, 101, 103–104,
    106–109, 121, 126, 129–130, 135,
    138–139, 141, 147, 149–151, 159,
    166, 191, 195
Airline reservation system, 60, 125,
    195
Amount of information, 109
Analysis of variance (ANOVA), 28,
    127, 141, 143, 150, 154, 179
APICS, 15, 17
APL, 184
Aspiration levels, 44
Attributes of information, 89, 129,
    153, 166, 174, 189, 190, 192
Audit, 99, 105, 187
Availability, 29, 41–42, 104–105, 197
Average cost, 83

Bayesian statistics, 47, 72, 115, 191,
    200
Bayes's theorem, 115, 119–120, 128,
    132
Behavioral aspects, 7, 102, 109, 113,
    127–129, 143–144, 151, 157,
    159–160, 190, 192, 201

Behavioral theory of the firm, 140
Benchmark, 20, 22, 29, 189, 196
Benefit-cost analysis, see Cost-benefit
    analysis
Bias, 136–137, 139
Bibliography, 47–48, 69, 86, 112–113,
    134, 203–243
Black box, 188. See also System
Bookkeeping error, 99. See also
    Accuracy
Booz–Allen, 11, 154
Bottom-up approach, 6–7, 102
Budget, 53, 67, 69, 83, 99, 137, 144,
    153, 159, 162–164, 182, 184, 197
  share, 60
  soft, 67
Business cycle, 98, 106, 108, 137,
    151–152
Buy-or-lease decision, 83
Buy-or-make decision, 56, 71

Case study, 42–43, 68, 71–72, 95, 102,
    106, 148, 154, 190, 193
Cash-flow discounted, 70, 199
Central limit theorem, 166, 199
Centralization, 56, 65, 106, 108,
    125–126, 129, 141
Charging, see Cost accounting, Pricing
Charging algorithm, 68
Chief programming team, 56
Closed loop, 125
Closed system, 9. See also System
Coarse IS, 121, 129–130, 133, 200
Cobb-Douglas production function,
    59–60, 82
Codasyl, 111

Coding, 99
Cognitive style, 104, 108. *See also*
    Behavioral aspects
Collusion, 143–144
Communication, 99, 123, 125, 129,
    131, 160, 188, 191
  cost, 53
  theory, 62, 147
  tele-, 7, 53, 199
Computer
  center, 69, 84, 105
  center management, 61
  error, 100, 106. *See also* Accuracy
  network, 7, 23, 30, 64, 69, 105, 111
  selection 33, 108
Congestion, *see* Queuing
Continuous, 139, 152–153, 190–191.
    See also Discrete-event simulation
Control engineering, *see* Control
    theory
Control theory, 96, 98, 112, 125–126,
    135, 138–140, 149, 157, 188,
    190–191
Conversion, 33, 63
Corporate simulation, 140, 174, 191
Cost, 162, 185
  average, 66, 82, 189
  of capital, 71, 75, 78, 84
  differential, 66
  fixed, 55–56, 65–67, 82–83, 85, 95,
    102, 137, 159, 162, 177, 182, 189,
    198, 201
  integral, 66, 82, 189
  joint, 66–67, 82–83, 85, 198
  marginal, 66, 82–83, 189, 198
  opportunity, 66, 105–106
  overhead, 64, 66, 68, 83, 91, 101,
    105, 198
  replacement, 66, 82, 198
  shadow, 67
  variable, 65, 162, 182
Cost accounting, 63, 65, 71–72, 83, 86,
    100, 189. *See also* Pricing
Cost-benefit analysis, 45, 62, 84, 187,
    191
Cost-volume relationship, 159
Criterion, 19, 35, 45, 108, 150, 158,
    161, 168, 183, 189
  hierarchy, 36

multiple, 33, 157
number of, 35, 44
overlapping, 20–21, 35, 47
CSMP, 137, 200
CSSL, 200
CYSDEM, 142, 190, 192

Data, 53
  descriptive, 109
  global, 106, 139, 151
  prescriptive, 109
Data bank, 7, 15, 85
  public, 7
Data capture, 90, 92, 94, 97, 100–101,
    111, 113
Data management, 22, 24, 30, 61
Database, 7, 9, 61, 63, 66–67, 84,
    90–93, 95–97, 104–107, 109, 111,
    129, 139, 151, 159, 161, 164,
    172–173, 201
  centralized, 111
  distributed, 108–109, 114
  external, 108
Database management system (DBMS),
    7, 10, 15–16, 20, 28, 91, 100–101,
    103, 105, 108–109, 113–114, 195
Datalogical design and analysis, 187
Deadlock, 83, 85
Decentralization, *see* Centralization
Decision, 6, 8, 89, 92, 130, 140
  operational, 6, 8, 15, 60, 97, 101,
    130, 142, 144, 152, 189, 195
  repetitive, 130, 146
  strategic, 6, 8, 15, 44, 96, 101, 144,
    152, 158, 189–191, 195
  tactical, 6, 8, 15, 96, 130, 142, 158,
    189–190, 195
  triggered, 92, 94, 97, 129, 138,
    141–142, 154, 172
Decision delay, 93, 138
Decision interval, 110, 142
Decision-making delay, 142, 144, 146,
    150
Decision support systems (DSS), 7, 189
Decision theory, 114–115. *See also*
    Bayesian statistics
Decision tree, 117, 119, 121, 123, 125,
    128, 190
Decision variable, 35–36, 40, 75–76

Decomposable system, 102. *See also*
     System
Delay, 12, 14–15, 45, 89, 91–92, 99,
     101, 104–110, 126, 129–130,
     136–139, 142, 144, 147–150,
     152–153, 160, 166, 189, 191–192,
     195, 199, 201
  exponential, 136, 138–139
  processing, 110, 139, 141, 149, 152
  reaction, 93
  response, 19, 29, 33, 37, 41–44, 46,
     90–92, 95–96, 104, 189,
     196–197
  retrieval, 92, 138, 196
DELPHI, 72
Demurrage, 68, 198
Depreciation, 65–66, 83, 159, 174, 176,
     182, 185, 199, 201
Descriptive data, 109
Design, *see* Experimental design
Detail, *see* Aggregation
Diebold Corporation reports, 3, 11, 17,
     60, 71, 85–86, 154, 185
Difference equation, 137, 140, 149,
     152, 200
Differential cost, 66
Diffuse, 132, 200
Discounted cash flow, 70, 199
Discrete event simulation, 138, 140,
     142, 191. *See also* Simulation
Domination, 133
Dummy variable, 76
Dynamic programming, 123
Dynamics, 96, 124–126, 128–129, 131,
     135, 137, 140, 142–143, 146, 157,
     159, 183, 190–191. *See also* System
DYNAMO, 137

Econometrics, 137
Economic order quantity, 13, 115, 147
Economics, 131, 159, 164, 189
  Keynesian, 53
Economies of scale, 53, 61, 82,
     95, 199
Editing, 99
Elasticity, 82, 163, 182, 198
Electronic funds transfer (EFT), 13
Empirics
  data, 137

methods, 135
  studies, 133, 148, 154, 157, 190, 192
Employment, 10, 60
Emulation of old hardware, 57
Entropy, 135, 147, 153
Environment, 81, 96, 98, 107–108,
     130–131, 141–142, 150–151, 158,
     160, 164, 189, 191–192
  variables, 35, 76, 90
Error, *see* Accuracy
Exception report, 89, 102, 104, 107,
     113, 129, 136, 142, 144, 149, 151
Experimental design, 41, 78, 146,
     149–150, 154, 167, 190, 192
Expert opinion, 72. *See also*
     Probability
Exponential delay, 136, 138–139
Exponential smoothing, 96, 107, 161,
     163–164, 175, 177–178, 182, 201
External effect, 62–63, 68–69, 189, 198

F-statistic, 153, 171–172, 179, 183, 186
Factorial design, 127. *See also*
     Experimental design
Fail-soft, 105, 111
Feedback, 107, 109, 131, 135, 137, 144,
     148, 152, 157, 163, 191, 200
Feedforward, 131, 135, 141, 148, 152,
     157, 191, 200
Field test, 148, 150, 154, 192
File, 142, 188
Financial, 1
Fine IS, *see* Coarse IS
Fixed cost, *see* Cost
Flexibility, 33, 46, 56, 64, 89, 107,
     109, 114, 130, 189
Forecast, 96, 101, 103, 107, 110, 124,
     130–131, 135, 142, 144, 147, 150,
     153, 161, 163–164, 173, 175,
     177–178, 182, 196, 199, 201
  subjective, 117, 128
Formal model, 1, 8, 10, 28, 33, 44,
     61, 71, 103, 107, 109, 127, 130,
     136, 151, 189, 191
Format, 89, 94, 102, 104, 113, 129,
     141
Formula timing, 20, 29
Free competition, *see* Monopoly
Fuzzy set, 44, 188

Game, 28, 96, 98, 114, 127, 131, 135,
    139–140, 143, 148, 150, 153, 157,
    184, 190–192, 201
    against nature, 117, 127, 143, 150,
    184
Game theory, 125, 131
Garbling, 129
General accounting office (GAO), 69,
    85–86
General system theory (GST), 10, 188
Global data, 106, 126, 129, 139, 151
Goal programming, 44
Goal variable, 160, 183. *See also*
    Criterion
Gossen's laws, 37, 46, 57, 66, 82
GPSS, 140, 142–143
Graceful degradation, 105
Graphics, 94, 104
Grosch's law, 53
Gross benefit, 2, 5, 119, 121, 130–132
Group decision making, 48

Heuristics, 14, 107, 141, 143, 151, 157,
    160, 163–164, 174, 184, 192. *See
    also* Rules of thumb
Honeywell, 114
Human engineering, 102, 113

IBM, 14, 63, 84, 109, 113, 131, 142,
    144, 148, 157, 163, 168, 182,
    184–185, 190, 201–202
ICL, 157, 161, 163, 166, 175, 184
Inaccuracy, *see* Accuracy
Indifference curve, 38, 40, 46
Industrial dynamics, *see* System
    dynamics
Inertia of technology, 90
Infological design and analysis, 187
Informal model, *see* Formal model
Informatics, xiii
Information attributes, *see* Attributes
    of information
Information economics (IE), 96, 102,
    107, 109–110, 113, 115, 135, 138,
    140, 146–147, 149, 153, 157, 183,
    190–191, 201
Information overload, 107
Information-requirements analysis, 92,
    187

Information theory, 62, 147
INFOTECH, 2, 8, 30, 86, 111, 113–114
Initial condition, 141, 150, 154, 168,
    171, 173, 183, 185, 201
Input time, 199
Input variable, 137, 140, 143
Inquiry system, 1
Instruction mix, 19
Intangibles, 2, 9, 190
Integral cost, 66, 82, 189
Integration, 56
Integrity, 100, 106
Interaction, 21–22, 41–42, 45, 76, 123,
    127, 139, 141–142, 144, 149–150,
    152, 154, 160
Interactive factors, 89, 106, 113, 128,
    130, 140, 151, 195, 199
Internal rate of return, 70–71
Inventory, 8, 11–13, 15, 56, 60, 63,
    66, 75, 93, 96–97, 100, 102–103,
    107, 110, 115, 123, 125–126,
    129–131, 137–139, 141–143,
    147–149, 152, 157–159, 161–162,
    164, 167, 172, 175, 177, 181,
    183–184, 189–190, 192, 195, 202
    evaluation of, 65
Investment, 69, 103–104
Investment analysis, 5, 68–70, 86, 195
IPSO, 106, 139, 185, 192, 201. *See
    also* Philips
ISDOS, 60

Job accounting, 68. *See also* Cost
    accounting, Pricing
Job satisfaction, 1
Job shop, 61, 84, 150
Joint cost, 66–67, 82–83, 85, 198

Kernel, 20–21, 196
Keynesian economics, 53
Kiviat graph, 36, 44

Lag, *see* Delay
Layout, *see* Format
Learning, 56, 124, 143–144, 190
Lease, 71, 190
Least squares, 75, 162, 167–168, 179,
    200–201. *See also* Regression
    analysis

Library services, 62–63, 94, 187
Life cycle, 75
Linear programming (LP), 7, 44, 46,
    56, 58, 61, 65, 67, 71, 75, 78,
    131, 135, 140, 146, 153, 184, 190,
    192, 197, 201
Literature retrieval, 103
Local data, 106, 126, 129, 139, 151
Logical error, 98, 100, 129, 166
Loss function, 126, 133, 200
Lottery, 43

Maintenance, 23, 198
Man-machine mode, *see* Interactive
Management by exception, 67, 133.
    See also Exception report
Management science, *see* Operations
    research
Marginal cost, 66, 82–83, 189, 198
Market, 51, 182, 189, 201
    information, 115, 184
    share, 161, 163–164, 168–169, 171,
        174–176, 179–181, 185, 190, 195,
        197
Marketing, 46, 75, 108–109, 127, 139,
    158–160, 163–164, 166, 175–178,
    183–185, 202
Markov system, 90
Material-requirement planning, 8
Maximin, 43, 128
Mean absolute deviation (MAD), 131
Meaning of information, 62, 109
Measurement error, 98–100, 109, 129,
    152, 166, 195
Measurement scale, 99
Mental model, *see* Formal model
Metamodel, 75–76, 78, 87
Microprogram, 57
Minicomputer, 56, 64, 91, 100, 111
Minnesota experiments, 144–145
Model, 1, 14
    continuous, 135
    formal, 1, 8, 10, 28, 44, 61, 71,
        103, 107, 109, 127, 130, 136, 151,
        189, 191
    implementation, 192
    meta, 75–76, 78, 87
    synthetic, 20
    validation, 28, 77, 99, 157, 164, 183

Modularity, 56–57, 108
Monitor, 28, 30, 56, 68, 196
Monopoly, 51–53, 62, 64, 82–83, 108,
    183, 189, 198
Monte Carlo sampling, 74–75, 140
Multiple criteria, 33, 157
Multiple decision makers, 123, 140, 160
Multiple users, 89, 98, 101, 104, 108

Net benefits, 5, 119
Net Present Value (NPV), 43, 62,
    70–72, 76, 84, 149, 190
Network of computers, 7, 23, 30, 64,
    69, 105, 111
Newsboy example, 116, 123, 128, 132,
    146, 190
Noise, *see* Accuracy
Nonprofit organization, 1, 67
Number crunching, 5, 7–8, 15, 64, 106
Numerical mathematics, 100, 113

Oligopoly, 52, 158
On-line systems, 137, 152, 184, 201
Open loop, 125
Open system, 9. *See also* System
Operational decision, 6, 8, 15, 60, 97,
    101, 130, 142, 144, 152, 189, 195
Operations research (OR), 7, 9–10, 13,
    16, 22, 43, 61, 105–108, 126, 151,
    158, 160, 184, 187–188, 191
Opportunity cost, 66, 105–106
Order quantity, 13, 115, 147
Overhead cost, 64, 66, 68, 83, 91, 101,
    105, 198

Pages, 22, 29
Payback period, 70–71, 84, 199
Payoff matrix, 116, 118, 127, 132, 147
Perfect information, 118, 121–122, 127,
    132. *See also* Attributes
Peripheral observation, 90
PERT, 72, 86
Petri networks, 123
Philips, 106, 138–139, 146, 151, 185,
    192
Physical subsystem, 9–10
Pilot project, 148, 154
Planning horizon, 70, 75, 101, 107,
    110, 124, 150, 152, 167

Planning-programming-budgeting (PPB), 187
Point of sale (POS), 8, 12, 14–15, 92, 100, 111, 117, 196, 199
Posterior probability, 115–116, 118, 120, 132. *See also* Prior probability
Pragmatics, 17, 188
Precision, 99, 103–104, 111, 129, 199–200. *See also* Attributes
Prediction, *see* Forecast
Prescriptive data, 109
Price, 163–164, 176, 178, 182
  differentiation, 164, 177
  discrimination, 67, 83, 182, 198, 201
  elasticity, 163, 182
Pricing, 55, 64–65, 83, 166, 189
  computer jobs, 53
Prior probability, 115–117, 120–121, 127–128, 132. *See also* Posterior probability
Privacy, 63–64, 89, 105, 107, 109, 130, 199
Probability
  objective, 72
  subjective, 34–35, 72, 74, 117, 128, 195
Process control, 149
Processing delay, 110, 139, 141, 149, 152
Production factor, 51, 58, 60, 64, 146
Production function, 58, 61, 82
Production smoothing, 162, 184
Production technique, 5, 46, 58–59, 68
Productivity, 59–60, 101, 113
Profit center, 52, 63–64, 68, 85
Programmed decision, 6, 102
Programming error, 100, 166. *See also* Accuracy
Prototype, 92, 135, 148, 154, 190, 192
Psychology, 7, 127, 144. *See also* Behavioral aspects
Public good, 62–63
Purging, 104
Purpose of information, 109

Quadratic cost, 136
Quadratic cost-volume relationship, 152

Quality control, 102, 130
Quality of information, *see* Attributes
Quantile, 29, 46, 73, 196–197
Queuing, 24, 30, 33, 46, 62, 69, 83, 91, 138, 140, 142, 152, 196–198, 201
  theory, 22, 95, 189
Query, 89, 94, 96, 102–103, 107, 129
QUEST, 40

RAND Corporation, 146, 150, 192
Random number, 168–169, 171, 173, 180
Rate of return, 70–71, 83–84, 199
Ratio, 187
Reaction delay, 93
Real time, 90–92, 111, 148, 150, 201
Recall, 103
Recency, *see* Delay
Recovery, 89, 105, 130, 199
Regression analysis, 28, 42, 72, 74, 77, 79, 82–83, 107, 133, 179, 182, 184, 190, 192, 198, 200–201. *See also* Least squares
Relevance, 102–103, 109, 114. *See also* Attributes
Reliability, 19, 23, 29–30, 54, 89, 100, 105, 109, 130, 195–196, 199
  engineering, 100, 105
Repetitive decision, 130, 146
Replacement cost, 66, 82, 198
Report format, 89, 94, 102, 104, 113, 129, 141
Report mode, 89, 94, 99, 102, 129, 141, 192
Research and development (R&D), 43, 49, 52, 62–63, 75, 159, 162–164, 167, 176–177, 185
Response time, 19, 29, 33, 37, 41–44, 46, 90–92, 95–96, 104, 189, 196–197
Retention period, 89, 95, 104, 106–107, 109, 129–130. *See also* Attributes
Retrieval delay, 92, 138, 196
Return on investment (ROI), 158, 161, 163, 168–169, 171, 174, 176, 179–182, 190, 195, 201
Revolving planning, 152
Risk, 71–72, 105, 109, 131, 143
  attitude, 43, 128, 132

Risk analysis, 9, 15, 47, 73, 75, 84, 146, 190
Roll-up procedure, 118
Round robin, 196
Rules of thumb, 130, 157, 192. *See also* Heuristics

Sampled data control system, 98
Sampling error, 98–100, 104, 109–110, 129, 152, 166. *See also* Accuracy
Satisficing, 14, 44, 62, 75, 78, 96, 128, 139–140, 190
SCERT, 27
Scientific method, *see* Formal model
Scope, 89, 106–109, 139, 141–142, 149, 151, 187. *See also* Attributes
Scoring method, 33, 44, 189
Screening, 99
Security, 63–64, 89, 105–107, 109, 130, 195, 199
Semantics, 17, 188
Semiotics, 188
Sensitivity analysis, 35, 46–47, 75, 110, 115, 128, 137, 147, 149–150, 154, 160, 174, 185, 190
Sequential information system, 125
Sequentialization, 78
Shadow price, 67
Shannon-Weaver communication theory, 62, 147
SIMSCRIPT, 140
Simulation, 7–8, 21, 24, 33, 41, 69, 73–74, 98, 110, 131, 135, 137, 139, 148–150, 152, 157, 189–191, 195, 201. *See also* Discrete event simulation
language, 27, 31, 101, 137, 140, 143
Smoothing, *see* Exponential smoothing
Social welfare, 48
Software engineering, 100
Software package, 56. *See also* Buy-or-make decision
Source of information, 109. *See also* Attributes
Specialization, 56, 108, 199
Spillover, 62–63, 68–69, 189, 198
Starting value, *see* Initial condition
Statistical analysis, 154, 173, 202

Statistical design, *see* Experimental design
Statistical quality control, 102, 130
Status variable, 93, 98
Steady state, 135, 190–191
Stock, *see* Inventory
Strategic decision, 6, 8, 15, 44, 96, 101, 130, 144, 152, 158, 189–191, 195
Structured decision, 6, 8, 28, 102, 195
Structured programming, 113
Subjective probability, 34–35, 72, 74, 117, 128, 195
Summarization, *see* Aggregation
Super Market Institute (SMI), 13, 17
Surprise, 102, 115, 130, 191–192, 202. *See also* Attributes
Syntax, 17, 188
Synthetic model, 20
System
black box, 188
closed, 9
decomposable, 102
dynamic, 96, 124–126, 128–129, 131, 135, 137, 140, 142–143, 146, 157, 159, 183, 190–191
open, 9
physical, 9–10
real-life, 174
System dynamics (SD), 69, 98, 135–137, 140, 142–143, 149, 151, 153, 157, 190–191
System life cycle, 71
System profile, 20, 29
System theory, general, 10, 188
Systems analysis, 1

Tactical decision, 6, 8, 15, 96, 130, 142, 158, 189–190, 195
Team theory, 64–65, 109, 123, 125–126, 129, 160, 190
Technological progress, 46, 53–54, 60–61, 105
Telecommunication, 7, 53, 199
Throughput, 19, 29, 33, 41, 46
Time lag, *see* Delay
Time resolution of uncertainty, 72
Time sampling, 99, 102
Timeliness, *see* Delay

Top-down approach,
6–7
Trace, 24, 100–101
Transcription error, 98–99, 129, 152,
166. *See also* Accuracy
Transformation error, 98, 100, 105,
129, 166. *See also* Accuracy
Transient, 191. *See also* Steady state
Trigger, 92, 94, 97, 129, 138, 141–142,
154, 172
Truncation error, 100–101, 166. *See
also* Accuracy
Tuning, 36, 44, 61
Turnaround time, 198
20–80 Rule, 103

Uncertainty, 62, 72. *See also* Risk
Unemployment, 10, 60
Universal product code (UPC), 12, 15
Update interval, 92, 109, 126, 138–139,

141, 146, 149, 151–153, 199. *See
also* Delay
Update processing delay, 92, 138, 142.
See also Delay
User-machine mode, 89, 106, 113, 128,
130, 140, 151, 195, 199
Utility, 16, 33, 36, 44, 57, 66, 86, 128,
130, 189

Validation, 28, 77, 99, 157, 164, 183
Variable cost, 65, 162, 182. *See also*
Cost
Variance analysis, 67, 85
Verification, 15, 99, 100
Von Neumann–Morgenstern approach,
43

Waiting, *see* Queuing
"What if?" approach, 75
Workload, 28, 68, 196
Working set, 22, 29, 196